The German Occupation
of Belgium
1940-1944

American University Studies

Series IX
History
Vol. 122

PETER LANG
New York • San Francisco • Bern • Baltimore
Frankfurt am Main • Berlin • Wien • Paris

Werner Warmbrunn

The German Occupation of Belgium 1940-1944

PETER LANG
New York • San Francisco • Bern • Baltimore
Frankfurt am Main • Berlin • Wien • Paris

Library of Congress Cataloging-in-Publication Data

Warmbrunn, Werner.
  The German occupation of Belgium, 1940-1944 / Werner
Warmbrunn.
     p. cm. — (American university studies. Series IX, History; vol.
122)
  Includes bibliographical references and index.
  1. World War, 1939-1945—Belgium.   2. Belgium—History—
German occupation, 1940-1945.   I. Title. II. Series.
D802.B4W37   1993   940.53'37—dc20   91-35882
ISBN 0-8204-1773-4   CIP
ISSN 0740-0462

Die Deutsche Bibliothek-CIP-Einheitsaufnahme

Warmbrunn, Werner:
The German occupation of Belgium, 1940 - 1944 / Werner
Warmbrunn. - New York ; Berlin ; Bern ; Frankfurt/M. ; Paris ; Wien :
Lang, 1993
   (American university studies : Ser. 9, History ; Vol. 122)
   ISBN 0-8204-1773-4
NE: American university studies/09

The paper in this book meets the guidelines for permanence and
durability of the Committee on Production Guidelines for
Book Longevity of the Council on Library Resources.

© Peter Lang Publishing, Inc., New York 1993

All rights reserved.
Reprint or reproduction, even partially, in all forms such as microfilm,
xerography, microfiche, microcard, offset strictly prohibited.

Printed in the United States of America.

Table of Contents

Foreword by José Gotovitch ix

Preface and Acknowledgements xi

Introduction 1

I   Before the Occupation 5

    The Land and the People 5
    Institutions and Society 6
    The Monarchy 13
    Politics and Government 1918-1940 17
    The "Language Question" 24
    Foreign Policy 34
    The Invasion and its Aftermath 43

II   Survey of the Main Periods of the Occupation 53

III   The Establishment of the New Administration 63

    National-Socialist Government and German
        Designs on Belgium 63
    The Establishment and Organization of the
        Military Command 68
    General von Falkenhausen and his Staff 77
    The Reports of the Military Administration:
        Intentionality and Reliability 93
    The Struggle Over the Introduction of a
        Civilian Administration (*Reichskommissariat*) 96
    The Germans and the Belgian Administration 104
    The Germans and the Administration of Law 114

IV German Political Activities 125

    General Policies 125
    Policy Toward King Leopold 127
    Nationality Policies (*Volkstumspolitik*) 130
    The Germans and the Mass Media 136
    Police and Security Measures 141
    The Persecution of the Jews 149
    Labor, Welfare and Culture 172
    The Germans and Belgian Prisoners of War 186

V The Economic Exploitation of Belgium 191

    General Observations 191
    Reconstruction and Transportation 193
    Stages of Exploitation 198
    Agriculture and Food 214
    Labor and the Labor Draft 225
    The Management of Finances, Wages and Prices 238
    External Trade 247

VI Summary and Conclusion: The German Occupation
    Regime in Belgium 1940-1944 249

    The German Administration: Personalities,
        Policies and Political Effectiveness 251
    Economic Exploitation 259
    The Moral Issue 263
    Final Conclusion 266

Glossary 269

Selected Abbreviations Employed in Notes
and Bibliography 273

Notes 275

Bibliography 325

Appendix: Bibliographical Essay
by Willem C. M. Meyers 347

Index 357

Foreword

Werner Warmbrunn has studied the history of the German occupation of Belgium during the Second World War over a period of twenty years. Therefore he cannot be charged with the criticism so often leveled by European historians against their American colleagues: the speed and superficiality of their research. It is true that since the work of Robert Paxton on Vichy France, European scholarship has been obliged to respect those American works which have dared to provide a synthesis of European society during the war. Warmbrunn's present study represents a significant step toward such a synthesis, following the patterns of his 1963 *The Dutch under German Occupation 1940-1945* which was the first scholarly attempt at an integration of the occupation experience of our neighbor to the north. His familiarity with German occupation policies in the Netherlands provides him with a perspective which enables him to analyze the similarities and the differences of German policies in Belgium as compared to those applied in Holland, differences which were based on German awareness of the distinctive historical background, and of the immense complexity of Belgian society.

The awareness of these complexities enables Warmbrunn to portray the interacting forces of the occupation regime: on the one side the occupying power with the conflicts between the military and the SS, between local and central Reich authorities; on the other, the Belgian establishment, including the king, the church, the civil service and Big Business. He reminds us of the crucial factor unique to the situation in Belgium in contrast to that in the other occupied countries of Western Europe: the memory of the earlier occupation of the country during the First World War which played a major role in creating a mind-set for rulers and ruled alike during the long years of the second occupation.

The frequent and extensive discussions which Werner Warmbrunn conducted with the scholars of our Center and his intensive use of our archives and of those located in Germany have provided him with a substantial basis for the present book. I hope that this study will be read widely not only in the English-speaking world but that it will also receive serious attention in Belgium and in other European countries. It is the work of a mature scholar which should fill an existing void, stimulate wide discussion and, it is to be hoped, encourage further research designed to integrate this unique period into the history of our country and to further illuminate the dynamics of the Second World War.

José Gotovitch, Director
Centre de recherches et d'études de la seconde
guerre mondiale, Brussels, and
Professor at the Université Libre de Bruxelles

Preface and Acknowledgements

January 1992

This book has been in the making since the autumn of 1967. The principal reason for its slow gestation has been the demand on my time arising from my primary commitment to teaching and to the business of Pitzer College. Another reason has been my reliance on primary archival sources in the relative absence of secondary scholarly publications, especially during the first decade of my research. As the attentive reader will notice, the final product shows some of the strengths and weaknesses of a study which has evolved over a long period and which has been revised numerous times over the years.

In 1967 I chose the second occupation of Belgium as my topic primarily because at that point in time, relatively close to the end of the war and to highly charged domestic controversies over questions of collaboration and resistance, it was difficult for Belgian historians working in an extremely politicized country to write objectively about the occupation without fear that future career opportunities might be affected by what they had to say. Therefore it seemed advisable, in my view and that of some of my European colleagues whom I consulted, for an outsider familiar with the languages needed for such research to undertake the effort to provide an unprejudiced picture of the occupation.

In the decades since 1967 a new generation of younger Belgian scholars has arrived who are less emotionally involved than their elders in the political issues of the occupation and the immediate postwar period. A number of sound scholarly studies have appeared since 1967 but few of these have attempted to provide a general single volume account of the occupation.

Although an objective account of the occupation is far easier to render now, some of the same political issues, especially the Flemish-francophone struggle and the return of certain rightwing tendencies, tend to agitate the country to the present day. Therefore an account of the occupation from a distant shore by a historian who has no particular emotional stakes or political prejudices in the portrayal of German policies and actions, or in the Belgian reaction to the German regime, may, it is hoped, have a place in the historiography of the Second World War.

This book owes its existence to the support of many institutions and individuals. A substantial part of the research was carried out in 1970-71 under the sponsorship of the Fulbright Commission in Washington and Godesberg which granted the author a year-long Senior Research Fellowship. During that year the Institut für Zeitgeschichte sponsored my stay in Munich furnishing office space and the assistance of its library and archives staff. Throughout the years since 1967, Pitzer College has supported the preparation of this book through a variety of sabbaticals and of research and travel grants. In addition, the College has been generous in contributing substantial staff time and material resources to the completion of this study.

The list of archives and research institutes and of their staffs and of other individuals without whose assistance this book could not have been completed is very long as it stretches over the years. First of all I owe profound gratitude to the Hoover Institution at Stanford University, above all to Agnes F. Peterson, Curator of Western European Collections, who has been a major source of counsel and advice since 1967. I also wish to express my special appreciation to Kirsten Gronbjerg, my research assistant during the summer of 1968 who laid much of the groundwork for this study identifying sources in the Hoover Library. Recognition should also be given to Helmut Krausnick and Martin Broszat, both deceased who were successive Directors of the Institut für Zeitgeschichte. Other members of the Institute staff who were particularly helpful include Dr. Anton Hoch, archivist, and Dr. Hellmuth Auerbach, research associate, and at one time librarian of the Institute. Special mention should also be made of Léon Masset, a Belgian scholar living in Holland and of Professor Werner T. Angress in Berlin who read the manuscript painstakingly. Both made valuable suggestions. I also wish to recognize Allen Greenberger, Professor of History at Pitzer College, who perused the text at an early stage.

The author of this book is under obligation to the Bundesarchiv in Koblenz, the Militärarchiv in Freiburg i/Brsg, and to the Politische Archiv of the German Foreign Ministry in Bonn for assistance rendered during my year in Germany. During that year too, I enjoyed the privilege of interviewing at her residence in Nassau, Germany the late Cecilie von Falkenhausen, the Belgian widow of the German Military Commander in Belgium during most of the occupation. During this visit Mrs. von Falkenhausen provided me with an opportunity to read the manuscript of her husband's memoirs which now rests in the archives of the Militärarchiv in Freiburg. Mrs. von Falkenhausen's remarkably objective and detached comments about her husband made him a particularly interesting figure in my mind.

Special mention should be made of the support of the Rijksinstituut voor Oorlogsdocumentatie in Amsterdam, for some years my second home in Europe and of the guidance and generosity of its then Director, Professor Louis de Jong, the dean of Dutch World War II historians, and of his successor Dr. Harry Paape. Mr. Zwaan, archivist of the Institute assisted me with my research on Belgium, and Edouard and Emmie Groeneveld, librarian and head of acquisitions respectively, remained reliable friends and advisers throughout the period of my work on the present study.

In the nineteen seventies and eighties the Centre de recherches et d'études historiques de la seconde guerre mondiale in Brussels became my European headquarters, with temporary excursions to the German and Dutch archives which I had used during my initial period of research. This study owes much to Jean Vanwelkenhuyzen and José Gotovitch, successive directors and research associates of the Center.

They arranged for office space and for the assistance of their staff during two two-month periods in 1974 and 1975, and during shorter visits in succeeding years. Among the staff of the Center first and foremost Willem C. M. Meyers, but also Frans Selleslagh and Rudi Van Doorslaer have made significant contributions to the book as it now stands. Albert de Jonghe, a former associate of the Center, has furnished the present writer with special insights into the mentality of Flemish nationalists during the occupation. His stories, his scholarly work, his genial interest in the work of this German-born American historian, and above all the story of his life provided me with a sense of the ambience of the Flemish milieu from which he came. In the final stages of the completion of the present book, José Gotovitch, the present Director of the Center deserves special mention as he and his assistant Lut Van Daele have assisted me in tying up loose ends that inevitably emerge at the end of such a long endeavor.

Back home, the book gradually took shape in the hands of a number of members of the Pitzer College staff who possessed the necessary competence with the word processor which the author still lacks at present. Foremost among them Beverly Scales who composed the typescript of the main body of the book, and Sandy Hamilton who prepared the end notes and the glossary. Sandra Corbett Jr., then archivist of the Pitzer History Project composed the bibliography. Without the generous assistance of these Pitzer College colleagues this book would never have seen completion.

And finally I wish to express the most profound thanks and gratitude to my wife, Loretta Champ Warmbrunn. Not only did she suffer the long hours of seclusion in my study, the inevitable raids on the refrigerator, and my long absences in Europe, but she also painstakingly proofread the final copy for typographical errors, inconsistencies and conformity to publication standards. In addition she has prepared the index for the book. For these long hours of labor over a work table covered with scores of reminders and rules of spelling, capitalization and such like, but above all for her patience and unfailing support, I owe her more than I can express in print.

While I wish to acknowledge the help and advice I have received over the years, I want to emphasize that the responsibility for any errors and weaknesses in the final product is entirely mine.

Werner Warmbrunn,
Pitzer College
Claremont, California

January 1992

For Loretta

Whose love and support enabled me to complete this book.

Introduction

Historians and their books have a history too, and a life of their own, and it may be useful to sketch the background of this book for the reader. When I first set out on a study of the German occupation of the Netherlands in August 1947, the Second World War had been over for only two years. There was a question in the mind of this graduate student whether events of such recent vintage would be considered a suitable subject for a doctoral dissertation in History. Fortunately they were, and one of my mentors, the late Harold H. Fisher, after inquiring about my language repertoire, suggested the Dutch Resistance as a topic since he had sixteen crates stored in the basement of the Hoover Tower containing uncatalogued documents and books collected in Holland for the Hoover Library during the war.

I soon discovered that it made little sense to write about the Dutch Resistance without taking first a good look at the context in which it arose. Therefore I widened the scope of my study and examined, first, German administration and policies during the occupation and, next, the Dutch reaction to them.

When I began the present inquiry into the German occupation of Belgium twenty years ago, the Second World War had receded into the past (and was to recede further during the more than two decades which this book has been in the making) and it had become a thoroughly accepted field of historical study with the rise of Contemporary History. With the passage of time it has become more acceptable to deal with this period of history objectively and dispassionately than it was in the immediate aftermath of the war. As a matter of fact, perceptions of the war and its most tragic dimension, the extermination of the Jews of Europe, have undergone considerable modification since 1947, and particularly since the nineteen sixties. Perceptions have become more differentiated leading to a more sophisticated understanding why the Germans and the occupied nations and their leaders acted the way they did.

As a result of this increasing sophistication, and of the primary documentation that has become available since the sixties, my present study experienced a shift which in a sense is the opposite from the shift which occurred with the Dutch project. While I started out with a broader focus, to study German actions and the reaction of the people of Belgium to German rule, my focus narrowed when I discovered that the personalities and policies of the German occupation regime in Belgium were far more complex than those of the German administration in the Netherlands. The complexities of Belgian society presented the Germans with a wider variety of problems and opportunities than those facing their counterparts to the north. This realization gave rise to a new set of questions which the present study will attempt to address: Did the historical context, the fact that there had been a previous German occupation of Belgium within the life span of many adults, influence the policies and actions of the German rulers? Did the Germans deal with the problems and opportunities presented by the tensions between the Flemish and their French-speaking Belgian compatriots more effectively during the second occupation than they had during the first? To which extent were the Germans able to implement consistent policies in Belgium given the conflicts and power struggles characteristic of the Third Reich? What were the moral and practical problems faced by administrators who were not blindly committed to the extreme notions of the transformation of Europe held by Hitler and Himmler and the radical wing of the Nazi party and SS? To which extent did the attempt of the German administrators in Belgium to postpone ideologically motivated political transformations (and propaganda advocating such changes) affect the climate of the occupation, and what were the practical consequences of such a policy? Specifically, was the "policy of the velvet glove", the attempt to proceed gingerly and avoid unnecessary confrontations, effective in maintaining law and order and in promoting economic exploitation? Did the reluctance of the German administrators to risk negative public reactions significantly slow down the deportation of the Jews? How can we explain the survival of the military administration throughout most of the occupation in view of Hitler's disapproval of its "moderate" policies and his growing dislike of the Military Commander, General Alexander von Falkenhausen? These are some of the questions about the German administration of Belgium that emerged from the studies for this book.

These questions and the new materials which have become available have produced the present book on the German rule over Belgium, with a narrower focus than originally intended. It is designed to provide what I hope will be an objective and dispassionate account of the structure, policies and actions of the German administration, taking into consideration the issues just raised. It will focus on the question how effective its actions were as judged against the goals set by Reich and local German authorities. Inevitably these questions will be framed and answered against the background of my familiarity with German occupation policies in the Netherlands. Therefore the present study will have an implicit (and sometimes explicit) comparative dimension.

Chapter One

Before the Occupation

At the beginning of the fifth decade of this century, Belgian government and society were characterized by such unique complexities that it may be helpful to discuss the people and their institutions in some detail because these complexities influenced important aspects of German occupation policy. Therefore this introductory chapter will present certain characteristics of Belgium, its people and its institutions which set the context for the policies of the German occupation.

The Land and the People

Just before the outbreak of the Second World War, in 1938, Belgium was the most densely populated country of Europe with 8.39 million inhabitants on 11,779 square miles of territory.[1] Over half of the population (in 1930) used Flemish as the first language, while less than half employed French as their mother tongue. Brussels, the capital with 910,154 inhabitants (in 1937)[2] housed eleven percent of the total population of the country, and provided work for additional tens of thousands who lived elsewhere.

In these prewar years Brussels attracted many Belgians and other Europeans as a government and economic center. Many Belgian and some foreign business establishments had offices or headquarters in the Belgian capital. However, unlike Paris, Brussels did not absorb all the energies of the country, leaving civic and cultural vitality intact in the many large and small cities and towns within an hour's train ride of the capital. Antwerp was Europe's largest port, and Ghent was a major manufacturing city. Liège and Namur remained active centers of a coal mining and manufacturing area.

The main industries of Belgium were metal products, mining, and textiles. These three branches of industry between them provided employment for about forty percent of the industrial labor force.[3] In the war economy that was to come they would play a major role. After Great Britain, Belgium was the most highly industrialized country in Europe. In 1930, 48.9 percent of the work force was employed in industry and mining, a percentage then exceeded only by Great Britain.[4] While this degree of industrialization made the high population density possible, industry was unequally distributed geographically in the prewar years. The heavy concentration of industry (with the exception of Ghent and Antwerp) was located largely in the (French-speaking) east and south of the country, in the provinces of Liège, Hainault, and Namur. The Flemish-speaking north and west was mostly agricultural with the exception of the industrial regions of Ghent and Antwerp. Hence, the wealth of the country tended to be concentrated in the south and the east, and in Brussels, whereas the rural northern provinces inhabited by the Flemish-speaking people tended to be poor and economically backward.

Heavy industrialization and a high level of food consumption made Belgium heavily dependent on food imports in the prewar years. According to one estimate, fifty percent of the national caloric intake was imported in prewar years (seventy percent if the amount of animal grain feed was included).[5] This heavy reliance on food imports was to create a major problem under the occupation.

Institutions and Society

Visitors to Brussels will find near the northern edge of the Parc de Bruxelles in the center of the city a fountain where office workers gather on a summer day during their lunch hour in hopes of catching a bit of sun. A number of passages fan out from the fountain that offer to the observer sitting on the edge of the fountain views of the buildings housing the fundamental institutions of the Belgian state. Directly to the north, at the shortest distance from the fountain, lies the Parliament building (*Le Palais de la Nation*) near the office of the Prime Minister, the head of the government. To the south, one promenade leads to the royal palace, the king's official city residence. The other southern promenade provides a view of the distant Palace of Justice (*Palais de Justice*) which in its utter massive ugliness towers high above the lower city and which houses the Supreme Court (*Cour de Cassation*) as well as many inferior courts. And to the west, through the trees and above them, the visitor can sense the presence of a row of office buildings which contain many of the great business establishments such as the *Société Générale de Belgique*, which, while not part of any governmental structure, control a large part of the Belgian economy and heavily influence governmental affairs. No special promenade view had been provided for them by the planners of the park back in the nineteenth century, but their presence is obvious to the visitor walking along the Rue Royale on the west side of the park past one name plate after the other of banks or business concerns that have played a major role in the control and development of the economy.

In this manner the design of the Parc de Bruxelles symbolizes the essential structures of the country. The ultimate source of authority and legitimacy, according to the Constitution and increasingly in practice, the people and their Parliament, are close by and fully visible from the fountain, as is the government whose work is dependent on the approval of the Parliament. Further away, at the other side of the park, the king's palace, seat of the royal power, the formal head of the executive, and as destiny would have it, the symbol of integration between two language families that had grown increasingly hostile to each other in the years before the occupation. Even further away the judiciary, highly respected in a business society where law always played an important role, not quite a third branch of government in the sense of the U.S. Constitution, but at least twice in the nation's history a spokesman for national sentiment confronting a foreign conqueror at a time when the other organs of government were no longer present and functioning.* And the business community along the Rue Royale not formally part of any constitutional structure and not as visible from the fountain as the other buildings, but yet present along the whole length of the park as it was present in many operations of government and society, in Belgium earlier and perhaps more decidedly so than in any other continental country. And a strong influence, too, during the second occupation when Parliament, cabinet and Crown were no longer in a position to govern the country.

Only one "power" in society is missing from our picture, with its Brussels "seat" located a few blocks off the Rue Royale, on the way to the lower town.** There stands St. Michael's Cathedral, popularly called "St. Gudule" before the war, the principal church of Brussels and of Belgium where kings and dignitaries of state come together to celebrate religious and patriotic occasions. Whatever the intentions of the planners of the royal park, the Catholic church played a vital role twice in the twentieth century when government and Parliament had departed.

But be that as it may, the visitor to the fountain in the Parc de Bruxelles can sense the presence of the major institutions of this complex country, near and afar, either fully visible, or partly and even totally hidden, but all playing their roles in normal times and in a modified form in the time of crisis which is the subject of this book.

It cannot be the purpose of the present study to present a history of Belgium during the first century of its national existence, but it may be helpful to mention a few aspects which have a direct bearing on the second German occupation. First of all, it should be noted that the Belgian state was established in 1831, as a result of a revolution triggered in part by the events of the July Revolution of 1830 in Paris. Thus a revolutionary spirit going back to the aspirations of the French

---

* During the first German occupation the Belgian judiciary went on strike in 1917 to protest against the deportation of Belgian labor.

** Part of Brussels, including the park, is located on a plateau (*la haute ville*) and part in a lower section (*le marais*).

Revolution of 1789-91 in its liberal phase, as interpreted by the property-owning upper bourgeoisie in 1830 and 1831 formed the conceptual framework of the Constitution of 1831.[6] However British constitutional arrangements also influenced the design of the Belgian constitution.[7]

Throughout the nineteenth century the Catholics and the Liberals formed the two main competing parties which controlled the government. While deeply divided over religious, clerical and social issues, the parties' leaders, sharing a common social and economic background, found sufficient areas of agreement and common interest leaving the basic constitutional arrangements unquestioned before the outbreak of the First World War.

The Constitution of 1831 established a constitutional monarchy. During the remainder of the nineteenth century two strong rulers, Leopold I and his son Leopold II stretched the limits of that constitution in their determination to effect a consolidation of the new state,[8] but they never openly breached the constitutional arrangement. Catholics and Liberals alternately controlled the government. The Catholics held control of the government for a thirty-year period before the outbreak of the First World War. The suffrage was extended very slowly. Only in 1919 was equal universal manhood suffrage granted, and women did not gain the right to vote until after the end of the Second World War.[9]

For the first century of its existence the Belgian state remained firmly in the hands of the French-speaking bourgeoisie. By the time the Socialists were first taken into the government they had become a reformist party, committed to the support of constitutional processes.[10]

One reason why Belgium was able to consolidate her institutions in the nineteenth century was that she remained at peace throughout this period until 1914. Her neutrality had been guaranteed by the European state system in 1839 by the Treaty of London. Great Britain in particular was committed to the defense of Belgian neutrality because the Low Countries were viewed by the British as a strategically vital barrier against potential aggressors who might wish to establish themselves on the Channel coast. Therefore,

Belgium on the one hand owed her existence and tranquility to her strategic location as long as no power sought to upset the European equilibrium. Yet, by the same token, Belgium became a primary target in 1914 and then again in 1940 when that equilibrium broke down.

During the nineteenth century the potential tensions built into Belgian society through its linguistic dualism did not yet create any major problems because the Flemish bourgeoisie was assimilated into the French-speaking culture of state and society.[11] The potential linguistic polarization was further attenuated by the development of parallel societies, the phenomenon of *verzuiling* or "compartmentalization of life within 'spiritual' families."[12] This term describes the phenomenon that the foremost political groupings (Catholics, Liberals and Socialists) created a network of voluntary associations such as schools, trade unions and athletic clubs which provided a way of life and a "home" for many Belgian citizens. These associations were local in character and national in scope. They succeeded in keeping alive the national ideal without weakening local traditions and ties. Yet despite these reinforcing factors—a liberal state, a strong monarchy, shared economic and social interests—it has been said of modern Belgium that there are few countries in Europe where the nationhood of the country is questioned so vigorously and so openly and where the sense of nationality is so weak as it is in Belgium.[13]

This same ambiguity confronts us as we search for national characteristics or "national character." One observer suggests: "The outstanding characteristic of Belgian national character is that there is none—there are only two peoples, the Flemish and Walloons"[14] (or as others might say three—adding the inhabitants of Brussels as the third "nation".) It has been suggested by a contemporary Belgian scholar that Belgians become aware of their "national character" only in their confrontations with other nationalities in peace or war.[15]

But other observers would disagree with such a "cynical" view. They could point to the unifying force of religion: ninety percent (or more) of the people of Belgium described themselves as Catholics.[16] As in many Catholic countries, and more so than in some, the church played an important role in political and social life, to the point where bishops were viewed "as the spiritual counterparts" of the provincial governors, according to one observer.[17] There existed a lively anticlerical tradition, particularly among Liberals and Socialists. Yet a profound respect for the authority of the Catholic church was widespread. It was reinforced when at the beginning of the occupation in 1940, the church remained the continuing authority least affected by combat, dislocation and exodus.

The cohesiveness of the family, not unrelated to the strength of religious authority, could be considered another outstanding characteristic of the Belgian people.[18] Parental influence remained strong, even over young adults in their twenties and thirties. One expression of this strong family feeling was the desire to own one's own house, to an extent unique among continental peoples at that time.[19] These family ties, together with the ties of the innumerable private associations and of local and communal life, gave the urbanite in prewar Belgium a matrix of relationships which stood him in good stead during the trials of war and occupation. This was not a society likely to come apart easily at the seams even under the strain of extreme wartime conditions.

One other "national character trait" sometimes mentioned in the literature which influenced behavior under the occupation has been called "the cunning of the oppressed." For centuries the people of the Southern Netherlands and Burgundy had lived under the sway of "foreign" rulers. Throughout these centuries, it is believed by some that a negative and contemptuous attitude toward the authority of the state had emerged, implemented by complex skills in evading the demands of government. This negative attitude toward government was reinforced after 1831 by the philosophy of a liberal state committed to laissez-faire economics, and to non-interference by the state in the lives of private individuals and associations.

This spirit of indifference or even "fraud"[20] may be related to a degree of materialism that some observers detect in the Belgian national character.[21] Certainly good food and drink, and plenty of it, have traditionally characterized life in Belgium, probably from before the days of Pieter Breughel and Peter Paul Rubens. Belgian per capita beer consumption was the highest in the world in 1939, and *frites* (French fries) and rich sauces remain the staples supplied with Brussels restaurant meals to this day. Perhaps all this says no more than that people of Belgium knew how to live well, but it is probably also true that the contemptuous and suspicious attitude toward government and high expectations of a materially satisfying life influenced the ways in which the population coped with the shortages and deprivations of the occupation.

The mention of the importance of stabilizing factors such as monarchy and church on the one hand, and of dynamic factors such as disrespect for the state and a taste for the good life on the other, leads us to make one more final characterization. Belgian society on the eve of the Second World War seemed to be a curious mixture of the old and the new, of tradition and modernity.

Belgium was the first continental country to industrialize on the British model. Its aristocracy was prepared to profit from the benefits of commerce, banking and industry, and a new aristocracy of business men and industrialists managed to merge with the old nobility during the nineteenth and twentieth centuries. In turn, industrialization and urbanization gave rise to an industrial proletariat which in time spawned a Socialist party and strong labor unions. And yet, opposed to these dynamic modernizing forces we find a narrow oligarchy running many branches of industry, business and government, with the same family names occurring over and over again in leading positions, a strongly entrenched conservative Catholic church, a stubbornly persisting family tradition, and a firm nexus of local community life. And finally in the thirties, we find an all-pervasive unresolved ethnic problem, labelled the "language question," conjuring up some of the nationalistic and even tribal emotions that on first sight have no place in an advanced modern industrial society. Thus it can be argued, that a strong degree of internal contradictions, between the old and the new, between tradition and modernization, was a significant overall characteristic of Belgian society in the nineteen thirties.

The Monarchy

The monarch who was called to the throne in 1831 to reign as Leopold I was a capable German prince, a member of the House of Saxe - Coburg - Gotha. He was the favorite uncle of the Princess Royal, who was to ascend the British throne in 1837 as Queen Victoria. When invited to become King of Belgium he managed to sever his concerns with the small principality from which he came and devoted his full attention and energies to the task of consolidating the new Belgian state.

The new monarchy was seen by many of the Belgian people, particularly the upper and middle classes as a guarantee of their newly-won liberty. After all, the people of Belgium now lived under a dynasty and a government of their own for the first time in centuries. Thus the notion that the ruling monarch, especially Leopold I, was the "Maker of Belgium," the *conditor Belgii*, contributed to the growth of loyalty to the new dynasty and state.[22]

Leopold I from the start "intended to rule as well as to reign". He personally presided over the sessions of the cabinet, served as the actual commander in chief and closely supervised the affairs of government departments.[23] His son Leopold II took an even more active role in the conduct of the government. He concerned himself especially with the army, foreign affairs and the colonial enterprise. In fact he acquired and for some decades ran as a private business what was later to become the Belgian Congo, creating such outrage by his exploitation of the Congolese that Parliament took over in the end, making it a Belgian colony. Leopold's arbitrariness and his personal extravagances brought royal rule into disrepute by the end of his reign.[24] However his nephew Albert retrieved the popularity of the monarchy by his courageous and patriotic conduct during the First World War.

Albert I was more discrete than his uncle but he was also determined to make an impact on public affairs. He no longer presided routinely over cabinet meetings, except during the war, but dealt with individual ministers on issues with which he was particularly concerned. When the Germans invaded Belgium in August 1914 he assumed personal command of the army in keeping with tradition and acquired tremendous popularity as the "Soldier-King"* (*Le Roi Chevalier*) who stayed and fought with his troops until final victory.[25] He retained this nimbus of glory and veneration throughout his life until his tragic end in 1934. At this point, his son, Leopold III ascended the throne, surrounded by the accumulated prestige of the monarchy, an heir to the personal veneration of his own father[26] whom he worshipped and tried to emulate to the best of his ability.

The tradition that the king would serve as the actual commander in chief had created by 1914 an anomalous constitutional situation little noticed at the time. Under the Constitution, the king could act only by securing the countersignature of a minister. By this signature, this minister became politically responsible to Parliament for the action concerned and thus "covered" the Crown. Hence the concept: "The king can do no wrong." As commander in chief, however, Albert issued instructions directly to the Chief of the General Staff of the Army, without the countersignature of the Minister of War. He, therefore, made himself responsible politically for orders given to the army.[27] This issue was never raised publicly, but the king's actions set a precedent for King Leopold in May 1940.

All in all, Belgium at the end of its first century of existence had developed into a twentieth century parliamentary democracy in which the cabinet in essence had become the creature of Parliament and of the major political parties. However, the king still played a somewhat stronger role, particularly in military and diplomatic affairs, than did his British, Dutch or Scandinavian counterparts.[28] In the view of one responsible observer, the Belgian rulers exerted an influence on government greater than that which the framers of the liberal constitution of 1831 had had in mind, but on the whole Parliament

---

* literally: "The Knight-King"

and public had acquiesced in the use of the royal prerogative made by the Belgian rulers.[29] Throughout this period Parliament had remained the supreme authority in matters of legislation and that authority had never been questioned, even if at times circumvented.[30]

Leopold III who ascended the throne in 1934 was made of a more contradictory mold than his predecessors. It cannot be the purpose of this study to enter in depth into the psychological makeup of the king, but some understanding of his personality is required for a proper appreciation of his conduct in 1940-44, and beyond. It appears that he was a shy, retiring, complex person, basically an introvert, with a high sense of personal duty and, in the years that concern us, high expectations of himself in his role as a ruling monarch. The extraordinary events of his life prior to 1940 may yield some clues to an understanding of his conduct during the war.

Leopold was twelve years of age when the First World War broke out. He spent some years at Eaton, but during the last part of the war he served on the Western front with the Belgian army. In that situation he observed from close proximity his father's actions as commander in chief. He was keenly aware of the veneration of which Albert was the recipient then and in subsequent years, and he shared these feelings. Leopold's veneration of his father and his desire to follow in his footsteps, to act as his father would (in Leopold's opinion) have liked to see him act,[31] probably provide the single most important psychological clue to an understanding of his motives in 1940.

After the war Leopold served as an officer in one of the crack regiments of the army, an experience not conducive to an avoidance of a certain kind of aristocratic snobbery.[32] He also attended university and developed a special interest in the natural sciences. He has been described as the happiest when absorbed in his work in his laboratory.

At the University of Ghent he also attended lectures of the dean of Belgian historians, Henri Pirenne. Pirenne is famous as the articulator of the *idée belge*, the notion that Belgium, on the basis of her history, culture and her geographical situation, had an ancient historical tradition and a historical mission at the crossroads of Europe. Pirenne thus viewed the Belgian state of 1831, far from being an artificial creation of Great Power politics, as the embodiment of a historic and organic community.[33] It is reasonable to assume that Pirenne's teaching only helped to deepen the sense of mission in the prince.

After completion of his formal education, Leopold was appointed to the Senate, the upper house of the Belgian legislature, acquiring some firsthand experience in government. In 1926 he married Princess Astrid, a niece of the Swedish king. Astrid, a beautiful woman and a warm human being, quickly acquired great popularity among the Belgian people, and three children were born to the royal couple.

Then in 1934 the first of the tragic accidents that were to mar Leopold's life struck unexpectedly when King Albert perished in a mountaineering accident in Switzerland. And only one year later, in 1935, Queen Astrid was killed in an automobile accident during a Swiss vacation, while Leopold was in the driver's seat. This quick succession of violent deaths of his two closest family members, and in particular his gnawing sense of responsibility for Astrid's death, caused, or deepened in Leopold an already existing sense of melancholy, withdrawal and isolation.[34] One does not have to go as far as Rudolph Binion, a psychoanalytically-oriented American historian who explains Leopold's conduct in 1940 as a classical instance of a reenactment of these two previous tragedies,[35] to conclude that they may have had profound psychological repercussions which were likely to affect Leopold's actions in a crisis.

Three other members of the Royal family played a role during the war and occupation. Queen-Mother Elisabeth, the widow of King Albert, a former Bavarian duchess, had become very popular in Belgian society particularly through her devotion to welfare work and her sponsorship of literary and artistic affairs.[36] She continued to be active during the occupation remaining in public view after the disappearance of the King from the public stage in 1940.

Of special political importance, particularly during the first months of the occupation, was Leopold's sister Marie-José who was married to Crown Prince Umberto of Italy. Marie-José was a sportswoman, an acquaintance and allegedly a "friend" of Hitler's. In 1940 she became the intermediary through whom Leopold's visit to Hitler was arranged.

Leopold's younger brother, Charles, was less in the limelight during the occupation. He was not committed to the king's policy toward the Germans and therefore a logical contact for the Allies and the Resistance. He went underground with the help of the Resistance in the closing weeks of the occupation and became Regent after the liberation in place of the absent king. After the resolution of the constitutional crisis in 1950, Prince Charles became involved in financial scandals and disappeared from the public stage.

Politics and Government 1918 - 1940

Belgian patriots often point with pride to the fact that Belgium has the oldest continuously functioning constitution on the continent which stipulates that the government is responsible to the Parliament.[37] But it must also be noted that suffrage remained extremely restricted at least until 1894. Hence, until the First World War Parliament and government remained the instrument of the affluent bourgeoisie organized in the Liberal and Catholic parties.

In the interwar years the Socialists joined the two old parties in the government. For much of this time, a coalition of two out of the three major parties could form a majority government. However, since the parties were in themselves associations of various interest groups it proved difficult to maintain stable majorities for government proposals, particularly in the thirties. Hence governments came and went. This instability was a major reason for dissatisfaction with the parliamentary regime.[38] But it should also be noted that after the First World War party affiliations were basically very stable. Voters did not easily shift party allegiance because of their membership in the network of associations attached to the major parties. Moreover appointments to government positions were often made on the basis of allegiance to a political party.

Hence political obligations and employment considerations stabilized party allegiance.

According to some observers, Belgian political life during this period was sometimes characterized by a lack of a sense of proportion, elevating relatively minor issues to matters of principle. As was the case in much of Western Europe many Belgian politicians and intellectuals were profoundly dissatisfied with the functioning of their political system during the thirties. Among many circles, from the Socialists to the more conservative Catholics and royalists, arose the desire for some fundamental change, a strengthening of government and executive authority around the king, in order to meet the economic and political challenges of the Depression and the rise of fascism.[39] According to conservative supporters of such ideas a more authoritative government would mean a reestablishment of the "original principles" of the Constitution, but to others these currents smacked of authoritarianism and fascism.[40]

The Catholic party (or Catholic Union) was a federation of many groups. It represented a wider range of different political and social points of view than the other great parties.[41] It included conservative elements opposing social change, but also a "socialist" wing which supported social reforms in the spirit of Leo XIII's encyclical *De Rerum Novarum*.[42] Likewise the party counted in its ranks fervent advocates of a unitary Belgian state and continued predominance of the francophone* element, as well as Flemish nationalists wanting at least some form of cultural autonomy for Flanders.[43]

On the whole the Catholics had their greatest strength in Flanders, particularly in the rural regions. They relied heavily on the advice and authority of the Belgian episcopate and even of the pope. The party stood united on such specifically religious issues as government support for parochial schools. It strongly supported the policy of neutrality in the 1936-40 period. The Catholic party and the church were fiercely royalist seeing in the monarchy the symbol of the

---

* French-speaking

unity of the country.⁴⁴ In the postwar evolution of the royal question it would become "the king's party" supporting Leopold's reinstatement on the throne.

The Catholic party did not have any one dominant leader in the interwar period. Frans Van Cauwelaert who headed its Chamber group was a moderate Flemish nationalist who sought greater equality for the Flemish within the existing framework of a unitary state.⁴⁵ Hubert Pierlot, another Catholic leader, was a man of firm, not to say rigid, principles and a stubborn sense of moral rectitude. He became Premier in 1939 and was destined to be the head of the wartime Belgian government.

In the interwar years the Catholic trade unions had grown substantially. They gained the allegiance of a significant section of the working class and offered the Socialist unions stiff competition.⁴⁶ They formed another structure, in addition to the church itself, through which Catholic initiative and actions could make itself felt at the local level during the war years when the parties themselves were suppressed.

The Liberal party was based primarily on the bourgeoisie of Brussels and of the French-speaking part of the country. The core of its beliefs had been its anticlericalism, and, in the 20th century, its opposition to government regulation of social and economic affairs. The party vigorously supported the military budget. Its parliamentary leader Devèze, was a decided militarist. Since the party represented the concerns of the French-speaking bourgeoisie, it tended to oppose legislation giving more rights to the Flemish and putting the Flemish language on a par with the French.

The Socialist party (*Parti Ouvrier Belge*) constituted even more than the Catholic party "a house of its own", a party with a complete set of social and economic organizations and institutions that could provide "a way of life" to its members. Before 1919 universal suffrage had been its primary political objective. After the achievement of universal manhood suffrage and basic social welfare legislation at the end of the First World War, it had advocated further improvement of the lot of the working class. It retained its prewar anticlerical stance and was pacifist, opposing greater appropriations for the army.[47]

Since its beginnings in the 1890's the Socialist party had enjoyed strong and permanent leadership in Emile Vandervelde, its leader in Parliament. The main regional strength of the Socialist party lay in industrial Wallonia, particularly in the province of Liège and in the industrial regions of the south, but it also had a sizeable Flemish wing based in the industrial cities of Antwerp and Ghent. Originally the party had been antimonarchist, but by the 1930's it had accepted the monarchy as a guarantee of the unity of the Belgian state.

On the language issue, the Socialist party, like the Catholics, was divided between its Walloon and its Flemish wing. In general the Socialists steered a middle course on the Flemish question, supporting the integrity of the Belgian state against Walloon and Flemish separatist movements.[48]

In the 1930's two younger leaders of the party had made their mark in politics. One of these was Henri De Man. De Man came from a francophone Flemish background. He had studied in Germany and had been deeply influenced by German thought. (He taught Sociology at the University of Frankfurt until 1933.) In 1933 he had come forth with his famous *Plan de Travail*, a comprehensive scheme of social and economic organization designed to secure the right to work which smacked somewhat of corporatist and Fascist social thought. After Vandervelde's death, De Man became the head of the Socialist party in 1939.[49] De Man was quite close to the king and was to be by his side during the invasion and the capitulation. For a few months in 1940 he was to play an important role in trying to move labor into the path of collaboration, but he soon vanished into the shadows spending the later years of the war in the Alps and escaping into Switzerland before liberation.[50]

Paul-Henri Spaak also belonged to the younger generation of Socialist leaders. He was sometimes viewed as the "crown prince" of the party. He was a member of the French-speaking bourgeoisie, and counted among his relatives many political and business leaders.[51] Bright, personable and gregarious, Spaak had moved up quickly in the hierarchy of the Socialist party and had been a member of the cabinet since 1934. He had specialized in foreign affairs and served as Foreign Minister since 1938. During the war Spaak became the leading figure in the Belgian government-in-exile in London next to Prime Minister Pierlot, and Belgium's chief spokesman in the Allied world. In the nineteen thirties Spaak had grown close to the king and there had been unusal personal compatibility and liking between the two men.[52] Together, they were viewed by many contemporaries as the chief architects of Belgium's new policy of "independent" neutrality.[53] But despite his warm feelings toward the king in the thirties, Spaak broke with Leopold in May 1940 and ten years later played a key role in the movement which eventually brought about the king's abdication.

In the interwar years the parties were faced with three broad sets of issues. The oldest of these was the religious issue on which the Catholic and Liberal parties in the 19th centuries had been the clear-cut spokesmen. With the school compromise of 1921 (providing for public support of Catholic schools) the religious issue had lost some but not all of its intensity.[54]

The second set of issues revolved around questions of economic and social reform. The Socialist party most clearly presented the demand of the working classes for an improvement in their situation, whereas the Liberal party tended to support the views of business and the property-owning middle classes.[55] As has been discussed above, the Catholic coalition included a wide variety of views on social issues.

The third group of issues revolved around the language question and the demands of the Flemish-speaking people for effective equality, and for greater autonomy. On the language question, the Catholic party (among the three great parties) most nearly represented the Flemish interest. In the 1920's it increasingly came under pressure from the Flemish nationalists for a more vigorous stance on the language issue.[56] As has been mentioned previously, the Liberal party was opposed to most Flemish demands while the Socialist party was split on the issue.

Thus it can be seen why it was difficult to maintain stable government. The two largest parties, the Catholics and the Socialists were divided on the two most important issues facing the country: how to solve the economic crisis and improve the lot of the working class, and how to deal with the Flemish question. Hence party leaders could not always count on the votes of their representatives, and governments sometimes resigned even without a no-confidence vote in the Chamber when their legislative projects failed.[57] The problem of government effectiveness and stability was exacerbated during the 1936-39 legislative period when it took the three major parties, Catholics, Liberals and Socialists to form a majority government and pass legislation.

The outcome of the elections of 1936, which created this situation, gave the country its major political shock of the decade. The newly founded proto-Fascist Rex party under the leadership of thirty year old Léon Degrelle, a flamboyant alumnus of the Catholic youth movement, captured eleven percent of the electoral vote, while the three old "democratic" parties lost seventeen percent of the vote they had received in 1932.[58] This sudden emergence of Rex sent a shudder down the spine of the democratic elements who remembered the meteoric rise of Italian Fascists in the early twenties and of the German Nazi party in 1930. However, this Rexist success proved to be a flash in the pan. In 1937, Degrelle was trounced thoroughly in a byelection in Brussels, the area of his greatest strength, where he ran as the sole opponent to former Prime Minister Paul van Zeeland who was supported by the three established parties, and by the Catholic church in the person of the Archbishop of Malines.

In Parliament too, the Rexist delegation of twenty-one members made a poor showing. These factors and tactical mistakes made by Rex led to its virtual disappearance from Parliament in the elections of 1939 when Rex dropped from twenty-one to four seats, and to four percent of the popular vote. The old parties recovered the votes they had lost in 1936 and between them held one hundred and seventy out of two hundred seats in the Chamber.[59] A majority government was formed by Catholics and Liberals with Hubert Pierlot of the

Catholic party as its Premier, with the understanding that the Socialists would join in the event of war to form a government of national union. This promptly happened on September 3, 1939. Thus Belgium was fortunate in having in its wartime cabinet representatives of the three major parties which between them had gathered over eighty percent of the popular vote. This made it legitimate for the government during its years in exile to consider itself the representative of the nation.

How deep and widespread was the dissatisfaction with the shortcomings of the parliamentary regime by the end of the decade? Interpretations as to the extent of political dissatisfaction differ. On the one hand, the well-known journalist and collaborator Raymond de Becker in a postwar memorandum blames the phenomenon of Collaboration on the inability of the prewar political leadership to make the necessary changes.[60] We also read elsewhere that:

> There was hardly anybody left in Belgium at the outbreak of the Second World War who did not thoroughly believe that our political institutions were going through an acute crisis, that Chamber and Senate no longer met their responsibilities, and that they should be replaced by a different constitutional system.[61]

The Rexist attack on the corruption of the politicians of the period proved quite effective since most politicians had engaged in some business dealings at one time or another which could be made to look questionable even if they were not.[62] On the other hand, it could also be argued that this Rexist attack on parliamentary government essentially strengthened parliamentary democracy because it induced the three major parties to join ranks (as they had in the 1937 byelection in Brussels) and that it had increased their capacity for compromise in the face of internal and external danger. Thus three acute observers of the period, Willequet,[63] Gérard-Libois and Gotovitch stress that after all the great majority of Belgians had pronounced itself in the 1939 elections faithful to parliamentary democracy and that the articulate and vocal anti-democratic extremists such as De Man and Degrelle had no substantial popular following.

Gérard-Libois and Gotovitch believed that most of the dissatisfaction with the regime was found in the royal court and in the francophone bourgeois intellectuals in the capital who dominated the Brussels press.[64] Their views lead them to conclude that "there was no reason on May 10, 1940 for the belief that there could be established a national unity party around the throne."[65]

The truth probably lies somewhere in between. In the opinion of this writer there is no question that there was widespread sentiment in the thirties that the parliamentary regime no longer functioned satisfactorily in Belgium. The dissatisfaction with the operations of the political system and the unresolved social, economic and Flemish questions was real enough to lend itself for exploitation by the Germans during the occupation. But it is also true that collaborationist and authoritarian movements could not count on widespread popular support (as the more perceptive Germans well knew after the summer of 1940) because the great majority of the Belgian people, Walloons and Flemish alike, were loyal to their own country and its democratic institutions, great as some of their dissatisfactions in the midst of the crisis of the thirties may have been.

The "Language Question"

Previous comments have suggested that the relationship between the Flemish and the French-speaking segments of the population saddled Belgian politics with a complexity unique in Western Europe. By and large the two language families not only occupied two different regions of the country but they also possessed different economic and social attributes. Most of the Flemish lived in the north and west of the country. Most of the French-speaking people lived in the south and east, and in the capital city of Brussels.

The "language frontier" had remained relatively stable since the fifth century A.D.[66] It ran along an old Roman road from Visé in the east through Waterloo just to the south of Brussels and from there westward to Dunkirk in France. To complicate matters, French-speaking Brussels lay clearly within Flemish language territory. Furthermore, French had become the language of the educated people everywhere, even in Flanders.[67]

A curious paradox existed with regard to the balance between French and Flemish-speaking people. On the one hand the Flemish-speaking people with their rural background and stronger religious commitments increased faster than the urban Walloon* population which experienced very little net growth in the decades before the war. On the other hand large numbers of Flemish people moved from "overpopulated" Flanders to the industrial centers of Wallonia where jobs were available. These people became therefore "lost" to Flemish language and culture as their children spoke French instead of Flemish. In addition, the French-speaking population of Brussels continued to expand into the Flemish countryside as more and more residents moved into the suburbs. Because of these contradictory tendencies both French and Flemish-speaking people viewed the future with apprehension.

In 1930, 42.92 percent of the population spoke Flemish, 37.56 percent spoke French and an additional 12.92 percent spoke Flemish and French.[68] Much of the bilingualism could be found in Brussels and, to a lesser extent, in the cities of Flanders.[69] Flemish-speaking and bilingual speakers clearly outnumbered French native speakers in the country as a whole, although more people could express themselves in French than in Flemish.

Whereas Flemish-speaking Belgians outnumbered their French-speaking compatriots, the French language traditionally had enjoyed a superior position in state and society. French had been the tongue of the educated as illustrated by the saying: "French in the parlor, Flemish in the kitchen."[70]

---

* "Wallonia" ("*La Wallonie*") and "Walloon" ("*Wallon*" in French, or "*Waalsch*" in Flemish) are terms which came into general use in the period before the First World War to designate the French-speaking regions of Belgium. Of the same derivation as the English term "Welsh", Walloon in its narrow sense refers to a Latin language related to French in a manner similar to that in which Provençal is related to the French national language. Most inhabitants of Wallonia speak French although "*Wallon*" survives as a dialect and in folklore.

Knowledge of French had been necessary for careers in public affairs or in government service, particularly at the higher levels, or as one writer put it: "in order to become Belgian one had to give up being Flemish."[71]

French was a world language with a great literary and cultural tradition in which French-speaking Belgians could fully participate: "There is no cultural frontier to the south."[72] Hence to teach French to the Flemish was viewed as one way of raising their cultural level. Flemish on the other hand had sadly deteriorated from its great medieval heritage. It had further been hurt by its separation in 1830 from the Dutch literary scene. After independence, the clergy had encouraged such a separation in order to protect the faithful from Dutch Protestantism. It also had opposed the use of French, the language of the Enlightenment, and of laicism and anti-clerical thought.[73] In fact by the nineteenth century there was no such thing as a Flemish language. Flemish was largely a collection of dialects, with Dutch being used as the literary language.

Although the Flemish-Walloon problem in its broader context was a product of nineteenth century European nationalism, its full dimensions were not yet felt in the nineteenth century. It was possible to argue that "no country was ever more homogeneous than the Belgium of 1830: The French-speaking and property-owning bourgeoisie formed the ruling class."[74] The *pays légal* of Flanders spoke French and absorbed French culture, perhaps as much as its counterpart to the south. To be "francophone" was a source of pride and prestige in Flanders.

Yet a plea for the rentention and development of Flemish was heard from a few individuals as early as the first decade of the existence of the new state: "The language is the entire people" as the Flemish writer Jan Frans Willems would have it.[75] But in the nineteenth century the Flemish movement remained in the main a literary and intellectual endeavor, restricted to a relatively small group of professional people of lower middle class background. They asked only for more respect for the Flemish language and for its recovery and development.

The broadening of manhood suffrage in 1897 transformed the Flemish movement. From a cause supported primarily by intellectuals, it turned into a popular movement; from being primarily concerned with the question of language, it now moved toward demanding equality for the Flemish-speaking part of the nation in all walks of life.[76] Foremost among these demands were the use of Flemish in secondary and higher education, in the administration of law and in government agencies, and the effective opening of public careers to the Flemish.[77]

Whatever the relationship of Flanders and Wallonia was going to be, Brussels presented a special problem. During the 19th century it had turned from a predominantly Flemish-speaking to a predominantly French-speaking city. Because of the French character of Brussels life, the Flemish-speaking person did not feel at home in the city. As one writer observed, "The capital of Flanders is not Brussels, but Antwerp or Ghent."[78]

The inhabitants of Brussels were viewed with an unsympathetic eye by some Walloons as well as Flemish: they were seen as materialistic, snobbish, and lacking in spiritual values.[79] Moreover, later during the nineteenth century, when city dwellers began to move into the suburbs, the inhabitants of Brussels tended to take their French preferences with them into the Flemish countryside: a movement which some Flemish viewed as the "Brussels oil slick" polluting the "pure" Flemish region.[80] Yet, Brussels supplied a unifying element in the Belgian state; the *Bruxellois* "views himself and his compatriots as the only true representative of the orthodox national unity" observed a conservative politician under the occupation.[81] "The impossible Belgian fusion has occurred in the capital . . . under the hegemony of the French language," wrote a postwar observer.[82] Here government offices and the great national institutions were located at the heart of an excellent railroad system. Thousands of persons from the provinces travelled to the capital each working day to work, returning home by train at the end of the day. Thus in the complexity of the linguistic and ethnic conflicts, Brussels remained an impediment to any simple regional solution.

But it was the reality of social and economic discrimination which formed the greatest single obstacle to a "neat" or sensible solution on the Swiss model. The basic elements have been mentioned: French was the language of the educated elite, Flemish the language of the poor and the uneducated; Brussels and Wallonia were "rich", "backward" Flanders was poor; French a world language, Flemish a collection of dialects borrowing the language of neighboring Holland as its *lingua franca* and its literary language. Careers, especially advancement into the higher positions, in government and any but local business were reserved for the francophones. For many decades education in Flemish was available only in the elementary grades. There was no Flemish university until 1917. Hence the number of Flemish students in secondary and higher education remained substantially below that of the French-speaking population. This meant that the Flemish elite was numerically weak until the 1930's.

And finally there was, for Flemish nationalists, the anguish of parents or grandparents who saw their offspring disappear into another language and culture, grandparents unable to talk freely to their grandchildren who were raised in the language of the "ruling class," for the sake of making sure that "doors will be open to them."[83] And on the other hand, on the part of Walloons and of the inhabitants of Brussels, contempt, often expressed with particular vehemence by the person of Flemish origin who had "made it" recently into French society, for the Flemish "simpleton", the peasant or servant or deliveryman. There existed a determination on the part of the French-speaking population to protect its privileged position in society and government against the demands "for a place in the sun" of what was to be a growing majority. And above all, a determination to protect their children's future by seeing to it that they learned "pure" French and a corresponding reluctance for them to learn the "inferior language," a language which was seen as being of no use to them. In the words of a postwar observer:

> For the Walloons accept it generally as an axiom that it is difficult not to say impossible, and rather unnatural for Walloons to learn Flemish while it is easy and natural for the Flemish to learn French.[84]

By way of caution it must be added that the ordinary Flemish-speaking person, the Flemish "common man" did not necessarily harbor strong resentments against his French-speaking compatriots in the days before 1914. Most of the ordinary people in the country and in the small towns lived in a totally Flemish-speaking environment and did not come into contact with many organs of the French-speaking bureaucracy. Only with the drafting of large numbers of Flemish soldiers into the Belgian army, to serve under officers who usually only spoke French, did the masses of the Flemish people come face to face with the Flemish-French duality. And it was out of the experience of the First World War that the nationalist movement began to acquire the political character it possessed in the nineteen thirties and under the second occupation.

We have taken so much space to discuss some of the sociological and psychological dimensions of the Flemish problem because they alone explain, especially to the foreigner, the degree of effectiveness of the German policy of encouraging Flemish separatism in two world wars.

It has been implied before that the progress of the Flemish cause was slow in the nineteenth century. However, by the 1870s the first laws were passed on behalf of the Flemish language. They gave permission for the use of Flemish in legal proceedings and in government services. Since 1898 laws and decrees were published in both languages.[85]

But the real progress came only as a result of the First World War. In the Great War Flemish soldiers constituted substantially more than half of the Belgian army. They had to serve under francophone officers most of whom did not understand Flemish and had the usual contempt for that language. Thus many conflicts developed between officers and common soldiers, aggravated by the endless suffering of trench warfare. These conflicts lead to serious agitation and even to mutiny. Out of this turmoil arose a new cohesion among the Flemish peasant soldiers which found its expression in the Front movement (*Frontbeweging*). The Front movement went as far as to send emissaries to the Germans.[86]

In response to this Flemish agitation, King Albert in 1918, on behalf of the government, promised equality of the two languages and the establishment of Ghent as a Flemish university.[87] It had become the king's personal conviction that full equality should be granted to the Flemish in recognition of their sacrifices on the battlefield. But the king also continued to plead the cause of national unity opposing a "narrow particularism" that might destroy the unity of the state.[88]

In the meantime a group of Flemish intellectuals and professionals called "Activists" had worked in German-occupied Belgium with the occupation authorities toward the fulfillment of their goals. They achieved a major triumph when Ghent was opened as an exclusively Flemish university in October 1917. At the same time a group of Activists under the leadership of Auguste Borms formed the so-called Council of Flanders (*Raad van Vlaanderen*) which proclaimed the independence of Flanders in December 1917.[89] After the end of the war the Flemish Activists were prosecuted for their wartime endeavors, and harsh sentences were passed out. Borms was sentenced to death, but the sentence was commuted to life imprisonment. One consequence of the harshness of these postwar judicial proceedings was that it further embittered supporters of the Flemish cause.[90] But on the other hand, the wartime policies of the Activists made the entire Flemish movement suspect in the eyes of francophones and also made it more difficult to implement immediately the reforms King Albert had promised in 1918.[91]

Another consequence of the Front movement was the creation of the Front party (*Frontpartij*), a radical Flemish group in Parliament which gained six seats in 1919 and eleven in 1929. Its goals included the old Flemish demands in addition to the insistence on amnesty for the Activists languishing in jail.[92] Progress remained slow in the twenties because of the prevailing climate which equated the Flemish national cause with treason. But the Flemish movement (as distinguished from the radical nationalists in Parliament) had now become a mass movement that could draw as many as one hundred thousand people to its annual pilgrimage to the memorial of the Flemish war dead (the *Ijzerbedevaarten*) at Dixmuide.[93]

Despite its growing popular appeal, the Flemish nationalist movement in the interwar years was weakened by internal disagreements on goals and the means to achieve them. Some Flemish spokesmen would be satisfied with effective equality of language and the adoption of Flemish as the only language for Flanders; others, a growing segment, wanted autonomy for Flanders within the Belgian state or a Federal statute for Belgium; still others wanted complete destruction of the Belgian state and the establishment of an independent Flanders or of a state for *all* Dutch-speaking people (*"Dietsland"*). And finally there was a group under the leadership of one Joris Van Severen, grouped in an organization called Verdinaso*, which wanted to unite all of Belgium with the Netherlands and parts of northern France to form a new state *"Groot-Dietsland"* along the boundaries of a Burgundian state that had existed in the late Middle Ages. It should be noted, however, that no group before 1940 advocated union with Germany.

Differences also existed in political philosophy. The great majority of Flemish nationalists were died-in-the-wool Catholics: "Everything for Flanders, Flanders for Christ," as the banners of the annual pilgrimages to the Yser proclaimed. Some of these politicians were prepared to support parliamentary democracy and a liberal state which had made many concessions to Catholic views. Others were increasingly influenced by the rise of fascism, particularly in Italy, and its corporatist tendencies. As the thirties progressed, more and more Flemish nationalists looked favorably toward Germany and the accomplishments of national-socialism. But there also remained within the nationalist movement many individuals and groups who were suspicious of Germany and fascism, and who basically wanted a Catholic Flanders autonomous or independent, left to itself to work out its own destiny, possibly within the framework of the Belgian state.[94]

---

* *Verbond van Dietse nationaal-solidaristen* or "league of Greater-Netherlands nationalist solidarity."

But whereas the radical *Frontpartij* made little headway with its demands in Parliament during the 1920s, an agreement in principle was reached in 1921 between the moderates in the Socialist, Catholic and Liberal parties called the "Compromise of the Belgians" (*Compromis des Belges*). This compromise stipulated the use of the native language in each of the two regions, and the bilingualism of national institutions and services. This formula in fact became the basis of the resolution of the language question in the thirties and in the early postwar period.[95]

The eventual adoption of the principles underlying the *Compromis des Belges* illustrates the fact that the main legislative progress in the Flemish cause was achieved by the Flemish sections of the majority parties, rather than by the radical Flemish nationalist parties. These acted as pressure groups keeping the issues fresh in the minds of the Flemish sympathizers in the majority parties, and by their very existence and potential appeal to Flemish voters reminded majority party politicians of the need to be responsive to the demands of Flemish voters.[96]

It took a major political upheaval to provide finally the momentum for the legal implementation of the promises made to the Flemish after World War I. In 1928, in a byelection in Antwerp, Borms, then still in prison, was elected to the Chamber of Deputies by a large majority. This event showed the depth of Flemish resentment of the government's failure to implement its postwar promises. It raised the prospect that Flemish nationalists might make heavy inroads on the traditional constituencies of the Catholic and Socialist parties. This threat produced the needed parliamentary support for a series of language laws passed between 1931 and 1935 which met most of the demands of the Flemish movement over the past decades; the exclusive use of Flemish in Flanders, the equality of Flemish in public life, the conversion of the University of Ghent into an exclusively Flemish-speaking institution, and a law requiring army officers commanding Flemish troops to know Flemish.[97]

Although the passage of the language laws met many of the demands of the nationalist movement, implementaton lagged in the thirties because the government bureaucracy and French-speaking public officials and individuals in the private sectors often remained reluctant to implement these laws in good faith.[98] Hence the resentment of the Flemish, particularly of the more fervently nationalist elements, was by no means allayed by the end of the decade despite many legislative accomplishments. Thus the Belgian state in the thirties lost some more of its credit among Flemish nationalists and made them more predisposed toward collaboration with the Germans than they might have been if the language laws had been put into force fully and generously. This state of affairs subsequently enabled the German administration to claim that its pro-Flemish activities during the occupation amounted to nothing more than the implementation of Belgian laws that were on the books.[99]

In the meantime, the old Front party had fallen apart in 1931 as a result of its internal dissensions. In its place a new party, the Flemish National League (*Vlaams Nationaal Verbond* or VNV) was founded in 1933 with a Flemish school teacher Staf de Clercq at its head. This movement became increasingly Fascist in orientation and engaged in extensive collaboration with the Germans under the occupation.

During the months of the Phoney War, wartime mobilization produced further radicalization of the Flemish because once again Flemish soldiers often found themselves commanded by French-speaking officers who did not know Flemish or were contemptuous of its use. In the purely Flemish regiments on the other hand, the Flemish soldier often was led by Flemish-speaking reserve officers of middle class background who were imbued with the spirit of Flemish nationalism. But it can also be argued that associations of Flemish and French-speaking soldiers sometimes increased understanding among the men drafted into military service.[100] Yet dissatisfaction was widespread among the Flemish, to be exploited later by the German occupation regime.

In the years before the outbreak of the First World War a Walloon nationalist movement also made its appearance, in part in response to the Flemish movement. In 1912, Jules

Destrée, a member of the Socialist party, founded the *Assemblée Wallonne* and held a Congress in Liège in hopes of gaining widespread support for Walloon culture. But the Walloon movement gained even fewer adherents than its Flemish counterpart; it too remained split among protagonists of different philosophies ranging from cultural nationalists advocating a revival of Walloon folklore and culture, to proponents of a Federalist system and even to outright protagonists of the annexation of Wallonia to France.[101]

The Walloon movement differed from its Flemish counterpart in that it drew its constituency largely from Socialist circles and from anti-clerical liberals. Its inspiration was the French Revolution of 1789 rather than the Catholic faith.[102] Unlike the Flemish movement, it was not, before 1940, animated by a concrete set of grievances and daily irritations similar to those that gave such force to the demands of the Flemish. Hence it never gained a representation in the national parliament before the Second World War but individual parliamentarians such as Destrée carried the concerns of the Walloons to a national audience. Although one small group explored annexation to France in 1940, the Walloon separatist groups did not collaborate with the Germans during the occupations to the same extent as their Flemish counterparts largely because of their socialist and liberal francophile orientation.

Foreign Policy

At the Congress of Vienna the Big Powers had created the Kingdom of the Netherlands (comprising the Netherlands and today's Belgium) in order to block a renewal of the expansionist movements on the part of France which had upset the European balance of power since the days of Louis XIV. Once the Revolution of 1831 in Brussels had succeeded in repelling the Dutch attempts to reunite the kingdom, the European powers sought to achieve the same result by stipulating and guaranteeing the perpetual neutrality of the newly created Belgian state in the Treaty of London (1839). The British saw their own security protected by having a stretch of the Channel coast controlled by a neutral country ruled by a close relative of their own royal house. They therefore took special interest in the independence of the new state. But despite the Treaty of London, the existence of Belgium was not necessarily taken for granted throughout the nineteenth century. As late as 1866 the possibility of an annexation by France formed the subject of discussions between Bismarck and Napoleon III.[103]

After the establishment of the German Empire in 1871, and particularly after the abandonment by the German government of Bismarck's foreign policy of self-restraint, the neutrality of Belgium was threatened by Germany rather than France. In 1904 and 1913, the German Emperor had made an attempt, "through dynastic channels" to seek Belgian cooperation and alliance, but he had received no encouragement.[104] General Bernhardi, the German military writer, in 1911 attacked the entire concept of permanent neutrality as contrary to the principle of national sovereignty.[105]

With the German invasion of August 1914, Belgian neutrality *de facto* had come to an end. Fritz Fischer, the revisionist German historian, has demonstrated convincingly that civilian and military German authorities throughout the war intended to secure some form of control over Belgium and her economic resources. Specific plans varied, depending on the author and the prospects of German victory, from outright annexation to the establishment of Belgium as a satellite state.[106] A study of these war aims can provide us with useful clues with regard to the origins of the German territorial aims in this region which emerged in 1940. Although Hitler may have been unaware of the 1914-1918 German aims and policies with regard to Belgium, it is clear that other high officials were conscious of German goals and experiences during the First World War.

In recognition of the failure of obligatory or absolute neutrality, and in awareness of the continuing potential danger from a revisionist Germany, Belgium after the war turned to the United Kingdom and France, the two allies which had defended her against German aggression. In anticipation of a similar agreement with Great Britain,

Belgium signed a military agreement with France in 1920. The Anglo-Belgian military agreement never materialized although verbal assurances were given.[108] Therefore Belgium went through the postwar years with a unique relationship with France, not quite a treaty, but a military understanding of what to do in the event of German aggression. In a wider context however, Belgium based her security on the League system and subsequently on the Locarno treaties which guaranteed the security of her eastern frontiers and made Belgium in turn a guarantor of the territorial *status quo* on the Rhine.

With the Nazi seizure of power in Germany in 1933 and the subsequent rearmament of Germany, existing arrangements no longer appeared satisfactory. In 1934 Belgium sought formal British guarantees or a treaty, but the British were unwilling to make any formal commitments. During this same period the special ties with France became less and less acceptable to Flemish public sentiment. Hence the government was under a good deal of pressure to repudiate the 1920 military accords with France.[109] Quite apart from Flemish objections, public opinion in Belgium feared that Belgium might become involved in a conflict in Central Europe into which France might be drawn in fulfillment of her alliances with the Soviet Union and the Little Entente.

Early in 1936 the Belgian government encountered great difficulties with its military appropriations in part because of objections to the Franco-Belgian Military Agreement by Flemish deputies. These difficulties finally induced the government to repudiate the Agreement and, after long and difficult negotiations with the French, letters terminating the Understanding were exchanged between the two governments on March 6, 1936, two days before the German occupation of the Rhineland and Hitler's denunciation of the Locarno Treaties. The termination of the Agreement was announced by Premier Paul van Zeeland on March 11 to "a cheering Chamber of Deputies." Apparently the enthusiasm over the termination was so great as to overshadow the impact of Hitler's action the previous days.[110]

However, German moves and the lack of French and British resistance gave final shape to the new "policy of independent neutrality" (*politique d'indépendance*) which had been in the making for years. This policy of absolute neutrality had wide support in Parliament, in the press, and from the Catholic church of Belgium.[111] It was sometimes associated with King Leopold because it had received one of its most persuasive articulations in a formal speech King Leopold had made to the cabinet in October 1936 as part of a plea to strengthen Belgian defenses. The cabinet had been so impressed by the king's address that it had requested his permission to have it published.[112] In fact, however, the king had only confirmed a policy which the government had evolved and for which a wide range of support existed in the country. It should also be noted that during this period Belgium became engaged in an unprecedented effort of strengthening her armed forces, a point which the king was trying to emphasize in his address.

In the period from March 1936 to the outbreak of the war in September 1939, or for that matter until the German invasion of May 10, 1940, the Belgian government valiantly attempted to maintain a neutral position. Within the framework of the "policy of independent neutrality" the Belgian government refused to respond to British and French proposals for preliminary staff contacts,[113] although some such contacts did in effect occur at the working level after the outbreak of the war.[114] For all practical purposes, as one Belgian observer commented, due to a series of "authorized leaks" and the general openness of Belgian policies the French staff was well aware of Belgian military dispositions in the months before the outbreak of the war.

The government's control over the army and the consistency of military policy were threatened during this period by the existing system of dual leadership. On the one hand, the government was constitutionally authorized and obliged to formulate and implement military policy through its Minister of Defense, General Denis. On the other hand, the king, as commander in chief, also had formal authority to issue instructions to the army and the General Staff. It so happened that the king took an active interest in military affairs, and that he was assisted by an ambitious and self-confident Military Counselor, Major-General Raoul Van Overstraeten. Thus there came into existence a system full of potential conflict and difficulties: ". . . a Chief of the General Staff formally responsible, but without real authority, and a Military Counselor of the King, without formal responsibility [to the government], but always listened to and obeyed."[115] This dual leadership was responsible for some of the difficulties during the Phoney War period which will be discussed below, and for the conflict between king and government in May 1940.

The Belgian policy of absolute neutrality met with formal approval on the part of all major European governments except France. Germany repeatedly, from March 1936 to September 1939, assured the Belgian government of its intentions to respect the neutrality of Belgium.[116] France and Great Britain at times expressed the wish for closer staff consultations or even for an agreement on preventive entry into Belgium, but they were consistent in their assurances that they would come to the assistance of Belgium if invaded by Germany.[117]

With the outbreak of the war in September 1939, the government redoubled its efforts to keep Belgium out of the conflict. It sought to accomplish this goal by fully mobilizing the army on the one hand, and on the other hand, by avoiding any action that might provoke the belligerent powers (in the first place Germany), or give them a pretext for involving Belgium in the war.

As the August 1939 crisis deepened, the Belgian government had begun to mobilize the army. By early 1940 when the army reached its full wartime strength, Belgium had over 600,000 men under arms.[118] This mobilization strength represented approximately eight percent of the population, a figure comparable to the percentage of men mobilized in Germany or France at the time.[119]

In sheer numbers, the Belgian army would seem to have constituted a powerful deterrent to a potential aggressor. However, its strength and weaknesses were similar to those of the French army: its leaders and many of its officers were veterans of the First World War, and strategy and equipment were based on the concepts of defensive stationary warfare prevalent during the latter phase of that conflict. While strong in manpower, the Belgian army was short of tanks, anti-aircraft guns, and above all, fighter planes.

Belgian strategy in the event of a German attack called for an immediate retreat to prepared fortified positions to the west. This strategy involved the surrender, without a contest, of the eastern part of the country. It was unpopular among the French-speaking population of eastern Belgium with its vivid memories of the German occupation during the First World War, but the Belgian High Command concluded that it had no alternative since it considered the eastern border indefensible.

Troop dispositions were made with an eye to both military necessity and the requirements of Belgium neutrality. While proclaiming publicly that troop dispositions were designed to repel equally an invasion from the south or the east, troops in effect were shifted in accordance with the government's sense where the greatest invasion danger was deemed to exist at a given moment. Therefore in September when the Belgians feared that the French might want to aid their Polish allies by attacking Germany through Belgium, the bulk of Belgian troops was deployed along the southern frontier. Thereafter, as signs mounted in the fall that the Germans were planning to invade Belgium, troops were shifted to eastern positions.[120]

In order to prevent any possible provocation of the belligerents (*de facto* Germany) the government went as far as to impose censorship on the Belgian press. It not only appealed to the press to observe appropriate caution, but it also confiscated and temporarily prohibited the publication of newspapers and periodicals which in the view of the authorities did not observe proper restraint. It has been noted by postwar observers that the government attempted to balance measures against publications so that opposing factions (right and left, pro-allied and pro-German) were equally affected, but that it tended to come down particularly hard on Communist publications.[121]

The official policy of neutrality was not changed in the fall and winter of 1939-1940 when it became increasingly clear that the Germans intended to invade Belgium as part of their plan of attack in the West. As a matter of fact, the question of invading Belgium had been raised in a German military staff memorandum as early as August 1938,[122] and by November 1939 Belgium had been included in the operational plans for the attack in the West.[123] During the fall and winter, Belgian authorities received warnings with regard to Germany plans from at least two different sources, Colonel Oster of the *Abwehr*, the military counterespionage organization in Berlin, and through "the Italian connection," Foreign Minister Ciano and Crown Princess Marie-José.[124] Concrete information on German intentions was acquired on January 10, 1940 when German operational instructions for the attack in the West fell into Belgian hands after the emergency landing of a German courier plane on Belgian territory near the village of Mechelen-sur-Meuse.[125]

The capture of German operational plans and intelligence reports to the effect that a German attack was imminent led to the so-called "January crisis." It appears that the government decided to maintain its stance of neutrality, but that the king and his military staff believed that they needed to take the initiative in anticipation of the apparently imminent German attack. Consequently, orders were given on January 14 by the Chief of the General Staff, Lieutenant-General Edouard Van den Berghe, with the approval and possibly on the orders of the Military Counselor of the King, Major-General Van Overstraeten, to prepare for the entry of French troops by removing the road barriers on the French frontier. When the crisis blew over, the government dismissed General Van den Berghe, for having taken this step without its approval. However, Prime Minister Pierlot writing in 1947, came to the conclusion that the original orders had been given with Leopold's consent, but that General Van den Berghe had decided to accept the blame in order to "cover" the king.[126]

The "Mechelen incident" led to another "unauthorized" action in high places. King Leopold himself took the initiative to inquire in London whether the Allies were still prepared to come to the assistance of Belgium if attacked and which "guarantees" they would furnish Belgium in that event. Apparently the British interpreted this inquiry as a "request for assistance." The Belgian government vigorously disclaimed any such intention when informed of the royal inquiry.[127] The entire affair was hushed up, but it represented another illustration of the potential conflicts about military and political authority.

Yet it should be recognized that whatever the internal difficulties, government, Parliament and king were firmly united in their determination to keep Belgium out of the war as long as possible, and, on the other hand, to defend the country against invasion.[128] The incidents that did occur, such as the removal of the barriers and the king's unauthorized inquiry in London, primarily reflected differences about responsibility and authority in the common task of maintaining neutrality and defending the country if it should be attacked. Although in one sense these differences amounted to no more than nuances in the implementation of a generally accepted policy, they also foreshadowed issues that would become major sources of conflict after the invasion.

In its efforts to bolster the Belgian posture of neutrality, the government found some strange allies. After the defeat of Poland, a group of French-speaking intellectuals who were to become leading collaborators during the occupation published the so-called "September Manifesto" which urged continued Belgian neutrality in spirit and in practice. It advocated a general European peace based on the *status quo* (i.e., the partition of Poland) and on an acceptance of German hegemony in Central and Eastern Europe.[129] One of the authors of this "Manifesto of the Thirteen" claimed during the occupation that it had been approved by Paul-Henri Spaak, the Foreign Minister. He claimed that Spaak had asked him to publish a weekly in support of the policy of neutrality.[130] The manifesto also allegedly had been approved by the royal court. After its publication its authors received the congratulations of Prime Minister Pierlot and of Foreign Minister Spaak. By the end of October a number of Flemish nationalists published a similar statement entitled "Peace through Neutrality" (*Vrede door Neutraliteit*).[131]

In response to these appeals, a countermanifesto was issued by a number of democratic "patriotic" figures who, without criticizing the official policy of neutrality, affirmed the right of citizens to express their opinions and sympathies with regard to the world conflict. The sponsors of this statement included such prominent figures as Jacques Pirenne, son of Belgium's great historian Henri Pirenne and after 1945 secretary to the king, Adolphe Max, mayor of Brussels since before World War I, and leaders of the Catholic and Socialist parties in Parliament.[132]

In addition to these activities in the press there existed in Brussels a "salon" run by a couple by the name of Didier. This salon served as the meeting ground for a variety of politicians and intellectuals committed to a pro-German neutralist position. A German diplomat, Max Liebe, one of the associates of Otto Abetz, the future German ambassador in Paris, frequented the Salon Didier. Thus the "salon" furnished German diplomats with an opportunity to influence Belgian intellectuals, publicists and politicians. Even Spaak appears to have shown up occasionally.[133]

The reason for the tendency of the government to seek support even in rightwing and pro-German circles must be found in the fundamental dilemma inherent in the neutralist position. While supporting diplomatic and military neutrality, the majority of Belgians, including the members of the government and their parties, detested Nazi Germany and hoped for the victory of the Western democracies. During the Phoney War period, it thus remained difficult to maintain the "proper spiritual balance." Therefore the government sought support wherever it could. By courting rightwing support, the government attempted to counterbalance the expressions of the general sympathy for the Western democracies in the press and in public opinion.

The Invasion and its Aftermath

During the early days of May 1940 the government received repeated reports from its contacts in Berlin that the invasion was about to take place. On May 7 the Archbishop of Malines, the Primate of the Catholic church in Belgium, received identical information from the Vatican.[134] Due to these warnings, and to reports about troop movements near the German frontier, key members of the government (Pierlot, Spaak and General Denis, the Minister of Defense) spent the night of May 9-10 in government offices.[135] About five o'clock in the morning, General Van Overstraeten received word that the Germans had crossed the frontier and that Fort Eben-Emael, a key fort in the first Belgian defense line, was under attack.[136] By that time the first German planes had appeared over the capital.

The Prime Minister, on hearing about the opening of hostilities, immediately telephoned the king to secure his approval for an appeal to the Allies. The appeal was dispatched to London and Paris after a short delay. The Allies responded affirmatively within the hour.[137] Allied troops began to enter Belgium during the morning of May 10.

At seven o'clock in the morning, more than two hours after the opening of hostilities, the German ambassador, Count von Bülow-Schwante asked to see the Foreign Minister. When they met at 8:30 A.M. the Ambassador started to read the official German note, but Spaak interrupted him curtly with the phrase that was to trail him throughout his life: *"Moi d'abord!"* ("I will speak first!").[138] Spaak then proceeded to read to the Ambassador a prepared note which pointed out that for the second time in twenty-five years Germany had attacked Belgium without the slightest provocation and that Belgium was determined to defend herself. Thus he anticipated and responded to the German note which asked Belgium to permit the passage of German troops promising the integrity of the Kingdom and of the monarchy if Belgium would not put up any resistance, while threatening the most dire consequences if Belgium were to oppose the Germans.[139]

At seven o'clock in the morning the king had received Pierlot, Spaak, and General Denis at the royal palace in Brussels prior to his departure for army headquarters at nearby Breendonck. On this occasion, Pierlot asked the king to address Parliament later that day. This the king refused to do, saying that his presence was required at military headquarters. The cabinet ministers were unable to persuade the king to follow the example of his father, King Albert, who on August 4, 1914, had rallied the nation with his address to Parliament. Writing after the war, Pierlot expressed the opinion that the king had refused to deliver a speech because he had not wanted to be identified with or to seem to approve of declarations of loyalty toward the Allies which were bound to be made on the occasion. According to Pierlot, the government felt that the king's absence from the May 10 session of Parliament deprived the nation as a whole of an inspiration which his presence would have provided.[140] The king on the other hand felt that his duties as commander in chief had to take priority, given the advanced stage of military operations.[141] In the mind of this observer, the king's decision revealed Leopold's sense of priorities.

When Parliament met that afternoon, the prime minister on his own authority expressed the regrets of the king that military necessity had prevented him from attending the Chamber session. He then proceeded with a government declaration, pledging resistance to the Germans and loyalty to the Allies, and reporting such government measures as the declaration of the state of siege and the institution of press censorship.[142] Frans Van Cauwelaert, the leader of the Catholic party and "Speaker" of the Chamber expressed special feelings of loyalty and comradeship-in-arms with the Netherlands and Luxembourg.[143]

The only item of substantive business before the Chamber was the passage without discussion of a law which authorized the government to pass laws if the Parliament would be unable to meet. This step came to be regretted by some in later years because it became one of the "legal" foundations for the issuance of decrees mandated by the occupation regime.[144]

In the meantime military events unfolded with breathtaking speed. The Germans advanced everywhere much faster than had been thought possible. Within five days they forced the Netherlands to surrender. In Belgium, Fort Eben-Emael which had been viewed as being "impregnable" fell on the first day. The main advance Belgian defense line, the Albert Canal, a holding position, was evacuated on the second day. Brussels, which had been declared an Open City by the Belgian government fell on May 18, a week and a day after the start of the invasion. The major fighting on Belgian soil took place along the Yser front in Flanders, but it too, served only a delaying function. What made the situation hopeless, however, was not the military action in Belgium, but the German breakthrough further to the south, through the Ardennes and past Sedan (in France). The German armored columns which broke through this gap raced through northern France to reach the Channel coast near Abbeville on May 21. By doing so they managed to cut the Allied forces in two, leaving British, Belgian and some French forces to the north separated from the main French armies.

The Allied High Command made no major effort to cut off these German armored units by breaking through the thin line established by the German advance. This failure left the Belgians and the British isolated to the north. When this situation became clear around May 20, Leopold and the Belgian High Command began to consider a surrender while the British started to organize the evacuation of the British Expeditionary Force from Dunkirk. The final decision to capitulate to the Germans was taken on May 27,[145] although the king had decided by May 25 that a prompt surrender was necessary.[146] The capitulation went into effect at 4:00 a.m. on May 28,[147] eighteen days to the hour after the launching of the German attack.

Beginning with the day of the invasion, the government arrested a number of persons whom it considered to be potentially subversive or dangerous in the emergency. This group included right-wing elements, such as Flemish nationalists, members of Rex with its leader Léon Degrelle, and left-wing radicals and Communists. In addition the police arrested German nationals and political and racial refugees of a wide variety of nationalities. In total the number of persons interned during the eighteen day campaign ran into the thousands. A German report prepared in August 1940 claimed that the number of Germans interned alone amounted to ten thousand but that number was almost certainly exaggerated.[148] Gérard-Libois and Gotovitch, writing in 1972, estimate the total number of internees at four to six thousand, about evenly divided between Belgian citizens and foreign nationals.[149]

The internees were eventually moved to France where they ended up in French camps. A group of prominent internees were packed into the so-called "phantom train" and shunted about in northern France. Twenty-one of these including Joris Van Severen, leader of the Flemish Fascist group Verdinaso were executed by French soldiers in Abbéville under circumstances which were never fully clarified.[150] Many of the political prisoners underwent hardships, and were maltreated by their guards. After the German-French armistice, these German nationals and right-wing elements were returned to Belgium. It has been claimed that the indignities suffered by some of the Flemish nationalist and Rexist leaders during their internment had a significant impact on their attitudes during the occupation[151] by making them more radical in their attitudes toward the Belgian state and more disposed to subscribe to national socialism and to collaborate with the Germans.

Despite the swiftness of the German advance many private citizens and many government officials managed to flee to the west and south into France. This "exodus" turned into a veritable mass movement. By the end of the campaign almost four million people or half of the population may have left their homes, although hard and fast figures are not available. Contemporary estimates ranged from 1.5 on to 2.2 million Belgian refugees in France, but a more recent evaluation suggests that the figure of two million may be accurate.[152] As a result of the mass departure of government officials, many

Belgian public services ceased functioning and public life came to a complete standstill almost everywhere. After the French surrender most of these refugees returned to their homes in Belgium although some German Jews[153] and politically exposed opponents of national-socialism may have remained in southern France.

Human losses during the campaign were light, amounting to less than one percent of the mobilized forces. According to figures supplied by the Historical Services of the Army in 1968, 5,481 men in uniform were killed or died as a result of casualties incurred during the campaign. Civilian casualties outnumbered those of the military: 6,552 civilian fatalities were recorded. The final battle in Flanders on the river Lys, with 2,549 dead, accounted for almost half of the military casualties.[154]

Material losses resulting from the campaign were extensive in some areas given the brevity of the hostilities, but they dislocated public life significantly only for a limited time after the surrender. The worst damage was repaired well before the end of the year. All in all physical destruction inflicted in 1940 did not significantly affect the life of the population under the occupation, beyond a few months needed for reconstruction.

It may be permissible to ask the question how well the Belgian army fought in May 1940. As we have suggested in our discussion of Flemish nationalism, some defeatism and even disloyalty may have existed among Flemish soldiers although defeatism was not limited to Flemish-speaking troops. On the other hand, the king and conservative opinion in the country in general went out of their way to praise the Belgian army for its "heroic performance."[155] British soldiers in the field took a more ambivalent view of the performance of the Belgian soldiery.[156] Paul Reynaud and the French in their days of agony tended to blame the Belgian leaders and army for the disaster which had befallen France. The Belgian government ministers, also, from May 15 on were struck by the air of defeatism in General Headquarters and around the king.[157] (In later controversies this defeatism was labelled as a "sense of realism" by defenders of the General Staff and of the king.)[158]

With the distance of time, a more dispassionate perspective emerges. It now seems fair to say that the Belgian army was as ill-equipped materially and psychologically as the French or the Dutch to fight successfully the kind of warfare the Germans launched in the West in May 1940. Neither the military leadership nor the ordinary soldier was able to cope with the new technology of mechanized warfare that the Germans had perfected in the preceding years. After the first disastrous days of the campaign, defeatism may have played some part in the poor performance of the military, and lack of loyalty a very minor part: however, the real problem was not the lack of "heroism" but the absence of proper training and equipment which would have given meaning to a will to fight. Yet it would be an equal distortion to surround the Belgian army with a nimbus of heroism at a time when confidence in the success of the patriotic cause was at such a very low ebb. Belgian soldiers performed as well or as poorly as did their Polish, Dutch and French counterparts when confronted with a new kind of warfare which they had been neither trained nor equipped to fight.

After the invasion the tensions and disagreements between king and government developed into a major political crisis under the strain of war and defeat. Soon after the German breakthrough at Sedan when the German tank advance toward the Channel coast threatened to drive a wedge between the Allied armies, the king and his military advisers began to plan for a retreat of the Belgian army toward the Flemish coast to establish a "national redoubt" to defend themselves against the Germans as long as possible with their back to the sea. Pierlot and Spaak on the other hand urged that the Belgian army make every attempt to join the bulk of the French forces to the south to continue the battle.[159]

Behind these different strategic proposals lay differences in perceptions of the military situation and of the nature of the relationship between Belgium and her allies. The king took the position that Belgium was only obliged to defend her own territory, but that no further obligation existed to fight with the Allies. In the view of the government, unanimous on this point, Belgium had become a full-fledged member of the alliance by accepting Allied assistance and had no right to terminate the fight unilaterally even though no formal treaty agreement to that effect had been drawn up.[160] Moreover, the king believed already by May 20 that the Allies had lost the campaign on the continent while the cabinet continued to have hopes for Allied recovery in France.

The second major conflict between king and government occurred over the king's growing determination to remain in Belgium after a surrender to the Germans. The government took the position that the king should do everything in his power to avoid falling into German hands. Pierlot and Spaak felt that the king should remain free to lead the continuing struggle against the Germans, that he would have liberty of action if established on French or British territory, but that on the other hand he would be powerless to do much for his people under a German occupation.[161] The cabinet viewed with particular distress Leopold's apparent determination to form a new government which would be under control of the Germans.[162] The ministers feared that by remaining in Belgium and lending his name to such a regime, Leopold would end up appearing to sanction a German puppet government, and bring Belgium into discredit in the Allied world.

Underlying this conflict between king and government lay different assessments of the future course of the war and of the nature of the Nazi regime. By the end of May the king believed that Germany had won the war in Europe. Whereas he undoubtedly detested some of the "cruder" outgrowths of the Nazi regime, he also admired other aspects such as the sense of order, authority and purpose Hitler had created in Germany. He considered it necessary and possible to work with a victorious Nazi Germany, given the circumstances of May 1940. There is little doubt in the mind of this writer that the king, like many other traditional figures in Western Europe, was also eager to seize this opportunity to reorganize government in Belgium along more authoritarian lines in order to make it work "more efficiently", free of the restraints and obstacles which a parliamentary system had placed on government in crisis in the thirties.

The ministers on the other hand in late May still believed in, or at least had not given up hope for, an eventual Allied victory. Most of them were parliamentary leaders committed to parliamentary democracy, men who realized that German victory would mean the end of democracy in Europe in general, and in Belgium in particular. Therefore, in May 1940 (notwithstanding a lapse the following month) they were slower than the king and his generals to accept accommodation with Germany as long as there was any hope left that the Allies might continue the fight.

These differences between government and king began to become apparent as the pattern of Allied defeat in the West emerged. On May 15 the king first mentioned to Pierlot the German breakthrough and the possibility of a Belgian retreat to the northwest. On the sixteenth this topic came up again, and the ministers argued for a move to the west and south to maintain contact with the French armies. They also urged the king to make sure he personally would continue the battle on the Allied side if Belgium would have to surrender. On May 21 at a meeting in Ypres in Flanders, the issue of the direction of the retreat formed the foremost topic. The ministers found themselves in agreement with General Weygand of France, the Allied Supreme Commander, in opposition to the position taken by the Belgian military and the king. The outcome was a compromise in which contact with the British troops was maintained, but no attempt was made to move south.[163]

The final dramatic interview between Leopold and four ministers (Pierlot, Spaak, Vanderpoorten and General Denis) at the castle of Wynendaele on May 25, dealt primarily with King Leopold's personal plans. By that time it had become apparent that the Belgian army would have to lay down its arms very soon ("in 24 hours" said Leopold),[164] and the ministers did not dispute the necessity of a surrender. But when the king stated that he now had definitely decided to remain in Belgium with his troops and allow himself to be taken prisoner, the ministers remonstrated with him vehemently, dropping the usual format of respectful intercourse with the royal person. They explained that they would have to repudiate him publicly if he were to persist. They asked the king whether he intended to form a government after his surrender. Leopold responded that he was not a dictator and would have to find a legal instrument of governance.[165] In the end they left the king, fully convinced that he intended to install a new government under the Germans.[166] There was no reconciliation of views other than Leopold's observation that both parties would have to follow their consciences. The ministers immediately went to London on a British vessel and from there back to Paris where they dealt with the Allied reaction to the Belgian capitulation that occurred on May 28.

The king's final official act on May 28 was to issue a proclamation to explain the course of events and defend his actions. He stated that the army had fought valiantly and honorably, but that German superiority made further resistance useless and irresponsible. He claimed that Belgium had fulfilled her obligations to her allies by defending her territory to the best of her ability. Now the time had come for soldiers to "return to their homes and for the country to get to work again."[167] This latter phrase was to be interpreted later by some as signalling definite acceptance of German victory and as authorizing economic collaboration with the Germans[168] even though the king stated in a letter (which did not receive wide circulation) that his declaration did not mean that Belgians should work for the Germans.[169]

The capitulation itself was a purely military instrument of surrender stipulating a ceasefire and the surrender of the Belgian armed forces. A supplement to the main instrument set forth the provisions for King Leopold and his household. Leopold was assigned the castle of Laeken just outside of Brussels as his residence.[170]

As Pierlot and Spaak had predicted, some of the reverberations of the Belgian capitulation in the Allied camp were violent. Paul Reynaud, the French premier, denounced Leopold and blamed Allied reversals on his betrayal. He accused (unjustly as it turned out) Leopold of having failed to notify the Allies of his intention to surrender.[171] The reaction in England was more moderate even though the Belgian surrender freed German troops for an attack on the British Expeditionary Force which was then in the process of being assembled for evacuation around Dunkirk. Lord Keyes, the British military liaison officer attached to King Leopold, defended the latter's actions, and Churchill and some British papers counselled withholding of judgment until all the facts were known.[172] In the United States, King Leopold found defenders in the face of a hostile public opinion in former President Hoover (who had headed the Belgian Relief Administration during the First World War) and in Hoover's associate, Hugh Gibson, former U.S. Ambassador to Belgium.[173] In occupied Belgium, however, in the immediate wake of the capitulation and throughout the summer of 1940, the "romantic" decision of the king to remain with his people and his soldiers as a "prisoner of war," was highly popular. It was contrasted favorably with the cowardly "desertion" of the Council of Ministers and other high government officials.

On May 28, Premier Pierlot presented over the French radio the Belgian government's view of the capitulation, in response to Reynaud's radio address earlier that day. Pierlot was under great pressure from the French who were using Leopold as a scapegoat for their own unexpected traumatic military reversals. Pierlot was also worried about what he perceived to be the king's willingness to form a government under the Germans and about French hostility toward the Belgian refugees in France who had been harrassed by angry Frenchmen during the day as a result of Reynaud's speech. In his radio talk, Pierlot characterized the surrender as a purely military decision taken by the king as commander in chief, and disassociated the government and the Belgian people from responsibility for his act. He furthermore pledged Belgium to a continuation of the struggle against the Germans and announced the levy of a new Belgian army in France. According to his own testimony, Pierlot's talk went far to calm the French people and lessen the hostility encountered by the Belgian refugees in France.[174]

Chapter Two

Survey of the Main Periods of the Occupation

The German occupation of Belgium in the Second World War can be divided into four periods. The first of these lasted from June to the end of September of 1940. It may be called the "honeymoon of the occupation." During this period almost everybody, the German conquerors as well as the population of the occupied territory, believed that Germany had won the war and would control the European continent for the foreseeable future. In early June the Germans set up their system of governance for Belgium, a military government headed by a 61-year-old Prussian general Alexander von Falkenhausen who claimed that he wanted to govern Belgium in such a way as to avoid the mistakes of German rule during the First World War.

During this period, the German military was able to administer the occupied territory with only a minimum of interference from other German government and party agencies. During the summer of 1940 the Germans could perform functions that were perceived as being helpful by the Belgian population: they facilitated the return of Belgian refugees from France, they repaired much of the physical damage caused by the war and encouraged the resumption of normal life. The Germans treated the king with courtesy and announced the release of the Flemish prisoners of war. Thus they could appeal for cooperation with a reasonably impressive record of accomplishments, especially since German dominance over Western Europe seemed unchallengeable and permanent.

Moreover during this period the political and economic policies which eventually would turn the population against the occupying power either had not yet commenced, or had not yet made a serious impact. From the beginning the Germans had started a vast program of economic plunder moving raw materials and goods to Germany as quickly as circumstances would permit. However, people were not yet seriously affected by these transfers since existing supplies did not become exhausted immediately. In this period the German military government kept its distance from Belgian collaborationist groups and took few steps to tamper with the administration of the country or with normal life.

As a result of this favorable climate engendered by their deliberately "conciliatory" policy, the Germans were able to secure in these first few months the cooperation, always within certain limits, of Belgian government agencies, of the leaders of business and industry, and basically of the population as a whole. This cooperation was offered more easily during the summer of 1940 because the population at large and the governmental and economic elites were in a state of shock over the rapid and apparently complete victory of the Germans on the European continent, although the paralysis, in view of the previous experience of World War I, may not have been quite as complete and paralyzing in Belgium as it was in neighboring Holland and France. But the shock was real enough, and in view of the apparently inescapable prospect of permanent German dominance of the Continent the task of rebuilding the country in cooperation with German authorities and returning to normal life was widely if not universally accepted as natural and inevitable.

Such a policy of cooperation was sanctioned in July 1940 by a group of business leaders meeting under the chairmanship of Alexandre Galopin, President of the *Société Générale*. The basic decision made was that Belgium would have to resume its industrial production in order to produce for the German war economy goods other than direct armaments and munitions. In return, Germany would import enough food to ward off starvation and would supply sufficient raw materials for Belgian industry. Since Belgian industry would work for the German economy, Belgian labor would not be forced to work in Germany, although it was considered acceptable for Belgian workers to "volunteer" for job assignments in the Reich.

One key explanation of the willingness of Belgian business leaders to enter into such an arrangement was the memory of the deportation of hundreds of thousands of Belgian workers to Germany during the First World War when Belgian industry had ground to a halt. If Belgian industry would produce for Germany (ran the rationale) Belgian workers hopefully could be kept working at home during the second occupation. A critical observer has suggested, not without justification, that less elevated motivations contributed to the compromise of the summer of 1940: By working for the Germans, Belgian employers could count on handsome profits and could retain and even increase their control over their enterprises and over their workers and employees.*

The highest government officials left behind in the occupied territory, the Secretaries-General, the administrative heads of each ministry, had expressed their willingness to cooperate with the German authorities early in June. Like their counterparts in business, the Secretaries-General also hedged their pledge of cooperation with reservations which were gradually eroded in the course of the occupation.

In this manner the foundation of German-Belgian cooperation in government and business was laid in the first few months of that memorable summer of 1940 when the entire continent seemed to have fallen under German control. This basic pattern of cooperation continued to function throughout the occupation even after many of the original premises had gone down the drain.

This "honeymoon of the occupation" came to an end with the waning of the summer. Most importantly, the continued resistance of England and her success in the Battle of Britain brought home the message that the war was not over yet. Closer at home, the impact of German economic spoliation

---

* See references to John Gillingham's views in Chapter Five below.

and the increasing scarcity of food made themselves felt. During the traumatic first winter of the occupation, many people went hungry and experienced near-starvation. Thus the second period of the occupation which lasted from October 1940 to September 1942 was above all characterized by increasing physical hardships. Its opening months saw the descent of Nazi party agencies on the country, the beginning of political collaboration and the start of political and racial persecution. The first laws against the Jews were promulgated in October 1940, and the campaign against the Jews made its inexorable progress until finally in August of 1942 the deportation trains started taking Jewish men, women and children to their death in the East.

This second period may be called a "period of transition" for a variety of reasons. It was a transition from a near-certainty of German victory to a situation in 1942 where the balance of world power and resources had clearly shifted against Germany with the continued resistance of the Soviet Union and England, and with the entry of the United States into the war in December 1941. In 1942 the scales still appeared to hang in the balance, but the expectation that German dominance would inevitably be permanent had largely evaporated.

In 1941 German policies became more radical in the wake of the invasion of the Soviet Union. Economic policies became more exploitative, particularly after the winter of 1941-42 when Germany began to gear up for a long war. This was also a period of transition in governmental affairs as the Germans during this period tried to place as many collaborators in government services as possible, and to bend these services to the authoritarian mold typical of the Nazi state. It was a period of transition in the field of labor recruitment, as voluntary and initially very successful recruitment for work in Germany was turned increasingly into a program of compulsion culminating in the introduction of the labor draft for work in Belgium in March 1942. By now deprivations and demands caused by the Germans reached into nearly every home.

This was also a period of transition in that Nazi party agencies and their Belgian cohorts became more active and that political pressures increased substantially. The cautious policies of the military administration were questioned by agents of the SS who called for more decisive political actions and for harsher punishment of political opponents. The SS now tried to sponsor a radical Flemish movement prepared to advocate annexation to Germany and to spread the racial philosophy of the SS among the Flemish population. The German police and SS established themselves in this period in Belgium and managed to gain increasing independence from the military administration and its restraints.

During this period Rex, the VNV and the Flemish movement sponsored by the SS became more actively involved in collaboration, particularly in connection with the war against the Soviet Union. These movements supported the recruitment for military service on the Eastern front and for auxiliary formations that were to support the German regime in Belgium. Degrelle himself took service in the East, and covered himself with military glory. Through such activities the collaborationists incurred increasingly the hatred of the patriotic majority.

During this period King Leopold lost much of the popularity he had enjoyed during the summer of 1940. His remarriage to a young woman, Lilian Baels, the daughter of a Flemish politician, was viewed by many of his subjects as an act of self-indulgence, particularly since affection for Queen Astrid had remained very much alive and since certain ambiguities existed about the family of the bride.

For the population, the second winter of the occupation was somewhat less traumatic than the first, since food distribution was better organized. However the extreme cold of the winter of 1941/1942 caused much suffering because of a scarcity of fuel.

This period also witnessed the great constitutional conflict of the occupation. At stake was the question whether the Secretaries-General had the authority to issue decrees and regulations having the force of law under emergency acts passed by the Parliament in 1939 and 1940. At one point in

March 1942 the *Cour de Cassation*, the highest Belgian court, invalidated a decree establishing the National Corporation for Agriculture, thereby putting into question the validity of the whole body of regulatory and quasi-legislative decrees promulgated by the Belgian authorities since the beginning of the occupation. For awhile it looked as if the Belgian judiciary might go on strike and the entire edifice of official cooperation might collapse. By June 1942 however a compromise was achieved which gave the Germans in substance what they wanted (the acceptance and implementation of regulations passed so far by the Secretaries-General in compliance with German requests) but provided some protection against future actions of individual collaborationist Secretaries-General.

The third period of the occupation lasted from the introduction of the compulsory draft for labor in Germany in early October 1942 to May 1944, the month preceding the Allied landings in Normandy. This period was characterized by the progressive breakdown of the pattern of cooperation established during the first few months of the occupation. The controlling factor was the shifting tide of war which forced Nazi Germany to place ever increasing burdens on the population of the occupied territories. The imposition of the compulsory draft for work in Germany in October 1942 was the turning point because it drove underground many of the men threatened with deportation to Germany. Now Resistance organizations sprang up in significant numbers in order to supply the necessary documents to the tens of thousands of people in hiding. Conversely the men and women in hiding were more likely to engage in resistance activities, and therefore the level of violence rose dramatically in 1943, as armed attacks on rationing offices and other government facilities multiplied.

This climate of violence was further intensified by the retributory actions of the Military Command and by the growing ruthlessness of the German policy. Assassinations of pro-German collaborators began in earnest and by the end of this period hundreds of Rexist and Flemish collaborators had been killed. These assassinations of collaborators gave rise to a campaign of counterterror in which Rexists and Flemish SS killed a number of prominent patriots. By the winter of 1943-1944 the Germans and the Belgian police had lost so much of their control of the country that in some regions they no longer could protect effectively industrial installations and communications and transportation lines. By early 1944 the economic life of the country had been substantially affected by this breakdown in internal security.

As a result of the declining fortunes of the Third Reich and of the prevailing climate of violence some of the most vocal early collaborationists, including a number of francophone journalists resigned from their offices in 1943. The VNV also made some feeble attempts to distance itself from the Germans, but it was too deeply enmeshed in collaboration to extricate itself. The Flemish extremists on the other hand and the Rexists embraced the Nazi cause ever more tightly in the face of approaching disaster.

During this third period of the occupation, the German police continued its campaign of deporting Jews to the East, rounding up Jews where they could find them. In September 1943 they conducted a great sweep of Jews of Belgian nationality who had been exempted from deportation up to that point. By the end of this period almost half of the Jews living in Belgium in 1940-1941 had been deported to the East.

Paradoxically, during this stage the food situation showed a decided improvement, as measures taken in the field of agriculture began to show results and as collection and distribution methods improved. Now the population often could find in the stores at least the meager food supplies allowed by the official rationing regulations. However the accumulated nutritional deprivations of years of occupation began to take their toll, and fuel remained very scarce.

During the months of April and May 1944, Belgium experienced weeks of concentrated Allied air attacks, especially on transportation facilities such as railroad yards and bridges. These allied air attacks were so intensive and widespread that the economic life of the country was paralyzed almost completely.

The fourth and final period of the occupation was the interval between the Normandy invasion and the liberation of the country. Now the Germans and the Belgian population clearly faced each other as enemies whose fortunes were dependent on the progress of military operations occurring only a few hundred miles away. The immediate German reaction to the Normandy invasion was to deport King Leopold and his immediate family to Germany.

In July 1944 the Military Command was finally replaced by a civilian administration (*Reichskommissariat*). This transformation of the German administration was the result of many years of efforts by Himmler and the Nazi party to acquire in Belgium the kind of influence and power they had secured in the Netherlands and in Norway. However, Himmler's success came too late to bear much fruit other than to increase the ruthlessness of a German police no longer concerned with the restraints the Military Command had placed on its conduct.

During these final months the control of German and Belgian government agencies over public life gradually unravelled as domestic violence continued at an ever increasing pitch. Assassinations and counter-assassinations proliferated, even though the Resistance was under restraint from Allied instructions to lie low and keep itself intact until the decisive moment. Toward September Resistance groups became more active as they readied themselves for that moment when, in conformance with their instructions, they would assist Allied forces upon their entry into Belgium. This entry occurred on September 1. Allied forces quickly swept through the country occupying Brussels on the evening of the third and Antwerp on September 4. Some serious fighting between Resistance groups and German troops took place in the eastern part of the country, but on the whole the liberation of the country was fast and caused relatively few casualties. Only in the territory northeast of Antwerp did the Germans hold on for a few months.

It was illustrative of the basic continuity of Belgian political life in the postwar period that in many places the former Belgian officials who had been dismissed by the Germans quickly reassumed their places on all levels of government without formalities. The government-in-exile itself entered Brussels early in September as the unquestioned political authority (functioning under Allied Military Government), to offer its resignation to a reassembled rump Parliament on September 17.

In this manner the long occupation had come to a mercifully quick end, although Belgium's last wartime trials such as the bombing of Antwerp with V-2 rockets and the Battle of the Bulge still had to be faced before the ordeals of the Second World War were finally over.

Chapter Three

The Establishment of the New Administration

National-Socialist Government and German Designs on Belgium

Scholarly analysis of National Socialist theory and practice has experienced (and continues to experience) significant changes since the end of the Second World War but some areas of basic consensus are emerging which have a direct impact on the study of German occupation policies in Belgium. The work of Fritz Fischer and his followers has demonstrated that a considerable degree of continuity existed between the imperialist aspirations of the Second Empire in the First World War and National Socialist foreign policy aims in World War II.[1] These "traditional" aspirations of German imperialism were kept alive in the government bureaucracy, the military, in German business, and in the academic world. In time these traditional expansionist aspirations would both merge and clash with the designs put forth by advocates of the more extreme Nazi racist policy such as Himmler.

More recent research has also continued to emphasize the impact on policy of the competition and conflict that existed within the Nazi power structure.[2] To be sure, Hitler's commands were rarely opposed and never openly refused. But it is now recognized that Hitler deliberately encouraged the competition of a variety of individuals and organizations, in part because this system left him as the unquestioned arbitrator, in part because he simply was a poor administrator. These conflicts over areas of competence compounded by differences in perspectives on policy became more pronounced after the start of the war: The regular ministries, the organs of the Nazi party, the SS and Police, the High Command of the Army, the Air Force all competed for their share of influence and power in Germany and in the occupied territories. These conflicts profoundly affected the administration of occupied Belgium.

At the center of power, in Berlin or at Hitler's wartime headquarters, each of these major structures had its representative or delegate who sought to advance his own personal influence as well as that of his organization: Martin Bormann, who after Rudolf Hess's flight to England, became the virtual head of the NSDAP and who became Hitler's Secretary in 1943, made himself spokesman of the party and controlled access to Hitler of all party figures; H.H. Lammers, Chief of the Reich Chancellery, tried to safeguard the views and interests of the permanent government bureaucracy. He controlled access to Hitler of nonparty civilians. Heinrich Himmler worked for the implementation of his racial vision and the expansion of his empire as head of the SS and Police. On the military side Field Marshal Wilhelm Keitel provided liaison with the Wehrmacht, and until December 1941 General Walther von Brauchitsch represented the army. Hermann Göring was in a special position as Hitler's successor, as Plenipotentiary for the Four Year Plan (the organization created in 1936 to oversee economic mobilization), and as head of the Air Force. And then finally there was Albert Speer whose star was on the rise after 1942 as head of industrial mobilization, and Joseph Goebbels, often Bormann's ally in party matters and a representative of the old pre-1933 party radicalism. All these figures played a role in the conflicts over the nature and policies of the German occupation regime in Belgium.

German interest in the Low Countries can be traced back to the rise of romantic nationalism in the nineteenth century. Most of this interest was centered around common historical, cultural and folkloristic themes, but with the rise of pan-German political aspirations in the twentieth century it took on a political and imperialist coloration.[3] Special ties with Flanders were stressed and exploited in the policies of the

German occupation of Belgium during the First World War. In the nineteen thirties the racial theme was added to the older nationalist and cultural tradition to become the foundation of the *Flamenpolitik* of German organizations and agencies operating in Belgium.[4]

During the First World War the German government, and military and business groups sought military and economic control of Belgium. The German chancellor Theobald von Bethmann Hollweg assumed in 1914 that the inclusion of Belgium in the German sphere of influence would be one of Germany's war aims. At one time he also considered giving the French-speaking part of Belgium to France.[5] Among the many plans that were discussed at the highest levels of the German government were annexation to Prussia of the region of Liège and Verviers,[6] the division of Belgium into a French and a Flemish-speaking state, the permanent or temporary occupation of the Belgian and French Channel coasts down to Boulogne or, at the very least, the maintenance of a Belgian vassal state "independent in name, but in practice at our disposal."[7]

German industry was not slow either to let its own aspirations be known. In September 1914 August Thyssen sent a memorandum to the government demanding the incorporation not only of all Belgium, but also of two French departments, the Département du Nord and the Département du Pas-de-Calais (which subsequently were included in the territory administered by the German Military Command in Brussels during the Second World War). The emperor himself proposed that the areas to be annexed from Belgium should be cleared of their present population and be "settled" with German veterans.[8]

Von Bethmann Hollweg tended to reject plans for outright annexation, but he remained intent throughout to secure at least indirect economic and military control of the country. According to Fischer, the chancellor's principal instrument for securing this indirect control was to be Germany's "Flemish policy" (*Flamenpolitik*), i.e., the encouragement of Flemish separatist aspirations.[9]

The German military were even more adamant than the civilians in their demand for permanent control of Belgium. As late as July 1918 Paul von Hindenburg and Erich Ludendorff demanded that Belgium should be divided into two states, Flanders and Wallonia, united only by a personal union, and that there should remain the closest possible association with Germany including a customs union and a joint railway system.[10] Earlier during the war Admiral Alfred von Tirpitz asked for outright incorporation of Belgium as a base for German naval operations on the Channel coast and went as far as to make that control the touchstone of German victory.[11] But whatever the specific shape of German demands, the military leadership right up to the fall of 1918 was determined to maintain control over Belgium after the war in one form or another.[12]

There is no evidence that Hitler himself or any other German government agency developed specific plans for possible conquests and boundary modifications in the West before the outbreak of the war.[13] However, the earlier cultural and nationalist ideas remained active in government circles, and in the academic and professional world where they received articulation through such agencies as the Institute for the Low Countries at Cologne University.[14]

Hitler himself had made it quite clear in *Mein Kampf* that the mere revision of the Treaty of Versailles was not an adequate goal of German foreign policy. But such utterances were taken to pertain to Eastern Europe. Yet as early as 1937 Hitler, in one of his speeches at a school for prospective party leaders, reiterated the vision of the resurrection of the Holy Roman Empire[15] (which had included Belgium until the end of the 18th century). It may be true that Hitler was not, until 1939, familiar with the German *Flamenpolitik* of 1914-18 (although he had spent most of the war in Belgium and northern France), but his aspirations included vague notions of expansion in the West (given an opportunity) based on his vision of German hegemony over Europe. He did not talk much about these goals before 1940 because they were not his primary aims and it would have been counterproductive to raise apprehensions in the West but they were latently present to be revived at the proper moment.

Once German troops had won victory in the West, a number of decisions were taken which suggest the existence of such a set of aspirations. Parts of Alsace-Lorraine, and Luxembourg and the Belgian districts of Eupen and Malmédy were *de facto* incorporated into Germany. There was talk at Göring's headquarters about the creation of a Burgundian vassal state. In Brussels itself, plans justifying the annexation of French West Flanders to Flanders or Germany on the basis of racial considerations were circulating within German and Flemish nationalist circles.[16]

We have another indication of the trend of Hitler's thoughts in a decision he made in October 1939 when presented with the choice whether Germany should proclaim her determination to maintain the independence of the Low Countries, in the event of an invasion, or whether this question should be left open. Hitler's emphatic preference for this latter alternative[17] indicated that even at that early date he wanted to keep his options open.

We have a further indication of Hitler's state of mind soon after the Belgian capitulation. An officer of the Supreme Command of the Armed Forces (*Oberkommando der Wehrmacht*, or OKW) reported to the Military Commander in Belgium that Hitler intended to appoint later (but not immediately) a civilian High Commissioner for Flanders (analogous to the appointment of Seyss-Inquart in the Netherlands), but that the French-speaking part of Belgium (Wallonia) would be left under a purely military administration.[18] This report suggests that at this particular point in time (June 4, 1940) Hitler envisioned annexation of Flanders, but that he was less definite about the eventual disposal of Wallonia.

Soon after the French armistice Hitler ordered Secretary of State Stuckart of the Reich Ministry of the Interior to prepare a study with maps showing possible future western boundaries of the Reich. On the basis of directions from Hitler, Stuckart eventually prepared a revised plan which incorporated into Germany all of the Netherlands, Belgium and northern France down to the mouth of the river Somme.[19] There is little doubt in the mind of this writer that this revised Stuckart draft represented Hitler's real ambitions, and that the retention of two northern *départements* of France in the Command Area had political motives.

Nothing in Hitler's actions during the rest of the war conflicts with this assumption and there is much that confirms it. The basic instruction to the Military Commander of July 14, 1940 stated explicitly that "the Führer has not yet made a definite decision with regard to the future of the Belgian state."[20] This remained official German policy despite the repeated efforts of the German occupation authorities in Brussels to persuade Hitler to guarantee publicly the integrity of the Belgian state. Instructions prepared in October 1941 in connection with plans for a transformation of the Military Command into a civilian administration make it clear that Hitler at that point in time entertained the possibility of splitting Belgium into Flanders and Wallonia, with Flanders possibly being made part of the Netherlands.[21] These indications in my opinion receive their authoritative confirmation from a notation in Goebbels' diary of May 30, 1943 to the effect that

> .... the Führer has quite concrete plans for the enlargement of our frontiers. It is self-evident for him that Belgium as well as Flanders and Brabant will be turned into German *Reichsgaue*.[22]

Thus there is little doubt that, given a free hand in the event of a German victory, Hitler would have annexed all of Belgium splitting that country into two or three *Gaue* or provinces (Flanders and Wallonia, or Flanders, Wallonia and Brabant, the latter to include Brussels and the surrounding regions), unless he would have allowed the "experts" to modify his decision on economic or political grounds.

The Establishment and Organization of the Military Command

The authority of the German Military Command in Brussels extended to all of prewar Belgium except for the districts of Eupen and Malmédy, and for the village of Moresnet which were annexed to Germany by the Führer decree of May 18,

1940.[23] It also extended to two French departments, the Département du Nord and the Département du Pas-de-Calais. For a few weeks the Military Commander in Brussels also governed the Grand Duchy of Luxembourg, but in July 1940 that country was removed from the Command Area when Hitler appointed a Chief of the Civil Administration paving the way for the *de facto* annexation of Luxembourg to Germany.[24]

Although this study is limited to Belgium (and only to those parts of Belgium placed under General von Falkenhausen's command) something needs to be said about the inclusion of the two French departments in the Military Command area. Originally the main reason for this arrangement may have been military (in connection with the pending invasion of England),[25] but very soon political factors came into play. Among these were Hitler's territorial ambitions and German imperialist aims dating back to the First World War which have been discussed in the previous section. As has been shown above, in the Stuckart draft the two departments were to be excluded from a future France whose northern frontier would run along the river Somme.[26] The German Foreign Office in turn expressed the view that the two northern provinces could be used as "bargaining chips" (*Faustpfand*) in a future peace settlement with France. The military authorities in Brussels soon developed a proprietary interest in these two departments, primarily because they included an important coal mining region. Von Falkenhausen went so far as to argue against a return of these provinces to France on racial grounds.[27] And finally a small group of Flemish nationalists supported by certain elements within the German orbit claimed that "West Flanders" was originally Germanic territory and that many people still used Flemish as their mother tongue.[28] But whatever the particular points raised at each turn of the discussion over the two departments from May 1940 to July 1944, they remained in effect under the control of the German administration in Brussels until their liberation in 1944.

Indignation over the activities of the SS Task Forces (*Einsatzgruppen*) during and after the Polish campaign induced the High Command of the Army (*Oberkommando des Heeres* or OKH) to ask Hitler in October 1939 to authorize the establishment of purely military administrations in the West.[29] The army specifically asked that party and government agencies be excluded from preparations for the occupation regimes in Western Europe. On November 1, 1939 Hitler agreed to these requests[30] knowing full well that he could reverse himself later if it suited his purposes to do so.

During the autumn of 1939 the army assembled a task force of civilians and military officers to design the military administrations for the West European territories to be conquered bearing the experience of the First World War in mind. This task force was headed by Eggert Reeder, the *Regierungspräsident* (provincial governor) of Cologne and Düsseldorf. It also included Harry von Craushaar, a reserve officer with business connections, Franz Thedieck, an assistant to Reeder in Cologne, and a Colonel Nagel, a specialist in economic affairs.[31]

This study group or *Studienkommission* worked during the ensuing months on the draft for a military administration which will be described below. By April 1940 the task force saw its recommendations approved by the OKH with some modifications. The documents outlining policies and procedures for a military administration were gathered in a folder nicknamed "The Red Donkey" (*Der rote Esel*).[32] The basic decree establishing the Military Command stipulated that every effort must be made to avoid giving the impression that Germany intended to annex the occupied territories. It also stipulated that a promise would be made to observe the Hague Convention on Land Warfare, that the population would be protected and that normal economic life be maintained.[33]

Three days after the attack in the West, Alexander von Falkenhausen, General of the Infantry, was informed that he was to be appointed Military Commander in the Netherlands. He met with Reeder and familiarized himself with the work of the Study Commission, but even before he could proceed to the Netherlands it was announced over the radio that Dr. Arthur Seyss-Inquart, the Austrian quisling, had been appointed *Reichskommissar* in the Netherlands, to head a civilian administration. At first, von Falkenhausen was ordered to remain in Germany, but on May 18 he was authorized to proceed to The Hague to preside over the establishment of a temporary military administration in the Netherlands.[34] Four days later, Belgian territory occupied by German troops was placed under his authority.

On May 29, von Falkenhausen handed over his authority for the Netherlands to Seyss-Inquart in a ceremony in The Hague. He then immediately departed for Brussels. On May 31 he was formally appointed Military Commander for Belgium and Northern France (*Militärbefehlshaber in Belgien und Nordfrankreich,*) a position he held until July 1944.

The German Military Command as designed by the Study Commission formed an uncompromisingly hierarchical structure. At its head stood the territorial Military Commander (*Militärbefehlshaber*) who controlled the two branches of the Command: the military staff (*Kommandostab*) primarily responsible for military affairs and for security, and the Military Administration* (*Militärverwaltung*) responsible, despite its name, for civil affairs. The head of the Military Administration (*Chef der Militärverwaltung*) was the direct subordinate of the Military Commander. This same hierarchical relationship was repeated at the lower administrative levels, with a clear and unquestioned chain of command reaching from top to bottom. This meant that despite the attempted interference of a number of central Reich agencies during the occupation, the formal authority of the Military Commander and of the Chief of the Military Administration was rarely questioned from within the command structure.[35]

The Germans considered the Military Administration a supervisory body (*Aufsichtsverwaltung*) which supposedly left the responsibility for the actual administration of the country to existing Belgian government services.[36] This division of labor was accepted early in June by the Belgian Secretaries-General, the highest administrative officials left in the

---

* The Term "Military Administration" will be capitalized in this study only when it refers to the "*Militärverwaltung*"

country.37 For the Germans this arrangement meant great savings in manpower, and, at least in the beginning, a legitimization of their rule and of the demands they were to make during the occupation.

The three major functions of the Military Administration were summarized as follows by Reeder:

(1) supervision of Belgian government services

(2) preparation of decrees and directives to German agencies in the Command Area, and

(3) negotiations with central Reich agencies to mediate between their demands and the requirements of the occupied territory.38

It must be stressed, however, that German intervention in the administration of the country by Belgian government services went much further than this outline suggests. Many of the ordinances promulgated formally by one or more of the Secretaries-General were originally requested or drafted by the Germans. The Military Administration involved itself most intimately in the day-to-day conduct of business of Belgian government agencies, including personnel matters. Therefore the concept of a purely supervisory administration must be taken with a grain of salt, even if it remains true that in Belgium existing government services were left more scope and autonomy than in the Netherlands.

The Military Administration was organized into three main divisions which were distinct from the collection of miscellaneous services and agencies, often delegated by central Reich agencies, which also came under Reeder's formal authority*.

The largest unit was the Economics Division (*Wirtschaftsabteilung*) which in turn was subdivided into sections for each of the major branches of industry. There were also separate sections for agriculture, forestry, banking, foreign trade,

---

* See chart A, below.

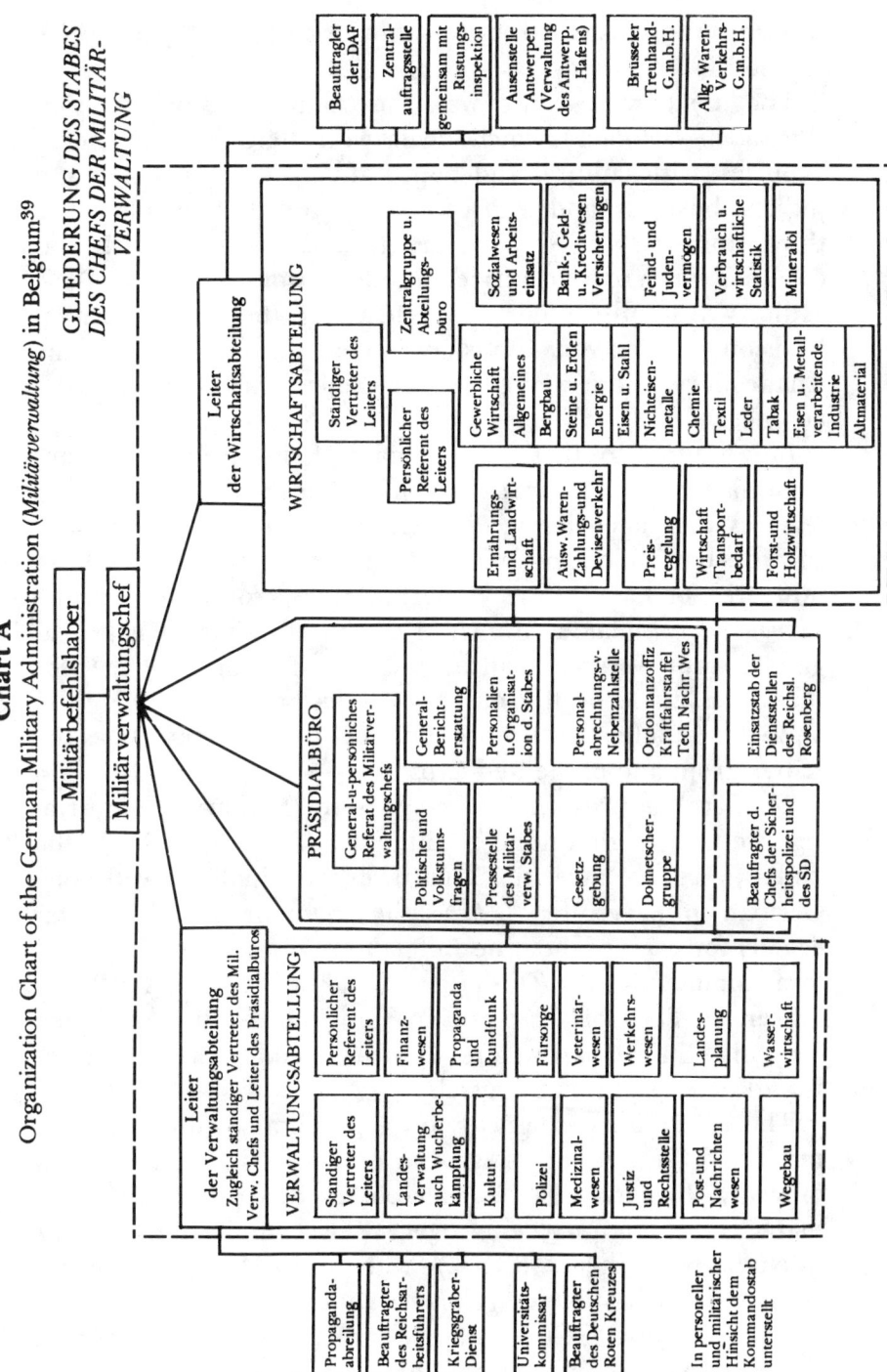

Chart A

Organization Chart of the German Military Administration (*Militärverwaltung*) in Belgium[39]

GLIEDERUNG DES STABES DES CHEFS DER MILITÄRVERWALTUNG

Militärbefehlshaber
Militärverwaltungschef

PRÄSIDIALBÜRO
- General-u.-persönliches Referat des Militärverwaltungschefs
- General-Berichterstattung
- Politische und Volkstumsfragen
- Pressestelle des Militärverw. Stabes
- Personalien u. Organisation d. Stabes
- Gesetzgebung
- Personalabrechnungs-v-Nebenzahlstelle
- Dolmetschergruppe
- Ordonnanzoffiz Kraftfahrstaffel Tech Nachr Wes
- Beauftragter d. Chefs der Sicherheitspolizei und des SD
- Einsatzstab der Dienststellen des Reichsl. Rosenberg

VERWALTUNGSABTEILUNG
Leiter der Verwaltungsabteilung
Zugleich ständiger Vertreter des Mil. Verw. Chefs und Leiter des Präsidialbüros

- Ständiger Vertreter des Leiters
- Persönlicher Referent des Leiters
- Landes-Verwaltung auch Wucherbekämpfung
- Finanzwesen
- Propaganda und Rundfunk
- Kultur
- Polizei
- Fürsorge
- Veterinärwesen
- Medizinalwesen
- Verkehrswesen
- Justiz und Rechtsstelle
- Landesplanung
- Post-und Nachrichtenwesen
- Wegebau
- Wasserwirtschaft

+
- Propagandaabreilung
- Beauftragter des Reichsarbeisführers
- KriegsgräberDienst
- Universitätskommissar
- Beauftragter des Deutschen Roten Kreuzes

+ In personeller und militärischer Hinsicht dem Kommandostab unterstellt

WIRTSCHAFTSABTEILUNG
- Leiter der Wirtschaftsabteilung
- Ständiger Vertreter des Leiters
- Persönlicher Referent des Leiters
- Zentralgruppe u. Abteilungsbüro
- Gewerbliche Wirtschaft Allgemeines
- Sozialwesen und Arbeitseinsatz
- Bergbau
- Bank, Geld- u. Kreditwesen Versicherungen
- Steine u. Erden
- Feind- und Judenvermögen
- Energie
- Verbrauch u. wirtschaftliche Statistik
- Eisen u. Stahl
- Mineralöl
- Nichteisenmetalle
- Chemie
- Textil
- Leder
- Tabak
- Eisen u. Metallverarbeitende Industrie
- Altmaterial
- Ernährungs- und Landwirtschaft
- Ausw. Waren- Zahlungs-und Devisenverkehr
- Preisregelung
- Wirtschaft Transportbedarf
- Forst-und Holzwirtschaft

- Beauftragter der DAF
- Zentralauftragsstelle gemeinsam mit Rüstungsinspektion
- Aussenstelle Antwerpen (Verwaltung des Antwerp. Hafens)
- Brusseler Treuhand-G.m.b.H.
- Allg. Waren-Verkehrs-G.m.b.H.

transportation, social services and employment and price regulation.

The next main unit was the Administration Division (*Verwaltungsabteilung*) which dealt with Belgian government agencies, with cultural and police affairs, with medicine and judicial business, and with censorship and propaganda. The third unit was the Chancellery (*Präsidialbureau*) which was designed primarily to service Reeder's work as Chief of the Military Administration. The head of the Administration Division, Harry von Craushaar, was also the head of the Chancellery. He served as Reeder's representative in Reeder's absence.

In addition to these three main divisions, the Military Administration comprised a miscellaneous collection of services and agencies which were formally under Reeder's control, but which in effect received their instructions from ministries or main offices in Berlin. This group included the *Propagandaabteilung*, a branch of Goebbels' Ministry of Propaganda, the German police, the coordinating agency for purchases made by the military services (*Zentralauftragsstelle*), and various other local representatives of such agencies as the Labor Front and of the Red Cross.

The local and regional structure of the Military Administration went through a number of modifications in 1940. By the end of 1940 a three-tier structure was finalized with one German military office (*Feldkommandantur* or *Oberfeldkommandantur*) for each of the nine Belgian provinces, and a series of local command posts (*Ortskommandantur*) headed by a military officer.[39] Each of these regional and local offices included specialists in civilian affairs who received their instructions from Reeder's office in Brussels.[40]

The supervisory character of the Military Administration permitted the Germans to govern Belgium with relatively few officials. In early 1941 Reeder observed with pride that he managed a territory with over twelve million inhabitants (including northern France) with only 472 professional administrators (*Beamte des gehobenen Dienstes*).[41]

The personnel of the military staff (*Kommandostab*) and of the Military Administration differed in background. The

Kommandostab consisted largely of active or reserve officers, often members of the nobility, most of them of nationalist and conservative but anti-Nazi persuasion.[42] The Military Administration, on the other hand, consisted primarily of civil servants or businessmen many of whom had joined the Nazi party for practical reasons. From the point of view of some of the aristocratic officers of von Falkenhausen's entourage, Reeder and his *Militärverwaltung* were "Nazis",[43] but Reeder himself claimed after the war that he had recruited the members of his staff, including many opponents of the regime for purely professional reasons.[44]

Despite these differences in background, the two services cooperated well. It is fair to say that the internal morale and cooperation of the German military services for Belgium and northern France were exceptionally high throughout the occupation. This smooth operation reflected in the first instance the respectful collaboration between von Falkenhausen and Reeder. It was also aided by the living arrangements for German officials in Brussels: most of them were required to live in the Hotel Plaza in the center of Brussels and to share dining and recreational facilities. Thus the two staffs from von Falkenhausen and Reeder on down, associated with each other on a daily basis instead of forming separate and mutually antagonistic cliques.[45]

While the differences in background between the two groups were real enough, it was an exaggeration to claim that Reeder's Military Administration consisted of fanatical Nazis. Rather, these men were chosen by Reeder primarily for their competence and usefulness. Although most of them were nationalists and many had joined the Nazi party, Reeder's staff was basically nonpolitical and intent primarily on governing the country competently in order to extract from it as large a contribution to the German war effort as possible.

In their work in Belgium, members of the Military Administration suffered from a number of disabilities which Reeder unsuccessfully tried to change. They were considered military personnel, had to wear uniforms and received only limited military pay according to their rank. They were not allowed to have their families join them and they did not get the recognition and awards that were attached to combat service. For instance Reeder, the second highest official in the Military Command area lived in two rooms in the Hotel Plaza drawing two hundred marks (fifty dollars) per month.[46]

Administrative relationships with many Reich agencies were less than satisfactory from the beginning of the occupation and became more difficult over time. Von Falkenhausen's direct superiors were the Quarter Master General (*Generalquartiermacher*) General Wagner, and the Commander in Chief of the Army (*Oberbefehlshaber des Heeres*) General von Brauchitsch. As long as he remained in office, von Brauchitsch, a former student of von Falkenhausen's at the Infantry School who had been responsible for von Falkenhausen's appointment in the first place, continued to give the latter some support against the infringement of government and party agencies. After von Brauchitsch's dismissal in December 1941 the chain of command on policy and competency questions led more directly to field the Supreme Command of the Armed Forces (OKW), headed by Field Marshal Wilhelm Keitel from whom von Falkenhausen received little or no support. For administrative and logistical purposes the *Militärbefehlshaber* continued to depend on Wagner who was generally sympathetic, but did not have sufficient authority or time to stand up to competing agencies at the higher government levels.[47]

Reeder felt the need for a direct chain of command from the highest policy level on down most acutely, particularly when comparing his own position with that of *Reichskommissar* Seyss-Inquart in the neighboring Netherlands who had direct access to Hitler. Reeder felt that his relatively subordinate administrative position deprived him of adequate authority in the disputes and conflicts with competing civilian and military services which will be described in this chapter.[48] Reeder may, however, have underestimated the advantages of this "lowly" administrative position: it provided him with protective cover since no civilian government or party agency (such as the SS) was able to issue direct orders to him without having to go through the Supreme Command of the Armed Forces. Be that as it may, the Military Command, so well organized internally, after 1941 found itself without much high level support in the struggle that was carried on in the administrative jungle of Hitler's Germany.

General von Falkenhausen and his Staff

In many ways the German administration of occupied Belgium bore the imprint of its two leading figures. Alexander von Falkenhausen was born in 1878 into a Prussian noble family which had emigrated hundreds of years ago into Silesia from Southern Germany. He was sent to a military academy at the age of twelve and from that time on followed a straight military career. As a lieutenant he participated in the suppression of the Boxer Rebellion in China in 1900. Subsequently he enrolled in the Seminar for Oriental Studies in Berlin and joined the General Staff. In 1910 he was sent to Japan to serve in Tokyo as German Military Attaché.

During the First World War he filled a variety of staff positions. In 1918 he was appointed the German military representative in Turkey. After the war he transferred to the new German professional army, the *Reichswehr*, with the rank of Colonel. In 1926 he became the head of the Infantry School at Dresden and in 1930 he retired from the *Reichswehr* with the rank of Lieutenant General. In 1934, he went to China as military advisor to Chiang Kai-shek, in part in order to get away from Hitler's Germany. (His brother had been murdered in the June 1934 Blood Purge.) After the conclusion of the Anti-Comintern Pact between Germany and Japan he was recalled in 1938, and he returned home with great reluctance only after threats had been made against his family.

He was ordered back into active service in August 1939 as Commander of the Military District of Dresden.[49] As has been mentioned above, his appointment as Military Commander of the Netherlands and Belgium probably was on the recommendation of von Brauchitsch. Curiously, a relative, Ludwig von Falkenhausen, had for a time been military governor of Belgium during the First World War.[50]

This sketch of von Falkenhausen's career suggests that while he came from the "correct" background and had gone through the proper training for a General Staff officer, his horizons were not limited to those characteristic of his caste. Von Falkenhausen himself and many observers attributed his wider views to his experiences in the Orient and to some of the values he had absorbed from oriental cultures.[51] These views included a strong sense of the shared values of Western Civilization and a more accurate assessment of world power relationships than that possessed by his colleagues whose experiences had been restricted to the European continent. He also possessed a certain sense of detachment from everyday tribulations and a sense of duty that may have blended a Prussian military with a Confucian tradition.

During his years in Belgium, von Falkenhausen presented an unusual and striking figure. Almost totally bald, he looked so emaciated that he was nicknamed "Gandhi"* by some of his subordinates.[52] His pince-nez gave him a schoolmasterly look and suggested a nineteenth century personality.

One of his collaborators testified to his superior intellect and his subtle understanding of world politics: "Perhaps he was wiser than the rest of us." ("*Vielleicht war er im Vergleich zu uns der Klügere.*")[53] While in Brussels, he was never ill, spending regular though not excessive hours at his desk. However he also enjoyed social life and used the social graces at his command to good purpose. He gave frequent parties (*soirées*) at the Plaza which he used to integrate his staff and to impress and win over visiting dignitaries. Reeder's comments made after the war, portray the mood of these occasions: "He .. (von Falkenhausen) .. liked these parties to the extent to which they were characterized by calm and achieved a certain level of sophistication."[54]

He frequently would spend his weekends at the Castle of Seneffe (confiscated from its owner, a Belgian Jewish banker) entertaining German, Belgian and other foreign guests in

---

* When interviewing the General's widow in her home in Nassau in 1971, the author was taken aback when he saw what he took to be a portrait of Gandhi on the wall. Cecilie von Falkenhausen explained that this was a sketch made during the last years of Alexander von Falkenhausen's life.

style. He justified this "fraternization" by claiming that it was necessary to maintain contact with the people of the country in his charge.[55] His favorite recreation was playing cards and when travelling about he was often seen chaperoning two dachshunds. All in all, von Falkenhausen was a somewhat eccentric figure having his roots in 19th century Prussia and in the pre-1914 world that was shattered by the First World War. There were times when he viewed himself as an anachronism,[56] probably more for the values he held than for his life style.

His values were basically traditional, but yet of a somewhat unusual mix. They were rooted in a nonsectarian Protestantism, and he was attracted to Buddhism which he viewed as "the most peaceful and tolerant of religions."[57] Degrelle was not entirely off-base when he called the general a "Voltairian spirit".[58] At the same time he was also a German nationalist, a monarchist and an authoritarian. He displayed some of the anti-Semitic prejudices common to his caste,[59] although he was opposed to the Nazi persecution of the Jews.[60]

His political views put him at odds with Hitler and the Nazi party, nationalist though he was. After his retirement in 1930 von Falkenhausen had joined the German Nationalist party (*Deutschnationale Volkspartei*) and its paramilitary organization, the *Stahlhelm*. He was elected a deputy in the Saxon diet on the Party's list. He opposed national socialism for its anti-Christian character. Like Rauschning, von Falkenhausen sensed at an early point the limitless nature of Hitler's aspirations which he feared would eventually lead Germany to disaster.[61] He blamed Himmler for his own brother's death in the Blood Purge[62] and was in touch with the military conspirators in the years before the outbreak of the war. He knew Carl Goerdeler, the chief civilian figure among the July 20 group, and was a personal friend of General Ludwig Beck, the original leader of the military conspiracy. He believed that the army should overthrow Hitler, but that the initiative should come from the Chief of the army. He opposed assassination[63] and more or less lost touch with the conspiracy after he assumed command in Belgium, despite occasional contacts with such men as Ulrich von Hassell and Helmuth James von

Moltke. Von Falkenhausen was considered by the conspirators as the future president of Germany.[64] In 1941, the British radio mentioned him as the prospective head of a military government that was to follow Hitler's overthrow.[65] After the attempt on Hitler's life on July 20, 1944 he was arrested by the Gestapo. He was imprisoned in Dachau and other camps for the remainder of the war but was never brought to trial because the Gestapo failed to find proof that he had participated in the conspiracy.

After the end of the war von Falkenhausen spent six years in a variety of Allied camps and in Belgian prisons. He was tried in 1950 and 1951 and sentenced to twelve years imprisonment for his part in the execution of hostages, all the other counts against him having been dropped. This sentence was reduced to time served and he was released immediately, at the age of seventy-two. He spent the remainder of his life in Nassau, Germany. In 1960, when he was eighty-two, he married a Belgian citizen, Cecile Vent who had looked after him in prison as a Red Cross worker. He died in 1966.[66]

Von Falkenhausen's policies in Belgium can be best understood against the background of his beliefs and experiences up to that time, although it must always be borne in mind that he was first and foremost the chief executive officer in Belgium of a totalitarian government. But it remains true that the General believed in a Europe of nation states on the nineteenth century model, presumably under German hegemony, which would have to cooperate in order to preserve Western civilization, particularly in the face of the Bolshevik threat.[67]

He believed from the start, and certainly since September 1940 when Operation Sea Lion was called off, that Germany might not win the war.[68] He therefore tried to govern Belgium (to the extent to which this was possible, given the nature of the war and of the Nazi regime), in such a way as to increase the likelihood that opportunities for postwar collaboration between Germany and Belgium would not be totally compromised.[69] He believed that the Belgian state, although originally an artificial construct, had come to serve best the interest of the country as a whole and that it was supported by a majority of its people.[70] He considered the Belgian monarchy the capstone of that state, and formed a relationship of respect and friendship with King Leopold and the royal family. In his memoirs written after the war he vigorously defended the policies of the king in 1940 against the accusations of the Pierlot government.[71] All in all, von Falkenhausen did what he could to prevent any changes in the existing political and social structure in his Command Area despite the attempts of Himmler and other Nazi party officials to initiate national-socialist reforms and set up Nazi institutions under the occupation.

There is no doubt that von Falkenhausen resisted his own superiors and the SS hierarchy from Himmler on down in an attempt to protect individual Belgians and groups from the excesses of German terror. He tried to exert control over arrests made by the police and over the length of confinement.[72] He intervened with limited success to prevent the maltreatment of prisoners. He delayed for a long time orders to execute Resistance workers despite heavy pressure from his own superiors in the OKW.[73] Yet he was not particularly effective in limiting the number of executions compared with the situation in France or the Netherlands.[74]

It is also known that he intervened in a number of individual cases, particularly on behalf of members of the Belgian nobility, but not exclusively so. Those aided included political prisoners, hostages, and individuals threatened by the Labor Draft.[75] He told members of the royal household that he could do nothing for Jewish people, referring them to Reeder's staff,[76] but on another occasion he intervened on behalf of a group of Jewish children at the request of Queen Mother Elisabeth.[77] At one point he reinterned Belgian officers to keep them from being sent to a concentration camp.[78]

His attempts to soften the excesses of German terror were based both on moral and on pragmatic grounds. Although a "law and order" man himself, he realized that excessive police terror was basically counterproductive and would only produce more disaffection and resistance. But beyond this, his religious and moral conscience also came into play particularly since he was aware sooner than most that Germany and the Germans would eventually be held responsible for what had transpired during the Nazi years.

Yet, given all these good intentions, it must also be recognized that von Falkenhausen did his best to help Hitler's Germany win the war. He oversaw the economic exploitation of the country in the service of the German war effort. In his situation he was bound to carry out in the main orders from the central government and party of which he personally disapproved but which he could not evade, such as the segregation and expropriation of the Jews, the forced labor draft and the execution of Resistance workers. Von Falkenhausen was conscious of this moral dilemma but tried to justify his action with the argument of "the lesser evil." He claimed that his resignation would have brought about the appointment of a *Reichskommissar* who would be a fanatical Nazi party member on the Seyss-Inquart or Terboven model and thus would have run counter to the best interests of the Belgian people.[79]

Thus there remained for von Falkenhausen, as for many "patriotic" Germans, an insoluble moral conflict. He never ceased to work for a German victory even though he believed that Hitler's victory would be the ultimate disaster for Germany and for mankind.[80] He continued to repeat even after the defeat that after all each German had to fulfill his duty to his country.[81] There is little doubt that he suffered considerable mental torture from this unresolved and ultimately insoluble contradiction.[82]

It remains surprising that an individual with such unorthodox (in terms of the Third Reich) views and attitudes could be appointed as governor of an important occupied country and that he could retain his Command over a period of more than four years while the Nazi regime became increasingly desperate and radical at home and abroad. It must be assumed that Hitler consented to von Falkenhausen's appointment in 1940 because he needed the full support of the army for the forthcoming offensive in the West.[83] Von Falkenhausen's retention until July 1944 is a complicated story which will be told in a subsequent section of this chapter. Hitler himself acquired a growing dislike for von Falkenhausen, primarily for his lack of ruthlessness and for his fraternization with the Belgian aristocracy. Von Falkenhausen on his side fought with determination for his retention in office despite moments of despair in 1943 and 1944 when he seriously considered resignation or suicide.[85]

Despite von Falkenhausen's success in retaining his Command, there is little doubt that his political position within the German hierarchy was weakened by two personal shortcomings. He was politically indiscreet voicing his anti-Nazi views and his contempt of certain party figures not only among intimates, but even in the presence of Belgian nationals whom he did not know personally.[86] It remains a mystery to this day why Himmler did not use these indiscretions, which were general knowledge among German dignitaries in Brussels, to persuade Hitler to remove von Falkenhausen. The general was also indiscreet in his personal life by maintaining very close personal associations with members of the Belgian nobility. He became the personal friend and probably the lover of a Princess Elisabeth Ruspoli, the Belgian widow of an Italian prince who was killed at El Alamein. A circle (the princess called it a "family") of Belgian baronnesses and other aristocrats around the princess and the general lead an intimate social life with von Falkenhausen and other officers of the *Kommandostab*. During one of the festivities held at the Castle of Seneffe, the Princess Ruspoli was reported to have been crowned "Queen of the Black Market" in the general's presence in recognition of her prowess of buying up food to help feed the Italian colony in Brussels.[87] Toward the end of 1943 the princess was arrested and accused of black market and illegal foreign currency operations, but she survived the war.[88]

How are we to explain such a lack of discretion and such a touch of frivolity in the midst of a terrible war when the stakes were so high in the power game of Nazi Germany? In part, the general proclaimed a deliberate philosophy that it was good and justified to play in the right time and place, but on the other hand, his political carelessness and his somewhat Bohemian lifestyle must be attributed to a certain arrogance and eccentricity that were characteristic of him. On some level, he simply did not care what others thought of him or what the political consequences of his actions might be. Be that as it may, there is little doubt that his careless personal conduct made him more vulnerable in Berlin and at Hitler's headquarters. It gave the impression to at least some of his subordinates that "he lived like a Pascha and left all the hard work to Reeder."[89] It also gave rise to the sentiment that he cared more about the Belgian aristocracy than about the common people.

During his years in Brussels, von Falkenhausen found a great deal of support among the members of his military staff who formed his closest associates. A sense of absolute loyalty to the Chief prevailed.[90] It was within this circle of congenial spirits that von Falkenhausen's gift of leadership showed most directly. As one subordinate described it: "He had the gift to let you know his thoughts and intentions without having to give orders. Nobody could escape the persuasive force which he communicated."[91] He expected and was given a great deal of work and loyalty because "it was an honor to work under such a Chief."[92]

The general's closest associate and head of the *Kommandostab* was Colonel Theodor von Harbou, a fellow officer and friend from the days before the First World War.[93] Descendant of a Huguenot family, von Harbou may have felt special sympathy for the Belgian elites. He had been in business between the wars and had a number of acquaintances among Belgian businessmen. He was a hard worker, but he, too, lacked political and personal discretion and restraint.[94] He had allegedly run into trouble with the SS early on when he opposed the establishment of the SS in Flanders and made an enemy of SS General Berger.[95] He, too, had a liaison with a Belgian countess.

In late 1943, a few weeks after the arrest of the Princess Ruspoli, von Harbou himself was arrested after a conflict with local SS officers. He also was accused of illegal foreign currency transactions and was taken to Berlin for investigation and a court martial. In December 1943 he died in prison in Berlin, presumably a suicide.[96] General von Falkenhausen considered the arrest of Princess Ruspoli and of Colonel von

Harbou, his two closest personal friends, an indirect attempt by the SS to destroy him.[97] It was the loss of these two close associates that brought von Falkenhausen to the edge of despair and suicide.[98]

Other members of the *Kommandostab* included an ex-Foreign Office official dismissed by von Ribbentrop for his anti-Nazi views,[99] a former member of an anti-Communist intelligence group born in England[100] and the future head of the Protestant Church in Germany.[101] Such men formed a solid phalanx around von Falkenhausen until some of them were transferred or otherwise removed in 1943 and 1944. Their personal friendship and moral support made it psychologically possible for the general to maintain his exposed position until very near the end of the occupation.

The other German official to put his imprint on the occupation regime in a major way was Eggert Reeder, the Chief of the Military Administration. He was born in 1894 in the North German province of Schleswig-Holstein. His father was a landowner who served as *Landrat* or County Administrator. Reeder's father was the unquestioned authority in his family circle in the stereotypical Prussian manner and Reeder was said to have inherited from him an authoritarian temperament, a military demeanor (*schneidiges Auftreten*), and a preference for strictly hierarchical organization.[102]

Reeder saw military service in the First World War as a commissioned officer. In the turbulent months following the war he joined a Free Corps. He subsequently studied law and joined the civil service. Reeder very quickly moved up the civil service ladder becoming provincial governor (*Regierungspräsident*) first in Aachen (1933), then in Cologne (1936) and finally also in Düsseldorf (1939).[103]

During the Weimar years his religious and political convictions placed him on the right. Like von Falkenhausen he was for a time a member of the German Nationalist party (DNVP). In 1933 he joined the Nazi party, primarily to protect and advance his career, but also because he was swept up in the "National Awakening" by a movement which professed many aspirations congenial to his own beliefs. He accepted an honorary rank in the SS after being assured by Himmler that his religious beliefs and his church membership would not be in conflict with his membership in the SS.

In the years after 1933 Reeder repeatedly ran into difficulties with Göring and Himmler over his insistence that police services should remain under the control of the regional government official, the *Regierungspräsident*, instead of receiving instructions directly from Himmler as head of the German police. In this conflict Reeder already exhibited the same commitment to a singleheaded hierarchical administration that was to characterize theory and practice during his years in Belgium. Reeder himself believed that it was this philosophy of his, and his success in resisting Himmler's demands for police independence that induced the High Command of the Army to select him in 1939 as head of the task force to lay plans for the administration of territories to be occupied in the West, and to pick him subsequently for his assignment in Belgium.[104]

He was drafted into the army in November 1939, but did not meet von Falkenhausen until May 1940. Reeder assumed his duties as Chief of the Military Administration in June and served in that capacity until the evacuation of the country, surviving into the days of the *Reichskommissariat*. After the German withdrawal from Belgium, he resumed his duties as *Regierungspräsident* in Cologne in September 1944. In 1945 Reeder was arrested by the Allies and turned over to Belgian authorities who kept him in prison until his trial. He was tried by a Belgian Military Court along with von Falkenhausen and also received a prison sentence, but like the general, was released for time served. After his return to Germany Reeder held a number of positions in business, but never rejoined government service. He died in 1959.[105]

Reeder's personality was different from that of the low-keyed, self-controlled General. Reeder was impulsive, given to rages, occasionally blowing up in meetings and subsequently regretting his lack of self-control. However, he also was an extremely competent administrator[106.] As one of his former associates put it in 1971: "He was viewed as the most capable administrator in the German civil service."[107] Reeder himself, (it must be admitted) had a high opinion of his own ability to the point of being conceited. During his years in Belgium he more than once referred to himself as the (one) person who could weigh and balance all the elements in the situation.[108]

Reeder held clear concepts about administration which he tried to spell out in detail and which he worked hard to implement. He was a dedicated worker and like von Falkenhausen was able to generate deep loyalty and devotion in his associates and subordinates even if he treated them roughly at times. Moreover, Reeder had a streak of stubborness and a full measure of personal courage which enabled him to stand up to higher officials and even to Himmler himself. He was also adept at using friends and allies in the German civil service in the old ministries to support his views against those of his opponents.

There has been some debate to which extent Reeder was a Nationalist Socialist. To this writer the evidence is rather clear. He was a nationalist and conservative to begin with, and in 1933, like so many others, joined the Nazi party not only to enhance his career, but also from conviction. His membership in the SS, however, probably was on a more pragmatic basis, to accommodate Himmler's wishes and advance his career. His subsequent experiences with the party and with Himmler in particular gradually disillusioned him as he watched party and SS corroding the foundations of traditional state and society.[109] On the other hand, despite his growing misgivings, his own identification with party and SS provided him with a measure of political clout. It was this identification and his prestige as a superior administrator that made him so effective in defense of the occupation regime.

Reeder's perception of goals and policies to be pursued harmonized with the general's. Like von Falkenhausen he felt that there should be only minimal changes in existing structures and institutions as long as the war was in progress. He was emphatic in this respect because he wished to preserve the existing Belgian government bureaucracy to administer the country under his supervision and at his direction. But this was mostly a pragmatic stance for him since he was more sympathetic than the General to Flemish aspirations for autonomy or independence.[110] It seems likely that at least in 1940 Reeder favored the eventual (well-understood: postwar) division of Belgium along linguistic lines with the resulting entities safely under German control.[111] It must be admitted, however, that he resisted all such moves during the occupation, and that he deplored the open advocacy of annexation by the SS.

Reeder's foremost assistant was his former personal counselor (*Persönlicher Referent*) Franz Thedieck, a man of deep religious (Catholic) convictions. Thedieck had originally studied agriculture, but had become politically active as a student during the immediate post World War I period in the struggle against the separatist movement in the Rhineland. Subsequently he worked for the Prussian Ministry of the Interior to promote resistance against the French and Belgian occupation of the Ruhr. He then became a "specialist for Western frontier territories," especially Eupen-Malmédy, a small area near Aachen which Germany had been forced to cede to Belgium in the Treaty of Versailles. Because Reeder suffered a severe automobile accident in May 1940, Thedieck had played a major role in "putting together" the Military Administration in June 1940. During his years in Belgium he was, as he described himself, Reeder's "Girl Friday" (*das Mädchen für alles*), with special responsibility for relations with the Secretaries-General, the Catholic church, and the Flemish movement.[112] He was the prime protagonist of the Flemish nationalist movement within the Military Administration. As a supporter of the VNV against the Flemish SS and the annexationists, and as a practicing Catholic, Thedieck came under heavy attack from Heydrich and Himmler. A reluctant Reeder was eventually forced to dismiss him in April 1943 at Himmler's insistence, after much bitter acrimony.[113]

Thedieck's role was somewhat balanced by that of another assistant of Reeder's by the name of Günther Heym who had also worked for Reeder in the thirties and who took over Thedieck's role after the latter's dismissal. Heym was a member of the inner SS circles and had connections with members of Himmler's personal staff. Nevertheless he was apparently genuinely loyal to Reeder even though some members of Reeder's staff felt that he tended to conceal his own convictions. Heym's ability to judge the climate within the SS at a given point in time made him particularly valuable to Reeder because his advice suggested the outer limits of resistance to Himmler and the SS.[114]

Reeder's official second-in-command Harry von Craushaar, was a moderate, a "reasonable" and basically non-political type who got along well with Reeder. He was less exposed politically since his main task was to lend administrative support to Reeder's operation.

Most of the department heads under Reeder were administrators rather than policy makers. One of them, however, Professor Franz Petri of Cologne University, deserves special mention because he was a person of a certain academic and intellectual stature who proposed theories which had some impact on occupation policies. Since 1936 he had been the Director of the Institute for the Low Countries (*Niederländisches Institut*) at the University of Cologne.[115] In 1937 he had published a book, *Germanisches Volkserbe in Wallonien und Nordfrankreich* ("Germanic Folk Heritage in Wallonia and Northern France") in which he put forth the theory that Germanic settlements in the Middle Ages had reached into northern France down to the river Somme, and that the current language line that crossed Belgium represented a retreat from positions the Germanic peoples had held earlier.[116] Whereas Petri denied before the outbreak of war that these findings legitimized any German claims to Belgian or French territory, it was clear that this kind of thesis could be used to provide a basis for future annexationist claims, particularly once language was equated with race. Petri himself opened the door to such possiblities in his speeches and publications after May 1940,[117] while admitting that eventual decisions would be made on a political rather than scholarly basis.[118]

As head of the section for Culture and Education Petri supported the use of Flemish as against that of French in schools and universities and promoted a variety of exchange activities between Flanders and Germany as one of the least controversial ways of importing German culture and scholarship.[119] When the crisis in the universities came over the labor draft he did his best to mediate and keep the universities open as long as possible. After the war he returned to his position at Cologne University.

With Petri, as with Reeder, one is tempted to ask how much of a Nazi this man was and our findings are not too dissimilar from those in Reeder's case, except that for Petri religious convictions and ties played a more central part than for Reeder.[120] Basically Petri was a German nationalist who found himself working in a politically "hot" area when he selected the "language question" in Belgium as his dissertation topic.[121] There is no doubt that he too was swept up in the emotions of the "national rebirth" of the 1930's and in the enthusiasms of the summer of 1940 when "everything seemed possible." During this period he openly if obliquely justified German expansion into Belgium and Northern France. However, within the spectrum of administrators working under Reeder he must be considered a moderate who wished to protect existing Belgian educational institutions to the best of his ability.

Although Reeder was inferior to von Falkenhausen in general education and in subtlety of character and style, in his own way he, too, managed to create a harmonious and loyal administrative apparatus. His associates and subordinates knew where they stood with him, policies and lines of authority were clear and remained essentially unchanged throughout the occupation, except in the case of the labor draft and of the police. The personnel of the Military Administration proper remained unusually stable, in large part at Reeder's insistence, at least until 1943 when growing manpower needs and policy conflicts brought about a number of personnel shifts during the last year of the occupation.

Given the fact that General von Falkenhausen and Reeder were such highly idiosyncratic individuals, the question arises how they could work together so effectively. A number of factors made this possible. First and foremost, they agreed on basic aims[122] even if at times they disagreed on methods and timing. Secondly, they shared a certain cultural and ideological space: They were both Lutherans, nationalists, authoritarian in temperament and philosophy, monarchists (Reeder less decidedly so) and both of them were "law and order" men used to working in a strictly hierarchical system, the army and the Prussian bureaucracy respectively. Reeder's sense of hierarchy made it easy for him to accept inwardly the authority of a man twenty years his senior, a General Staff officer of superior birth, education, experience and rank.[123] The general in turn, in his self-assurance had no difficulty in accepting Reeders competence and aggressiveness. He sought and listened to Reeder's advice[124] and gave him a free rein, within a mutually understood framework, to administer the country.

According to their postwar testimony, they quickly established a clear working relationship in 1940. The general retained ultimate authority and responsibility for the actions of the Military Administration, but he delegated the day-to-day authority to Reeder, including the right to sign decrees in the name of the Military Commander. Reeder, in turn, developed a sense of where von Falkenhausen stood and what he wanted. The general has testified that Reeder never put him in a position where he had to accept a *fait accompli*[125] and Reeder never felt disavowed by von Falkenhausen.[126]

Within this context a clear division of labor occurred. The general and the *Kommandostab* were primarily responsible for security, including sabotage directed against the armed forces. The general was also responsible for such external relationships with other countries as continued to exist after the expulsion of the diplomatic corps in 1940 and for relations within the military hierarchy in the Command Area and in the Reich. Von Falkenhausen also retained a personal interest in the Belgian prisoners of war, the food situation and the forced labor draft, and in relations with the king.

Reeder and the Military Administration in turn dealt with Belgian government agencies from the Secretaries-General on down and with all civilian affairs including economic problems, police, collaboration and the Flemish movement. Reeder was also primarily responsible for negotiations with German civilian government agencies and with party and SS.[127]

There is a good deal of evidence that Reeder on the whole was the one who took the initiative in areas not exclusively preempted by the Military Commander and his staff. In general, Reeder proposed and von Falkenhausen approved.[128] It probably was true that Reeder was the real work horse in the German administration of occupied Belgium.

The effectiveness of the Reeder-von Falkenhausen team was further enhanced by a certain complementary dimension in style and competence. The general provided the broad philosophical framework while Reeder was primarily a practitioner and a systems man. On the other hand, von Falkenhausen was a "babe in the woods" in the Third Reich jungle of competing personalities and competencies, whereas Reeder was thoroughly familiar with the realities and complexities of Hitler's Germany. The general tended to be indecisive in political matters, whereas Reeder had an excellent sense of timing, when to act and place Berlin before an accomplished fact[129] and when to give in when demands from the center could not be ignored. Reeder also assumed the responsibility for defending the policies of the Military Command against criticism in government and party circles, always declaring himself fully in accord with the general's policies.[130] At his trial von Falkenhausen testified that in his opinion he and von Harbou with their intransigent and contemptuous attitudes could not have lasted "two weeks" without Reeder's sense of realism.[131]

Despite this excellent cooperation there remained differences and distinctions based on their dissimiliar social backgrounds and on the nuances in their political milieu and outlook. In the immediate postwar period the general seems to have displayed a tendency for a while to burden Reeder with responsibility for some of the least defensible actions that took place within the Military Command area such as the execution of hostages, but by the time of the trial the general accepted full responsibility for the actions of the Command. It appears that after their repatriation their relationship mended again in the years before Reeder's death.

During the occupation, Reeder on his side was critical of the idiosyncracies of the general which weakened the political position of the Military Command in its struggle with party and SS[132] At one point Reeder went so far as to request a visiting diplomat, Ulrich von Hassell, to ask von Falkenhausen to be a bit more discreet.[133] But despite this criticism Reeder remained loyal to the general even though he could have easily overturned the military regime had he sided with Himmler. He did not do this because, as he said at his trial, he felt that the general's policies were "in the best interest of Germany and Belgium."[134] That is why it is probably no exaggeration to say that at the command level the German occupation regime in Belgium was one of the more stable and harmonious German administrations in occupied Western Europe through the cooperation of these two very different but in their own ways very competent men.

The Reports of the Military Administration: Intentionality and Reliability

An important part of the information about the structure and activities of the German military regime used in this study is drawn from the periodic reports which the Military Administration prepared for its superiors in the Reich. These reports, which after a while came to be called *Tätigkeitsberichte* or Activity Reports, were produced at first on a ten day or fortnightly basis. After May 1941 they were prepared on a quarterly basis and finally in 1944 again at a rate of one per month. In addition we have an Annual Report (*Jahresbericht*) which provides a good deal of information about the first crucial year when most of the patterns of the occupation were set. These reports were formally addressed to the Quarter-Master General (Wagner) in the High Command of the Army, but approximately two hundred mimeographed copies were distributed among government and party agencies in the Reich.[135]

Usually these reports opened with a general section written by Reeder himself which provided an overview over political, economic and social problems and trends during the period concerned. The other sections were written by the heads of the competent divisions of the Military Administration or by their associates, subject to Reeder's approval.[136] It appears that von Falkenhausen reviewed and approved the introductory section and presumably read the entire report, but that the reports were in the main the handiwork or Reeder's *Militärverwaltung*. The *Kommandostab* sent its own periodic reports to the High Command of the Army but they did not have as broad a scope as the *Tätigkeitsberichte*.

The introductory sections, and, on a lesser scale, the Activity Reports as a whole provided Reeder with an important forum for the advocacy of policies espoused by the Military Command and for their defense against adversaries in the government, and in the party and SS. Thus the reports contain pleas in 1940 for the return of the Walloon prisoners of war, for additional imports of grain and other foodstuffs from Germany, and for some assurance of continued Belgian independence. Later during the occupation, issues advocated included the need for central control of policies within the Command Area, for the control of the unrestrained purchases by German personnel and agencies and for a moderate and integrated Flemish policy. In 1941 and 1942 incidents of sabotage were played down and the successes of the German police in catching perpetrators of anti-German acts were played up in order to obviate the need for harsher repressive measures urged by Hitler, the OKW and the SS. From 1941 on, the reports warn against the introduction of a compulsory labor draft on the grounds that voluntary recruitment had been successful. Throughout these reports the reader is encouraged to recognize the effectiveness of the Military Administration in harnessing the occupied territory to the German war effort.

In many Activity Reports Reeder and his associates attempt to take the pulse of public opinion and to assess the mood of the country. While these sections too are weighted in support of the policies of the German occupation authorities it must be admitted that the assessment of public opinion reflected in the *Tätigkeitsberichte* strikes even the presentday reader as realistic and sophisticated, particularly with respect to the intellectual and civil service milieus most accessible to German agencies. A comparison of these German assessments with the foremost contemporary Belgian assessment of public opinion, Paul Struye's *L'évolution du sentiment public en Belgique sous l'occupation allemande* (which Reeder received, read and may have utilized) reinforces the impression that Reeder was sensitive to changes in the public sentiment of the country.

It is impossible to assess the practical effectiveness of the *Tätigkeitsberichte* in their primary goal of securing support in the Reich for the policies of the Military Command. On the one hand, we read about Hitler's irritated comment that Belgium is not to be governed with lots of *Briefschreiberei* (letter writing),[137] but on the other hand, the Military Command gained general acceptance in the Reich of its own view that it was the most efficient occupation regime in Western Europe which should not be dismissed lightly. The historian reading these reports is struck with the cohesiveness of the policies advocated and with the vigor of the language. The reports provide an enormous amount of data and it must have taken an immense effort to secure and present this vast array of information.

Given the fact that these reports had a definite purpose (they were sometimes called *Zweckberichte*[138] or "Reports with a Purpose") the question arises whether they are sufficiently accurate and objective to serve as a reliable source for an understanding of the period. It is clear that the reports have to be used with a degree of sophistication with regard to their "intentionality." After the war Reeder claimed that the facts and figures given were accurate, but that the emphases were slanted to achieve the desired result. Intentionality becomes particularly important in statements which contain a significant element of subjectivity. In particular, many reports were designed to give a relatively optimistic outlook in order to counteract more alarmist reports prepared by the SD and other party agencies.[139] At other times, the reports emphasized the distress and growing antagonism of the population when doing so suited a particular purpose of the Military Command such as to encourage the return of the Belgian prisoners of war or to urge increased food imports from Germany. Because of this intentionality these reports have to be used with special caution and savvy. They obviously are most reliable when their content is confirmed by independent Belgian statements.[140]

Another important source of information on the activities of the Military Administration is to be found in the surviving sections of the Final Report (*Abschlussbericht*) which members of Reeder's staff started preparing in Germany in 1944 after the German withdrawal from Belgium. This team (*Abwicklungstab*) had the files of the Military Administration at its disposal.[141] Most of the factual data in these Final Reports are reliable, but the reader must beware of a new tendency: With the approaching defeat of Germany clearly just over the horizon, these reports are in large part designed to show that the Military Administration had the best interests of Belgium and of its population at heart and that it tried to proceed on the basis of voluntary cooperation which was, according to the reports, given freely, particularly in the early years of the occupation. These reports also have another self-justificatory dimension: they stress in retrospect the correctness of the centralizing and coordinating policies of the Military Command and deplore the interference from government and party agencies. But with proper allowances made for these special considerations, these Final Reports too constitute another useful source for the study of the occupation regime.

The Struggle Over the Introduction of a Civilian Administration (*Reichskommissariat*)

Previous comments have suggested that Hitler probably intended from the outset to institute as soon as practicable a civilian administration headed by a high party official on the Dutch, Norwegian and East European models. What makes the Belgian case so special is that despite Hitler's original intention the final imposition of a civilian regime did not occur until July 1944, only a few weeks before the end of the occupation.

Since more detailed accounts of the struggle over the replacement of the Military Command by a *Reichskommissariat* are available[142] this study will provide only a relatively brief summary of the conflict that took place. Active consideration of a changeover to a civilian administration took place on four distinct occasions.

The first of these occurred during the early weeks of the occupation. Three days before the Belgian capitulation, on May 25, 1940, Himmler proposed to Hitler the establishment of a *Reichskommissariat* in Belgium within the context of discussions over the German regime in the Netherlands.[143] As has been mentioned previously, early in June information arrived in Brussels that Hitler intended to appoint a *Reichskommissar* for Flanders, but not for the French-speaking section of the country.[144] It appears that he had picked (at least tentatively) *Gauleiter* Karl Kaufmann of Hamburg to be the new *Reichskommissar*.[145] General von Falkenhausen vigorously rejected attempts by a representative of *Gauleiter* Kaufmann to arrange for a transition schedule. On June 25, 1940, in a letter to the High Command of the Army he protested against this unauthorized interference and urged the retention of the Military Command.[146] The OKH supported this position with Hitler but it took some weeks before a decision was handed down. Then, on July 20, 1940, the High Command advised the Military Commander in Belgium of a Führer decision: "Belgium will be administered by the *Militärbefehlshaber* until further notice (*bis auf weiteres*)."[147]

What were the main considerations that kept Hitler from carrying out his original intention? In the summer of 1940 the main factor probably was the strategic location of Belgium in the context of the plans for an invasion of England (Operation Sea Lion). The presence of Leopold III, brother-in-law of the Italian Crown Prince, presented an additional complication. Appointment of a High Commissioner might have signalled to the king and to Belgian political circles that Germany intended to annex Belgium and thus might have placed into jeopardy the cooperation of Belgian government services and business so crucial to the success of the occupation regime.[148] Retention of a Military Command structure served best to cloak ultimate intentions and "to keep all options open."[149]

But despite this decision matters were not allowed to rest. Rumors about the impending replacement of the Military

Command floated about in Berlin and in Brussels throughout 1941 as Hitler grew increasingly disenchanted with the von Falkenhausen regime. In October 1941, H. H. Lammers, Chief of the Reich Chancellery who was to occupy the key position in the deliberations on this issue, reported that Hitler intended to establish a civilian administration in Belgium.[150] However, in a consultation of the Supreme Command of the Armed Forces and of the ministries concerned initiated by Lammers in November, all the agencies queried favored retention of the military regime.[151] In May 1942 Lammers reported that Hitler, undoubtedly in reaction to these responses, did not want to deal with the issue. Lammers therefore postponed its consideration until the fall[152] bringing to a close the second episode in the struggle over the replacement of the military regime.

It is not quite clear at whose initiative the third round of discussions at the Reich Chancellery level commenced. Possibly Lammers was observing his own timetable, but it is more likely that reconsideration arose from the struggle over the introduction of the compulsory labor service. It is also possible that, ironically enough, Reeder himself started the ball rolling with his complaints over the obstacles put in his path, since we know that State Secretary Stuckart of the Reich Ministry of the Interior, after an interview with Reeder and at the latter's suggestion, proposed in October 1942 the establishment of a *Reichskommissariat* which would have greater clout in the German hierarchy.[153] Lammers had another memorandum prepared in the Chancellery which posed the question whether it was advisable at this point in the war to tackle the political transformation of Belgium at the risk of political turmoil and economic loss to the war effort.[154] On October 23, 1942 Lammers reported once again that Hitler did not consider this the opportune moment to introduce a civilian administration and here the issue rested for another year.[155]

The fourth move to replace the military regime may have been initiated by Keitel himself who had become distrustful of von Falkenhausen over the von Harbou affair and over reports about the general's personal life. More importantly perhaps, he may have believed that the security situation in occupied Belgium was getting out of hand and that a harsher regime might deal more effectively with the Resistance. Furthermore, *Gauleiter* Fritz Sauckel, Plenipotentiary for the labor draft by this time had turned into a fierce opponent of the occupation regime and of the general personally. At any rate, after a consultation with Keitel, Hitler told Lammers late in December 1943 that he had decided to go ahead with the installation of a civilian administration. He ordered Lammers to prepare the decrees necessary to institute a *Reichskommissariat*.[156] This time once more Lammers instituted a round of interagency consultations, presumably to delay the replacement of the military regime. These consultations again dragged on for a few months, but this time only the Foreign Office retained its opposition to the proposed change.[157] However, it appeared that even then Hitler was not yet quite ready to make a final decision and as late as June 29 the Führer was reported to remain undecided. But whatever the immediate cause, Hitler finally made up his mind in early July and the decree instituting a *Reichskommissariat* was signed on July 13. It provided for the appointment of a civilian *Reichskommissar* (*Gauleiter* Josef Grohé of Cologne and Aachen, Reeder's home ground), a territorial Military Commander (*Wehrmachtsbefehlshaber*) not named in the decree, and of a Higher SS and Police Leader (*Höherer SS und Polizeiführer*), to be designated by Himmler. At the insistence of the Foreign Office the decree left the two French departments within the boundaries of the new *Reichkommissariat*.[158]

On July 12 a conference took place with Hitler in which Lammers, Bormann, Keitel and Himmler participated with Grohé and General Grase, about to be appointed as *Wehrmachtsbefehlshaber*. After some introductory remarks by Lammers, Hitler made a speech which is important because it reveals more clearly than any other document his real feelings about Belgium. He set as the goal of German policy "to get the Belgian territory (*das Gebiet Belgiens*) [i.e., not the state or the Kingdom of Belgium] into our hands for good, with the best solution being that of the establishment of a Flemish and a Walloon *Reichsgau* [province of the Greater German Reich after a proposed territorial reorganization]."[159] It was the task of the new *Reichskommissar* to implement German national interests "ice-cold . . . and totally ruthlessly and selfishly." (. . . *eiskalt zu verfolgen und ganz rücksichtlos und egoistisch zu vertreten.*")[160] He also urged the new administration to rely on lower class Flemish people and above all to make certain that the Belgian nobility would not ". . . subjugate the occupying power intellectually and spiritually,"[161] an obvious reference to the von Falkenhausen regime. Here we have Hitler's true sentiments (in 1944) about the rule of Military Command, and about German goals in Belgium, not much modified since the early days of victory, except that now the French-speaking part of the country was also to be annexed to Germany.

Himmler then added some remarks to the effect that the Flemish National League (VNV) did not offer a proper basis for cooperation because it advocated a Greater Netherlands (*Diets*) view. Instead he praised the radical Flemish group Devlag and its leader Jef Van de Wiele as the only reliable basis of support for a Greater Germanic policy and expressed the hope that its men would be used to replace less reliable elements in the Belgian government services. Degrelle was also recommended as a potentially useful if somewhat more unreliable ally.[162]

The struggle over the introduction of a civilian administration can best be understood as a reflection of the basic power conflicts in Hitler's Germany. The older traditional elements in the government and in the armed forces who found a supporter at the Reich Chancellery level in Lammers tried to administer and exploit the occupied country as efficiently as possible by minimizing wartime political or administrative changes that could arouse unnecessary opposition and resistance. Himmler on the other hand, with Hitler's wavering support, wished to bring about such transformations already under wartime conditions in order to expand his empire and gain more direct influence in Belgium. Bormann on his part favored a civilian administration under a *Gauleiter* because such an arrangement would strengthen the hand of the NSDAP, but he opposed in Belgium (as he did in Holland) the expansion of Himmler's empire. Therefore the belated establishment of a civilian administration headed by a *Gauleiter* and including the office of a Higher SS and Police Leader reflected on the one hand a compromise between Bormann and Himmler, but on the other hand a victory of party and SS over the military and the "old ministries," particularly the Foreign Office.[163]

The surprising durability of the military administration was due to a number of special circumstances: (1) Belgium's strategic location on the Channel coast, first as a jumping-off point for an invasion of England, and then from 1942 on as potential invasion territory,[164] (2) the presence of the king who was a close relative by marriage of the Italian monarchy which was allied with Germany until September 1943, (3) the economic accomplishments of the Military Administration, (4) Reeder's success in avoiding the sort of major political confrontations with the population that occurred in the neighboring Netherlands and in Norway, and finally, (5) the location of the Military Command in the hierarchical ladder, so often deplored by Reeder, which placed von Falkenhausen and his regime under the protection of the leadership of the Army and of the OKW (feeble and unreliable as this protection was on specific issues) and which kept the Military Command in Belgium far removed from Hitler's immediate purview (" . . . *zu weit ausserhalb des Blickfeldes Hitlers.*")[165] In addition, the retention of the Military Command obviously continued to suit one of Hitler's objectives until it no longer mattered: to camouflage for as long as necessary his ultimate intention to annex Belgium to the Reich. The reasons for the final dismissal of the Military Command can also be listed, but they are far less rational in the face of the Allied landing in Normandy than the reasons for retention. By July 1944 a number of the previous obstacles had been removed: (1) the invasion had occurred in Normandy (and *not* in Belgium) and the Allies were still (for another week) bottled up in the Normandy peninsula, (2) the king had been removed to Germany in June and the reaction of the Italian monarchy no longer mattered, (3) the economic yield from the occupied territory had taken a huge downturn in 1944, (4) the security situation was becoming increasingly destabilized with the rapid increase in the activities of the Resistance, and (5) Keitel, by December 1943, had removed his protective shield (such as it was) over von Falkenhausen and his regime.

During the long years that the fate of the military administration hung in balance, the uncertainty created by the situation had a contradictory impact on the political climate in Belgium and on the effectiveness of the von Falkenhausen-Reeder regime. It was well-known in many responsible milieus in Belgium that the Military Command might at any time be replaced by a *Reichskommissar*. To some extent this knowledge naturally undermined the position of the military authorities with respect to the radical collaborationist groups such as the Flemish SS, Devlag, and Degrelle's Rexist party which tried hard to play off their SS connections against Reeder. The latter often complained bitterly about the indiscretion of Party and SS circles who told their Belgian allies as early as 1941 that the regime would soon be replaced by a *Reichskommissariat*.

But while these rumors and uncertainties may have weakened Reeder's authority over the Belgian allies of the SS, the military regime also derived considerable benefit from the threat of its replacement by a more radical party and SS dominated administration. The very precariousness of its position and the threat of worse things to come made individuals in the Belgian power structure such as government officials and leading businessmen more ready to compromise in order to avoid confrontations that would further weaken the Military Command in the eyes of Berlin. Such considerations played into the hands of the military regime by strengthening the argument in favor of collaboration as the policy of the lesser evil (*la politique du moindre mal*). The Military Administration, in turn, subtly used this issue in its negotiations with the Belgian leadership. There was a recognition in high German government circles in Berlin that this line of reasoning was effective in lowering the level of Belgian resistance to German demands.[166] This insight in turn became an argument in favor of the retention of the Military Command.

After four years of behind the scenes struggles the Military Command finally came to an end on July 18, 1944, when

General von Falkenhausen officially transferred his authority to *Gauleiter* Grohé, the new High Commissioner.

Once installed in office, *Reichskommissar* Grohé informed the officials of the *Militärverwaltung* that he intended to retain the existing staff. He specifically asked Reeder, an old acquaintance from the Rhineland whom Grohé held in high respect, to stay on. Reeder said he would accept on the assumption that the *Reichskommissar* approved of the policies followed by him so far. Grohé's appreciation of Reeder went so far that he appointed him his deputy in all areas of competence except the police.[167]

It was known that Himmler had secured Hitler's approval for the appointment of Jungclaus, the SS representative in Brussels, as Higher SS and Police Leader. Since this appointment was delayed in Berlin, Grohé appointed Jungclaus Commissioner General of Security within the *Reichskommissariat*.[168] His designation as Higher SS and Police Leader finally arrived on August 1.[169]

General Grase's appointment as Military Commander (*Wehrmachtsbefehlshaber*) was of short duration. He was dismissed early in August 1944 after Grohé reported to Hitler that Grase had refused to add his signature to Grohé's telegram congratulating Hitler on his survival of the assassination attempt.[170] On August 11 Jungclaus was appointed *Wehrmachtsbefehlshaber* in Grase's place,[171] a curious move since Jungclaus had no executive or military experience to speak of.

Now Himmler had achieved on paper the objective he had pursued all these years. His man in Brussels had become the Military Commander as well as the independent police executive for Belgium, (except that Jungclaus' political activities remained formally under Grohé's, i.e., Reeder's supervision) while a faithful party stalwart stood at the head of the territorial administration. Unfortunately for Himmler, this turned out to be a very hollow victory indeed (quite apart from the shortness of the time left to the Germans in Belgium) since Jungclaus did not possess the necessary qualifications to command troops in the face of an advancing enemy, or to deal with the crisis situation soon to arise with the approach of German withdrawal.

Moreover, to Himmler's disappointment, Grohé did not embark on any startling new policies during the few short weeks of his regime. SS General Berger was probably correct when he claimed Grohé appeared to have come under Reeder's influence.[172] We know that in a conversation with Lammers on August 4, Grohé echoed Reeder's long-standing view that neither Degrelle nor Van de Wiele had sufficient backing in Belgium for the Germans to bank on their support. Lammers quoted Grohé as saying that "the political basis for a German regime in Belgium and northern France was as limited as could be (*denkbar schmal*)." Grohé expressed his suspicion that Degrelle would seek to establish a separate Belgian client state in the end. He was also convinced that the VNV remained committed to the concept of a Greater Netherlands.[173] All these factors led him to counsel caution in the push for political transformation, just as Reeder had over these past four years.

Due to this perhaps unexpected moderation of the new High Commissioner and to the retention of the staff of the old Military Administration, the policies of the new civilian administration in general did not differ significantly from those of its predecessor. Only in the struggle against the Resistance, there may have been some toughening in part because of the more independent operation of a police now definitely removed from von Falkenhausen's and Reeder's restraining influence. However, it could be argued that the dramatic increase in the number of arrests, executions and removals to concentration camps during August was primarily the result of the advance of the Allied armies.[174]

The Germans and the Belgian Administration

From the outset the Germans pursued a clearly formulated policy with regard to the Belgian administration. They intended to use the existing Belgian government services to run the country under the supervision of a relatively small German supervisory administration (*Aufsichtsverwaltung*). Unlike in neighboring Holland, however, the Germans felt that in view of the "petty legalistic narrow-mindedness of the

Belgians"[175] it was advisable to base the authority of the Secretaries-General on powers accorded to them by existing Belgian law rather than on powers conferred on them by German authorities. By anchoring wartime decrees in Belgian law, the Germans expected to protect the legitimacy of the Secretaries-General and make them and their subordinates more effective tools in carrying out German orders.[176]

This desire to protect legitimacy induced Reeder to do what he could to prevent mass resignations of Secretaries-General in the face of unacceptable German demands. Instead he intended to replace less cooperative officials one by one,[177] and, whenever possible, for "non-political" reasons. This policy meant that replacements would be made by following established procedures which allowed the resigning official to nominate and the Committee of Secretaries-General as a whole to designate his successor. This process was followed formally throughout the occupation, but the Germans usually "strongly suggested" a candidate, particularly during the first two years when most replacements were made. In the instances they cared most about, the replacements in the Departments of Economic Affairs, Justice and of the Interior, they engaged in sometimes protracted negotiations to make sure that their nominee was finally appointed.[178] And throughout the occupation they retained the right to approve or reject nominations made by the Secretaries-General which in practice amounted to a preventive veto.

The German desire to preserve the legitimacy of the Secretaries-General limited their ability to put blatantly pro-German or collaborationist officials into place,[179] especially since as a rule Secretaries-General were drawn from high level civil servants within each department. Reeder, with his civil service background, was reluctant anyway to back individuals who did not have the necessary experience and competence.[180] As a result of these restraints, the Germans imposed only two clearly pro-German collaborationists on the College of Secretaries-General, Victor Leemans in Economic Affairs and Gérard Romsée in Interior.

Within the framework of these limitations Reeder pursued his program of staffing the College of Secretaries-General with individuals reasonably responsive to German demands, and by the end of the occupation only three out of the eleven original Secretaries-General had survived. As part of his policy to avoid political confrontations, he issued instead a decree lowering the retirement age to sixty on the pretext that younger men were needed to meet wartime pressures. Howevever the main purpose of this decree was to get rid of Secretaries-General whom the Germans considered "uncooperative"[181] and its application allowed Reeder to replace five of these top officials.[182] Subsequent replacements occurred both as the result of resignations and dismissals. In one department, Labor and Social Welfare, a whole succession of Secretaries-General had to be appointed and dismissed because none could be found who was acceptable to the Secretaries-General and at the same time sufficiently pliable to cooperate fully with the German labor draft.

Since the Germans viewed the Committee of Secretaries-General a quasi-government and as their main instrument for the imposition of war related measures, they sought to strengthen its authority at the expense of elected and appointed national, regional and local bodies. To that end they suspended the operations of all elected bodies such as the national and regional parliaments. They also introduced the leadership principle, particularly at the local and regional levels, and saw to it that some of the authority formerly held by local and regional officials and bodies was now reserved to the Secretaries-General or to the provincial governors under the control of the Department of the Interior.[183] In addition, they transferred to the Department of the Interior, where they had placed their most reliable collaborator, Gérard Romsée, a number of functions and services that had been located elsewhere.

In defense of their basic policy of governing the country through the Committee of the Secretaries-General, the Germans beat back all attacks on the authority of that body. When the highest court of the country, the *Cour de Cassation*, or *Verbrekingshof*, held in 1942 that the Secretaries-General lacked the power to "legislate", the Germans on their part issued a decree on May 14, 1942 denying Belgian courts the authority to review the legality of decrees issued by the Secretaries-General.[184] This May 14 decree in effect substituted German authority in place of the authority of Belgian law for the actions of the Secretaries-General, something Reeder had been trying to avoid since the beginning of the occupation. This German action threatened to precipitate the biggest political crisis of the occupation, the termination of the activities of the Belgian judiciary analogous to what had happened during the first occupation, but the dispute was eventually settled on a basis of mutual compromise. This settlement gave the Germans their most important goal, an acceptance by Belgian courts and authorities of the decrees passed so far, but it limited the extent to which they could manipulate individual collaborationist Secretaries-General because the compromise set up the requirement that all future "important" decrees would have to be approved by the Committee of Secretaries-General as a whole. This sometimes made it possible for the more traditional officials to restrain their collaborationist colleagues.[185]

This policy of collective responsibility was acceptable to the Germans because they had viewed from the beginning the Committee of the Secretaries-General as a sort of cabinet[186] to serve as a counterweight to the government-in-exile.[187] While this policy offered the Germans certain advantages, it also placed some restraints on their freedom of action because it created, particularly after the initial effect of German victory had worn off, a forum of resistance to the more extreme acts of economic exploitation and political persecution.

The reliance placed on the Belgian administration and on its heads, the Secretaries-General, was entirely pragmatic. It was somewhat ironical in view of the fact that Reeder and his associates initially had a very low opinion of the Belgian civil service claiming that it represented an "unimaginably low standard."[188]

From the German point of view, the collaboration of the Secretaries-General was relatively satisfactory in the early years of the occupation when there was a considerable area of agreement with regard to the reconstruction of the country, the elimination of unemployment and the need to increase agricultural output. The Germans saw that spirit of collaboration weaken as their own demands on the Belgian economy and manpower grew harsher while at the same time the likelihood of German victory diminished. By 1943 the Germans became increasingly aware of the fact that some of the mounting opposition and inefficiency of the Belgian administration was due to political resistance and to fear of retribution in the event of Allied victory.[189]

In May 1942 another grave conflict developed between the Germans and Belgian officials over a variety of issues having to do with the economic exploitation of the country. This was the one time General von Falkenhausen himself was brought into the picture in a confrontation with three Secretaries-General (Plisnier in Finances, De Winter in Agriculture, and Claeys in Labor and Social Affairs) whom the General berated for specific instances of obstruction raising the question whether the present regime remained viable.[190] Von Falkenhausen's and Reeder's outbursts were in large part the result of pressures to which they were subjected by Berlin[191] but there is no indication that they ever seriously considered dismissing the Secretaries-General in favor of a more pliable government of outright collaborators. The issues at hand, such as the problems of the food supply, the labor draft, and how to cope with increasing Resistance activities continued to be negotiated with the Secretaries-General on a pragmatic basis for the duration of the occupation. Except in the Department of Labor and Social Affairs, no further substitutions took place in 1943 and 1944.

The question remains: how well did the system work for the Germans? The answer must be affirmative on the whole, given the overall record of the German administration in the exploitation of the country which will be discussed in Chapter Five. It enabled the Germans to govern with a handful of men a territory containing twelve million people. The authority of the Belgian administration on the whole remained relatively effective, at least until 1944, just as Reeder had hoped it would, despite attacks on the Secretaries-General in the underground press and despite a good deal of administrative sabotage at the lower levels, some of which was conducted with the knowledge of the department heads in Brussels. But while the cooperation of the Secretaries-General facilitated the exploitation of the country, it is also true that the German willingness to respect the limits on collaboration set by the Secretaries-General forced them to carry out some of their programs without the assistance of Belgian authorities. This applied to the removal of the Jews to the East, the final steps of the deportation of labor to Germany, and the hunting down of saboteurs and escapees from the labor draft, areas of activity in which the Germans could use indigenous services in the neighboring Netherlands.

While Reeder himself never expressed any doubt about the wisdom of his basic policy, one German official, writing the Final Report after the end of the occupation, raised the question whether the German regime might have been more effective if the Military Administration had appointed collaborators as Secretaries-General.[192] The present writer tends to think not. The use of a group of top administrators drawn from Rex and the Flemish SS would have produced a good deal more popular resistance to economic exploitation early on and could easily have provoked some of the major political confrontations that occurred in Holland and Norway. The basic willingness of the von Falkenhausen-Reeder regime to preserve, in the words of Professor Willequet, the *"ançien régime"* provided the Germans with a maximum opportunity for economic exploitation[193] while imposing on them the limitations that have been discussed in these pages.

Quite apart from the dismissal of most Secretaries-General, the Germans also replaced as many other "uncooperative" government officials as possible with more pliable and reliable elements. In this endeavor the Germans initially used two tools. The first of these was the decree of July 1940 concerning the exercise of public functions (*Verordnung über die Ausübung öffentlicher Tätigkeit*).[194] This decree subjected government officials who had left their posts during the May invasion to a review by a committee constituted of Belgian officials, and made a permanent resumption of their public functions subject to ultimate approval by German authorities.[195]

On the whole, the Germans were dissatisfied with the operation of these Belgian review boards which they considered too lenient. By the spring of 1941 only thirteen percent of the eight hundred mayors[196] and only approximately six hundred officials nationwide had been dismissed.[197] Therefore, the Germans decided to use another excuse for cleansing the Belgian government services by ordering in March 1941 government officials over sixty years of age to retire.

This Decree against the Superannuation of the Public Administration (*Verordnung gegen die Überalterung der öffentlichen Verwaltung*)[198] had been designed initially, as has been mentioned above as a device to dismiss a number of the older Secretaries-General considered uncooperative. It was, however, employed subsequently throughout the public services. Since many government officials were over sixty (according to the Germans half of the mayors and of the second level officials in the ministries)[199] this decree gave the Germans a much wanted scope. By December 1941, 2,500 officials had been replaced on the basis of this decree[200] and in 1943 this figure stood at 2,800.[201] But even these extensive replacements did not provide the occupying power with a genuinely cooperative Belgian administration, partly because suggestions for replacements came in the first instance from regular Belgian officials, but more significantly because the pool of genuinely collaborationist personnel who had any sort of qualification was very limited. In a relatively small number of instances, primarily in the case of vacancies in the position of mayor, did the Germans proceed independently by appointing their own nominees outright.

The Germans had special difficulties finding replacements for mayors in the French-speaking parts of the country, particularly after a series of assassinations of Rexist mayors. Therefore many mayoralty positions in Wallonia remained vacant during the latter part of the occupation and their functions were carried out by some of the aldermen.[202] All in all, the Germans estimated after the end of the occupation that three-quarters of the mayors in Flanders and one-half in the country as a whole were replacements designated under the occupation.[203] Numerically the Germans achieved success in the appointment of eight (out of nine) provincial governors, but while basically satisfied with their cooperation, they still did not find them efficient instruments in their attempt to centralize provincial and municipal services.[204]

Because it turned out to be so difficult to penetrate Belgian public service on a broad front, the Germans had to make the best possible use of the few thoroughly pro-German officials prepared to collaborate with the Germans without reservations. As has been mentioned before, their most useful collaborator, in their own eyes, was Gérard Romsée whom they placed in the Ministry of the Interior. Romsée was so useful to the Germans that Reeder commented in 1941: "It was possible to make the [Department of the Interior] headed by Romsée into the real instrument of the war economy."[205] They placed as many services as possible under his control, particularly police and gendarmerie and other agencies responsible for the enforcement of wartime regulations such as rationing and Black market control. In their effort to place reliable men in communal governments they gave Romsée the authority to appoint mayors and aldermen.[206]

In their search for cooperative and loyal personnel the Germans naturally tended to look toward members of what they called "movements of renewal" (*Erneuerungsbewegungen*), a relatively neutral term coined to bring under one hat members of the VNV, Rex and Devlag, and the Flemish SS. Despite his basic suspicion of Degrelle, Reeder noted with appreciation the relatively high number of Rexists (about four hundred in all), given the small membership of the movement, who had become available for administrative positions. Writing in 1943, he expressed his admiration for the fact that these Rexists did not lose courage "despite the hopeless position of the movement in the country as a whole."[207]

But even during the heyday of collaboration in the first years of the occupation, Reeder made it clear to his superiors that by placing members of these movements into administrative positions he was far from turning the government over to the VNV or to Rex.[208] To Reeder, the men of the VNV and of Rex were primarily instruments he used to administer and to exploit the occupied country more effectively. He well knew that in the event of German victory these men too would be eventually disappointed in their hopes of governing their own country with any degree of independence from Germany.

The introduction of the *Führerprinzip* and the centralization of the administration mentioned above were completed in 1941. The suspension of the Belgian Parliament and of the provincial and municipal councils left the entire machinery of public services at the provincial and communal level (theoretically) under the control of the Secretary-General of the Interior, Romsée, and of the provincial governors who were dependent on him. In practice, particularly in the smaller communities where the old mayors continued in office, the municipal councils often continued to function much as they had before.

In order to overcome the resistance of traditional government ministries, the Germans at the beginning of the occupation, took to the establishment of special commissariats on the model widely practiced in the Reich. Such new commissariats included the Commissariats for Reconstruction, Wages and Prices, for Provincial and Communal Finances, and in 1944, for Refugees (to look after evacuees from coastal areas).[209] In order to bring Belgian agriculture up to the needed level of wartime performance the Germans initiated a special Corporation for Agriculture which will be discussed in greater detail in Chapter Five.

Perhaps the most controversial of all German sponsored administrative changes was the consolidation of the big city administrations. This was an issue which actually did not involve any compelling German interests even though Reeder claimed at the time that this centralization was in the interest of wartime management.[210] The large cities of Belgium had never been unified administratively, but instead had varying systems of borough government. These "*grandes agglomérations*" included Brussels, Antwerp, Ghent, Bruges, Liège and Namur. The pluralism inherent in these arrangements reflected historical tradition and the spirit of liberal government typical of prewar times. Some efforts to consolidate the government of large cities had been made before the war but had failed in the face of political opposition. In the German view these traditional administrative arrangements presented an obstacle to effective government.

The plan to streamline city government appealed to the Germans because it conformed to their notions of a centralized authoritarian administration, and because it reflected notions about city government that had been prevalent in Germany even before the Nazi period. It was viewed as simplifying the task of police work and fire protection and as providing opportunities for the dismissal of uncooperative officials in the constituent communities and the appointment of "reliable" men to positions in the new centralized agencies. For all these reasons the Germans decided to proceed with the consolidation of the largest municipalities. Beginning with the city of Antwerp, the administrations of Ghent, Brussels, Liège and Namur were unified. These consolidations met with much opposition among government officials and judicial authorities because they were viewed as being politically motivated and as being unconstitutional "unnecessary" tampering with Belgian institutions. This conflict came to a head in December 1942 when the *Cour de Cassation* declared the consolidation of Antwerp to have been unconstitutional.[211] Despite this decision, the big cities remained under unified governments for the duration of the occupation, but after the war returned to their previous administrative status.

In summary it appears that the Germans left Belgian public services substantially intact in their attempt to utilize them in the administration and exploitation of the country. They tried to increase this utility by planting as many pro-German officials in the government services as they could find, and by making the modifications that have been described in this section. It should be noted that most of the new organizations the Germans created were to perform economic rather than political functions, in distinction to policies pursued in the Netherlands. All in all, it can be said that the Germans were reasonably effective, particularly in the early years, but that they never succeeded in making the Belgian government services a totally compliant and a willing tool in their own hands. In their reliance on traditional government services and structures they found that they had to accept the limitations of the arrangements which grew more apparent as the expectation of German victory on the battlefield faded over time.

The Germans and the Administration of Law

In line with their basic decision to rely as much as possible on Belgian institutions in the governance of the country, the Germans left to the Belgian judicial system the responsibility for administering Belgian law, including the enforcement of wartime regulations issued by the Secretaries-General.[212] However, the Germans also instituted a system of military courts based on German law which handled infractions by Belgians of decrees passed by the occupying power and dealt with legal proceedings against German nationals.

From the beginning the Germans held ambivalent views of the Belgian judiciary. They (correctly) considered it anti-German and frequently hailed judges before military courts for anti-German activities and comments.[213] They complained that Belgian courts worked too slowly and imposed punishments that were too lenient, especially with regard to violations of wartime regulations.[214]

In order to make the Belgian judiciary more pliable, the German administration dismissed many of the judges over sixty years of age on the basis of its 1941 decree. It also sought to influence the selection of new judges and public prosecutors by urging the Department of Justice to appoint more Flemish and otherwise "reliable" lawyers to existing vacancies.[215] In 1940 the Germans reserved to themselves the right of approval of high judicial appointments. In 1944 they extended this provision to all judicial appointments.[216]

From the German point of view the most serious deficiency of the Belgian judiciary was its failure to deal promptly and vigorously with infringements of economic regulations, particularly in the areas of rationing, black market operations, and of wage and price controls. In an attempt to overcome these shortcomings the Germans persuaded the Secretaries-General to authorize the establishment of an administrative judicial system for economic offenses (*Ordnungsstrafverfahren*).[217] Under these regulations Belgian officials were entitled to levy fines up to a maximum amount, to confiscate property and to restrict or prohibit the exercise of a profession or business.[218] Mayors and other local authorities were delegated this power as courts of the first instance, with provincial governors acting as a court of appeal.[219] The Secretaries-General implemented this legislation despite its doubtful constitutionality[220] out of their desire to enforce economic regulations to protect the population. In view of the tightening economic situation, these administrative courts were very busy. According to German sources, 226,057 cases were referred to them in 1942[221] and 247,500 in 1943.[222]

On the political level the relationship between the German authorities and the Belgian courts remained one of watchful tension. Despite occasional crises the Germans succeeded in their primary objective of keeping the Belgian judiciary at work. They managed to contain the major conflicts that occurred without having to back down on any of their programs while making a number of formal concessions to the Belgian sense of constitutional legality.

The German military court system was meant to supplement the Belgian judiciary in recognition of the fact that the Belgian courts would not enforce decrees and regulations passed by the occupying power unless transformed into Belgian regulations by the Secretaries-General. In particular, offenses against the occupying power ranging from derogatory remarks about the Germans and their confederates to acts of sabotage or assistance to Allied aviators and Jews would be brought before the military courts.[223]

For most of the occupation, the German military court system consisted of eleven courts with three branch offices. Each court had three members with a commissioned officer presiding.[224] Defendants were allowed to engage Belgian defense lawyers who were given considerable freedom in pleading their case.[225] One of the Belgian lawyers admitted to plead before German military courts came to the conclusion that the German courts did not view the defense lawyers as purely private individuals but as representatives of the

Belgian Bar.[226] The same lawyer expressed the opinion after the war that the German courts on the whole tried to be legally correct and that the judges often were not in sympathy with the Nazi regime.[227] However they obviously had to defend the interests of the army and of the occupying power and therefore often dealt severely with anti-German actions. They also had to be wary of not being too lenient since the German police could always keep the prisoners and whisk them off to a concentration camp. Toward the end of the occupation, an increasing number of resistance workers never came before a military court because the police deported prisoners before their cases came to trial. Some of these were tried in Germany while others were simply sent to a concentration camp.

General von Falkenhausen had the final authority of review of sentences pronounced by the military courts[228] except that the OKW had reserved the right to commute death sentences. He generally tried to moderate sentences although he admitted after the war that he had occasionally increased their severity.[229]

In view of the ever growing number of prisoners, the Germans requisitioned two Belgian prisons, St. Gilles in Brussels and the Fortress of Huy in the eastern part of the country.[230] In addition they established a concentration camp at Breendonck, a former Belgian army base, halfway between Antwerp and Brussels. Yet there existed throughout the occupation a shortage of prison space both within the German and the Belgian prison systems. The number of inmates in the latter tripled during the occupation.[231]

In summary, it can be said that criminal justice was administered in a more orderly and restrained manner in Belgium than in the neighboring Netherlands. Von Falkenhausen and Reeder were primarily concerned with pragmatic arrangements that would provide the maximum law enforcement possible under the circumstances. In this endeavor, they at one point went as far as to turn over to Belgian courts individuals caught with firearms or accused of harming or killing Belgium collaborators, provided no German personnel or direct German interests had been harmed. Von Falkenhausen promised in December 1943 that such individuals, if sentenced by Belgian courts, would not be turned over to the German police, but could serve their sentences in Belgian prisons.[232] By agreeing to this measure, he hoped to persuade the Belgian police and prosecutors to take a more active role in the investigation and persecution of criminals in the categories concerned. To Reeder's and von Falkenhausen's distress, Hitler overturned this arrangement in 1944.[233]

In the field of law enforcement as elsewhere the Military Administration tried to use Belgian agencies and services as much as possible. Therefore, it left to the Belgian police the task of enforcing Belgian laws and decrees including those passed by the Secretaries-General at German request. However, in contrast to the situation in neighboring Holland, the Germans did not expect the Belgian police to enforce German regulations which were not covered by decrees issued under Belgian law. For the enforcement of such decrees the Military Command relied primarily on its own police forces.[234]

From the start of the occupation the Military Commander had two military police organizations at his disposal. The Secret Field Police (*Geheime Feldpolizei* or GFP) included among its original assigments the control of espionage, sabotage, treason, enemy propaganda, censorship and "the general supervision of the population."[235] The Field Gendarmerie (*Feldgendarmerie*) was the executive or enforcement branch of the Secret Field Police. It dealt in the first instance with German military personnel, but it also supervised and supported the Belgian police in its work, and later on in the occupation conducted raids and searches in an attempt to ferret out people who had gone underground or refused to go to work in Germany.[236] Its size was small (only about two hundred men in early 1941) and it was further weakened when some of these were transferred to the East in anticipation of the invasion of the Soviet Union. The methods of the GFP and of the Field Gendarmerie in dealing with suspected opponents of the regime were not necessarily any gentler than those of Himmler's police, and beatings and torture were well within their repertoire.[237]

Although it had been the original intention of the military authorities to exclude Himmler's SS and police from the administration of the occupied territories in the West, Reeder soon discovered that the military police was unable to deal adequately with the tasks at hand. Moreover the GFP was under the command of the *Kommandostab* and therefore not under his immediate control. Therefore he asked for (or accepted at Heydrich's urging) a contingent of the Security Police (*Sicherheitspolizei* or SIPO) whose agents arrived in GFP uniforms toward the beginning of July 1940. This contingent soon expanded into a fullfledged office of the *Sicherheitspolizei* and SD (*Sicherheitsdienst* or Security Service, the political investigative branch of the SS and police) installed by Heydrich on July 27, 1940 with the approval of the OKH and of the Military Commander.[238] After an initial period of subordination to the Paris office of the SIPO, the Brussels office after December 1941 reported directly to its Berlin superiors in the Reich Main Security Office.[239]

The Reich Main Security Office (*Reichssicherheitshauptamt* or RSHA) had been established by Himmler in 1939 to amalgamate the German police with the SS. Here indeed the fusion of party and state reached its most far-reaching implementation. Officials in the RSHA usually held a rank in the SS as well as in government service. However, internally a distinction remained between more "moderate" career police officials and the more "radical" and ideologically motivated members of the SS proper. The main police functionaries in Brussels were all career police officials, whereas Jungclaus who eventually became Higher SS and Police Leader in August 1944 had advanced through SS channels.

The internal organization of the Brussels office of the German police closely followed that of the parent RSHA. Section III dealt with ethnic affairs, and with culture and economic matters. The two sections most directly concerned with police work proper were sections IV "Enemies and Counter- Espionage" headed by Kriminaldirektor Franz Straub, and Section V "Criminal Police." Responsibilities of Section IV included Communists and Jews, and Resistance and sabotage. Most of the police activities described in this study emanated from Section IV. Section V dealt primarily with ordinary non-political crimes committed by German civilians, but it was also responsible for the struggle against the black market and infractions of German economic regulations.[240]

During the first few months of its operations in Belgium the German police had only investigative authority. During this period it had to ask the GFP to make arrests and act as its investigative arm. This was changed in February 1941 when, presumably on the basis of an agreement signed by the OKH and Himmler,[241] the SIPO was given full authority to act as a political police. From that point on the GFP was limited to military tasks such in investigations of Allied espionage, sabotage against military installations, as well as the apprehension of Allied aviators, the escape attempts of Belgian patriots seeking service with Allied forces in London, and the control of German military personnel.[242] As Reeder put it, the SIPO and SD had now become the political police of the Military Command and the main political intelligence service of the occupying power.[243]

In the formal organizational chart of the Military Administration the SIPO chief reported directly to Reeder. The ongoing supervision of such business as the control of arrests made by the SIPO was carried out by the *Gruppe Polizei* of the Military Administration.

In the post war trials of German officials, a controversy developed about the degree of responsibility for the actions of the police for which each of the defendants should be held accountable.[244] Certain facts are clear: Reeder asked for the assistance of Himmler's police and von Falkenhausen acquiesced in the situation. Reeder tried to keep the SIPO under his control, but he knew from experience that Himmler and Heydrich would try to operate as independently as they could. They made a concession to Reeder in that they sent relatively "moderate" and professional officers to Belgium[245] while at the same time trying to remove their Brussels office from Reeder's supervision, and from the restraints placed on the SIPO in such matters as making arrests and keeping suspects in custody. Over the years, the authority of the Military Administration over the police weakened,[246] but it continued to exist formally, and to some extent in practice, until July 1944. Because of this continuing restraint, police rule in Belgium never went to the extremes that it attained in neighboring Holland, let alone in Eastern Europe. Himmler and his subordinates in Berlin even worried that their representatives in Brussels were coopted by Reeder and von Falkenhausen.[247] But by the same token, the Military Command from von Falkenhausen on down remained to a large extent responsible for the actions of a police organization which it had chosen (or been willing to accept) as its executive organ in 1940.

Conditions at the Breendonck concentration camp became a source of friction between the Military Command and the SIPO in 1941. Acting on Belgian complaints over the mistreatment of prisoners, Reeder twice visited the camp which was operated by the SIPO. As a result of his visits food rations were increased at least temporarily and the system of prisoner foremen (KAPOs) was abolished. However, Reeder's request for the replacement of the camp commander was turned down.[248] Unfortunately, conditions at Breendonck reverted to their previous deplorable state after a while.[249]

Another instance of conflict between the Military Administration and Himmler arose over the counter-terror, the assassination of Belgian patriots authorized by Himmler. Reeder opposed this policy, but he had to give in because by 1944 Himmler's power had grown to the point that Reeder was unable to prevail on this kind of issue.[250]

Whereas the Military Administration sought to restrain the German police, its problem with the Belgian police was the opposite. The Belgian police proved reluctant to take measures against persons violating wartime regulations such as rationing and price controls which were being perceived as being imposed by the Germans and serving German interests. Except during the first year[251] the Germans found the work of the Belgian police unsatisfactory.[252] Despite a number of attempted reforms, the Belgian police remained an inefficient instrument in the enforcement of occupation policies. Worse, Belgian police officers became increasingly involved in anti-German activities, and throughout the occupation, they frequently were arrested for anti-German remarks and actions.

The decentralized structure of Belgian police forces formed one obstacle to thoroughgoing reform. In fact, there were three distinct Belgian police forces: (1) the municipal police forces attached to the local authorities, (2) the criminal police (*police judiciaire*) attached to the public prosecutor's office (*procureur du roi*) within the judicial system, and (3) the national gendarmerie (*gendarmerie nationale*) primarily under the control of the Department of Justice. The Germans were unwilling to take the political risks of a radical centralization of police forces in Belgium such as took place in neighboring Holland. Therefore their reforms remained limited and piecemeal.

The largest and most unwieldy force was the municipal and rural police (*police communale* and *gardes champêtres*). In an attempt to make these local police forces more responsive to the enforcement of wartime regulations, the Germans established police training schools and special courses[253] in order to wean Belgian officials away from their "legalistic" approach to police work. But despite all these efforts it became increasingly clear that the bulk of local police forces remained unreliable and anti-German in spirit.

The Military Administration was similarly unsuccessful in its attempts to subvert the criminal police. The latter remained under the control of the Department of Justice whose head was less pliable than Romsée at Interior. By 1943 the Germans had to admit that the criminal police was useless in the suppression of the increasing amount of violence and economic transgressions.[254]

In view of these failures, the Germans concentrated their reform efforts on the one genuinely national police force they found in place, the National Gendarmerie. Before the war the National Gendarmerie had been trained and equipped along military lines by the army and stationed in barracks across the country. The Ministries of Justice and of the Interior had the authority to use the gendarmerie as an enforcement agency.[255]

In order to plant pro-German elements in the gendarmerie, the Germans in 1940 decided to increase its numbers and to dismiss unreliable officers. They improved the pay scale and maintained tight control over new appointments, particularly at the officers' level. In 1941 they replaced the old commander with a pro-German officer, a Colonel van Coppenolle. Above all, they placed the National Gendarmerie under the exclusive authority of the Department of the Interior thereby giving Romsée a free hand to appoint collaborationists.[256] A number of pro-German Flemish army officers released from P.O.W. camps for that purpose were appointed to officers' positions within the gendarmerie.[257] But even with all these efforts the Germans succeeded only to a moderate extent in their endeavor to bend the gendarmerie to their purposes. Therefore, they continued to view this organization with a high degree of ambivalence.

During the few months when the Germans promised that Belgian offenders would not he hauled before German courts the gendarmerie became temporarily more effective[258] but after the repudiation of that agreement by the Germans, the gendarmerie reportedly no longer engaged in actions against the Resistance,[259] and desertions increased significantly.[260] In the summer of 1944 the Germans concentrated the gendarmerie in a few barracks which was viewed by Belgian officials as a first step toward deportation to Germany.[261] This suspicion in turn produced more desertions and in the end, as the Allies overran France, the Germans disarmed the gendarmerie[262] thus giving final expression of their lack of trust in their supposedly most reliable police force. But at the same time it must be mentioned that, while the Germans viewed the Corps with a good deal of ambivalence, Belgian patriots and particularly the Resistance and the underground press considered the Corps and its Commander Colonel van Coppenolle German stooges.

The relative unreliability of the various Belgian police forces, and the extreme shortage of German manpower induced the Germans to recruit Belgian personnel for more than a dozen auxiliary and special purpose law enforcement and guard formations. These new formations were used primarily for law enforcement activities that had no precedent in peacetime, such as the protection of German installations, the enforcement of wartime economic regulations and the protection of agricultural crops. Auxiliary police forces created by the Germans included the Auxiliary Field Gendarmerie (*Hilfsgendarmerie*) formed to assist the German Field Gendarmerie[263] and the Supplemental Communal Police Force (*Kommunale Ergänzungspolizei, Police Auxiliaire* or *Hulppolitie*) created to assist local authorities in the event of internal disturbances or invasion.[264]

These auxiliary police forces remained small, but much larger organizations were created to guard and protect economic assets such as crops, factories and railroads, and to enforce economic regulations. The largest of the guard troops was the Rural Guard (*Garde Rurale* or *Boerenwacht*) formed by the National Corporation for Agriculture (CNAA) It was reported to have 117,000 members by the end of 1942. Its task was to protect crops and farms, including those owned by collaborators.[265]

Other guard troops included the Flemish and Walloon guards with a few thousand men each. In addition the Germans also organized factory guards, and auxiliary guards and fire fighting services for the Air Force. The Organization Todt, the German military construction organization, likewise recruited guard troops for its own installations from among the Belgian population. Most remarkable of all, in a sense, was the recruitment of a Flemish guard unit wearing German police uniforms for the purpose of guarding and servicing the Brussels headquarters of the German SIPO and SD.[266]

Finally, two economic enforcement services should be mentioned in this category of auxiliary groups. The first of these was the corps of rationing controllers (*controleurs de ravitaillement*) which had enlisted about six thousand men by March 1941 for the purpose of catching violators of rationing regulations. Supervision of the corps was located in the Ministry of the Interior. By contrast a German service established to catch up with violators of the labor draft, the Civilian Investigative Service or *Zivilfahndungsdienst*, counting a few thousand men was placed under the control of the Group

Labor in the Military Administration. All in all, German figures indicated that apart from the Rural Guard, almost nineteen thousand Belgian citizens were serving in these various auxiliary formations by June 1943.[267]

Early during the occupation the Germans filled the ranks of these auxiliary formations as far as possible with ideologically motivated collaborators. However as the war progressed and manpower became increasingly scarce German authorities were forced to recruit other Belgians who were willing to serve not for ideological reasons but for the pay and benefits offered and as a protection against being dispatched to Germany as slave labor. Eventually the earlier reliance on ideologically motivated collaborators became an obstacle to the effectiveness of these formations which were torn apart by political dissension. Moreover these organizations also became increasingly hated and despised as traitors and collaborators. Therefore the Military Administration decided in late 1943 to deemphasize the ideological character of these organizations and to transform them into quasi-military units wearing German army uniforms marked by special insignia.[268]

The description of the structure of the German administration in Belgium in this chapter reveals a certain paradox. At the top and on paper, the German administration was organized with hierarchic efficiency reflecting a basically military model, while at the middle and lower levels, particularly in the economic realm and in the area of security a variety of competing and overlapping structures were created reflecting differing ideological concepts of administering the occupied territory. In addition, wartime shortages and realities created by economic exploitation encouraged the creation of a hodgepodge of specialized agencies designed to cope with specific concrete problems. This paradox of strict formal organization at the top and a host of competing agencies at the operational level was reflected in the conception and execution of the German policies described in the next chapter.

Chapter Four

German Political Activities

General Policies

The political activities of the military authorities in occupied Belgium were less far-reaching than those of the occupation regimes in the Netherlands and in Norway because the political objectives of the military regime in Belgium were more limited. The main priorities, security and economic exploitation, were basically nonpolitical. As articulated by Reeder in 1941: "[The Military Administration]... has in the first place a present task to serve the war economy and not primarily the task to fulfill a Flemish mission."[1] Therefore, the German military authorities deliberately avoided political pronouncements or actions which might fan the spirit of patriotic or ideological opposition. Time and again they warned other German agencies such as the SS against agitation about future political or territorial arrangements which would activate the latent resistance to the German regime. All such issues, it argued, would fall into place naturally after a German victory.[2]

Over time the Military Administration developed a remarkable degree of sensitivity to popular moods and attitudes. It realized that the Secretaries-General would not easily be induced to make major structural changes which would not be justified as meeting wartime exigencies. It also decided to use great caution and discretion in dealing with the powerful Catholic church.[3] In this attempt to avoid arousing unnecessarily the patriotic and anti-German sentiments of the population the Military Command tried to overlook certain anti-German activities which occurred during the early years of the occupation. It reminded military and civilian officers in the Command Area not to take minor provocations too seriously. In one communication von Falkenhausen branded the tendency to overreact to minor incidents as "a sign of inner insecurity not worthy of a German." He urged his subordinates to investigate each incident carefully and not to jump to conclusions, and he particularly warned against reporting accidents as acts of sabotage.[4]

In defense of this "policy of the velvet glove" (*Politik der weichen Hand*) the Military Command repeatedly invoked the unfortunate memories of the previous German occupation which had left in its wake a heavy burden of hatred.[5] It also drew attention to the experiences of the Rhineland occupation when the harsh policies of the French and Belgians had awakened violent opposition whereas the greater casualness of British and American policies had left much better memories.[6] It reminded its superiors and other agencies of the need to take into account the particular mentality of the Belgian people which required suppleness and sophistication if major confrontations such as the judicial strike of 1917 were to be avoided.[7] As Reeder put it in April 1941: "The Military Administration has tried... not to provoke the heroism of the masses [*den Heroismus der Masse nicht zu reizen.*"][8]

There is no question that the German authorities in Belgium also acquired a proprietary and protective feeling for the Belgian population. After the war Reeder had this to say about General von Falkenhausen: " ... even though it was his duty to defend the interests of the Reich he felt himself to be (*se sentait intérieurement*) very strongly the protector of Belgium."[9] When attacked as "being more Belgian than the Belgians", von Falkenhausen replied that he was acting in the German interest because it was important to maintain a spirit of friendship with the Belgian people whose destiny would be tied to that of Germany regardless of the particular shape the postwar world would take. Reeder frequently pointed out in his reports to Berlin the underlying contradiction in German occupation policies, in Belgium as elsewhere, between the appeal to support Germany in her effort to organize the Continent, and the harsh exploitation of the country.

Given its basic determination to avoid raising potentially divisive political issues the Military Administration tried to silence discussion about a division of Belgium along linguistic lines or about annexation to the Reich.[10] The military had accepted the fact that the great majority of Belgians, regardless of the complaints they might have on account of the language question, were loyal to the Belgian state and to the monarchy.[11] Therefore it would be counterproductive to antagonize this majority unnecessarily through the discussion of hypothetical issues. Moreover, from a practical point of view, delay of such considerations would keep all options open, in conformance with Hitler's expressed wish.

But while keeping the state intact and under its control, and while suppressing consideration of the future as much as practicable, the German administration intended to take full advantage of Flemish-Walloon antagonisms.[12] By favoring the Flemish cause the Germans sought to secure the support of the Flemish nationalists and use them for their own purposes. At the same time they invited the collaboration of pro-German Walloons by permitting Rex and its leader Léon Degrelle to hope that they might play a major role in the future. Both collaborationist groups were told that they would have to "earn their passage" into the Greater Germanic Reich.[13] Thus the German administration tried to use the underlying nationalistic tensions without making any specific promises for the future and without giving actual power to any of these movements or to their leaders.

Policy Toward King Leopold

The same dilatory tactics charactized German treatment of King Leopold. It took Hitler a few weeks to articulate a policy toward the king. By July 20, 1940 instructions had been issued which remained the basis of German policy toward the king for the next four years:

(1) The king was to be treated with courtesy, but care should be taken that he would not engage in political activities. His personal contacts were to be limited to private

matters (in effect this limitation was not observed) and were to be supervised carefully.[14]

(2) Questions about the eventual disposition of Belgium and about the position of the Royal House were to be treated evasively with reference to Hitler's authority to make the ultimate decision.[15]

In June 1940 German attitudes toward the king from Hitler on down were favorable. The Germans praised Leopold for arranging the armistice and for remaining with his soldiers against the advice of his government.[16] During this period Hitler hoped to use the king to develop a climate of collaboration in Belgium.

Therefore the possibility of a personal interview with Hitler was raised early. The first initiative may well have come from the German side. SS General Karl Gebhardt, a physician in Himmler's confidence who had treated members of the royal family, and Otto Meissner, Chief of Hitler's Presidential Chancellery, discussed such a meeting in early June on the occasion of a visit to Brussels.[17] Leopold, while eager to explore what concessions he might secure from Hitler, was wary of the consequences of publicity and asked that the meeting be kept secret. Hitler was unwilling to agree to that limitation[18] and after the French armistice his own interest in an interview with Leopold decreased.

Finally a meeting was arranged in November 1940 through the initiative of Leopold's sister, the Crown Princess of Italy. It was held in Berchtesgaden on November 19, 1940. On that occasion Leopold raised three questions: 1. Would Hitler guarantee the continued independence of Belgium? 2. Could Germany do more to assure an adequate food supply? 3. Would Hitler be willing to release the remaining, predominantly Walloon, prisoners of war? To these three questions Leopold received an evasive, that is basically negative, reply.[19]

It appears that as a result of this interview Hitler gave up any hope of using Leopold for his own purposes. Reportedly he said immediately after the interview "that he did not think much of this king either and that he would have to do away with him as with the other remaining European monarchs."[20] By the year 1943, he expressed irritation over the fact that the king had remained in the country in 1940 because his presence constituted an obstacle to the reorganization of the Belgian territories.[21]

But while Hitler displayed basically negative sentiments about Leopold after November 1940, local German representatives such as von Falkenhausen and Werner Kiewitz, the German liaison officer stationed with the king, were and remained most supportive of Leopold and his wishes. Von Falkenhausen, old monarchist that he was, greatly admired the king as a man and a soldier and treated him with exquisite courtesy to the extent of sending flowers on the occasion of the king's remarriage and of the arrival of the first child.[22] Kiewitz supported in writing and in a personal visit to Hitler several requests made by Leopold in 1940 and 1941. They both defended the king's motives and actions in their reports to Berlin. Their devotion to Leopold became so obvious that they were subject to criticism on that count in Berlin.[23]

As the war went on, German authorities became increasingly concerned over Leopold's security. As early as 1941 rumors circulated that Belgian patriots were making plans to abduct the king and take him to England.[24] In 1943 Himmler issued special orders that measures should be taken to guard against Leopold's escape.[25]

Finally on the day of the Normandy invasion Kiewitz was ordered to inform the king that he would have to leave for Germany the following morning. Von Falkenhausen, summoned by Leopold, confirmed that these were orders from Berlin that would have to be obeyed. Leopold's wife and children were taken to Germany shortly afterward. For the balance of the war the king and his family were assigned a residence in Germany, to be liberated by the Allies in Austria in May 1945.

Undoubtedly security considerations played the predominant part in the decision to deport the king. The Germans did not wish to risk letting their most prominent prisoner fall into the hands of the Allies, to become the head of a reconstituted Belgian state. But at the same time it is probable that Hitler and his entourage also saw Leopold's removal as the first step toward the institution of a civilian regime and eventual annexation. Therefore, the deportation of the king to Germany was also a political measure designed to free the hands of the Germans to reorganize their administration of the occupied Belgian territory.

Nationality Policies (*Volkstumspolitik*)

The German authorities in Belgium never succeeded in the development of a consistent or even minimally effective nationality policy because too many irreconcilable forces came into play. These included:

(1) The memory of the failure of the German occupation policy during the First World War which had attempted to encourage Flemish separatism in an attempt to bring Flanders under German control.

(2) Hitler's instructions to "favor the Flemish" over the French-speaking population.

(3) The need to secure the cooperation of the largely French-speaking elite in government and business in the economic exploitation of the country, and to retain the collaboration of Rexist and of the francophone rightists of the Brussels press.

(4) The desire of the German SS, to convert Flanders as quickly as possible into a German *Reichsgau* by supporting the radical pro-German National Socialist minority group around Devlag and the Flemish SS.

Because of these conflicting goals, the chief German figures who influenced German policies in Belgium were at variance with each other. General von Falkenhausen favored the French-speaking nobility and traditional elites, and he supported the retention of the Belgian state and monarchy. Reeder, while favorably disposed toward the Flemish soon recognized that he would have to depend on the collaboration of French-speaking as well as Flemish elements. Himmler favored giving immediate political support to those elements among the Flemish people who were open to the racial ideals of the SS and to the future incorporation of Flanders into a Greater Germanic Reich, but he (sometimes) recognized some of the limitations of the Flemish radicals and the need to make political compromises in the interest of the German war effort.[26] SS General Gottlob Berger, Himmler's chief deputy for nationality policy, on the other hand, was totally committed to the concept of turning Flanders into a German *Gau* at the earliest possible moment.

The original OKH instructions that the Military Government should not exacerbate existing ethnic and linguistic tensions[27] were repudiated by Hitler's July 1940 instructions to favor the Flemish population. As a result, the Military Command, which during the first weeks of the occupation had virtually ignored the Flemish Nationalist Movement (VNV)[28] began to lend it some support by the end of the summer. In August, General von Falkenhausen received Auguste Borms, the Grand Old Man of the Flemish movement.[29] Soon thereafter the Military Administration appointed a Restitution Commission (*Wiedergutmachungskommission*) with Borms as its head. This commission was charged with the task to compensate Flemish Activists for losses and deprivations suffered at the hands of the Belgian state in retribution for their pro-German activities during the First World War.[30] The Germans also instructed the Secretaries- General to reactivate the Linguistic Commission which was charged under Belgian law with the responsibility for implementing the language laws of 1932-1935.[31] The Military Administration arranged to have a Flemish nationalist by the name of Florimond Grammens designated as the head of the commission over the objection of the Belgian Secretaries-General, and they saw to it that the commission acquired more far-reaching powers than Belgian legislation had assigned to it.[32]

By the fall of 1940 the Military Administration turned to the VNV as the best available representative of the Flemish people and the Flemish idea. It may be true (at least in part) that

Reeder did so largely for practical reasons as he claimed in 1943 in a letter to Himmler. The VNV was the only existing political organization in Flanders from which the German administration could expect significant political and practical support.[33] Reeder needed such a source of reliable manpower as he began to remove "unreliable" elements from Belgian government services.

In this attempt to strengthen the VNV the Germans subsidized the organization and its publications. They forced minor Flemish organizations to merge with the VNV.[34] In the years to come Reeder would support the VNV in its struggle against the more radical Flemish groups sponsored by the German SS. But while supporting the VNV politically and financially, Reeder throughout the occupation expressed his concern that the VNV should not be too closely identified with the German regime in the popular mind. In his 1943 letter to Himmler, he reaffirmed his belief that the VNV would have a better prospect of recruiting additional adherents if it were viewed as an indigenous political movement.[35]

Himmler and Berger, on the other hand, did not consider the VNV a promising ally. They knew that most of the leaders of the VNV subscribed to the "Greater Netherlands" idea, the notion of uniting all Dutch-speaking people in one state. This notion ran counter to Hitler's intention to annex Flanders (and the Netherlands for that matter) eventually, and to the SS determination to begin immediately with the political transformation of Flanders. Moreover, Himmler and Berger disliked the strongly Catholic orientation of the Flemish leadership which was bound to conflict with the essentially anti-religious neopagan thrust of the SS. In an attempt to change the character of the movement, Berger tried in vain at various times to gain control of the VNV. At the same time, however, he created his own political organizations which would be more pliant instruments in the political transformation of Flanders. To that end, Berger in August 1940 organized the Germanic SS in Flanders, without foreknowledge of the Military Command. This Germanic SS was seen as a branch of the German General SS devoted to the work of political education and to the creation of Flemish support for eventual annexation.

In order to gain an even broader base for political reeducation, Berger in 1941 seized control of the *Deutsch-vlämische Arbeitsgemeinschaft*, (or Devlag) a German- Flemish intercultural association which had been created in the 1930s at the initiative of German circles for the purpose of improving German-Flemish cultural cooperation and exchange. In 1941 Berger designated himself president of the organization. This gave him an opportunity to spread political propaganda further in Flanders, particularly through the Devlag weekly *De Vlag* ("The Flag").

In the following months and years, Berger attempted to build up Devlag into a rival organization to the VNV, along with his continued support of the Flemish SS. The ranks of his movement were weakened after June 1941 by the recruitment for the Flemish Legion, a military volunteer organization organized as a unit of the Waffen-SS, but throughout the occupation it remained in competition with the VNV for the hearts and minds of the Flemish people.

Berger's position was strengthened with the establishment of the Service Jungclaus (*Dienststelle Jungclaus*) in April 1942 as an extension of the *Germanische Leitstelle* which Berger headed in Berlin. This new SS agency sponsored political and cultural activities in Flanders on a larger scale. These activities, aside from recruitment for the Waffen-SS consisted of publishing a string of periodicals, establishing a publishing concern, and organizing a variety of cultural activities including a puppet theatre and other folkloristic enterprises. Berger felt a peculiar emotional commitment to Flanders, probably because two of his brothers had fallen there during the First World War. This may provide an explanation why Berger spent more money on Flanders than on any other occupied territory.

Despite these varied efforts German political accomplishments in Flanders were meager because of the existing policy conflicts and because of the eventual deterioration of Germany's military situation. Neither Reeder nor the SS succeeded in creating substantial support for an incorporation of Flanders into Germany. Instead Flemish nationalistic sentiments were intensified within the VNV in its struggle with Devlag and the Flemish SS,[36] while the latter groups failed to gain a significant number of adherents despite claims to the contrary. Only in one respect was German nationality policy partially successful: it did succeed in recruiting substantial numbers of Flemish people into civilian and military services in support of the German war effort.

German policies towards the French-speaking population were beset by a set of difficulties different from those that troubled the Flemish policies of the occupying power. Hitler's directive not to give any special advantages to the Walloons and especially his decision to keep French-speaking prisoners of war in Germany impeded German efforts to win over the French-speaking population. The small Walloon groups that advocated annexation of the French-speaking part of Belgium to France were suppressed.[37] The German administration tried to discourage the cultural ties that existed between the French-speaking intellectual elite and France.[38] The use of the French language was discouraged in the schools, particularly in Brussels and the linguistic border areas, and French-speaking teachers were at a disadvantage since Flemish-speaking applicants were given preferential appointments.

Apart from the prisoner of war question, however, these "anti-francophone" policies did not cut very wide or deep. For there existed an entire conflicting set of considerations which made a radical anti-francophone policy inopportune. The economic exploitation and the political management of the country required the cooperation of the French-speaking elite which held most of the leading positions in business, in the government services, and in the Brussels press. That elite contained many leaders in business and government who, while devoid of any great sympathies for national socialism, were prepared, at least in the early years to cooperate with the occupation authorities in their endeavor to align Belgium with Germany economically and politically. This elite also included ideological collaborators such as Degrelle and certain rightwing elements in the intellectual and journalistic world of the capital who could be considered actual or potential allies in the attempt to integrate Belgium into the New Europe envisioned by German planners. The German authorities in Brussels had to provide an acceptable basis of cooperation to these non-Flemish elements and therefore could not afford to ally themselves exclusively with the Flemish or to push anti-francophone moves too far.[39]

Léon Degrelle and his Rex organization presented a special problem to the Germans. Although Degrelle became a most enthusiastic supporter of the German cause particularly after the invasion of Russia, Reeder well recognized that Rex commanded only a minute and diminishing amount of support among the Walloons and the francophone population of Brussels. Therefore Reeder could not back Degrelle too emphatically without running the risk of alienating more moderate francophone elements whose assistance the occupying power needed in the management of the country.

In addition, Reeder became increasingly suspicious of Degrelle's personal ambitions and reliability. He recognized that Degrelle above all sought to carve out for himself a position of personal power and to become the leader of whatever political structure Hitler would design eventually. In 1941, Reeder called Degrelle a "Belgicist"[40] which meant a person in favor of the continued existence of a Belgian state. However, despite Reeder's warnings, Himmler made Degrelle his personal protegé, concurring by 1943 with Degrelle's claim (based on Petri's 1937 book) that the Walloons and some of the people of northern France were essentially of Germanic origin even though historical circumstances had forced them to adopt the French language.

While the Military Administration gave limited support to Degrelle, it organized a number of pro-German groups such as the *Communauté Culturelle Wallonne* and a youth group *La Jeunesse Romane*, in order to broaden its base of support in Wallonia. However, these groups, too, failed to attract significant numbers of followers and never acquired a real life of their own. The bulk of the French-speaking population outside of Brussels, apart from the Rexists, remained firmly anti-German, opposed in its basic orientation to fascism and national socialism.

German *Volkstumspolitik* in Belgium was bound to fail because of the conflicting aims and policies of the German agencies concerned and because of the conflicts within each of the nationalist groups themselves. It was bound to fail because the real ultimate German aim, to annex either Flanders or preferably all of Belgium had the support of only the tiniest minority among either the Flemish or the French-speaking segments of the population.

The Germans and the Mass Media

From the beginning of the occupation the Military Administration determined to control Belgian mass media and to use them in the German interest. The Belgian press with its multitude of daily and weekly publications was the most important and most complex object of German attention.

Prewar Belgium had supported a large and variegated press as might be expected from a highly politicized and deeply divided country, with seventy daily publications and 350 weeklies,[41] apart from the sizeable number of newspapers and periodicals imported from France. All Belgian papers had ceased publication as soon as the Germans occupied Belgium.

In order to establish their control over the press, the Germans set up a process of licensing the newspapers and periodicals they would permit to be published during the occupation.[42] In order to simplify control over the press they limited the number of publications and the number of copies that could be published. By the spring of 1941, according to a German report, the daily and periodical press published a total volume of 2.3 million copies or one-fifth of the prewar volume.[43] As the paper shortage grew more severe, the number of publications decreased and their size shrank until by 1943 only fourteen dailies made their appearance,[44] most of which consisted of only four pages. In 1944 the size of the issues, with the exception of the leading collaborationist publications such as *Volk en Staat* and *Le Pays Réel*, was further reduced to two pages.[45] The amount of editorial comment dwindled to next to nothing by the summer of 1944.

The guidance and control of the Belgian press was entrusted to the Propaganda Division or *Propagandaabteilung*, one of the hybrid organisms attached to the Military Administration. Although the *Propagandaabteilung* was formally subordinated to Reeder's Military Administration, in effect it received its instructions from Goebbels' Ministry of Propaganda in Berlin.[46] According to an agreement worked out in January 1941, the application of these instructions to Belgium was subject to the approval of the Military Administration.[47] Some division of labor was worked out: The *Propagandaabteilung* supervised the daily press, whereas the Cultural Section of the Military Administration was responsible for periodicals.[48]

Early on the Germans established a news monopoly through a German-controlled Press Agency, the Belgapress which for all practical purposes became the mouthpiece of the official German News Agency, the DNB (*Deutsches Nachrichtenbüro*). The acquisition of the *Agence Dechenne*, an agency responsible for most of the physical distribution of printed media across the country, gave Germans additional control over the press.[49]

In order to tighten their control over Belgian journalists the Germans tried a number of measures which would enable them to determine who would be allowed to publish. They included journalists among the groups whose right to resume work after June was subject to review.[50] They tried to persuade Romsée in 1941 to establish an Association of Journalists on the German model with compulsory membership for all practicing journalists. When Romsée, for once, at the urging of his colleagues, declined to establish such an organization[51] the Germans at first desisted but eventually in early 1943, on their own initative, established two such associations, one for Flemish and one for French- speaking journalists. Membership in these organizations was not made strictly compulsory.[52]

The complexity of the prewar Belgian press called for a corresponding flexibility in German press policies. The prewar press had been largely dominated by liberal elements which needed to be eliminated. Therefore the Germans at first established a complete system of preventive censorship.[53] They also began to sponsor in May 1940 a daily *La Nation Belge* published by a former Rexist which was such an obvious mouthpiece of the German propaganda machine that it failed to gain enough readers and had to be shut down at the end of September 1940. (It became known popularly as *La Nation Boche*.)[54]

Subsequently, the Germans acquired control over the two largest mass circulation dailies, *Le Soir* and *Het Laatste Nieuws*. In addition they encouraged and probably subsidized a number of collaborationist newspapers, the best known of which were the daily *Le Nouveau Journal* and the weekly *Cassandre*. They also subsidized indirectly the organs of the VNV (*Volk en Staat*) and of Rex (*Le Pays Réel*).

The preventive censorship established at the start was relaxed partially in the first year of the occupation. Close guidance of the Belgian press was achieved through frequent press conferences and through daily instructions issued by the *Propagandaabteilung*.[55] In order to create the impression that these publications enjoyed some independence and in order to attract readers' interest, the Germans granted editorial writers a degree of latitude, although always within well-defined limits. Belgian journalists could give some but not too much expression to disagreements existing within the milieu of the Collaboration, and sometimes they could even criticize German policies. From time to time slips occurred that led to reprimands and to the removal of journalists unwilling to toe the prescribed line. Certain topics such as the future of the Belgian state or the creation of a Greater Netherlands state remained taboo.[56] But while supporting collaborationist papers, Reeder was unwilling to turn them over to VNV, Rex or Devlag since he wanted to keep control safely in German hands.

In addition to their sponsorship of collaborationist publications, the Germans published a daily newspaper of their own, the *Brüsseler Zeitung*. This paper in the first instance addressed itself to the military and civilian German community in Belgium. It became the mouthpiece of the Military

Command, publishing decrees and speeches by leading German personalities, but Reeder also used this house organ to launch the discussion of sensitive topics among the public of the occupied territory. By reprinting or commenting on a speech or an article from the *Brüsseler Zeitung*, a collaborationist periodical could start consideration of a topic in the Belgian press which it could not have easily launched as its own idea without being accused of blatant subservience to the Germans.[57]

The control of the Belgian radio was easier to achieve since it involved replacement of a much smaller number of people than was needed for the press. The Germans proceeded with such replacements in 1940, but apparently only with limited success since as late as 1944 twenty employees of the Brussels radio were arrested for anti-German activities. However, the German authorities also faced the same problem of giving the Belgian radio some degree of credibility so that the stations would not be simply regarded as mouthpieces of the Germans.[58] The poor translation of many programs which betrayed their German origin was no help.[59]

But apart from these shortcomings, the main obstacle to credibility was the fact that the majority of the population listened to the British radio and to other neutral or Allied stations. Listening to such stations in groups had been prohibited since the beginning of the occupation, and listening by individuals was outlawed in December 1941[60] but even increasingly harsh penalties did not deter patriotic Belgians from listening to the B.B.C. and its French and Flemish broadcasts. The physical location of Belgium so close to the British isles made such listening relatively easy even though the Germans tried their best to jam Allied broadcasts.

The Military Administration never took the final step of confiscating the radio sets of the population as had been done in neighboring Holland in 1943, even though confiscation of sets in specific localities was authorized under certain circumstances.[61] The main reason for this decision against mass confiscation was von Falkenhausen's and Reeder's desire to avoid the mass confrontation that such a confiscation would bring about. Moreover they considered confiscation a declaration of moral bankruptcy and claimed that it would deprive the Germans of an important way of influencing the population. The military authorities were too realistic to believe that such an action would effectively cut off the Belgian population from the British radio since many sets would undoubtedly be hidden as was indeed the case in the Netherlands. Under these circumstances the British rather than the Belgian radio continued to inform public opinion.

The Germans used the Belgian press and radio as conveyors of their changing propaganda themes, along with brochures, pamphlets and posters published by the *Propagandaabteilung*. Their directives often included the smallest minutiae such as the proper placement of photographs and articles.

The themes emphasized by German propaganda in Belgium at any one time reflected the changes in the political and military situation. In 1940 German propaganda emphasized the advantages that would accrue to the population from the development of the New Europe which Germany was in the process of creating. A little later the Germans organized a Viktoria-campaign to demonstrate faith in German victory in response to the V-for-Victory signs painted all over Belgium by patriots.

Anti-Semitic propaganda made its appearance during the first year of the occupation in an attempt to prepare the population for the anti-Jewish measures to come.[62] With the invasion of the Soviet Union in June 1941, the theme of anti-Bolshevism became dominant and the population was urged to enlist in the Flemish and Walloon Legions that were being formed.

From the beginning of the occupation German propaganda had encouraged Belgian men and women to volunteer for work in Germany. This propaganda emphasized the practical advantages as well as ideological reasons for accepting such work. With the introduction of compulsory labor in 1942, glorification of work in Germany was emphasized even more in German propaganda. In one poster, labor in Germany and military service were linked: After a tour of labor service in Germany the Belgian workman in the poster decides to enlist in the Legion - and his family is portrayed as receiving great material benefits from these decisions.[63]

As Germany's military position deteriorated in 1943, the defensive theme of the Fortress Europe (*Festung Europa*) came to the fore. Given the strategic location of Belgium as a prospective battleground, German propaganda warned against the danger to health, life and property in the wake of Resistance and military action.[64] The Germans made use in their propaganda of a call of the Archbishop of Malines for a cessation of Allied bombing of Belgium. In this context the *Propagandaabteilung* also produced fake underground publications calling for cessation of "terrorist" activities in the interest of the population.[65]

All in all, German propaganda was more effective in the early years of the occupation when victory seemed certain or probable than later when the course of the war began to contradict German propadanda themes. Propaganda may have increased in the early years the willingness to accept work in Germany or even to enroll in German military or paramilitary formations, but in the long run it failed as it was bound to in the face of approaching German defeat. For most of the occupation, the majority of the population believed the Allied radio, its national programs and the underground press rather than the German-controlled media.

Police and Security Measures

The maintenance of internal security was the first priority of the Military Command. General von Falkenhausen and Reeder were no less determined to maintain law and order than their military superiors or Himmler. They differed from Hitler and Himmler in that they believed that internal tranquillity could best be achieved by a flexible and cautious approach rather than through harshness and ruthlessness. With the experiences of the First World War in mind, they wished to maintain order without antagonizing unnecessarily a largely cooperative population.

Moderation definitely was not apparent in the penalties spelled out for a wide variety of anti-German activities in a torrent of decrees some of which had been drawn up by the army before May 10. Offenses subject to the death penalty included not only sabotage, espionage and unauthorized possession of fire arms,[66] but also attempts to leave the country in order to take service with the Allies, to give assistance to prisoners of war[67] or to Allied personnel,[68] or the possession of radio transmitters.[69] Later during the occupation severe penalties were threatened for Communist activities,[70] forgery of rationing cards[71] and acts of violence against collaborators.[72] German decrees also authorized the arrest and execution of hostages, the imprisonment of families of persons suspected of anti-German activities or charged with failure to comply with German regulations. In May 1943 many of these ordinances were codified in a general "Security Decree of 1943" (*Schutzverordnung von 1943*).[73] However, the penalties listed in these German ordinances were intended primarily as deterrents. In Belgium they were not applied in their full severity, for fear of producing further alienation of the population.

In its reports to Berlin, the Military Command tried to secure support for its policies by stressing the strictness of the regulations passed and by downplaying the seriousness of such incidents as did occur.[74] It pointed out that such incidents were caused by a minuscule minority and that the great majority remained cooperative. The reports emphasized the success of German police investigations in an effort to anticipate demands for indiscriminate mass punishments that would be likely to alienate the population.[75] In order to appease the advocates of toughness in Berlin, they reported in great detail such acts of retribution as were taken. These tactics were relatively successful in the beginning of the occupation as long as acts of resistance occurred indeed on a limited scale. They became increasingly ineffective when the rising tide of resistance could no longer be disregarded and when German policies towards inhabitants of the occupied territories became radicalized under the influence of warfare in Russia.

From the beginning of the occupation, the Military Command took steps to limit and control the free movement of the population. It imposed a curfew from midnight to five o'clock in the morning, with earlier hours in small towns.[76] It tried to control illegal border crossings, and made a special effort after October 1942 to catch escapees from the labor draft. After a patriotic demonstration that occurred on Armistice Day 1940 (November 11) the Military Command took special precautions to anticipate and prevent unauthorized demonstrations on national holidays.[77]

The Communist party and its activities naturally occupied the special attention of the German police. For the duration of the Nazi-Soviet Non-Aggression Pact the situation was characterized by mutual suspicion and increasing supervision by the German police. When Germany invaded the Soviet Union in June 1941, the German police in Belgium rounded up between three hundred and four hundred alleged functionaries of the Belgian Communist party as part of a Europe-wide operation called "Operation Solstice" (*Aktion Sonnenwende*).[78] Despite the German hope that the Communist organization had been destroyed, a clandestine second-line leadership designated prior to June 1941 directed an increasingly active propaganda and sabotage campaign in 1941 and 1942. However, arrests of real and alleged Communists continued, and in the first half of 1943 the German police succeeded in penetrating the Central Committee and Secretariat of the Communist party, and in arresting most of its leaders.[79] This blow seriously weakened Communist party activities for a while, but the Communists rebuilt their organization again in subsequent months and expanded their activities during the last year of the occupation despite their truly terrible casualties.

A study of the reports of the Military Administration, of the Secret Field Police and of Belgian underground and postwar publications reveals that the German police was very effective in penetrating and destroying Resistance organizations, and in apprehending individual patriots engaged in anti-German activities. For the period from March 1, 1943 to February 15, 1944, a total of 4,700 arrests were reported by the Germans,[80] with approximately 1,000 arrests for each of the remaining months of the occupation.[81] Yet, time after time when the Germans claimed to have destroyed underground organizations such as the *Légion Nationale* (originally "legal" but later a forerunner of the *Armée Sécrète*), the Communist party, and the Independence Front, these organizations revived in one form or another. It is probably true that the German police pursued leftwing Resistance groups more vigorously than groups located in the center or on the right of the political spectrum,[82] but the center-right Resistance groups also experienced serious losses and interruptions of their organizations and activities. Resistance activities increased with the approach of liberation despite all the arrests made by the German police, because, as the Germans themselves acknowledged regretfully, a continuously growing reservoir of escapees from the labor draft and other patriots furnished new Resistance workers to replace those caught in the German net.[83]

The impressive success of the German police in Belgium was due to the "professional competence" of its Brussels office supplemented by the brutality of the Nazi regime. The utilization of police informants (V-men or *Vertrauensmänner*) who penetrated Resistance organizations by posing as patriots lay at the heart of German successes. Time and again German documents and underground papers reported the destruction of groups due to their penetration by German agents. Apart from V-men, arrestees often were made to talk either by convincing them that the Germans knew everything about their organizations anyway or by the torture methods officially known as "intensified interrogation" (*Verschärfte Vernehmung*).

During the last three months of the occupation, German police brutality became more pronounced. In line with existing orders, German police now frequently shot on the spot Resistance workers caught in the act and executed increasing numbers of prisoners without formal trial. Most political prisoners were now moved to concentration camps in Germany in anticipation of an Allied advance.

In the postwar trial of General von Falkenhausen the use of hostages as a preventive measure and their execution in retribution for anti-German acts received special attention. The German High Command considered the arrest and execution of hostages permissible under the 1907 Hague Convention on Land Warfare.[84] General von Falkenhausen was opposed to this procedure, but was forced, under orders from Berlin, to arrest hostages as early as 1940. Special regulations were issued for the treatment of these hostages, often prominent citizens drawn from the nobility, from political parties or the judiciary. Most of these hostages remained in detention only for a few months. In order to protect these "genuine" hostages, von Falkenhausen declared all political prisoners in German custody to be hostages in 1941.[85]

Hostage executions began officially in December 1942[86] with the shooting of ten alleged Communists. At his trial General von Falkenhausen testified that these men and all other so-called hostages executed subsequently had engaged in activities that would have made them subject to the death sentence if they had come to trial.[87] It appears to be true that the Germans in Belgium never executed any "genuine hostages" (*Wahlgeiseln*), and that von Falkenhausen carried out these retributory executions with the greatest reluctance under extreme pressure from Keitel and the OKW. This observation should not obscure the fact that such executions were carried out on an increasing scale in 1943 and 1944, nor does the exemption of "genuine hostages" provide moral justification for the execution of others.

It appears that approximately 350 persons were shot as hostages during the occupation while 450 individuals were deported to Germany. Approximately two thousand persons were held as hostages at one time or another during the occupation.[88] Figures from German sources contained in a report of the Belgian War Crimes Commission give the following picture of the total number of executions under the occupation:

Table 1[89]

Number of Hostages Executed

Year	Number
1942	18
1943	98
Jan. 26 - July 10, 1944	124
August 1 - 24, 1944	65
	305
Additional special executions July - August 1944	45
Total number executed	350

Even more reprehensible than the execution of hostages was the "counter-terror" (*Gegenterror*) campaign conducted under the auspices of Jungclaus and of the SD during the closing months of the occupation. This campaign was officially sanctioned by Himmler in June 1944,[90] but it had begun much earlier. The actual killings usually were carried out by members of the security organization of Rex or of Devlag - SS, allegedly in retribution for assassinations of members of their movements. The victims usually were prominent Belgian patriots, members of the judiciary, former high officials or politicians or other citizens known to be opposed to collaboration. They usually were shot at night in their homes or wherever they could be located. The assassins were squads of Rexists or Flemish SS who carried documents provided by the SD certifying them as auxiliary police.

According to a postwar statement made by the President of the Court trying Reeder and von Falkenhausen, the first assassination that could be considered a part of the counter-terror occurred in December 1942, but most of the counter-assassinations took place in 1944 as the number of killings of collaborators increased. The most notorious assassinations were those of Alexandre Galopin, the Governor of the *Société Générale*, in February 1944, and a wave of killings in Charleroi in mid-August 1944 in retribution for the assassination of the Rexist Mayor.[91]

Himmler's directives charged Jungclaus and the SD with exclusive responsibility for the organization of the counter-terror. He considered these murders "politically desirable" and ordered Jungclaus to support them with money and weapons. The SD was to take charge of the criminal investigation whenever possible and to delay any findings. In cases where the Belgian police or organs of the Military Administration conducted their own investigations, formal cooperation was to be rendered, but always with the goal of protecting the assassins. If none of these measures prevailed, the culprits were to be dispatched to Germany beyond the reach of Belgian or territorial German authorities.[92]

Reeder and the Military Administration were opposed to this campaign which Reeder viewed as leading toward "a war of all against all."[93] Reeder believed that the punishment and retribution for assassinations of collaborators should remain in the hands of official authorities. As early as mid-1943 he assured the leaders of the collaborationist movements that German authorities would apply the same punishments to the perpetrators of attacks on Belgian collaborators as to individuals who had committed attacks against German personnel.[94] He insisted that retributions for unresolved killings should be applied by German authorities against individuals in German custody[95] rather than arbitrarily by private persons. In view of Reeder's well-known position Himmler instructed his subordinates to organize the campaign without informing Reeder and that Reeder could be told only with Himmler's personal permission.[96] Nevertheless, it is likely that Reeder knew what was going on, even without being informed explicitely.[97]

The continually increasing number of prisoners made it necessary for German authorities to find additional prison space. The main places of confinement used for political prisoners were the concentration camp Breendonck, St. Gilles in Brussels, and the Fortress Huy in the eastern part of the country. Other prisons were located in Courtrai, Hasselt-Merxplas and in Louvain. Jewish detainees were placed in the transit camp in Malines prior to their deportation to the East. Late in 1943 arrangements were made to place political prisoners in the concentration camp 's Hertogenbosch in the southern Netherlands with the proviso that these prisoners would remain under the control of the Military Command in Brussels.[98]

General von Falkenhausen and Reeder claimed at their trial that they had tried their best to prevent the deportation of prisoners to German concentration camps,[99] but such deportations took place anyway.[100] However, orders from the RSHA in 1944 to move all political prisoners to Germany[101] were not carried out completely in the end.

Among all German places of detention in Belgium, the concentration camp Breendonck acquired special notoriety. It was located in an old Belgian fortress twenty miles from Antwerp. Space was extremely limited and many facilities were located underground. After an initial period of military control the camp came under the administration of the SIPO, and of an especially harsh Commandant by the name of Philipp Schmitt.[102] As a concentration camp, Breendonck served primarily as a place of detention for prisoners accused of anti-German Resistance activities, but in the beginning it also housed a number of Jewish prisoners. In 1940 it contained four hundred inmates, half of whom were Jewish. In 1942 it reached its peak occupancy with 830 inmates.[103]

Complaints about conditions in the camp and about the mistreatment of prisoners began to circulate in the Belgian community during the first year of the occupation. In September 1941 Prince Albert de Ligne, President of the Belgian Red Cross, drew General von Falkenhausen's attention to the problem. As has been mentioned above, an investigation ensued which led to a temporary alleviation of the problem but conditions remained harsh although they seem to have improved somewhat during the last year of the occupation under a new Commandant when the Belgian Red Cross was allowed to send in additional food for the prisoners.[104] Nevertheless Breendonck remained the most notorious and feared of the German places of detention in Belgium. By contrast conditions at Huy and Louvain where most of the genuine hostages were detained remained relatively tolerable.

According to a report by the Belgian War Crimes Commission submitted at the postwar trial of von Falkenhausen and Reeder, 102 prisoners perished at Breendonck during the years of 1941-1944 from a variety of "natural causes," whereas 179 were executed by a firing squad and seventeen met their death by hanging.[105] The majority of the executions took place in 1944.

In general, German police and security measures in Belgium in practice were almost as harsh and ruthless as they were in the other territories in the West. After all the German police everywhere in Europe received many of the same instructions from Berlin. But granting this general proposition, it also remains true that General von Falkenhausen and Reeder managed to restrain this ruthlessness to a marginal and decreasingly effective extent, motivated by their greater sensitivity to the political cost of unrestrained police terror than that shown by Seyss-Inquart in the Netherlands or Terboven in Norway.

The Persecution of the Jews[*]

The persecution of the Jews in Belgium must be viewed within the context of the German campaign against Jews in all European countries under German control or influence. It is now commonly (if not universally) accepted that concrete plans for the Final Solution, the systematic deportation and annihilation of European Jewry, were developed in 1941 in connection with the planning for the attack on the Soviet Union, or in the months following the invasion, and that they were instrumentalized in the Wannsee conference of January 1942. While some anti-Jewish measures were delayed in Belgium for a period due to the political caution of the Military Command, on the whole the time table of persecution

---

[*] Much of the material in this section is based on Maxime Steinberg's path-breaking three volume *L'étoile et le fusil* (1983-1986) which is cited in detail in the Bibliography. The present author wishes to acknowledge in this space his deep obligation to Maxime Steinberg in the composition of the final version of this section.

and deportation did not differ substantially from that applied in other Western countries.

At the beginning of the occupation an attempt was made to deny special designs on the Jews. The original instructions for the military government drawn up by Reeder in 1939-1940 contained the injunction to avoid special measures against the Jews, allegedly "in order to avoid giving the impression that Germany might plan annexation."[106] It is significant however that even then higher authorities, presumably on Hitler's orders, inserted the word "temporarily" (*"vorläufig"*) into the text.[107]

During the early months of the occupation, the military government pursued this line of policy of leaving the Jews alone. In the summer of 1940, General von Falkenhausen went out of his way to assure the Socialist leader Henri De Man that no special measures against the Jews were intended.[108] As has been mentioned above, the Military Administration in its early reports to Berlin emphasized the point that the Jews were few in number and did not present any particular problem in public life.[109] It warned against any unnecessary moves against the Jews that might cause an adverse political reaction. This fear of adverse reactions which might compromise cooperation with the Belgian elites, animated the Military Administration through the occupation, even though by the end of October 1940 it began to implement the persecution of the Jews under orders from Berlin. By and large it succeeded throughout the occupation in its endeavor to avert public and politically troublesome Belgian protests, and to prevent a breakdown of the basic framework of cooperation over the persecution of the Jews.

In their desire to avoid political complications, von Falkenhausen and Reeder found themselves in conflict with Himmler and the RSHA. On the local level this conflict was reflected in the struggle betweeen Reeder and his subordinates in the Military Administration on the one side, and the Brussels office of the SIPO and SD on the other. Once the deportations started, the local SIPO and SD took charge, acting on direct orders from Berlin,[110] while the Military Administration tried to postpone and limit measures planned by the police. The police officials in Brussels were susceptible to the influence of the Military Administration to which they were formally subordinated, but in the final analysis they were bound to obey orders from the RSHA in Berlin. The conflict between these German agencies and the degree of cooperation achieved by them, determined to a large extent the methods, timing, and parameters of the persecution of the Jews in Belgium.

Within the Military Administration, Reeder himself tried to maintain close supervision of anti-Jewish policies because of their potentially explosive political implications. Until the summer of 1942, Jewish affairs were handled by the Police Division (*Gruppe Polizei*), but in August 1942, soon after the start of the deportations, the responsibility for Jewish affairs was transferred to the Political Division (*Gruppe Politik*) headed by Günther Heym, himself, as mentioned above, a member of the SS and sometimes a liaison person with Himmler and the RSHA.[111] This transfer was intended to promote smoother cooperation between the military and the police.

In March 1942, Reeder established a Bureau for Jewish Affairs headed by a Baron von Hahn which was designed to implement anti-Jewish policies[112] and to minimize their political impact. The bureau dealt with appeals for exemptions from deportations, especially for individuals in mixed marriages and for Jews of Belgian nationality connected with the Belgian elites. Hundreds of Belgian Jews received exemptions through this office. Von Hahn, according to his postwar testimony destroyed the lists of exempted persons in July 1944 after the dismissal of the Military Administration, in order to prevent their utilization by the German police.[113]

The Jewish Section occupied only a relatively lowly place in the command hierarchy of the German police in Brussels, operating under the supervision of the Brussels Chief (Canaris or Ehlers) and that of the head of the Division (Straub). In its first two years, until the end of November 1942, it was headed by Lieutenant (*Untersturmführer*) Kurt Asche who put the machinery of deportation into place. Asche was a self-educated man without completed secondary education who had worked in a drugstore before joining the S.A. in

1931. He was a fanatical anti-Semite and participated in the *Kristallnacht* action of November 1938. He had been a member of the Special SS Task Forces (*Einsatzgruppen*)[114] in Poland since 1939 and arrived in Brussels at the end of 1940. At the end of November 1942 he was replaced by an SS Captain Fritz Erdmann because he had overplayed his hand favoring German as against Belgian Jews. Subsequently Asche was tried and sentenced by a Police and SS Court for having appropriated Jewish property.[115] The same fate befell his successor, Erdmann, who in turn was replaced in command in October by a succession of two SS officers, Felix Weidmann and Werner Borchardt who served in that function for five months each. In contrast to the rotation in the Brussels leadership, one SS officer Erich Holm headed the Antwerp office of the police for the entire period of the occupation carrying out persecution and deportation with special ruthlessness and success.[116]

The anti-Jewish section of the German police did not only occupy a lowly position in the German hierarchy, but it also possessed only limited personnel. Throughout the occupation Asche and his successors at any one time commanded at most twenty German police officers, approximately ten of whom were stationed in the Brussels office. This minuscule number of officials managed to orchestrate the deportation of over 25,000 Jewish men, women and children. In the execution of the deportation, they had limited additional assistance from Military Police (*Feldgendarmerie*), and the Currency Police (*Devisenschutzkommando*),[117] but above all from Flemish SS and guard troops, and from Rex security forces (in 1944). In one instance, in Antwerp in 1942, Holm even employed Belgian police in a raid on Jews, but that utilization was not repeated.[118] Despite this assistance from a variety of services, the German police remained extremely shorthanded. In its September 1943 raids, for instance, a typical raiding team would consist of one German police official and two Flemish guards, with one or two German police officials and half a dozen Flemish guards stationed at the assembly point.[119]

One reason the Germans succeeded as well as they did was that they managed to secure, up to a point, the assistance of

Belgian government agencies and of the Jews themselves. Municipal offices executed the original Jewish census in 1940-1941, and a second census in the summer of 1941.[120] In the spring of 1942, Belgian Labor offices participated in the summons of Jewish men to work in labor camps in northern France. However, Belgian government agencies refused to participate in the registration and sequestration of Jewish property or to distribute the Yellow Star,[121] and Belgian cooperation ceased almost entirely with the start of deportations in 1942.

The persecution of the Jews may be divided into three periods: The first period lasting from October 1940 to July 1942. During this period the Germans registered and progressively isolated the Jews living in Belgium, virtually confiscated their property and eliminated their opportunities for earning a living. The second period encompassed only three months, August, September and October 1942. During these three months the Germans carried out their initial and most concentrated drive to deport as many Jews as possible through a campaign of summonses and raids. The third period, from November 1942 to August 1944 witnessed a persistent effort by the German police to catch and deport individual Jews and their families, through routine checks, responses to denunciations, and a variety of other methods. During this final period, no additional mass raids took place, with the exception of the roundup of Belgian Jews in September 1943.

The first step in the campaign against the Jews was the prohibition of ritual slaughter on October 25, 1940.[122] Three days later, the Germans published the basic set of decrees directed against the Jews, the *Judenverordnung* of 1940. It established for the occupied territory the Nuremberg Law definition who was to be considered a Jew. The decree prohibited the return to Belgium of Jews who fled in May 1940. It required Belgian authorities to register Jews living in the occupied territory, and ordered Jews to register by November 30, 1940 (this date was later extended to January, 1941). The identity cards of Jews were to be marked. Jewish business enterprises had to be registered and sales of Jewish property required the approval of German authorities. Jewish owners of hotels and restaurants were required to designate their business as being owned by Jews. Jewish religious communities were ordered to help implement these regulations.[123] In a separate decree issued on the same date Jews were suspended or dismissed from public office, including public schools and universities. They were prohibited from practicing law or from occupying positions in the press and radio.[124] In one fell swoop Jews were placed in a separate category, and the process of segregation and isolation had begun.

A subsequent decree dated May 31, 1941 ordered Jews to register their property. It made its disposal subject to German approval. The proceeds from the sale of Jewish business enterprises or other property had to be placed in blocked accounts. Jews were also prohibited from exercising supervisorial or management functions in business.[125] They had to hand in their radio sets.

In order to implement this economic despoliation the Military Administration was forced to create its own agency for this purpose when faced with the refusal of the Belgian government to lend a hand.[126] The registration and liquidation of Jewish business enterprises were carried out through a subsidiary organization which was called the "Fiduciary Company" (*Treuhandgesellschaft*). It registered 7,700 Jewish enterprises and 3,000 pieces of real estate.[127] Most business enterprises were liquidated since Belgian businessmen by and large were reluctant to buy up Jewish companies and German buyers became disinterested in them once their inventory had been dissipated. Only eight percent of the Jewish business enterprises registered with the Germans continued in existence under "Aryan" management or supervision.[128] Proceeds from the sale of Jewish property were placed in blocked accounts under German control, and the Jewish "owners" were allowed to withdraw only limited monthly amounts to defray their living expenses.

Separate provisions were made for the disposition of radios and furniture owned by Jews. Radios confiscated in 1941 were distributed to German troops stationed in Belgium. Furniture left behind by deportees was first assigned to Germans settled in the East, but was redirected subsequently to bombed-out families in the Reich.[129] The German bureaucracy carried out this plunder with painstaking care, worrying over proper receipts and making sure that "legality" and "accountability" were maintained all along the way.[130]

Late in August 1941 an 8 p.m. to 7 a.m. curfew was instituted for Jews, and Antwerp, Brussels, Liège and Charleroi were designated as the only locations to which Jews would be given permission to move.[131] At the end of 1941, the Germans eliminated Jewish students from Belgian institutions of education at all levels. Jewish students were ordered to attend Jewish schools and Jewish university students were told to withdraw by the end of the year.[132]

Since the start of the campaign against the Jews the Military Administration, undoubtedly at the suggestion of Eichmann's office, had attempted to persuade Belgian Jews to form a Jewish Council. Although Jewish leaders proved reluctant to form such an organization, the Germans established "The Association of Jews in Belgium" (*L'Association des Juifs en Belgique* or AJB) in November 1941, almost ten months later than in neighboring Holland. The purpose of the Association, according to the German decree, was to promote "emigration" and to take charge of other Jewish affairs in Belgium. Existing Jewish organizations except for religious bodies were to be transferred to the Association or face dissolution. The Association was entrusted with the responsibility for administering Jewish schools and welfare organizations, and for managing the totality of organized Jewish life except for purely religious functions.[133]

The other purpose of the Association was to promote "emigration", by the end of 1941 a euphemism for deportation to the East. In carrying out that assignment, the AJB registered and re-registered Jews and it assisted with the registration and sequestration of Jewish property.[134] It distributed summonses to report for deportation in the summer of 1942 and it provided personnel for the processing of deportees. In August 1942 it urged Jews to report for deportation and as late as the spring of 1943 encouraged self-delusion by collecting and passing on to the German police for transmission to the East thousands of letters addressed to deportees most of whom had been killed by that time.[135]

During the first few months of 1942 the Germans completed the step by step process of isolating Jews. Increasing pressure was put on Jews to sell or liquidate their business enterprises and their property. Physicians and other medical personnel were prohibited to practice except for ministering to Jewish patients. In April 1942 German Jews were declared stateless and their property was confiscated outright.[136] In May the employment of Jews was further restricted and Belgian employers were authorized to dismiss Jews instantly without regard to Belgian labor regulations.[137]

Then finally in May 1942, on the order of the RSHA and after months of delaying tactics by the Military Command, Jews living in Belgium were ordered to wear the Yellow Star[138] and to stay overnight at the residence listed with the German police.[139] The noose had finally closed and the Jews of Belgium had been readied for deportation. The first phase of the persecution of the Jews had come to an end.

Even though General von Falkenhausen and Reeder may not have relished the task of segregating and despoiling the Jews of Belgium, they were well aware of the next stage of the process in which they played such a key part: the deportation of the Jews to the East. As Reeder wrote in the early summer of 1942:

> With these measures the legislation dealing with the Jews in Belgium may be considered complete. The Jews have only extremely limited ways of earning a living. The next step now would be the evacuation from Belgium which will, however, not be initiated locally but will be started by the competent offices in the Reich within the context of a general plan.[140]

The second phase of the persecution of the Jews in Belgium, the "Hundred Days" of Deportation, extended from the beginning of August to the end of October 1942, but German planning had begun much earlier. At a conference in Berlin on June 11, 1942, Eichmann had set a quota of ten thousand Jews to be deported from Belgium. This quota was increased to twenty thousand at the end of August.[141] Reeder learned about the deportation plans late in June and went to Berlin to secure exemption or postponement. On July 9 he met Himmler who made the concession that Jews of Belgian nationality would not be deported for the time being.[142] This concession was consistent with German policy in France where Jews of French nationality were also largely exempted from deportation.

On July 15, the German police ordered the AJB to establish an office for the labor draft (*Arbeitseinsatz*), another code name for deportation. A week later, the Germans had the AJB distribute approximately five thousand convocations notices to report by a given date to the assembly point in Malines.[143] Each summons bore the letterhead of the Military Commander for Belgium and Northern France. They were prepared by Flemish auxiliaries in the office of the SIPO.[144] In order to preserve the pretense of labor service in the East, the first round of convocation notices did not include children and old people.[145]

Naturally these summonses produced panic among the Jewish population. In order to counteract this panic the leadership of the AJB, at the behest of the German police, issued an appeal on August 1 to comply with the summons and to report for evacuation. This appeal conveyed the assurances of the German authorities that the current action was designed to put the evacuees to work, and that it was not a measure of deportation. It also threatened retribution against families and against the entire Jewish community in the event of noncompliance.[146]

At first, in late July and early August, most individuals and familes who had received convocation notices reported to the Caserne Dossin, a former military barrack in Malines used as the assembly point for deportees. However, the number of people who reported "voluntarily" drastically decreased as more and more persons were engulfed. In response, the German police began to raid homes, to make individual arrests and pick up people in the streets in order to meet the quota set by Eichmann. In cases where the police failed to locate Jews on the deportation lists in their apartments, they would carry away members of their family or Jewish neighbors instead. Obviously, these raids increased the sense of panic among the Jewish population.

During the month of August, these raids became the most important source of Jewish deportees to fill the trains leaving for the East although convocation notices continued to be delivered. Now the pretext of labor service was dropped as children and old people were included in the summons. Even though an increasing number of Jews went into hiding, the German police succeeded in its endeavor to fill the deportation trains on schedule. In four major raids on Jewish ghetto areas in Antwerp and Brussels between August 15 and September 12, the Germans captured more than four thousand victims.[147] In a final effort, in Antwerp on September 22-24, they raided rationing offices and schools. That action produced such vigorous protests from Belgian authorities that Reeder instructed the SIPO to cease its largescale operations in order to prevent further unrest among the Belgian population.[148] From this point on, the German police concentrated on the hunt for individual Jews in their homes, at work, on the street or in their hiding places.

By the middle of August the usefulness of the AJB to the German police began to lessen as more and more Jews refused to report "voluntarily" for deportation. The assassination of the Jewish head of the "labor draft" office of the AJB by a Communist resistance group made the leaders of the AJB more hesitant to expose themselves.[149] In response the SIPO arrested six of the leaders of the AJB including its head, the Grand Rabbi Ullmann, for "sabotage" and sent them to the Breendonck concentration camp. However, following protests by the Queen Mother, the archbishop, and the Secretary-General for Justice, Reeder ordered their release after a week's internment.[150]

During the period of police raids, Jewish people who were caught in Brussels were first taken to the main office of the SIPO and SD in the Avenue Louise. (In Antwerp they were assembled in a former movie theatre.) There they were kept only for a short time, at most up to three days, to be transported by truck to Malines. In the Caserne Dossin, German police officials would screen the prisoners and classify the captives into one of several groups. The largest of these groups was made up of Jews to be deported to the East on the next available train (*Transportjuden*). Then there were the "deferrals" (*Entscheidungsfälle*), or Jews whose cases were to be examined for possible exemption from deportation. The *Z-Juden* included Jews whose foreign nationality protected them from deportation for the time being, and finally there were the *S-Juden* or punishment cases, Jews accused of infraction of German regulations, often Resistance workers who were to be sent to special punishment camps such as Mauthausen where they were destined to suffer a painful death.[151]

Despite the obstacles encountered, the German police, during the Hundred Days of Deportation, succeeded in sending to the East almost seventeen thousand Jews or approximately two-thirds of the Jewish population deported during the entire occupation.[152] However by the time the dispatch of deportation trains was suspended on October 31, 1942 it had failed to meet the goal of twenty thousand deportees set on August 28.

Special mention must be made of a labor draft for younger Jewish men organized by the Economics Division of the Military Administration. Under the authority of the Labor Draft Decree of March 6, the Military Administration placed 2,252 Jews in the camps of the military construction company *Organisation Todt* in Northern France.[153] As mentioned above, the Belgian Labor offices called up the Jews assigned to such work, and in Antwerp the Belgian police delivered the summonses. In this manner, the Todt action seemed to bear the stamp of approval of Belgian authorities and appeared to be separate from the deportations organized by the German police. Once deportation got underway late in July, Todt labor service was viewed by many as providing protection against deportation to the East. In effect, however, at the end of October, the 1,833 persons then left in the Todt camps were rounded up and deported through Malines. In the intervening time, 196 deportees or seven percent of the total had escaped from the camps, fifteen had died, and 148 escaped from the deportation trains in Belgium subsequently. Many of these young men went into hiding and joined the Resistance.[154] But despite this relatively high rate of escape the Todt action separated out and put under German physical control many of the younger men who would have been most likely to engage in anti-German actions and to offer resistance to deportation.

The third phase of the persecution of the Jews in Belgium, the slow but steady hunt for Jews who had so far escaped the German dragnet lasted from October 1942 until the closing days of the occupation. During these twenty-three months, the Germans caught and deported approximately eight thousand Jews, or on the average a dozen persons per day. This number included approximately one thousand Jews of Belgian nationality[155] most of whom were caught in a two-day special action in Brussels and Antwerp on September 3 and 4, 1943.

After the raids of the summer of 1942 the German police was forced to hunt down Jews individually in part because the Military Administration viewed large scale raids as risking potentially undesirable political consequences. In the second place, many Jewish people had moved underground and could no longer be located in the dwellings registered with the police. Many had found shelter, often with the help of the Jewish *Comité de Défense des Juifs* or of non-Jewish friends or acquaintances.

Therefore the German police had to resort to new methods in their hunt for Jews. They encouraged denunciations by setting a bounty on each Jew betrayed to the German police.[156] It has been claimed that most Jews captured in their hiding places during this period fell into Germans hands as a result of such denunciations.[157] The police would also patrol the streets of the big cities and pounce on individuals who looked Jewish. To that purpose they employed Jewish informers such as the notorious "Jacques" (a.k.a. Icek Glogowski) who allegedly were particularly qualified to identify fellow Jews.[158] Other Jews were caught as the result of ideologically motivated denunciations or they were seized during routine checks in railroad stations, in trains, cinemas or other public places. In all these activities the German police was heavily dependent on its Flemish SS auxiliaries, and especially so in Antwerp.

In a relatively few instances it was possible to buy protection and release from the German police. In one case the Germans released an arrestee in return for a payment of BFrcs 25,000. Another report lists a ransom of 1.5 million. It also appears that a number of children were released to a childrens home upon payment of BFrcs 150,000-300,00.[159] It is probably true that the German police became more venal after 1943 when German morale was generally declining while the continuing temptation of opportunities for corruption made its impact. Above all, it must be remembered that these kinds of ransom payments could be arranged only in a limited number of instances and that none of them provided real assurance of safety unless the persons concerned were able to reach neutral or Allied territory.

The one major exception to the protacted hunt for individual Jews was the "*Aktion Iltis*" of September 3-4, 1943. From the start, the promise that Reeder had secured from Himmler early in July 1942 to the effect that the Belgian Jews would be left alone for the time being was not kept consistently by the police. In one spectacular sweep over three hundred Jews of Belgian nationality were arrested in Antwerp in the summer of 1942. Most of these people were kept in Malines until June 1943, at which point they were released in response to protestations by Queen Mother Elizabeth. However, they were ordered to reside in a common residence in Antwerp where they could be rounded up easily in the future.[160] Other Jews of Belgian nationality who had been captured during the summer of 1942 also were kept in Malines and released eventually, unless they were accused of unlawful activities.

At the end of June 1943 the German police in Brussels received instructions from the RSHA to incorporate Belgian Jews in its evacuation of Jews from the occupied territory. Once more, Reeder journeyed to Berlin to obtain cancellation or modification of the measure, but in vain. After his return, he continued to delay the implementation of the order in the Command Area. During a temporary absence of Reeder,

General von Falkenhausen on July 20 agreed to the deportation of Belgian Jews, provided the police would first make an attempt to catch individuals in hiding or persons otherwise guilty of infractions of German regulations. He also asked that children and old people be exempted.[161]

In the weeks that followed the German police began to arrest a number of Jews of Belgian nationality but denied that a fundamental change in their policy toward Belgian Jews had taken place. Finally, however, on the night of September 3-4, the night of the Jewish New Year, they organized a coup to capture a large number of Belgian Jews all at one time. Under instructions by Reeder to notify in advance the Military Administration of any major action against the Jews, the head of the German police at the time, Ernst Ehlers, dispatched a letter to the Military Administration dated September 1 which was delivered to Reeder on September 4, after the action had been completed.[162] In its directives to their operatives of the September 3 raid in Brussels, the German police specifically instructed their teams not to bring their activities to the attention of the Military Administration or to solicit the help of the military unless absolutely necessary. Jews in whom the Military Administration had shown a special interest were to be left alone.[163]

On the night of September 3, fourteen teams of German police and auxiliaries raided the apartments of Belgian Jews in Brussels using lists based on their own files and those furnished by the AJB. In these raids they managed to arrest 750 Belgian Jews who were taken to Malines.[164] In Antwerp, Erich Holm, the local police official in charge of Jewish affairs, employed ingenious trickery inviting the Belgian Jews recently released at the request of the Military Administration, and officials of the AJB to report to German police headquarters allegedly to transact business. In fact however, the 225 persons who reported were arrested and held for transportation to Malines.[165]

During the removal of 145 of the victims of this Antwerp action to Malines an "accident" occurred which for a moment appeared to put into jeopardy the whole framework of official cooperation between Belgian and German government agencies. Through carelessness and callousness, these 145 people were placed in a furniture van which was virtually hermetically sealed. For some reason, the journey from Antwerp to Malines which would normally take thirty minutes, took almost three hours. When the truck arrived, nine passengers were dead, eighty were unconscious and a number had gone insane.[166] News of this tragic event quickly circulated throughout the country, and Belgian authorities, from the royal court to the Secretaries-General threatened the cessation of the system of political cooperation that had been in place since the beginning of the occupation. Reeder was furious at this turn of events which appeared to produce exactly the kind of political confrontation that all along he had tried to avoid. He ordered the immediate end to all largescale actions and arranged the release of a number of Belgian Jews. In mid-September 88 persons or eight percent of the number arrested on September 3-4 were released from Malines,[167] but most of the remaining Belgian nationals were deported on September 20. Belgian authorities were informed that mass arrests were suspended and nothing came of the threat to terminate cooperation.

For the balance of the occupation the German police had to be more circumspect. Aside from its continuous pursuit of individual Jews not protected by the Military Administration, it conducted two minor raids, one in Namur, and the other in Liège in June 1944. It also laid the groundwork for some future major strikes at a time when the protective hand of the military might be removed or be made ineffective. To that end, the police agreed to the establishment of certain categories of protected Jews. These included Antwerp diamond workers who were at first exempted but subsequently deported toward the end of 1943. It also included approximately one thousand Jewish workers in the clothing industry manufacturing goods for the German military. This group remained in Belgium until the end of the occupation. The protected group also contained Jews, mostly of Belgian nationality who enjoyed the protection of the Military Administration. Then there were the members of the AJB and their families, a total of 331 persons in March 1944. In addition, at the urging of Queen Mother Elisabeth and other highly placed Belgian figures, the Germans exempted some children and older people from deportation to the East. These latter two groups were placed in residential establishments managed by the AJB. All of these protected people, a total of approximately four thousand persons, were registered with the German police.[168]

The establishment of protected categories had two kinds of potential utility to the German police. In the first place the exemptions granted the members of the AJB made available such services as the AJB might still be able to render. Secondly, the establishment of protection gave people in the protected categories a false sense of security which in the end would make it easier for the German police to seize and deport them when the time was ripe.

That moment appeared to have arrived in July 1944 when the Military Administration was replaced by the *Reichskommissariat* under *Gauleiter* Grohé. In this reorganization the German police was given the independent position it had long since occupied in Holland. During the month of August, a major roundup including the older people and children housed in establishments run by the AJB was planned by SS Lieutenant Anton Burger who had helped to stage the raids in 1942. He planned for the new raids to take place on August 27, but was unable to secure needed transportation. In addition, the Brussels SIPO office was moved to Hasselt in eastern Belgium on August 27 in the face of the Allied advance. Therefore Burger's raids never materialized. Moreover, as a result of negotiations between Belgian agencies, neutral diplomats and German authorities, the final evacuation train, the so-called twenty-seventh convoy which was to have been dispatched to Bergen-Belsen at the end of August never left Belgium.[169] Thus in the end, during the last month of the occupation, the German police was thwarted in its efforts to deport more Jews to the East.

Brief mention needs to be made of the harsher German policies pursued in the Antwerp region where the SS and German police enjoyed a degree of independence from the restraints of the Military Command and where anti-Semitic actions enjoyed a larger measure of support from the population than elsewhere. As has been mentioned, as early as November 1940, German authorities in Antwerp took it upon themselves to expel several hundred Jews to the eastern province of Limburg. On the second day of Easter 1941 the Flemish SS with the obvious connivance of local German authorities staged a pogrom after the screening of the anti-Semitic film "Jud Süss," smashing and looting Jewish shops and burning synagogues, while the Belgian police was ordered to stand by and let things take their course. A report of the Military Administration noted that the riot was "well-conducted" in that Aryan shops adjacent to Jewish stores were not damaged in the least.[170] Nevertheless the Military Administration in Brussels saw to it that this incident was not repeated. However the Easter riots led to a series of restrictions on Antwerp Jews such as a six o'clock curfew and the exclusion of Jews from public recreational facilities.

Some comments are in order with regard to the differential treatment given to Jews of foreign nationality. Stateless Jews, German Jews who were declared stateless in 1942, and Jews from countries under German occupation such as Poland and the Baltic countries were the earliest targets of deportation. At the other extreme, Jewish nationals of countries with which Germany was at war (other than occupied territories) in principle were exempt from deportation to concentration or extermination camps[171], at least until 1944. The fate of the nationals of other European countries depended largely on the attitude of their home governments. Jews from neutral countries such as Sweden and Turkey were given a deadline early in 1943 to return to their home country or face deportation.[172] The Hungarian government in 1942 tended to protect at least some of its nationals and the Germans afforded them an opportunity to return to Hungary.[173] Rumanian Jews, however, were deported.[174] The Bulgarian government adopted delaying tactics while agreeing to deportation in principle.[175] The German police in Paris urged their colleagues in Brussels by the summer of 1943 to deport as soon as possible Jews of French nationality residing in Belgium.[176] But beyond these general guidelines the fate of the individual often depended on the vagaries of the specific situation.

There remains the task of summarizing the result of German persecution. In order to judge the degree of success or failure of the German campaign, we first need to determine the size of the Jewish population in Belgium before the start of persecution. Unfortunately, we do not have reliable figures prior to the occupation because the Belgian census did not include the categories of religion or race. Although earlier estimates suggested a prewar Jewish population of 90,000 to 95,000,[177] it has not been possible to establish the original source of these estimates. The Belgian scholar Maxime Steinberg in 1986 presented an estimate of a prewar Jewish population of 64,600,[178] although he conceded the possibility that the prewar Jewish population could have been as large as 70,000 persons. He based his estimates primarily on German police files which list 56,186 persons[179] and on low estimates of the number of individuals and families who never came to the attention of government authorities.

The present writer believes that Steinberg's figures may be too low because Steinberg so largely relies on official statistics. It is possible that a larger number of persons than suggested by Steinberg fled to France in 1940 and failed to return, or entirely escaped registration. They would have included people who went underground in Belgium and France without ever being caught up in German police files, or who managed to escape to neutral or Allied territory. We must admit, however, that we do not have adequate concrete data to support this contention.

We are on firmer ground when we examine the number of Jews whose names appear in official files. The first registration in November 1940 - January 1941 of Jews under the Nuremberg definition yielded 42,642 names of individuals sixteen years or older.[180] By general agreement the number of children under sixteen is estimated at ten thousand. According to official figures, fewer than 2,332 Jews under the Nuremberg definition failed to list their names during that first registration.[181] By adding these three categories, we reach a total of 54,974 or approximately 55,000 Jewish persons in Belgium at the beginning of the occupation. This figure coincides for all practical purposes with the figure of 56,186 listed by the German police, particularly if the number of Dutch Jews caught in Belgium in their attempt to escape to neutral territory is included in the total. Even though we believe, for the reasons stated above, that this figure may be on the low side, we will use Steinberg's figures in the discussion which follows.

According to Steinberg, 25,124 Jews, or forty-three percent of the 58,186 persons represented in the files of the German police by the end of the occupation were deported from Belgium by August 1944. Only 1,323 or five percent of these deportees survived the war. In addition to the Jewish people deported from Belgium, 1,242 Jews who had fled Belgium after the occupation were deported from France, of whom only seventy-seven survived. Therefore it can be stated with considerable accuracy that 24,966 or forty-four percent of the Jewish population identified by the German police under the occupation perished in the East, while 31,220 or fifty-six percent of the total survived. This percentage remains approximately the same if the number of persons who were deported from France after having fled from Belgium in May 1940 is included in the count.[182]

Most of these survivors lived in hiding in the occupied territory since only four thousand Jews were in the protected groups in 1944.[183] Therefore, in the view of the present writer, Steinberg is correct in asserting that for most Jews it turned out to be significantly less dangerous to go into hiding than to follow the orders of the German police,[184] especially if it is assumed that the protected Jews would have been deported if the German occupation of Belgium would have lasted a little longer.

It is clear from the information on hand that Jews of Belgian nationality had twice as good a chance of escaping deportation and death as did the Jews who were not Belgian citizens. According to Steinberg, 1,203 Belgian citizens or twenty-seven percent of the total were deported from Malines from among the 4,341 Jews of Belgian nationality[185] as compared with forty-six percent of the total of registered non-citizen Jews who suffered the same fate. More Belgian than non-Belgian Jews survived because the Germans needed to exercise restraint primarily with regard to Jews of Belgian nationality since Belgian authorities in the main limited their intervention to the protection of fellow citizens. The delay in the deportation of Belgian Jews until September 1943 made it more likely that hiding places could be located, particularly since assistance was more forthcoming after the turn of the war in 1943. In addition it seems reasonable that Belgian Jews would find it easier to disperse across the country than Jews who could be identified more easily as recent immigrants from Central and Eastern Europe. On the other hand, Belgian Jews who trusted German assurances and remained in their registered residences by September 1943 fell an easy prey to the German police during the September raids.

Summarizing the figures on deportation and survival, it can be said that slightly more than half (over fifty-five percent) of the Jewish population listed in the files of the German police survived the war, and that almost half (somewhat under forty-five percent) were deported and perished. If the present writer's assumption is valid that the actual Jewish population within the Nuremberg definition living in Belgium before and under the occupation was larger than reflected in government figures, then an even higher proportion of Jews survived than official files suggest. It probably will never be possible to establish this information with absolute certainty.

In conclusion, the present writer wishes to confess to a sense of ambivalence in presenting the figures that have been listed. On the one hand, this kind of information is needed in order to assess the degree of success and failure of the German effort to exterminate the Jews living in Belgium. On the other hand, there is an element of callousness in these statistics because these figures represent human beings who experienced years of extreme agony and tragedy. Even the lives of those persons who survived German persecution were filled with daily fear and anxiety that they would be caught in the dragnet of the SS and deprived of their liberty, their families and of life itself. And there remains a degree of obscenity in speaking in numbers and statistical terms of those tens of thousands human beings from Belgium, or the millions from all over Europe whose lives were snuffed out in the extermination camps of the Third Reich.

The following two tables will provide summary views of the deportations and their ultimate results. Table 2 furnishes a listing of the 26 convoys sent to the East from Malines. Table 3 provides a total assessment of the fate of the Jews registered in Belgium after May 1940. The small discrepancies in the total number of Jews deported from Malines must be attributed to the adjustments made in the time since the year (1967) in which table 2 was prepared.

Table 2[186]

Transports from Malines to the East

Transports	Date	Number of deported persons	Special Comments
	1942		
1	August 4	1,000	
2	August 11	1,000	
3	August 15	1,000	
4	August 18	996	
5	August 25	996	
6	August 29	1,000	
7	September 1	1,000	
8	September 8	1,001	
9	September 9	1,000	
10	September 15	1,047	
11	September 26	1,745	
12	October 10	1,000	
13	October 10	676	
14	October 24	997	
15	October 24	476	
16	October 31	904	
17	October 31	887	

Table 2 (cont.)

Transports from Malines to the East

Transports	Date	Number of deported persons	Special Comments
	<u>1943</u>		
18	January 15	994	
19	January 15	614	
20	April 19	1,455	
21	July 31	1,556	
22 a	September 20	625	
22 b	September 20	793	
	<u>1944</u>		
23	January 15	655	
24	April 4	625	
25	May 19	507	
26	July 31	563	
	Transports of Jews of Foreign Nationality (Z-Juden)
	13 December 1943	132	Sent to Buchenwald
	15 January 1944	351	Sent to Auschwitz
	19 April 1944	14	Sent to Bergen-Belsen
Total Numbers Deported		25,559	
Special Deportations		72	Sent to Vittel
		25,631	

Table 3[187]

Summary of the Final Solution in Belgium*

Jewish Population after May 10, 1940	Deported from Malines			Percentage of Deaths
in Belgium	to Auschwitz	Survivors	Deaths	
55,670[a] Gypsies from France 516[b]	25,257 (-)351	1,205 (-)12	24,052 (-)339	
56,186	24,906	1,193	23,713	42.2%
	to Buchenwald, Ravensbrück and Vittel			
	218[c]	130	88	
56,186	25,124	1,323	23,801	42.3%
	Deported from Drancy (France) to Auschwitz			
	1,242[d]	(77)	(1,165)	
56,186	26,366	(1,400)	(24,966)	44.4%

(a) Without "Aryan" spouses.
(b) Deported from Malines in 1942.
(c) Jews of foreign nationality deported to concentration camps instead of extermination camps.
(d) Jews escaped from Belgium after 1940.

* Reproduced by permission of Maxime Steinberg.

Labor, Welfare and Culture

The German treatment of the Belgian labor movement furnishes a striking illustration of a halfhearted and eventually unsuccessful attempt by the Germans to create an artificial organization on the Nazi model. Before the war Belgium, as an intensively industrialized country, had been highly unionized. One out of every eight inhabitants was a member of a trade union. The two largest labor organizations were the Socialist union (*Confédération Générale des Travailleurs de Belgique*) with some 650,000 members and the Catholic union (*Confédération des Syndicats Chrétiens*) with a membership of 350,000. A much smaller union associated with the Liberal party, the C.G.S.L. (*Confédération Générale des Syndicats Liberaux*) claimed approximately 60,000 members. A Flemish labor organization called the Labor Order (*Arbeidsorde*)[188] with allegedly 30,000 members in April 1940 was modelled after the German Labor Front. It was a creation of the VNV and sought to rally Flemish labor to the cause of Flemish nationalism. Unlike the other trade unions which were organized along federative lines, the *Arbeidsorde* was a highly centralized organization.[189]

The Belgian trade unions provided their members with a large variety of services, including credit unions, saving banks, health insurance, and with a wide range of social and recreational associations. Because of these auxiliary enterprises the bigger unions possessed complex bureaucracies and substantial assets.

The German objective in Belgium as elsewhere was to neutralize politically those unions that had been associated with political parties, to subvert them gradually and finally to establish a centralized labor organization on the model of the German Labor Front which would inherit the assets and membership of the old unions. In order to accomplish this goal, a special service for labor affairs the so-called *Dienststelle Hellwig*, staffed by personnel of the German Labor Front, was created within the Military Administration in October 1940.

A first attempt to unify the labor movement was made in the summer of 1940 by the former head of the Socialist party,

Henri De Man, in a manifesto which called for the unification of the trade union movement. In response, the Socialist and Catholic unions entered into discussions about closer association in the fall, but their plans were modified by the Germans. The new central organization that emerged in November 1940 under the name of the Union of Manual and Intellectual Workers (*Union des Travailleurs Manuels et Intellectuels*, or UTMI) was presented by the Germans as an umbrella organization for the existing four unions, including, at German insistance, the VNV *Arbeidsorde*. The organization was headed by a Board of eight members, two from each of the four constituent organizations, with the presidency rotating among the members of the governing board.[190] This arrangement was seen only as a first step by the Germans and their collaborators.[191]

In the months that followed the Germans brought about the replacement of the old leadership. The Catholic union proved particularly intransigent and in the summer of 1941, the Germans appointed a Commissioner for the entire union,[192] thus removing a last obstacle, in the German view, to the creation of a genuine unitary organization. Late in 1941, they placed Edgar Delvo, a former associate of Henri De Man who had joined the VNV and the *Arbeidsorde*, on the governing board of the UTMI and in April 1942 they appointed him its singular head.[193] At that point the UTMI was reorganized on the leader's principle and now resembled the German Labor Front in many respects. This process was completed with the decree of August 26, 1942 which provided for the formal dissolution of the old unions and for legal transfer of their assets to the UTMI.[194]

Thus the Germans had succeeded in effecting on paper the organizational transformation they had desired, but to little avail: most workers refused to join the new organization despite the German attempts to give the UTMI credit for the eight percent wage increase granted in 1941. According to a count made in 1942, union membership dwindled from over one million in the immediate prewar period to a mere 109,000, with a bare 17,000 left in the French-speaking part of Belgium.[195] Thus practically all Walloon members had withdrawn, with 92,000 Flemish workers left to make up the bulk of what was left of the union movement. Upon Delvo's appointment in 1942 and the reorganization of the UMTI on the authoritarian principle, Henri De Man ceased his collaboration with the Union[196] and in 1943 Delvo himself resigned in order to become an officer in the Flemish SS.

By 1943 the UTMI had become largely an administrative agency whose paid officials worked with government departments and with Belgian employees on problems dealing with wages, working conditions and recreation projects. It made propaganda for labor recruitment for Germany, and in general it had become a tool of the Germans taking a consistently pro-German stance without becoming involved in the factional struggles of the Collaboration.

In the end, the Germans found their capture of the labor movement a hollow victory. Their attempt to establish in Belgium an institution on the National Socialist German model had ended in total failure. The Germans experienced a similar fiasco when they tried to organize a voluntary labor service along Nazi lines.

The concept of a voluntary labor service had arisen in Germany in the late twenties as an attempt to bring together young people of different social classes in manual labor projects. The original concept was inspired by a search for community that had become a part of the German reaction to modernity. The Nazis appropriated this idea and modified it to suit their own purposes. After coming to power in 1933 they established a German Labor Service headed by Konstantin Hierl, an old party stalwart. Under Hierl, the German Labor Service quickly became a tool of Nazi indoctrination. In 1935 six months of labor service became compulsory for German youth.

The original idea of voluntary labor service had caught the attention of some elite circles in other West European countries. In Belgium a voluntary labor service had come into existence in the nineteen thirties as a private organization. After the capitulation of May 1940, a group of conservative and royalist Catholic reserve officers headed by a certain Henri Bauchau had banded together to promote a voluntary labor service as a rallying point for a national revival after the defeat. Supported by the Catholic church and by certain prominent individuals in business and finance, and with the approval of the court, they had started setting up a small number of camps in the summer of 1940.

The Germans considered it necessary to secure a measure of control and established an office staffed by a member of the German Labor Service. They insisted on the integration of the voluntary labor service into the regular Belgian administration, to provide better supervision and control.[197] In November 1940, two labor services, one Flemish and one for French-speaking volunteers, headed by Henri Bauchau, were established under the authority of the Commissioner for Reconstruction. At German insistence, the labor services were transferred in August 1941 to the Department of the Interior in the hope that Gérard Romsée, the new Secretary-General, would be more amenable to German direction. In October 1941, Romsée established a labor service for women which, as it turned out, operated largely in Flanders.[198]

On the German side, the German Labor Service, through its local representative in Brussels, was the driving force within the Military Administration. The Brussels representative since the end of 1941 was a Colonel Avenarius who tried to enlarge his organization's influence over the Belgian services.[199] The German Labor Service and the SS wished to use the Belgian labor services for propaganda purposes,[200] and after June 1941, as recruiting grounds for the Flemish and Walloon Legions.[201]

The Flemish organization, the Voluntary Labor Service for Flanders (*Vrijwillige Arbeidsdienst voor Vlaanderen*) and the francophone Voluntary Labor Service for Wallonia (*Service Volontaire du Travail pour la Wallonie*) soon developed in different directions. The Flemish organization fell under Flemish nationalist and later Devlag-SS influence and worked closely with the German Labor Service becoming clearly an instrument of collaboration. The Walloon Labor Service on the other hand stayed under the control of Henri Bauchau until early 1943, and remained relatively resistant to German or Rexist influence.[202]

Both services were rather unsuccessful in their recruitment efforts. By mid-1942 each of the labor services for men enrolled six hundred men, with two hundred women in the Flemish Women's Service.[203] By mid-1943 the Walloon service reached its peak with eighteen hundred men whereas the Flemish service counted twelve hundred volunteers in September.[204] All in all not very impressive results, despite the fact that enrollment in the voluntary labor services provided at least temporary deferment from the labor draft and opened up career opportunities in government services.

In the meantime, a struggle between German agencies erupted in 1942. Two key issues were involved: The leadership and control of each of the services and the question whether labor service should be made compulsory as it was in the Reich and in neighboring Holland.[205] Himmler and Berger wanted to turn over the Flemish Labor Service to the Devlag-SS faction so that it could be used unabashedly for propaganda for a Greater Germany and for recruitment for the Waffen-SS. They also wanted to turn over the Walloon Service to Rexists, primarily for military recruitment purposes. Reich Labor Leader Hierl allied himself with Himmler in this struggle hoping to extend the authority of the Reich Labor Service over the Belgian organizations.

At first the Military Administration opposed these demands in order to avoid difficulties with the Secretaries-General. It tried to encourage recruitment by offering positive incentives. It did not favor a compulsory approach which would in its opinion only lead to new problems. By early 1943, this conflict reached its peak with a blast from Himmler accusing Reeder of insubordination.[206]

As a result of all this pressure, the Military Administration in March 1943 ordered the Secretaries-General to establish six-month compulsory labor service, allegedly because recruitment had fallen off, but it did not force the issue when the Secretaries-General refused to comply. In the meantime, Hierl changed his mind, allegedly in the interest of Sauckel's labor draft, and now advised Himmler against making labor service compulsory.[207]

In early 1943 the Military Administration, under pressure from Himmler and Hierl, had made an attempt to subvert the Walloon Labor Service by forcing it to accept in positions of leadership a number of Rexists who had served in the Walloon Legion. In response Bauchau resigned and many leaders followed his example. Recruitment fell off rapidly and the organization lost many members. Even Romsée, under pressure from his colleagues, eventually promised to resist the subversion of the Walloon Labor Service.[208]

In view of these fiascoes, all the principals, Himmler, Hierl, Reeder and Romsée, finally agreed to abolish the two voluntary labor services as public institutions, to be replaced by two labor services which would be organized as private organizations with the assistance of the German Labor Service.[209] Himmler and Hierl agreed to this arrangement because they hoped it would allow them to place their own people in control and to use the labor services for propaganda and recruitment without interference by Romsée and more traditional elements.[210]

Given the relatively minute number of Belgian youth to enroll in the two labor services, the attempt to establish a public labor service in Belgium remains a minor episode in the history of the occupation. However it illustrates well the policy conflicts within the German hierarchy and the limits the Military Administration placed on the Nazification of public life, given its overriding objective to avoid unnecessary conflict. For the sake of avoiding political repercussions it resisted pressures from more radical elements in the Nazi party structure by suggesting a solution which would avoid difficulties with those elements in the Belgian administration whose cooperation it considered necessary for the exploitation of the country. The failure of the labor service project also represents another example of the ineffectiveness of an attempt to recreate artificially in Belgium a Nazi organization rooted in German political culture but without genuine roots in Belgian society.

The Germans met with a similar failure in their halfhearted attempt to create a new social welfare organization on the German model when they established in November 1940 a centralized organization called the Winter Help (*Secours d'Hiver* or *Winterhulp*). The Germans gave a number of reasons for desiring a unification of charity activities but in essence they wanted to be in a position to control welfare work which was easier to do through a single organization run on an authoritarian pattern. They wanted to make sure that anti-German elements were excluded from the management and that benefits reached recipients in line with German policy ".. not to allow the situation of the socially disadvantaged to sink below a certain level..."[211] during the difficult first winter of the occupation. They saw an opportunity to create in capitalist Belgium the spirit of "Folk Community" (*Volksgemeinschaft*) which in the long run might pay political dividends. One final political objective was to neutralize the Belgian Red Cross which had close associations with the army, high society and the court.[212]

At the suggestion of the Germans, Paul Heymans, former Minister of Economic Affairs and governor of the *Société Nationale de Crédit à l'Industrie*, a banker thought sympathetic to the Flemish cause, was appointed president of the Winter Help. At first, the Germans found Heymans cooperative, probably because there could be little dispute about the necessity of rendering immediate relief during the difficult first winter of the occupation. In time it became apparent that Heymans was trying hard to overcome the impression that the Winter Help was a tool of the Germans, and that he wanted to build up the Winter Help as an autonomous welfare organization that deserved the trust and cooperation of Belgian patriots at home and abroad. He apparently was reinforced in this endeavor by representatives of the government-in-exile with whom he conferred in Lisbon in the autumn of 1941.[213] He succeeded so well in this effort of gaining the confidence of the Pierlot government that by 1943 the government-in-exile guaranteed credits for purchases abroad made by the Winter Help. At home too Heymans managed to gain the support of a large segment of Belgian society from the court on down, including the Catholic church,[214] the Belgian local and national administration, and even Rex and the VNV.[215]

The Germans themselves viewed the work of the Winter Help with mixed feelings. To be true, General von Falkenhausen after the war praised the leaders of Winter Help and Red Cross as "men who allowed themselves to be guided only by reason and real humanitarianism."[216] But other German officials viewed the Winter Help in a more differentiated manner. They realized that leadership and financial support came from Belgian patriots and that appeals were made on the basis of patriotic "Belgicist" sentiments,[217] which the Military Administration hoped to weaken in favor of a separate Flemish and Walloon consciousness. They watched with apprehension the staffing of the Winter Help with former military men who from time to time were found to be active in the Resistance.[218] After 1942 they used the labor draft to remove such men and to replace them with individuals viewed as being more "neutral." The Germans recognized that the Winter Help, despite these purges, remained under the control of Belgian patriots whose attitudes towards the Germans were "dubious" (*"undurchsichtig"*). They admitted after the end of the occupation that the Winter Help had been of no use to them in their *Volkstumspolitik* as originally hoped.

Why then did the Germans allow the Winter Help to acquire such independence and to frustrate the political objectives they had set for the organization? Probably because Heymans proved so effective in providing relief to a large section of the Belgian population. At one point during the first winter of the occupation, more than one out of six Belgians were reported to receive food or fuel from the Winter Help.[219] Moreover, it was very important to the Germans to retain the support of the Belgian elites which had traditionally been in the forefront of charity work, which made it necessary to leave in charge patriots with the proper connections. In order to be able to make purchases in neutral countries underwritten by the government-in-exile, the organization had to possess a degree of independence from the occupying power. Hence the Germans settled in the end for an agency which, far from being a German tool, became in the hands of Belgian patriots an important instrument for helping the economically weakest elements of the population to survive the deprivations of the occupation.

The Germans met with similar resistance and only minimal success in their attempts to impose pro-German and National Socialist ideas and structures on Belgian cultural and educational institutions. To begin with, German cultural activities in Belgium had only a limited number of objectives. In the first place, the Germans wanted to supplant the dominant cultural influence of France with that of Germany. They also sought to discourage the concept of a "Belgian" civilization, substituting for it the cultures and languages of Flanders and Wallonia. Finally, they sought to tie the Flemish cultural elites to Germany and to champion the development of Flemish cultural activities. In that context, they promoted the use of Flemish over French in public institutions.[220]

German cultural activities in Belgium were orchestrated by the Cultural Division (*Gruppe Kultur*) in the Military Administration headed by Professor Petri. As in other fields, the Military Administration had to compete with the more heavy-handed policies advocated by the SS and with the programs launched by Jungclaus' office. In view of prevailing anti-German sentiments it sought to work through existing organizations and institutions.[221] Only in a few instances did the Germans create new structures on the German model such as the Cultural Councils (*Kulturräte*)[222]. Petri in particular tended to stress the longrange aspects of cultural cooperation. His favorite method of promoting that goal of cooperation was through the exchange of professors, teachers, students, and of cultural programs and artifacts.

The German efforts extended into a number of fields. In literature they gave special recognition to pro-German writers such as Stijn Streuvels and Felix Timmermans who had traditionally had a large reading public in Germany. They also established German bookstores and promoted book exchanges and poetry readings. They supported Flemish dramatic activities and sought to introduce German plays into their repertoires. They sponsored the establishment of a Flemish Symphony orchestra after their attempt to control the programs of the Brussels Symphony had failed.[223]

The Military Administration evinced a special interest in the preservation of Belgian art and of structures that had historical or artistic value. Historical buildings were protected and repaired where damaged by war. Steps were taken to protect works of art against future war damage, and troops were not allowed to billet in historical buildings and museums.

The Military Administration assisted, and at the same time tried to control and limit German Reich authorities and private German art collectors in their attempts to buy up as many art objects as possible. It unsuccessfully opposed the removal to Germany on Hitler's special orders of two famous pieces of Flemish religious art, the Ghent altar tryptich by the brothers van Eyck and an altar piece by Dirk Bouts.[224] The Military Administration also tried to supervise and to restrain to some extent the art purchases of private German art collectors and of German museums including those of the Führer Museum in Linz.[225]

At the beginning of the occupation, World War I war memorials drew the attention of the Cultural Section of the Military Administration because many of these monuments contained anti-German inscriptions referring to alleged German atrocities. Orders went out to erase these inscriptions where possible or to remove the entire monument in cases where this was not feasible.[226]

Another painful issue to occupy the attention of the Germans was the question of responsibility for the second destruction of the library of the University of Louvain. That library had been destroyed in the First World War by German artillery and had been rebuilt in the twenties with the assistance of Herbert Hoover and his American committee. It had been damaged again in May 1940, and the question of responsibility arose. The Germans blamed British troops for the damage even though one internal report made that conclusion dubious.[227] A postwar Belgian commission fixed the responsibility on the Germans.[228]

In its Final Report written after the end of the occupation, the Military Administration had to admit that its cultural activities had only very limited impact. While the report blamed the poverty of resources at the disposal of the Cultural

Section for this outcome, the lack of cooperation on the part of the Belgian cultural community and the reluctance of the Military Administration to take unnecessary risks in a politically volatile area provide more convincing explanations of this failure.

In the field of education too the Germans made only a relatively minor effort to bring about changes. Their scope of action was limited because they had to work through the Department of Education whose head, Secretary-General Nyns, did not prove very cooperative. The effectiveness of any proposed changes was further diminished by the great influence over education wielded by the Catholic church. More than half of Belgium's elementary pupils attended parochial schools, and the Catholic University of Louvain was the largest and most prestigious of the four Belgian universities.

In view of its own limited resources and of the structural problems of making an impact on elementary and secondary education, German efforts tended to focus on the universities, in part in the hope of influencing the future intellectual leaders whose attitudes the German Military Administration considered crucial. This perception of the importance of Belgian elites meant that the Germans would try to win over these elements by influencing the universities and that they would endeavor to avoid unnecessary conflict. This was one of the reasons they exempted university students from labor draft obligation as long as they could.

German goals with regard to Belgian education were therefore limited. In elementary and secondary schools the Germans sought the removal of anti-German personnel and materials and their replacement with pro-German teachers and texts.[229] They wanted to increase the number of Flemish teachers and administrators and the number of classes taught in Flemish. Finally they sought to make German the first foreign language and to increase the number of hours devoted to German in the secondary schools.[230]

Some practical steps were taken to implement these goals. Lists of prohibited textbooks were distributed and the schools were told to eliminate their use. Most public schools complied but many Catholic schools did not. An attempt was made to provide more acceptable texts, particularly in history. By September 1941, 210 textbooks had been banned and changes had been ordered in another 180 titles.[231] Flemish was given a more prominent place in instruction, particularly in the Brussels school system. Anti-German teachers were dismissed (seventy-five cases in 1943), or even arrested if accused of anti-German statements.[232] In order to facilitate the appointment of Flemish and pro-German teachers, the power to appoint new teachers in public schools formerly reserved to local governing bodies, was given to Romsée in the Department of the Interior.[233]

Despite these measures the German impact on elementary and secondary schools was negligible, since the few pro-German inspectors whom the Germans managed to get appointed could not make much headway in the schools against the stubborn resistance of the great majority of patriotic teachers and administrators.[234] In the Catholic schools, most of the German-imposed regulations were disregarded on orders from the ecclesiastic authorities.

At the university level German plans were more specific and more far-reaching. The Military Administration was determined to keep the universities open, contrary to the World War I precedent and to the orders of the Pierlot government. According to German plans, Ghent was to become the primary repository of Flemish scholarship, and Liège its Walloon counterpart. Louvain, the Catholic University, was to be restricted to Theology, and the Free University of Brussels, that "bastion of liberal thought and Free Masonry," was to be converted eventually into a German "Frontier University," (*Grenzlandsuniversität*), a "Germanic bulwark against Latin Western Europe."[235] In the end very little came of these grandiose plans, but some attempts along these lines were made.

As in other areas the Germans initially concentrated on the question of personnel. Through the application of the decree requiring the screening of individuals who had left for France in May 1940, approximately twenty-five percent of the university teachers were eliminated by the end of 1940,[236] three-quarters of whom were from the Free University of Brussels.[237]

In order to control the appointment of new faculty members, the Germans made such appointments subject to their approval. Through the use of this authority the Germans imposed a number of Flemish or pro-German teachers on the universities, particularly in the case of the University of Ghent which they considered the institution most responsive to their initiatives. They also appointed a German Commissioner for the Free University of Brussels and for the Colonial University in Antwerp, in preparation of the transformation of these institutions in line with German aspirations.

Attempts to influence the nature or contents of courses taught at the universities remained minor. Original goals had included the introduction of new courses emphasizing racial and *Volkstum* scholarship, but very little came of this except at the University of Ghent. At the Free University of Brussels courses taught in Flemish were introduced in the fall of 1941.[238] At the University of Ghent the use of French as a language of instruction was prohibited.[239]

The Military Administration also placed great hopes on the exchange of scholars. It was hoped that visiting German professors could influence the development of Belgian universities "along the lines which had proved themselves to be effective in the Balkans.."[240] In October 1940, the Germans designated ten professors to be assigned to Belgian universities while eleven Flemish scholars were to give guest lectures at German universities.[241]

But whereas the Free University of Brussels had been willing to accept German exchange professors, the case was quite otherwise when the German University Commissioner Professor Ipsen in 1941 attempted to impose on the university three Belgian Activists who had been sentenced for their pro-German activities during the First World War.[242] When Ipsen insisted, the Belgian Board of Governors ordered the cessation of teaching activities on November 25, 1941. The Germans arrested ten members of the Board, but to no avail.[243] In 1942 the German authorities decided to make the closure of the university permanent, when it became apparent that the majority of the faculty would be unwilling to resume instruction.[244] The Germans made this decision at least in part because they concluded that the continued operation of this liberal institution would not be in the German interest. However, the permanent closure of the university also marked the end of their plan to transform the Free University of Brussels into a New Order institution.

The final conflict with the universities occurred in 1943 in connection with the labor draft. In line with its policy to avoid conflicts with the Belgian elites, the Military Administration had continued to exempt university students from the Labor Draft until the end of 1942. Under pressure from the Sauckel organization it finally required students to report for six-month labor service within Belgium.[245] It demanded student lists from the universities as a basis for checking compliance with German labor regulations but except for Ghent, the universities refused to furnish such lists.

In the end this conflict was resolved without any additional institutional closures. Therefore, the Military Administration achieved until the spring of 1944 its basic goal of keeping universities in operation. It can be argued that the continued operation of Belgian universities (compared for instance with the Netherlands where university teaching ceased after May 1943) prevented an influx of Belgian university students into the Resistance on the scale on which it occurred in the Netherlands.

By 1943 Belgian universities had to face yet another threat. German universities began to scour Belgian institutions in search of equipment under regulations issued by Speer's ministry. Petri's office tried to cooperate in this replacement program, while also attempting to protect Belgian institutions against the avarice of German universities. It suspected German scientists of trying to get their hands on the most modern equipment rather than just trying to replace equipment lost as the result of Allied bombing, the justification given for the replacement program.[246]

The Military Administration proposed that equipment transfers should be considered "loans" within the scientific community, but Belgian officials preferred to have the removals designated as requisitions under The Hague Convention, in order to escape the appearance of collaboration. Under this program a good deal of equipment of all kinds was removed, most importantly the Meridian Circle from the Royal Observatory in Uccles.[247]

Thus, the policies of the Military Administration in the field of culture were primarily designed to avoid unnecessary friction and conflict. The two breakdowns that occurred can be considered departures from the main policy envisioned by Petri. After the war, he attributed the crisis over the Free University of Brussels to a "lack of tact" on the part of University Commissioner Ipsen,[248] while the crisis over the labor draft in 1943 was brought about ultimately by the pressure put on the Military Administration by the Sauckel organization. Yet all in all, the limitations which the Military Administration imposed on itself in dealing with Belgian education payed off in that major confrontations were avoided with the two exceptions that have been mentioned.

The Germans and Belgian Prisoners of War

The record makes it clear that the basic policy with regard to Belgian prisoners of war was set by Hitler himself.[249] From the outset, Hitler intended to treat French-speaking prisoners of war differently from their Flemish compatriots. Therefore German troops on May 10, 1940 already carried with them instructions to separate Flemish from French-speaking P.O.W.'s.[250] On June 6th Hitler ordered the release of Flemish soldiers in German custody. Soldiers from Wallonia and French-speaking residents of Brussels were to be sent to Germany as prisoners of war, as were professional soldiers. Exceptions could be made for "specialists" whose services were needed in the occupied territory.[251]

On July 15, German authorities in Brussels announced that a decision had been reached to release all Belgian prisoners of war. This announcement, the result of a misunderstanding by higher military authorities, turned out to be in error.[252]

Hitler stuck by his original decision throughout the war, as he did in the case of the French P.O.W.'s.

There cannot be the slightest doubt about the attitudes of General von Falkenhausen and Reeder toward the prisoner of war issue. In their opinion the discrimination against French-speaking prisoners had a disastrous effect on public opinion and on the attitudes of the non-Flemish segment of the population toward the German regime.[253] In 1940 and 1941, German officials in Brussels considered this issue, second only to the food shortage, the key problem within the Command area. General von Falkenhausen noted with particular bitterness that Flemish politicians were more effective than the Military Command in effecting the release of prisoners of war from German camps.[254]

The purpose of the distinction between Flemish and French-speaking prisoners of war was clearly political. By releasing the Flemish soldiers, as in the case of the Dutch, Hitler wanted to create goodwill among the Flemish population slated eventually for annexation. On the other hand he kept the French-speaking prisoners of war, as in the case of the French, because they could provide cheap labor in Germany. Moreover, racial considerations played a role. By sending Flemish and Dutch men home to their wives they might father children to increase the reservoir of Germanic stock. Conversely, by keeping French-speaking men in Germany, the birthrate in the Walloon provinces would be lowered, for the sake of improving the edge of the Germanic races over their francophone compatriots.

In Belgium, however, the distinction had a special political effect: it served to drive another wedge between the francophone and the Flemish-speaking population in line with then-existing German plans for an eventual annexation of Flanders. Degrelle at least suspected that much, believing Himmler and the SS to be behind this scheme.[255]

Fortunately, Hitler's order was never applied in full to the approximately 600,000 men in the Belgian army. Most soldiers (probably as many as two-thirds of the mobilized army) simply returned to their homes and to civilian life after the capitulation. The Germans never made a systematic effort to seize the men that had vanished. However, soldiers who had been captured in uniform, especially while fighting was still in progress, usually were sent back to Germany. After the capitulation, Hitler's order was applied by the military authorities to soldiers in German custody, although one gains the impression that officers of the Military Command interpreted liberally the provision authorizing the release of specialized personnel in Belgium.

The return of Flemish soldiers from Germany seems to have been implemented by the end of 1940. The Military Administration reported on May 31, 1941 that 79,302 prisoners of war had been returned to Belgium.[256] Most of these men were Flemish, but not all Flemish P.O.W.'s had been returned even by that date. A number of them were reported to have remained in the Reich as late as 1944.

Professional soldiers generally were taken to Germany and placed in P.O.W. camps. However, a number of them were released subsequently on a variety of grounds.[257] One such group, headed by General Keyaerts, was freed in order to run an organization in Brussels to look after the welfare of demobilized Belgian soldiers and of prisoners of war. In 1941 the Germans also released a group of pro-German Flemish commissioned and non-commissioned officers to strengthen the gendarmerie. The Keyaerts group was eventually reinterned in early 1944.[258]

According to Belgian figures published in 1970 by Professor Jean Léon Charles, approximately 225,000 out of the 600,000 men in the Belgian Army were prisoners of war at one time or another. This number included 150,000 Flemish soldiers and it included a number of men who were picked up by the Germans after they had returned to civilian life. Over 165,000 former soldiers received official recognition having been prisoners of war (the *brevet des prisonniers*) after the war.[259]

Professor Charles also reported that seventy thousand Belgian prisoners remained in Germany in 1943. The Belgian government in 1945 estimated the number of prisoners of war then in Germany at 65,000 men.[260] Statistics from German sources submitted by the French government at the Nuremberg trial reported 53,000 Belgian P.O.W.'s other than commissioned officers present in Germany in the fall of 1943.[261] These figures provide us with a sense of the order of magnitude of the numbers of Belgian prisoners of war in Germany. This number was not static but may be assumed to have dwindled gradually as P.O.W.'s were released on an individual basis or as they managed to escape from the camps. Professor Charles reports that 6,770 such escapes took place during the war.[262] These figures justify the global statement that only somewhat above ten percent of the men constituting the Belgian army in May 1940 remained in Germany as prisoners of war by 1943.

Chapter Five

The Economic Exploitation of Belgium

General Observations

From the beginning to the end of the occupation the Military Command had one clear priority in its governance of the country (apart from the maintenance of law and order). It hoped to "...make available and preserve for the war economy of the Reich...the potential of the so highly developed [Belgian] economy."[1] To this priority it sought to subordinate all other objectives to whatever degree it was allowed to do so by its superiors and by competing German services and agencies.

In order to carry out this task effectively, the Military Administration recruited officials from German business and civil service into its ranks. The importance of economic management was highlighted by the fact that the Economics Division (*Gruppe Wirtschaft*) included more than half the total professional personnel of the Military Administration.[2]

It has been stated before that from the start the Military Administration sought to enlist the cooperation of Belgian businessmen and government officials. It realized that it would be necessary to appeal to their self-interest and patriotic sentiment in order to create a climate in which economic cooperation could be justified by the expectation of mutual benefits.[3] The underlying understanding reached in 1940 with Belgian government and business elites was that Belgium had to produce for the Reich in return for (1) receiving sufficient food and other supplies to maintain tolerable living conditions, (2) being able to employ Belgian workers at home to prevent the forcible deportation that had occurred during the First World War and (3) permitting Belgian business and industry to continue operating under their own management and, as far as possible, its own institutions and practices.* The Military Administration was sincere in its desire to maintain adequate living conditions since it realized that full economic utilization of Belgium would be productive only if living conditions remained tolerable.[4] Its reports to Berlin were full of such homilies as "you cannot expect to get milk from the cow you have butchered" or "to get eggs from a hen that has been killed."

Unfortunately, as the occupation progressed, it became increasingly obvious that continuation of this *modus vivendi* required a number of compromises on both sides. The Germans had to minimize structural reforms they would have liked to impose in order to remake Belgian economic institutions in the image of those that had come into being in Germany under the Third Reich. Belgian businessmen and government officials on the other hand found themselves locked into a pattern of economic cooperation even after it had become obvious that the Military Administration was unable to keep adequately its part of the bargain to provide an acceptable level of nutrition or to prevent the forcible deportation of labor to the Reich. Yet despite the multiple stresses and strains that evolved over the years the fabric of economic cooperation agreed upon implicitly in 1940 held together throughout the occupation because both sides continued to believe that it constituted the lesser evil among available alternatives. The Germans did not have the necessary manpower to exploit Belgian industry directly without the assistance of Belgian government officials and business

---

* An American scholar, John Gillingham, has maintained that the Belgian business elite on its part was eager to embrace German business methods and organizations and that they used the occupation to further their own ends. (John Gillingham. *Belgian Business in the Nazi New Order*. Ghent. 1977.) Without wishing to deny that such tendencies existed, the present writer cannot follow Gillingham in his single-minded argument that this attitude was typical of Belgian business and industry as a whole.

leaders, while Belgian elites viewed the policies of the Military Administration as preferable to the even more ruthless exploitation they would face if the existing regime were to be replaced by a civilian administration dominated by Nazi party officials. This "marriage of convenience" may be said to have lasted throughout the occupation on the basis of an "appreciation of each other's vulnerability."[5]

However, the potential opposition of Belgian business was not the main and certainly not the only obstacle the Military Administration faced in its attempt to maximize the economic potential of the occupied territory. It found its most formidable opponents in the host of German services and agencies which tried to pursue their own economic objectives without regard for the overall German interest. Foremost among these competitors for Belgian resources and products were the military procurement services, especially those of the Air Force,[6] the agencies of Göring's Four Year Plan and of the German Economics Ministry, German industry and business and, since 1942, the Sauckel forced labor draft (*Arbeitseinsatz*). The Military Administration pitted against these competitors an unceasing plea for coordination under its own aegis, pointing out in endless memoranda the destructive impact of uncoordinated action on the comprehensive mobilization of the Belgian economy.[7] In general it fought a losing battle against these competing forces, at least until the last year of the occupation when Speer's effort at economic coordination began to make itself felt to some extent in the occupied territories.

Reconstruction and Transportation

Before the economic exploitation of Belgium could get underway in earnest, damage inflicted during the May 1940 hostilities had to be repaired. This was an endeavor in which German and Belgian agencies, after some initial hesitations on the part of the latter, could cooperate without major reservations. Once the basic premise had been accepted that the Belgian economy would operate under the second occupation, Belgian officials had no objection to working with the

Germans in the reconstruction effort. To carry out this task, the Secretary-General of Labor and Social Welfare, Charles Verwilghen, was designated as Commissioner for General Reconstruction.[8]

For the Germans the restoration of the transportation and communication facilities had the highest priority because railroad lines, roads and waterways had been severely damaged by war actions and especially by demolitions by Allied troops. Reconstruction proceeded so quickly that railroad and postal services were restored by September, and bridges and waterways were repaired by May 1941, by which time most transportation other than private cars and public busses operated near prewar levels.[9]

Even quicker progress was made in the restoration of electric power and other utility services. By the end of 1940 the task of reconstruction was considered basically completed and utilities functioned at 80 percent of peacetime levels.[10] By the spring of 1941, industry in general had overcome the effects of the destruction caused by the hostilities, although this rarely meant full return to prewar levels of production.

The reconstruction of damaged private dwellings, occupied a lower priority. The main effort was directed toward the repair of buildings which had undergone only minor damage. It appears that despite early concern over the large number of dwellings destroyed and damaged, the total supply of private dwellings was not seriously impaired during the hostilities of May 1940.

The repatriation of the Belgian refugees constituted the major task facing German and Belgian authorities in the summer of 1940. As has been mentioned above in Chapter One estimates of the numbers of people who had been dislocated varied from 1.5[11] to 2.8 million,[12] but it may be assumed that something on the order of two million people were involved. At the suggestion of the Germans, Belgian authorities appointed a Commission for Repatriation functioning under the supervision of the Secretary-General for Social Welfare, Delhaye. This Commission consisted of four prominent Belgians, including Paul Heymans, the future President of the Winter Help, and Gérard Romsée, the future Secretary-General of the Interior.

On the whole, the repatriation of the refugees proceeded promptly and smoothly, once regular trains and fuel for automobiles were made available by the end of July. At first, Belgian authorities in France sought to impede the return to Belgium of young men of military age,[13] but in the end practically all refugees who wanted to do so returned. Jews in the unoccupied zone of France may have formed a partial exception because of their reluctance to return to a territory controlled by the Germans. After September 1940 the Military Administration refused to let them return to Belgium.[14] Between July 31 and the last week of September, the bulk of the refugees returned in about eight hundred trains. By the end of September 1940, repatriation was virtually completed.[15]

At the conclusion of the first year of the occupation, the Military Administration had good reasons to take pride in the speed and efficiency with which it had guided the physical reconstruction of Belgium and the repatriation of Belgian refugees. It felt that it had earned its share of good-will among the people living in the occupied territory by the manner in which it had helped Belgian agencies to perform this task.[16]

The prewar Belgian railroad network was the densest system in Europe. Satisfactory performance of the Belgian economy depended on its smooth operation and that of the Belgian canals which carried a substantial amount of freight traffic. Therefore the restoration of Belgian transportation systems described in the preceding section laid the basis for the resumption of normal life and for the economic exploitation of the country.

In order to maximize the utilization of existing transportation facilities the authorities established a division of labor between different transportation systems. The railroads carried interurban "long distance" passenger traffic and about seventy-five percent of all freight traffic,[17] with most of the remaining freight being carried by water. Streetcars handled local transportation, and local railroad lines some of the interurban transport. Buses were used only sparingly, mostly for taking workers to and from work.

All in all the railroads carried the bulk of passenger and freight traffic. Their task had been made more difficult by the removal to Germany during the first two years of the occupation of hundreds of locomotives and about fifty thousand freight cars.[18] For the balance of the occupation, the railroads had to manage with the locomotives left in the country, but a few thousand of the sequestered cars were returned in 1941.

Thus, in 1941 and 1942 Belgian transportation ran smoothly in support of the economy, with the exception of a few weeks in January and February 1942, when frost caused by the unusually cold winter led to a partial shutdown of the system.[19] However, by 1943 the picture began to worsen, largely due to sabotage, and to the bombing of transportation facilities by the Allies. Moreover, additional locomotives and rolling stock had to be delivered to Germany at a time when Belgian equipment was aging and in need of repair. By the winter of 1943/44, the situation had deteriorated drastically. The final blow came with the Allied air offensive of April 1944. These air attacks destroyed the most important rail yards, and reduced the shunting capacity of the Belgian railways by over fifty percent. They destroyed almost two-thirds of the remaining locomotives and temporarily cut off the rail traffic with the Reich by making inoperative a key rail yard on the German border.[20]

During the month of May, the Allies inflicted even heavier punishment on the transportation facilities of Belgium. During the first half of the month they continued to concentrate on railroad stations, rail yards and repair facilities, but during the second half of May they targeted their attacks on moving trains, locomotives and railroad bridges. For the month as a whole, freight movement on the railroads was reduced to one-seventh of its October to December 1943 average.[21]

The month of June brought a welcome respite, since Allied air attacks ceased almost completely after the Normandy invasion. Now water and road transport were revived, many railroads stations were reopened at least for through traffic, and freight circulation became sufficient to allow a revival of the economy which had been paralyzed almost completely.[22] However, the improvement in railroad service remained limited, since now the sabotage actions directed against rail transport (which had almost ceased while Allied bombing had been in progress) revived on a larger scale than ever before, with fifty attacks being recorded in one day during the month of June. These sabotage actions were so effective (even though damage wrought by sabotage could be repaired more quickly than the destruction wrought by air attacks) that on the average forty lines remained closed during June. Entire regions such as the Ardennes and the industrial regions of Charleroi and Mons remained closed to rail traffic.[23]

In order to save gasoline, which was in shorter supply than coal, the Germans from the start imposed stringent restrictions on the use of automobiles. Cars, trucks and motorcycles had to secure special permits. Authorization to purchase gas was granted only to eight percent of the prewar number of private cars[24] and overall only about ten percent of the prewar number of vehicles driven by internal combustion engines were given permits in 1940.[25]

Buses, which were allowed to operate temporarily in the summer of 1940, while other means of transportation were out of commission, were withdrawn just as soon as streetcars and railroads began to operate again. Moreover, throughout the war, vehicles were encouraged to convert to the use of natural gas, such as methane and propane. Later in the war, the Germans imposed further restrictions on vehicle circulation, such as the prohibition against the use of cars after dark or on Sundays.[26]

In summary, it can be said that the German and Belgian authorities succeeded in quickly restoring the damage done to Belgian transportation system by the military operations of May 1940, and that the Belgian transportation system provided the necessary facilities for the wartime exploitation of the Belgian economy. The system began to break down in 1943, and suffered almost complete paralysis in April and May 1944, making only a limited recovery in the remaining months of the occupation.

Stages of Exploitation

It was the policy of the Reich to extract from the occupied territories as many goods and services as possible in support of the German war effort while maintaining the standard of living of the German people as close to the prewar level as feasible. In the case of Belgium this meant the export to Germany of a maximum amount of raw materials, finished products and consumer goods and, over time, the exploitation of industry to the best of German ability, while importing from Germany the minimum amount of food and other supplies necessary to the survival and work performance of the population. On the other hand the Germans recognized that they could not call on Belgium to export food to any significant extent to the Reich.

Within this context, the exploitation of Belgium under the occupation went through two major stages. The first stage lasted from the summer of 1940 to the winter of 1941-1942, during a time span when Germany expected victory in a series of short wars. During this period, German authorities concentrated on the removal to the Reich of available raw materials, military supplies and consumer goods. The Germans also began to make limited use of Belgian industrial capacities by placing military and civilian orders in Belgium, but the removal of supplies on hand had priority. At the same time, the Germans also made attempts at integrating the Belgian economy into their "New Europe" by endeavoring to purchase Belgian firms (through a process called *Kapitalverflechtung* or "merging of capital"), and by creating in Belgium corporate business and industrial organizations analogous to those existing in Germany.

The second stage of the economic exploitation lasted from the spring of 1942 to the end of the occupation. It was prompted by the realization that the war might last for a long time and that therefore a greater effort to utilize the industrial potential of Belgium for war production would be required.

Within this second stage, it may be useful to distinguish two phases. During the first phase, from the spring of 1942 to the spring of 1943, the higher degree of urgency was manifested in a series of relatively uncoordinated efforts to place more orders with Belgian industry and in efforts to recruit workers for Germany on a quasi-voluntary and later patently compulsory basis. During the second phase, starting in the spring of 1943, a major but only partially successful effort was made to coordinate industrial production in Belgium, by controlling procurement and by putting Belgian workers to work in Belgian factories by establishing "blocked" factories (*Sperrbetriebe*) whose personnel could not be drafted for work in Germany. This policy was a part of Albert Speer's Europe-wide effort to coordinate war production and procurement, and to employ more workers "at home" in plants located in the occupied territories.

It was only during the second stage that the utilization of Belgian industry began in earnest. It should be noted however that the removal of raw materials and supplies did not end in 1941, and that both modes of exploitation coexisted throughout the occupation. However, the utilization of Belgian industry acquired an ever increasing priority as the German military and economic situation deteriorated after 1942.

In the expansive mood of the summer of 1940, German business interests with the encouragement of Göring[27] had started negotiations to acquire shares in Belgium business enterprises and industries in order to secure control of such concerns. Despite the benign title of *Kapitalverflechtung* with its appearance of mutuality, the campaign was clearly intended to give German enterprises control over Belgian business[28] as an integral part of the program of German economic imperialism that characterized the "New Europe" concept in vogue in 1940 and 1941.

The German Military Command in Belgium viewed this undertaking with suspicion. It feared that a vigorous campaign of expropriation would interfere with its primary goal of utilizing the Belgian economy for the German war effort. Moreover, as von Falkenhausen observed in his memoirs, the campaign was ill-timed and unnecessary. If Germany was going to win the war, the integration of Belgian business would occur inevitably. If the war would be lost,

German investments in Belgian business would also be lost. In short, this was a matter that should be deferred until the end of the war.[29]

In its attempts to ward off these takeovers the Military Administration sought the assistance of the German Economics Ministry. By September 1940, the ministry promised to restrain the negotiations of individual German firms. Supposedly, German business and government agencies were in agreement that such mergers should be voluntary.[30]

In the end, most of the agreements that were concluded applied to Belgian investments in enterprises located in Eastern Europe and in the Balkans. Estimates of amounts invested in Belgian enterprises as of 1941 varied from RM 13-15 million[31] (probably the realistic range) to the RM 25 million claimed by the Military Administration in its report on its first year of activities.[32]

By the fall of 1941, German interest in Belgian firms had decreased since the end of the war was no longer in sight. Activity in this area therefore slowed down. In general, the attempt to buy up Belgian enterprises was viewed as a failure by all sides concerned, particularly if compared with more successful German campaigns in neighboring France and in the Netherlands.[33]

The Military Administration refrained at first from making any major structural changes in the existing Belgian business and industrial organization which might interfere with the quick revival of industrial production. However in 1941 the Germans introduced some innovations. The first of these was the establishment of a system of "Purchasing Offices" or *Warenstellen* designed to direct the flow of raw materials and supplies. The *Warenstellen* which were located in the Department of Economics of the Belgian administration, appear to have been reasonably successful in serving as conduits for industrial supplies.

The second attempt at structural reform of industry was also initiated in 1941, under pressure from Berlin. It envisioned the foundation of a hierarchical organization of business and industry on the German corporate model. The alleged purpose of these new *Hauptstellen* (Central Offices) was to provide guidance on questions of internal management.[34] The Military Administration was lukewarm about this attempt to reorganize Belgian industry in the German image from fear that Belgian resistance to it might imperil smoothly functioning patterns of cooperation with existing indigenous structures. Belgian businessmen and industrialists, with some possible exceptions, likewise proved unenthusiastic and, by and large, the groupings created by decree in 1941 remained largely paper organizations without life or real influence, with the possible exception of organizations created for the production and marketing of coal and steel.

Throughout the occupation, the Military Administration tried to avoid the direct operation by German administrators of Belgian industrial enterprises in the belief that industry would function more efficiently under Belgian management. When several factories refused to accept arms and ammunitions orders because they were outlawed by the Hague Convention and by Article 115 of the Belgian Constitution, the Military Administration sought to camouflage these purchases to make it easier for Belgian management to accept these orders.[35] Only when this proved impossible, and only as a last resort, did the Military Administration proceed to place industrial enterprises under direct German management through the appointment of German administrators. By December 1941 only eleven such enterprises had been transferred to direct German management.[36]

In order to control and maximize Belgian industrial production more easily, the Germans deliberately reduced the number of industrial enterprises. In the beginning years, this goal was accomplished largely through the denial of raw materials and supplies to smaller enterprises. Smaller and less efficient firms often were forced to close, as they were unable to secure needed supplies. For instance, in the textile field, the number of firms decreased from 635 in 1940 to 175 in 1942.[37] Beginning in 1942, the Germans went further. They proceeded to close smaller and less efficient plants by fiat, reassigning their work force (in as far as it was not deported to Germany) to the larger more efficient industrial enterprises working for export to Germany.

As mentioned above, during the first year of the occupation when the end of the war seemed in sight, the immediate task at hand was to seize and export to Germany the ample stock of raw materials and other supplies on hand in this highly industrialized country which had piled up a variety of reserves as insurance against war time shortages. The Germans did not wait long to implement this strategy. Special military and civilian commissions followed closely behind the advancing German troops in 1940 in order to seize existing raw materials and supplies. Representatives of private industry soon arrived furnished with some kind of authorization to purchase raw materials and even industrial installations.[38]

It quickly became apparent that these independent operations led to chaos and that they would interfere with the ability of Belgian factories to work for the Reich. Therefore, the Military Administration, the army and the German Ministry of Economics attempted to create some order in the arbitrary operations of plunder that had been carried out in the first weeks of the occupation. Instructions were issued by the Ministry of Economics on Göring's authority to the effect that all deliveries to the Reich had to be approved by the Military Commander,[39] but these directives were often disregarded.

The Military Administration tried to take stock of existing supplies by sending out questionnaires and dispatching inspection teams to check on Belgian inventories. The task of making purchases was assigned to a limited number of German firms who had previously done business in Belgium.[40] A decision was made on paper to leave in Belgium enough raw materials to allow Belgian factories to work for the German war economy,[41] but it proved impossible to carry out this policy consistently.

Moreover, such restraints did not apply to consumer goods. German personnel in Belgium in 1940 was allowed to engage in a wild buying spree, which they did particularly with regard to articles such as textiles and leather goods which were already rationed in Germany.[42] This conduct was sanctioned by Göring who, as "high apostle of German consumerism"[43] in October authorized German soldiers to take back to Germany as many goods as they could physically carry on their persons. To the people of Belgium, the picture of the German soldier in 1940 returning homeward laden down with supplies purchased in Belgium remained a lasting bitter memory.[44]

In August 1942 Göring reaffirmed the principle that the German standard of living was to be maintained at the expense of the people in the occupied territories, particularly as far as food was concerned, and that stores in the occupied territories should be emptied in order to enlarge the supply of goods available to Germans during the Christmas season. To facilitate this plunder, by the end of 1942, all export restrictions to the Reich were removed, as were German custom levies on imports from the occupied territories.[45]

In order to regularize the initial wave of attempts by German firms and agencies to purchase Belgian goods, the Military Administration established toward the end of July 1940 a central export agency, the *Allgemeine Warenverkehrsgesellschaft* or AWG. This agency was formally organized as a private corporation, but its Board was made up of officials of the Economics Division of the Military Administration and its funds furnished by the Germans. The task of AWG was to coordinate the purchase of Belgian goods, to make the necessary financial arrangements, and to arrange transportation to Germany.[46] In 1940 it was given a monopoly over financial transfer arrangements, but this attempt at coordination and control soon broke down under the pressure from German business. Already by 1941 German firms could make purchases directly by using branches of German banks established in Belgium. The AWG accordingly performed the bulk of its transactions to the tune of RM 200 million during its first year of operation, but continued to do some business on a much reduced scale in the remaining years of the occupation.[47]

Payments of goods exported under the auspices of the AWG were made in German currency which was deposited in the AWG account in the Belgian *Banque d'Emission* within the context of the Clearing. On instructions from AWG, the bank then made payments to the Belgian seller in Belgian currency.

The list of raw materials and goods taken from Belgium under these arrangements and through other channels was extensive. It included almost all military supplies on hand[48], raw materials such as coal, iron, steel and nonferrous metals, and eventually also diamonds. Plans were made to deliver seventy-five percent of existing textile materials and products[49] on the assumption that the remainder would allow the Belgian textile industry to operate at thirty percent of its peacetime capacity.

All in all, during the first year of the occupation the Germans managed to carry off to Germany a vast amount of raw materials and other goods, estimated by the Military Administration at RM 789 million (including the value of finished products), compared to a prewar average total annual export of RM 277 million.[50]

The second stage of economic exploitation which got underway seriously in 1942 involved "using the total productive capacity of Belgian industry in the service of the German war effort."[51] Implementation of this concept involved direct placement of orders in Belgium and the displacement or subcontracting to Belgian firms of orders received by German industry. This latter process was called *Auftragsverlagerung* (or "relocation of production") in German bureaucratic jargon. As in so many other instances, the guiding policy of the Military Administration in this area was frequently sabotaged by other German agencies and services, and by German industry itself.

The central agency for the coordination of the utilization of Belgian industrial capacity was the *Zentralauftragsstelle* (Central Production Placement Agency) or "ZAST" established in August 1940 under orders from Göring as Plenipotentiary for the Four Year Plan.[52] ZAST was to function under the joint direction of the OKW and of the German Ministry of Economics. Its assignment included the establishment of a balance between purchases of (1) raw materials and semifinished products, and (2) the placement of orders for finished products. All orders of amounts above RM 5,000 were to be registered with ZAST. Supposedly they could take effect only if ZAST had raised no objections within a two-week period.[53] ZAST was closely allied to and also competitive with the *Rüstungsinspektion* (Army Procurement Agency) and it was to be responsive to its requests. It operated under the administrative supervision of the Economics Division of the Military Administration.[54] In practice its authority was not always accepted by other German services.

The placement of orders with Belgian firms faced a number of obstacles throughout the occupation. The first, and in the early years the most important obstacle was the attitude of German industrialists[55] who feared the loss of their own markets and who did not want to see their regular profits disappear. As early as August 1940, the German Anilin and Dye Trust (*I.G. Farben*) warned against any policy that might affect German markets adversely and even pleaded for opening up new markets in Belgium.[56] The *Rüstungsinspektion* complained that in 1940 and early 1941 it "literally had to peddle available productive capacities," in the face of resistance by German industry. The attitude of German industry became somewhat more favorable in 1941, as German plants lost more manpower to the military within the context of the acceleration of the war.[57]

The second obstacle to the success of a Belgian production program was resistance by Belgian industry. It played a lesser part, especially at first, although the Germans believed that they perceived danger signs in 1941 in the wake of a warning against economic collaboration by the Pierlot government.[58] No significant opposition developed in the early years however, in large part because the Germans exercised some restraint by avoiding the placement with Belgian firms of such overtly military orders as arms and munitions, and possibly because (some) Belgian industrialists hoped to make substantial profits and strengthen their position in relation to labor and consumer.

The third obstacle to the utilization of Belgian industry was the growing shortage of raw materials. Central Reich authorities were reluctant to replenish Belgian supplies of raw materials such as steel and nonferrous metals in the belief that there were sufficient supplies hidden in Belgium which could be acquired on the black market. As a result of this attitude, raw materials allocations often were received only belatedly or not at all. These delays interfered seriously with the prompt fulfillment of orders placed in Belgium.[59]

A fourth and indeed steadily increasing obstacle to full utilization of industry and to increases in production was the gradual deterioration of the Belgian industrial plant and equipment which could not be replaced under wartime conditions. The deterioration of the health and stamina of industrial workers under the cumulative impact of wartime deprivations also tended to lower production. In the later years of the occupation the increasing reluctance of management and labor to assist the German war effort after the turn of events in the winter of 1942-1943 may also have played a role in the declining man-hour output in 1943 and 1944.

The fifth, and by 1942-1943 perhaps most critical, obstacle to an increase in production, was the growing shortage of labor due to the initial impact of the Sauckel policy of deporting skilled labor to Germany. That problem was alleviated after the middle of 1943 as the direct result of the rationalization of the German war effort attempted by Albert Speer. Now new orders for finished products were placed in occupied Belgium on an increasing scale.[60] The value of finished products exported to the Reich therefore continued to grow until the spring of 1944.

All in all, the contribution of Belgian industry to the German war effort was substantial, even if it fell below German expectations and below the existing potential. According to a report prepared by ZAST, Belgian industry furnished Germany within the framework of *Auftragsverlagerung*, with products worth RM 4.341 million between May 10, 1940, and July 31, 1943, while RM 1.034 million worth of orders were still pending on the latter date. The largest contribution in monetary value was made by the construction industry, to the amount of RM 1.075 million, largely for military construction projects. The textile industry came second with RM 756 million, while shipbuilding and machine construction were third and fourth with RM 379 and RM 342 million respectively.[61] The total contribution of Belgian industry to the German war effort, including direct orders placed outside of ZAST, was significantly larger.

The Germans recognized from the outset that the maintenance of coal production was a prerequisite for successful exploitation of Belgian industry. Belgian coal provided the basic energy source for the manufacture of steel, iron and metal products, and for the electricity and home fuel supply of the working population. Soon the German goal to supply Belgian industry with coal, and to provide sufficient domestic fuel to maintain work morale and political stability came into conflict with demands of central Reich authorities for coal to be used in the Reich, at the expense of Belgian requirements.

On the other hand, the large number of coal mines of varying sizes, an estimated 168 in all,[62] and of coal distributors made control and supervision difficult. Therefore, as a first step the Germans reduced what they considered an excessive number of dealers. Distribution was centralized by granting monopolies to two existing Belgian industry agencies, the *Comptoir Belge des Charbons* for coal, and the *Comptoir Belge des Cokes* for the sale of coke. Despite this reorganization, the Germans never succeeded in eliminating the black market in coal.[63]

In the first months of the occupation, the restoration of coal production proceeded apace once the miners and managers who had fled to France had returned. Coal production increased rapidly during the fall reaching near prewar levels by November.[64] Despite temporary transportation problems during the winter, enough coal was mined and delivered to make coal rationing unnecessary.[65] However, it became increasingly difficult in 1941 to maintain, let alone surpass this early success. Instead, coal production declined in 1941 and in the following years from the peak attained early in 1941.

This decline was the result of many factors. The first of these was the growing shortage of mine workers due in part to forced recruitment for work in Germany and in part to earlier medical retirements resulting from deteriorating health. The second was the growing reluctance to work underground, declining work morale, and the replacement of older experienced workers with younger unskilled recruits. Finally the deterioration of equipment which could not be replaced under wartime conditions and the shortage of certain materials such as mine timber lowered productivity. All these factors combined to produce a gradual decline until April 1944, when the Allied air offensive caused a precipitous drop in production.

A variety of steps were taken to reverse the decline of mine productivity. These measures included the award to miners of maximum and special food rations, supplemental canteen meals, fuel and wage premiums for Sunday work and for seniority, and special clothing allotments. These inducements had only limited success, but undoubtedly the biggest incentive, after October 1942, was exemption from the labor draft for work in Germany.[66] In order to combat absenteeism and "desertion", the Germans also used threats of various kinds of punishment such as fines, imprisonment or deportation to Germany. In the end they even employed slave labor from Eastern Europe in order to prevent a collapse of coal exploitation.[67] As a result of all these measures the decline in coal production remained relatively moderate in 1941-1943 prior to its radical decrease in 1944.

Table 4[68]

Coal Production (Hard Coal) 1939-1944

Year	Tons (x1,000)	Percentage (1939=100)
1939	29,838	100
1940	25,600	86
1941	26,608	89
1942	24,929	83
1943	23,694	79
(Jan-May)1944	7,318	58 *

* Based on monthly average

The coal-based metallurgical industries of Belgium formed another important part of the Belgian economy. With a prewar production of 3.1 million tons of pig iron and 3.2 million tons of steel,[69] Belgium had been the biggest exporter of pig iron and steel in the world before the war,[70] sending about seventy-five percent of its production abroad.[71] Most of its raw iron ores had been imported, primarily from France and Sweden.

The Germans established a relatively smoothly functioning organization in the field of iron and steel production during the first year of the occupation. On the German side, a German steel industry executive by the name of Otto Steinbrinck was appointed Plenipotentiary for the Steel Industry in Western Europe. At German suggestion, a Belgian umbrella organization, called *Le Syndicat Belge de l'Acier* or SYBELAC, was created under Belgian law. The task of SYBELAC was to arrange for the import of raw materials, set production quotas, distribute orders to its member firms, collect bills, and distribute net income to the firms concerned according to their share in production. Allegedly, it did not concern itself with the internal management of Belgian steel firms.[72] The head of SYBELAC was appointed the head of the *Warenstelle* for steel in the Belgian Ministry of Economics.[73] Steinbrinck's representative occupied a desk in the Economics Division of the Military Administration. Through these parallel appointments the usual friction between competing agencies was largely avoided.

On the whole, cooperation between German and Belgian agencies was satisfactory, due to the common milieu and shared interests of the officials and businessmen concerned. The German steel industry did not try to take over Belgian firms through *Kapitalverflechtung*,[74] and on the whole prewar working relationships were preserved, although SYBELAC itself was a copy of the German *Stahlwerksverband*, the German industry organization.

Given this favorable climate, steel production was resumed quickly in the fall of 1940, as soon as technical and managerial personnel had returned from France and utilities and transportation facilities were restored.[75] According to a German source, by December 1940 monthly production reached 150,000 tons, the peak production under the occupation. It remained at a level of between 110,000 and 140,000 tons per month until April 1944, when it collapsed under the impact of Allied air attacks. The following table, compiled from a variety of sources, tells the story:

Table 5

Monthly Steel Production

Month/Year	Quantity (Tons)
1939	253,000[76]
Dec. 1940	150,700[77]
1942	110,000[78]
1943	133,000[79]
Mar. 1944	142,295[80]
June 1944	17,070[81]

The relatively low steel production in comparison to prewar yield had a variety of causes. Foremost of all was the problem of securing iron ores. German and Belgian steel industries were dependent on the same limited raw material sources (primarily France and Sweden), and it was the German steel industry through its control of the German allocation machinery that was in a position to decide how much iron ore Belgian firms would receive.[82] The decision to reduce Belgian steel production below its prewar level reflected German industry concern over markets and profits although Belgian sources after the war tended to attribute the reduced level of steel production primarily to patriotic resistance.[83]

The manufacture of products based on iron and steel was limited primarily by the amount of raw materials made available. In 1942, the Military Administration noted regretfully that the Central Order Office (ZAST) had to refuse approximately fifty percent of the orders received from Germany because of the shortage of raw materials.[84] This meant that highly specialized capacities such as railroad and shipbuilding yards went unused. Despite these complaints, the volume of metallurgical production delivered to Germany increased through 1943, as shown by the following table.

Table 6[85]

Metallurgical Products Delivered to Germany 1940-1944

Year	Tons	Value (Million RM)
1940-41 (June 1, 1940-Dec 31. 1941)	347,544	240.0
1942	357,760	351.2
1943	438,935	521.4
1944 (to June 30)	156,973	228.1
TOTAL	1,301,212	1340.7

In prewar years, Belgium also possessed an important up-to-date industry for the production of nonferrous metals, such as copper, lead, zinc and tin. When the Germans first arrived in 1940, they found only small amounts of nonferrous metals on hand, since the Belgian government had exported most of these metals in anticipation of the German invasion.[86] Such supplies as were found in 1940 were largely taken to Germany, on the assumption that the Belgian nonferrous metals industry should draw on recycled supplies and on its waste products.[87]

Production was resumed in 1940 primarily within the framework of *Auftragsverlagerung*. It reached its peak in 1941, but dropped steeply in 1942 because existing supplies now had really been exhausted. Despite this scarcity of nonferrous metals, Belgium continued to be considered the main contributor among the occupied territories of such materials to the German war economy.[88]

In the field of precious metals, German policy was largely one of outright spoliation. Precious metals such as platinum, gold and silver that could be located in Belgium in 1940 were shipped to Germany immediately without consideration for the needs of Belgian industry. At the insistence of the Military Administration, some needed metals were subsequently allocated to Belgian industry, in particular silver for the Belgian chemical industry.[89]

The construction industry worked almost exclusively for the Germans. Most of the German construction work was carried out for airfields and fortifications both in Belgium and in northern France. The Reich also ordered in Belgium temporary housing for bombed-out Germans, with Belgium being reported the second largest producer of such prefabricated homes among all the occupied territories.[90]

German policies toward other major Belgian industries were similar to their policies toward the mining and iron and steel industries. The Germans sought to deal with Belgian industrialists on a "businesslike" basis, trying to secure voluntary collaboration, and using threats and force only when voluntary collaboration broke down. As in coal and steel, the *Warenstellen*, i.e. the responsible desk in the Belgian Department of Economics, played the key role through the power of making allocations of raw materials. Although in theory practically all of Belgian industry was supposed to serve the German war economy, one gains the impression that Belgian managers, sometimes with the connivance of the Military Administration, managed to divert a not insignificant portion of their production to Belgian civilian use.[91]

In general, production proceeded at the pace permitted by the supply of raw materials supplies available during the first two years of the occupation. By early 1942, and very definitely after Stalingrad, production became more difficult as more and more German orders were placed in Belgium at a time when manpower, raw materials and energy were in ever shorter supply, and as managers and workers began to have second thoughts about collaboration. Despite these difficulties, levels of production were maintained at a reasonable though declining level until April 1944.

The trends that have just been outlined also applied to the chemical industry which could be of particular use to

Germany because it had always exported a high percentage of its production.[92] (The Germans felt that they had to be particularly circumspect in their dealings with the Belgian chemical industry because it was especially susceptible to technical or "cold" sabotage.) In 1940 the industry experienced some temporary problems since valuable parts of the production apparatus such as platinum cathodes had been hidden or taken to France, but most of these were returned once the policy to resume work had generally been accepted.[93] By the end of August 1940, one-half to two-thirds of the industry was reported to be working again.[94] By the beginning of 1943 Gaevert, the single most important firm and one of Europe's foremost producers of photographic film and paper, was working at ninety percent of capacity despite the shortage of silver,[95] the basic material for the production of photographic supplies. Belgian nitrate plants supposedly were used to make mining explosives and artificial fertilizer rather than munitions, supplying (in 1941) ninety to one hundred percent of the needs of Belgian agriculture.[96]

The Belgian textile industry, with almost half a million employees, also worked largely for the Germans. Although the industry initially was allowed to resume work at only thirty percent of its 1938 level, a more flexible policy was soon instituted, and by May 1941 the textile industry was working at approximately sixty percent of its prewar capacity.[97] It was allowed to produce minimally for Belgian civilian needs, particularly work clothes, garments for new families, children and young people, but approximately seventy percent of its production went to Germany, primarily for military purposes.

The leather industry likewise served German needs. Only a small and shrinking allocation for shoes was made for the Belgian population. The Germans tried to preserve existing supplies by encouraging concentration on shoe repairs rather than on the production of new shoes. However, the production of wooden shoes was taken up as a specialty, with a total annual production of 8.3 million pairs in 1943.[98]

The operation of all industries required an adequate supply of electricity, gas and water. Total energy production reached its peak at the end of 1941. It then began a slow but steady decline which became precipitous at the start of 1944.[99]

In the early years of the occupation a surplus of electrical power existed,[100] and the Germans could afford to divert some electricity to power grids in western Germany until April 1942. Later, in 1943, with the increased placement of German orders, Belgian plants ran short of energy, and power was transferred to Belgium from the power grid of western Germany to a limited extent.[101] In November 1943, power allocations to industry had to be curtailed by ten percent.[102] The Allied air attacks of April 1944 paralyzed power production. Nevertheless, power was restored during the remaining months of the occupation to a level of seventy-five percent of capacity, reached in August 1944. Despite the admittedly limited restrictions on the use of electric power imposed on industries, no attempt was made to ration its use to private consumers until 1944.[103]

Gas for cooking and heating, however, was in more limited supply, particularly since gas was also used as an industrial fuel. Beginning with the winter of 1942-1943, use in private households was limited to about two-and-one-half hours per day during the coldest winter months.[104] At times of crucial shortages, gas was shut off for industrial enterprises which did not work directly for the German war economy.

Agriculture and Food

The basic goal of German agricultural policy was to make Belgium sufficiently self-sustaining in food to enable the Germans to put the population to work without significant food imports from the Reich or from German-controlled territories. The implementation of this policy faced major difficulties in 1940 because of the "unbalanced" structure of Belgian agriculture.

Prewar Belgian agriculture had been devoted largely to the production of animal food such as meat, poultry, and dairy products. Only twelve percent of its acreage had been employed in the production of plant food for direct human consumption.[105] This emphasis had made it necessary to import large amounts of bread grains and fodder from overseas exceeding one million tons per year.[106] With these imports cut off, Belgian agriculture had to be reoriented toward the direct production of such plant foodstuffs as bread grains and potatoes (which provide the highest calorie yield per acre possible). This meant that a large amount of pasture land would have to be ploughed up to grow grain and potatoes. Effective use of Belgian resources would also have meant drastic curtailment of its livestock which should not have been allowed to compete with human beings for needed plant carbohydrates.[107]

In theory, the German Military Administration instituted just such a policy. In order to make Belgium self-sufficient in food it called for the conversion of 200,000 acres of pasture to grain and potato production, and for a corresponding reduction in livestock, poultry and hogs.[108] In practice, however, most of the livestock (except for hogs) was retained even as more potatoes and grain crops were produced in the middle and later years of the occupation.

As a first step toward the management of a wartime agricultural economy, the Germans in August 1940 asked the Secretaries-General to establish a Department for Agriculture and Food Control (*Département de l'Agriculture et du Ravitaillement*), with responsibility for all functions dealing with the production, distribution and consumption of food.[109] Under its aegis a new comprehensive compulsory agricultural organization called the National Corporation for Agriculture and Food Supply (*Corporation Nationale de l'Agriculture et de l'Alimentation* or CNAA) was to take charge of the production and distribution of agricultural products.[110]

The authority granted to the CNAA was comprehensive in nature. It was empowered to assign production quotas, close or open agricultural enterprises, and to regulate distribution and prices. It had the power to impose fines administratively, and to confiscate products illegally withheld from official distribution channels.[111] In actual fact, its major effort went into the task of persuading farmers to deliver their products at legal prices, so that they would become available to the population through regular rationing channels.

From the beginning, the CNAA was viewed by the population and by Belgian farmers as a tool of the Germans and as a means of exploiting the country. So many legal challenges were posed to the CNAA that it led a highly embattled existence throughout the occupation. But while the Secretary-General of Agriculture De Winter bitterly complained about the lack of cooperation from farmers, local government authorities and the public, and while the Belgian economist Baudhuin considered the work of the organization a failure,[112] in this writer's opinion it contributed significantly to the improvement in the food situation that occurred during the later years of the occupation.

An evaluation of the results of agricultural policies during the occupation encounters a number of difficulties. Statistics are frequently inconclusive or contradictory. For instance, ten to fifteen percent of total agricultural acreage disappeared from the agricultural census during the occupation, probably as a result of the tendency of farmers to underreport acreage in use in order to lower their delivery quotas. One observer estimated that approximately thirty percent of the acreage devoted to production of items for which a delivery obligations existed went unreported in 1941.[113] Yet despite these contradictions certain generalizations are possible.

It is clear that the Germans did not bring about quickly or completely an implementation of their policy to convert an adequate amount of pasture land to the production of carbohydrates for human consumption. According to German statistics, the acreage under cultivation during the occupation actually dropped below that of the prewar years,[114] but this apparent drop was probably a result of the underreporting previously mentioned. As late as 1943 only half the land ordered to be plowed under had actually been converted.[115]

Yet a slow growth in the production of bread grains did take place after the 1940-1941 harvest year (as shown in table 7) from 700,00 tons in 1941 to 888,000 tons in 1943, a twenty-seven percent increase over a three-year period. Probably these statistics underrepresent the increase in grain production that actually occurred.

Table 7

Cereal Grains Yields (1940-41 - 1943-44)

	1940-1941	1941-1942	1942-1943	1943-1944 (est.)
Quantity (Tons)	700,000[115]	750,000[115]	811,000[115]	888,400[116]
Index (1940-1941=100)	100	107.1	115.9	127

A larger percentage of the grain grown in Belgium during the occupation years was used for human rather than animal consumption than had been the case in prewar years. The most telling success was the improvement in the delivery and distribution of cereal grains for human consumption as shown in table 8, amounting to a 144 percent increase over the three-year period. In other words, by the last year of the occupation, the amount available for human consumption had more than doubled.

Table 8

Grain for human consumption available through official distribution channels

	1940-1941	1941-1942	1942-1943	1943-1944
Quantity (Tons)	205,000[115]	371,500[115]	384,000[115]	500,000[116]
Index	100	181	187	244

The production, delivery and distribution of potatoes, the other basic source of cheap plant carbohydrates, increased even more drastically during the war years. In two years the production of potatoes increased by 182 percent to 2.2 million tons.[117] By 1943, sufficient potatoes had become available through regular channels to kill the black market in potatoes.[118]

However, the failure of the German policy of radically converting Belgian agriculture from animal to plant production is most clearly illustrated in the statistics on livestock during the occupation. In fact, cattle livestock in 1941 appeared to have increased by sixty-nine percent over the average of the 1935-1938 prewar years, but this again must be a statistical distortion. It appears, however, that cattle declined only moderately (by a total of twenty percent) over the three years from 1941 to 1944.[119] Some of that decline may be due not to the slaughter of mature animals but to the quick delivery of calves to the market in 1942.[120] The number of milking cows declined only by fourteen percent in 1941 over the prewar average, and remained at that level for the balance of the occupation.[121] Poultry did decline more substantially, by approximately thirty percent from 1941 to 1943. The supply of hogs took the steepest drop, at about fifty percent from prewar days.[122] Table 9 provides more specific detail, but it should be noted that the decrease of livestock in all areas except hogs and poultry remained relatively marginal.

Table 9[123]

Heads of animals (in thousands)

	1935-1938	1941	1942	1943
Horses	255.9	272.6	269.4	268.9
Cattle*	1,755	2,969	1,764	1,504
Cows (in above)	972.9	842	810	857
Hogs	1,022.8	502	444.4	525.6
Sheep		198	185.8	216.4
Poultry	1,361.5**	3,281.6	2,629.9	2,227.1

* After 1941, counted from the middle of May.
** 1935-1938 only laying hens.

The evidence at hand suggests that the Germans failed at first but subsequently succeeded in their objective to make Belgium essentially self-sufficient in food, although admittedly at a quantitatively and particularly qualitatively marginal level of consumption. The reasons for the original failure are not difficult to identify. During the first year of the occupation (1940-1941) the Belgian food supply was based on the prewar production pattern that produced the 1940 harvest. It took some time to put the new agricultural plan into place which meant that it failed to be sufficiently effective during the 1941 harvest year.

In the face of Belgian resistance, the Germans compromised in this area as in a number of others. They gradually put the administrative machinery into place which would eventually convert Belgian agriculture and consumption patterns to a wartime food economy at least partially. By the last harvest year of the occupation, they had come close to achieving a tolerable food balance in the occupied territory, ending the dependence on grain imports from Germany,[124] without causing any fundamental dislocation in Belgian agriculture. In fact, Belgian farmers managed by the summer of 1942 to produce additional potatoes, and cereal grains for human and animal consumption, not only to feed the population at a minimal level (admittedly below that of neighboring countries) but also to preserve the bulk of their livestock.

The problem of redirecting agricultural production had a serious impact on food consumption very soon after the start of the occupation. Even though the Germans failed to supply the Belgian population with sufficient food during the first two years of the occupation, the failure was not for lack of trying. During this period, the Military Administration pleaded incessantly with the central Reich authorities for more food imports. Unfortunately Berlin was rather uncooperative and the actual situation in Belgium remained grim until the summer of 1942.

It has been mentioned previously that cereal grains and potatoes constituted the two fundamental pillars of the wartime diet of occupied Europe. Therefore, bread and potatoes were rationed immediately in May and June 1940 through the rationing machinery put into place by the Belgian government before May 10, 1940. The daily bread ration was set in June 1940 at 225 g, and the potato ration at 500 g.[125] With only two months of grain supplies (100,000 tons) on hand by the end of May, imports from northern France closed the gap until the 1940 harvest came to market.[126] Sufficient cereal grains were imported during the first year to provide by and large enough bread to meet the existing 225 g ration. But this bread ration by itself provided insufficient calories for a normal person.

Potatoes were a different story. For one thing, military operations in May 1940 had coincided with the planting season for potatoes, and therefore the 1940 harvest was below normal.[127] Moreover, under wartime conditions, potatoes were becoming a more important part of the diet. Hence, the amount of potatoes imported and available for distribution was entirely inadequate during the first two years of the occupation. In December 1940, for instance, only forty percent of the amount needed to meet the level set by rationing was available for distribution.[128] The situation remained problematic in 1941 but eased in 1942 when the Germans allowed the urban population to make contracts with farmers for direct sale and delivery.[129]

Meat supplies had held up at the level authorized by rationing until December 1940, since farmers marketed an increased number of animals, as they could no longer secure adequate feed for their herds. By January 1941, however, this source of supply had dried up, and for the next few months it proved practically impossible to buy any meat in regular stores, let alone the amount allowed by the official rationing.[130] By the summer of 1941, enough meat became available again to supply the meager ration.[131]

With the spring of 1942, the food situation finally began to look up. From now on, stores usually would receive enough food to allow the population to get the amounts stipulated in their rations. Fruit and vegetables which were not rationed also reached the market in larger amounts. In the winter of 1942-1943 herring became plentiful providing a protein food supplement that had not been available heretofore.[132]

These improvements continued in 1943. The fat ration was increased by a total of twenty-five percent, from about 300 g to an eventual 400 g per month, while in June the sugar ration was increased by fifty percent. Most importantly, however, the bread ration was raised from 225 g per day to 300 g.[133]

The final months of the occupation witnessed again some worsening in the food situation, due to the dislocation of transportation in the wake of the Allied air offensive, and to the reluctance on the part of the farm population to market its products. At times even bread was again in short supply, and the fat ration was lowered by thirty percent.[134] In the eastern part of the country, food temporarily became so scarce that renewed food strikes broke out in July.[135]

In summary, German policies failed during the first two years of the occupation and partially succeeded during the last two years (except for the final months in 1944) to provide a minimally adequate intake of calories, although many marginal individuals were gravely undernourished, and although the nutritional value of available food was very poor.

The high level of prewar beer and tobacco consumption presented the German and Belgian authorities with a special set of problems. Before the war, Belgium had the highest per capita consumption of beer of any country in the world,[136] and Belgian per capita tobacco consumption had been one-and-one-half times that of Germany.[137] These habits made all attempts at control more or less ineffective.

However, the Germans tried. They ordered beer rationing in January 1941, requiring the delivery of a stamp providing for one day's bread ration for the consumption of one liter of beer.[138] As a result of this regulation, the consumption of beer almost ceased, and existing stocks began to spoil. Since this situation aroused a storm of complaints it was abolished in April 1941. At the same time, the Germans ordered a decrease in the alcoholic content of beer to minimize the need for grain.[139]

The Germans met similar problems in their attempt to regulate tobacco consumption. The original distribution system based on store-by-store rationing proved ineffective since tobacco growers sold most of their production to the black market. Finally a new rationing system was instituted in 1943, giving male inhabitants over eighteen a certain number of points, analogous to the system prevailing for other consumer goods.[140] Allegedly this system functioned effectively during the last year of the occupation, but according to German estimates for the occupation as a whole, at most fifty percent of Belgian tobacco products were sold through regular channels, while the balance went into the black market. However, deliveries to the German military, set in 1940 at between ten to thirty percent of estimated Belgian production, were met in full.[141] Overall, it has been estimated that tobacco consumption during the war amounted to 125g per month per capita,[142] or approximately one third of prewar consumption.[143]

Since most goods, and particularly food items were in such short supply, the black market became an almost universal fact of life during the occupation. German services and businessmen, and almost every consumer in Belgium participated in black market transactions at one time or another.[144] Black market dealings were more widespread in Belgium than in other occupied territories in Western Europe because of the special circumstances prevailing in Belgium.

To begin with, food shortages were more severe than elsewhere in the West. Moreover, Belgian authorities were unwilling to impose sufficiently high taxes or exact compulsory savings to siphon off the extra liquidity created by German orders under conditions of utter scarcity.[145] Above all, the people of Belgium, raised in a spirit of individualism and suspicion of all government, had very little respect for rationing and price regulations, especially since existing shortages were attributed to German plunder.[146] Finally, German authorities insisted on maintaining a rigid official price level which, given the shortage of food and other consumer goods, and the absence of a common ethic with regard to regulations, made the appearance of a huge black market virtually inevitable.

Quite apart from the lack of Belgian cooperation, the Germans themselves were far from displaying unified attitudes or policies. To be true, the central Military Administration consistently pleaded for rigorous enforcement of rationing and other economic regulations in the interest of an orderly exploitation of the country and of social justice. But while the Military Administration tried to limit illegal transactions and to provide for a coordinated guided economic system, other German agencies engaged in large scale purchases at cross purposes with the policies of the Military Administration. Time and time again, the Military Administration complained that the transactions of German agencies rather than the illegal purchases of Belgian consumers formed the backbone of the black market.

In order to effect some control over German black market purchases, a special Coordinating Purchasing Agency, (*Zentralmeldestelle*), was established in March 1942, to be replaced in August by an agency with more comprehensive power (*Überwachungsstelle*). During the ensuing period, supposedly all German purchases in Belgium regardless of agency or branch of service had to be submitted to the approval of that agency, but those regulations too were evaded.[147] Finally, in March and April 1943, Göring, at the urging of the Military Administration, decided to prohibit all German black market purchases.[148] This new policy brought some relief in the situation, but it did not extinguish the black market.

This ambivalence on the part of German authorities made enforcement of economic regulations by the Military Administration difficult. Prosecutions instituted against Belgian black market operators often had to be terminated or were dismissed because the Belgian defendants enjoyed the protection of German customers. The German desire to secure needed supplies was simply too great to allow an orderly process in the face of the willingness of Belgian producers and businessmen to engage in black market transactions.

The failure of the Military Administration to combact the black market and other economic transgressions more effectively was not from lack of trying. A stream of German and Belgian regulations were issued, but only to limited avail. The Military Administration tried to restrain illegal profiteering by increasing penalties for the violation of economic regulations, particularly for large-scale black market dealings. Already in 1941 an attempt was made to induce military courts to impose the death penalty as a warning and deterrent, but this attempt ended in failure, when it turned out that German agencies were involved in the transactions for which Belgian black market operators were to be punished.[149] No executions for economic penalties are on record, but some black marketeers ended up in prison and in concentration camps.

The measures to restrain the black market made a major impact only after the spring of 1943, following the cessation of large-scale German purchases on the black market. From that point on, the Military Administration noted a significant decline in black market activities, but is is impossible to determine to which extent the penalties threatened or imposed for economic trangressions were responsible for this reduction.

In order to enforce economic regulations, the German Military Administration at first relied on the various control services attached to the responsible Belgian government agencies. In August 1941, these several control services were concentrated into one organization in the Department of Interior under a Director-General named Woestijn, and the personnel of this new service was eventually augmented to over five thousand men.[150] However, this new centralized control service disappointed German hopes. Therefore, the Germans in October 1942 established a control service of their own, the *Wirtschaftliche Fahndungsdienst* (Economic Investigative Service), under the Economics Division of the Military Administration. This new service was led largely by German officers some of whom were SIPO officials, but the rank and file was made up of Belgian nationals.

In addition, the Military Administration created a Control Corps, composed of Belgians but attached to the *Fahndungsdienst*, which received as its special assignment supervision of restaurants and small retail outlets. The functions of the Control Corps were purely investigative, whereas the *Fahndungsdienst* had executive authority, with power to arrest individuals and confiscate goods. The Security Police limited its involvement to large-scale black market operations which came to its attention through special information, whereas the *Fahndungsdienst* tried to deal with infractions of all kinds.[151]

None of these services had any authority over German personnel involved in black market operations, and experience showed that military courts tended to protect Germans accused of violation of economic regulations. Restaurants in particular remained a sore point with the Military Administration, since they were protected by other German agencies, and by Göring's wish to maintain peacetime appearances as much as possible. Only in 1943 and 1944, when Göring's protection was withdrawn, could the Military Administration take effective steps against these "sacred cows," closing a number of establishments permanently or for a stated period of time, and levying large fines against their operators.[152]

Labor and the Labor Draft

The German campaign to exploit Belgian labor can be divided into three periods. The first period lasted from June 1940 to March 1942. During this period, recruitment for work in Belgium and Germany was supposedly "voluntary" although increasing pressure was applied to persuade workers to accept assignments in Germany. The second period lasted from March to October 1942. During this interval workers could be assigned to jobs in Belgium, but recruitment for work in Germany remained "voluntary". The third period, the period of the Sauckel "slave labor" draft, lasted from October 1942 to the end of the occupation. Now Belgian workers could be ordered to accept jobs in Germany and forced to do so if necessary.

The basic administrative machinery for manpower utilization had been created during the first year of the occupation. Within the German Command structure, the direction of manpower rested with Group VII (*Gruppe Arbeit*) of the Economics Division, headed by a certain Dr. Schultze. Group VII had under its supervision and control the local German labor offices or *Werbestellen* which were largely staffed by Belgian employees. Over time, Schultze and his service acquired an increasing decree of independence from Reeder's direction, especially after 1942 when Schultze was appointed Sauckel's representative for Belgium.

Within the Belgian administration, the Department of Labor and Social Welfare (*Département du Travail et de la Prévoyance Sociale*) was responsible for Belgian employment services. It established in June 1940 a special employment office called *Office National de Placement et de Contrôle*.[153] In April 1941, this office was given a monopoly over all employment and placement activities, and was renamed National Labor Office (*Office National du Travail* or ONT).[154]

In November 1940 Fr. J. Hendriks, formerly the personnel director of the Belgian branch of the Philips firm and a member of the VNV, was appointed to head the ONT. It soon turned out that Hendriks was decidedly pro-German, that he admired German institutions and methods of comprehensive state management of job placement and of an inclusive social welfare system.[155] Because of his admiration for German methods of labor management, he was willing to collaborate with German authorities over the heads of his superiors and of the cabinet of Secretaries-General. The Germans protected their protegé against attempts by successive Secretaries-General of Labor to remove him and made it possible for him to do their bidding in almost complete independence from his hierarchical superiors. With Hendriks' approval and assistance, the German *Werbestellen* exerted ever closer supervision over local Belgian Offices, until the ONT became virtually the executive branch of the German administration with respect to compulsory placement in Belgium, and a subordinate but cooperative partner in the administration of compulsory labor in Germany.[156]

At first, in the summer of 1940, the German administration claimed that it viewed the reduction of unemployment as its most immediate task. It has been estimated that initially unemployment stood at 600,000,[157] almost fifty percent above the previous peak reached in 1938.[158] The Germans expected to put most of the unemployed back to work primarily in Belgium, but from the very beginning they also hoped to recruit sizeable numbers of Belgians for work in Germany. In June 1940 they threatened to deport 15,000 miners to the

Ruhr, but were deterred from doing so by the protest of the Belgian Secretaries- General.[159] These threats of deportation of smaller groups of skilled workers continued to crop up during the early years of the occupation, usually at the instigation of Reich authorities, but the Military Administration, mindful of the antagonisms created by the World War I labor draft, emphatically preferred to rely on voluntary recruitment. The same memory of wartime deportations also inclined the Belgian administration at first toward cooperation with the Germans. That attitude explains in part why it was prepared to assist the Germans in 1940 with recruitment for voluntary work in Germany.[160]

Within this mutually understood framework, an agreement was worked out between Belgian and German authorities in June 1940, which stipulated that:

(1) workers would be free to accept or refuse work in Germany,

(2) such refusal would not lead to the withdrawal of unemployment or welfare payments in Belgium,

(3) Belgian workers in Germany would not have to work in armaments or munitions factories,

(4) they would receive the same welfare and social benefits as German workers.[161]

Instructions designed to implement this agreement were sent out by the Department to regional employment offices by the end of July. These employment offices were ordered to post German announcements and provide information and advice about work in Germany as requested. The same circular also reminded local administrations of the existing regulation denying unemployment benefits to unemployed persons refusing to work in Belgium. In view of subsequent developments, it has been argued that these instructions had an ultimately detrimental effect by setting local employment offices on the course of collaboration with German services.[162]

During the first year of the occupation, German and Belgian agencies were so successful in reducing existing unemployment, that by July 1941 the number of unemployed had declined from 600,000 to 110,000, despite the large number of individuals who had returned from France and from prisoner of war camps. At that point (July 1941), 189,000 persons had volunteered for work in Germany according to German figures.[163] However, after the invasion of the Soviet Union on June 22, 1941, enlistments dropped drastically. Despite a modest recovery the limits of what could be considered genuinely voluntary recruitment had been reached by the summer of 1941.[164]

Therefore, the Germans applied increasing pressure to persons not regularly employed. To accomplish this, they used prewar regulations requiring able-bodied recipients of unemployment benefits to perform part-time work on projects of public utility. In 1941, special public work projects were organized for such people within the framework of the reconstruction program. The Germans, through the ONT, made sure that these projects provided work under conditions of considerable hardship, in an attempt to induce the unemployed to volunteer for work in Germany as the lesser evil. They also sought to classify individuals unwilling to accept work anywhere in Belgium as being "asocial" and subject to forcible placement in the projects described. Refusals to cooperate were to be considered sabotage.[165] In violation of the June 1940 agreement, "contract breakers" were refused unemployment benefits, and by 1941 local employment offices under German pressure sometimes denied benefits and even threatened to prevent the issuance of rationing stamps to persons unwilling to accept work assignments.[166]

This deteriorating situation raises the question how "voluntary" labor recruitment for Germany was during this allegedly voluntary period. It is safe to say that recruitment was more voluntary at the beginning of the occupation than in 1941-1942, particularly since contracts without time limits replaced term contracts by early 1941.[167] Increasingly direct and indirect compulsion was employed in 1941 and during the early months of 1942. However, it is also true that persons securely employed on a full-time basis by and large were not threatened, although the Germans attempted to force Belgian business concerns to replace younger single people with older personnel and with men with families who were less likely to "volunteer" for work in Germany. The prime targets for labor recruitment during this period were younger people and persons not fully or permanently employed, or those dismissed by Belgian enterprises on German orders. For this group, pressure intensified to such an extent that toward the end of the period supposedly "voluntary" recruitment for work in Germany had largely lost its voluntary character.

The imposition of compulsory labor service to be performed in Belgium had been under consideration by German authorities ever since February 1941, when this step was taken in neighboring Holland. The strong preference of the Military Administration for "voluntary" methods short of legal compulsion had delayed imposition of the draft for a year. However, the shortage of labor in Germany became ever more pressing with the prolongation of the conflict in the East. This urgency found its expression in the appointment of *Gauleiter* Sauckel as Plenipotentiary for Labor in March 1942 and led to the imposition on March 6, 1942 of compulsory labor service in Belgium. In reality, this measure was designed to increase pressure to accept work in Germany and to set up the machinery for the forthcoming labor draft to be performed in Germany.[168]

The March 1942 decree established the authority of the Military Administration to assign residents of the occupied territory to designated places of work within Belgium. It required employers to secure prior approval for the hiring of workers and employees. German authorities could also order Belgian employers to release workers. The German labor offices (*Werbestellen*) were given ultimate authority over the implementation of the decree, but the ONT was required to carry out the instructions of local German authorities, thus by-passing central Belgian officials.

In its discussions with the Secretaries-General, the Military Administration tried to minimize and soften the implications of the decree. First of all, they promised that Belgian workers would not be forced to work in Germany or northern France and that exemptions would be granted to persons in such categories as government employees, priests, mineworkers, and the dependents of Belgians serving in German military units. The Germans also asserted that they did not intend to draft "intellectuals" and others unsuited for factory work.[169]

Regulations implementing the labor draft required Belgian employers to file lists of their workers and employees with the Belgian labor offices, and to report promptly any proposed hirings or dismissals. Local Belgian Labor Offices were assigned the task of delivering summonses to persons assigned to designated places of labor.[170] At first, Belgian employers were slow to deliver the required personnel lists, since they were well aware of the fact that these would provide a basis for future deportations to Germany. When the Germans threatened fines and imprisonments, most Belgian employers eventually complied and the few who failed to do so were fined heavily.[171]

In May, the Germans futher tightened the screws, by prohibiting unemployment and welfare payments to persons unwilling to accept labor assignments, and to persons out of work or employed only on a part-time basis.[172] Since the Belgian Department refused to lend its cooperation to this measure the Germans ordered the ONT to proceed with its implementation. Most local Belgian labor offices cooperated with the *Werbestellen*, although a few ONT officials resigned in the wake of the decree.[173]

During this period, from March to October 1942, recruitment proceeded in the following manner: Local Belgian labor offices sent job applicants to the German *Werbestellen* for registration and additional information about work available in Germany. The persons concerned were told that they would not be forced to work in Germany, but the names of individuals who refused to report to the *Werbestellen* were sent to German authorities by the ONT. They were classified in the "asocial" category and became subject to forced placement in reeducation camps. As has been mentioned before, conditions in these camps were deliberately made unpleasant to encourage inmates to volunteer for work in Germany after all.[174]

The final imposition of compulsory labor service in Germany came about as the result of a Europe-wide attempt by Sauckel to increase the number of foreign workers in German factories. On Sauckel's insistance, the Military Command reluctantly issued on October 6, 1942 the decree which established the compulsory labor draft for Germany.[175] This decree authorized the Military Commander to impose the obligation to work in Germany on men aged eighteen to fifty, and on single women between the ages of twenty-one and thirty-five.[176] The minimum age of the draft for women was later lowered to eighteen.[177] In order to free labor for work in Germany, all employers except government services were required to secure prior approval of the Belgian labor offices for dismissals and for the hiring of new workers. Persons not in possession of a definite work contract were required to register with a Belgian labor office.

The German labor offices attached to the local Military Command were responsible for the administration of the labor draft for Germany, while the Belgian labor offices retained their responsibility for the implementation of labor assignments in Belgium. However, they also were required to assist the German agencies indirectly with the recruitment for work in Germany.[178]

During the first phase of the labor draft for Germany, the Germans tried to recruit primarily skilled labor from Belgian industry by "combing out" Belgian industry for potential labor draftees (*Auskämmungsaktion*). During this period German teams visited Belgian factories to identify workers suitable for work in Germany. Next, officials from the local Belgian labor office interviewed persons so designated at their place of work to determine whether there existed any special hardship conditions which would preclude their dispatch to Germany. On the basis of the amended list, the German *Werbestellen* would then call up the persons concerned. The person so designated had at least seven days before actual departure for Germany.[179] In the beginning months, the great majority of workers called up did depart from fear of reprisals against themselves and their families.[180]

By the spring of 1943 it became apparent that the pool of skilled labor that could be drawn from Belgian industry had began to run dry. Now the Germans increasingly turned to call-ups by age groups, concentrating on workers in their early twenties. For a while in 1943 both actions, the recruitment from industry , and the designation by age groups, went on side by side, but by September 1943 the focus clearly was on the draft of men born in 1920 and 1921. By that time, older workers had become virtually exempt from labor recruitment, provided they found employment in Belgium, and provided they were not already under contract or had not been called up already. Later on, these latter groups, too, increasingly were left alone.[181]

To implement the basic October 1942 decree, the Germans published a number of subsidiary measures. A minimum work week of forty-eight hours was established,[182] and employers were required to release workers no longer needed as a result of the lengthening of the work week.[183] In November, six-month prison sentences were provided as a penalty for persons refusing to work in Germany.[184] In March 1943 the Military Administration, under pressure from Sauckel, issued an order to deny rationing books and stamps to such persons,[185] but this decree was soon suspended, since the Belgian administration refused to participate in its implementation.[186] In June 1943, the Germans tried to introduce a "Labor Book" (*Arbeitsbuch*),[187] but this measure too was never implemented because Belgian officials refused to cooperate.[188]

In response to the protests of the Secretaries-General, the Germans promised to desist from the deportation of women, with the exception of domestic servants. However women were drafted for work in Belgium starting in 1943. Women who refused to respond to such summonses were arrested and sent to prison or to labor reeducation camps.[189] Pregnant women and women with children were exempt from the draft.

Despite problems with German statistics on the labor draft, it is apparent that the new measure was successful in the first six months of its implementation. According to German records, over one hundred thousand Belgian workers departed for Germany during that period.[190] Starting in May

1943 however, the number of persons recruited for work in Germany began to drop, despite the new policy of drafting entire age cohorts of young men. It appears that in the period from May 20 to December 1, 1943, only approximately 49,000 workers were recruited for Germany, or half of the number of the preceding six-month period. In the closing months of the occupation the Germans managed to increase moderately the number of men sent to Germany by conducting large scale raids, but despite this limited success the number of contracts issued between December 1, 1943 and August 15, 1944 amounted only to 38,000, or fewer than five thousand workers per month.*

In line with its long standing policy of treating intellectuals and the Belgian elites leaders with discretion, the Military Administration at first used great caution in applying the labor draft to secondary school and university students. Students in secondary and vocational schools remained exempted from the labor draft until the end of the occupation,[191] but in March 1943 the Military Administration, under heavy pressure from the Sauckel organization,[192] required them to serve in Germany or in Belgian industry for one year upon graduation. They were to be allowed to register at institutions of higher education only after completing their year of labor duty.[193] First-year university students were required to perform six months' labor service in Belgium between May 1 and October 1, 1943, at which time they could be readmitted for their second year of study. First-year students failing to report for labor service as specified would be liable to being sent to Germany for an indefinite period of time.[194] Threats were also made that their families would be drafted if the students themselves could not be located. No work requirement was imposed on second and third-year students.

The implementation of this decree ran into difficulties. At the instruction of the Secretary-General of Education, the heads of the educational institutions concerned refused to communicate these regulations to their students.[195] Therefore

---

* See table 10 for numbers of workers in Germany.

the Germans had to take recourse to publishing their mandates in the press, and having students report to the labor offices directly. When the Germans next asked the heads of secondary schools and for lists of their graduates or first-year students respectively, these officials refused to furnish the lists concerned. In a number of instances, uncooperative educational administrators were arrested and imprisoned for a period of time.[196] The head of the University of Liège, and the Rector of the Catholic University of Louvain who had destroyed or removed student lists, were tried and sentenced to serve time in prison.[197]

A further difficulty arose in the fall of 1943 over the control of the enrollment of second-year students. Belgian authorities declared themselves unwilling to ask students to produce a certificate that they had worked for six months as a condition of allowing them to register for the second year. Instead, it was agreed that the Germans would check the publicly posted examination lists in order to make certain that students registered for the second year had met their obligations.[198]

Through these various compromises, the Military Administration had met more or less the demands placed upon it by the Sauckel organization. One group of students had been forced to work for the German war effort for six months. It was reported that, on an overall basis, seventy-one percent of all first-year students had signed up for their six-month stint, with the largest number of refusals coming from the Universities of Louvain and Liège, and with almost one hundred percent compliance at Ghent. According to German records, almost four thousand university students were put to work in the summer of 1943, three-quarters of them in industry.[199] Most of these students returned to their studies in the fall.

Through its relatively "cautious" policy the Military Administration managed to keep the Belgian universities functioning until the spring of 1944 in contrast to the situation in the Netherlands and in Norway where the application of the labor draft to university students had led to the virtual closing of institutions of higher education.

The Economic Exploitation of Belgium 235

It is difficult to assess with any degree of accuracy the results of the German effort to recruit labor for work in Germany during the occupation. In order to impress Berlin the figures supplied by the Military Administration were inflated, because they counted cumulatively each new enlistment and re-enlistment and because they disregarded the substantial number of workers returned from Germany. The figures furnished by central German agencies such as the Ministry of Labor are much lower than those supplied by the Military Administration. Data supplied by the *Rüstungsinspektion Belgien* generally tally with those of the Military Administration, and reflect the same desire to maximize the achievements of German recruitment efforts.

Despite these difficulties, a number of conclusions can be drawn from such figures as are available. Table 10 below is based on a table compiled by the German scholar Mathias Haupt.[200]

The examination of table 10 permits us to state with some assurance that, during the period of voluntary labor recruitment which ended in March 1942, approximately 280,000 labor contracts (including some renewals) had been issued and that by the end of this period approximately half of the number recruited (130,000-150,000) were at work in Germany. The other half must have returned from Germany legally or illegally. It may be assumed that during the seven months following the imposition of the required labor in Belgium (March-October 1942) the number of new recruits dispatched to Germany at best equalled the number of returnees, and that consequently the number of Belgian workers in Germany either remained static or declined. The implementation of the labor draft for Germany in October 1942 at first led to a substantial increase in the numbers recruited for work in Germany. The cumulative half million mark of workers recruited from the Command Area was reached by May 1943. For the entire twenty-two month period during which the compulsory October 1942 labor draft was in effect, approximately 200,000 contracts were issued, as compared to 250,000 - 280,000 issued during the period of voluntary recruitment.

Table 10

Belgian workers with contracts and Belgian workers in Germany

Date	With Labor Contracts	In Germany	Source*
7 Dec 1940	90,423		T 12, p.70
18 Jan 1941	100,000		Wi/IA4 .34 - MAF
25 Apr 1941		86,349	R 41/166 - BAK
20 Aug 1941	200,000		Wi/IA4 .21 - MAF
15 Jan 1942	250,000		Wi/IA4 .23 - MAF
20 Jan 1942		131,000	R 41/141 - BAK
31 May 1942	300,670		T 20, p. C-12
31 Aug 1942	325,235		T 21, p. D-15
19 Dec 1942	398,270		T 22, p. D-12
14 Jan 1943		250,000	R 41/141 - BAK
20 May 1943	500,000		Wi/IA4 .27 - MAF
July 1943		310,000	R 41/276 - BAK
Autumn 1943		228,000	IMT, Suppt A, 876, also cited in Homze,[201] p. 195
15 Nov 1943		220,621	Homze, p. 148**
1 Dec 1943	548,937		Wi/IA4 .29 - MAF
Mid Aug 1944	586,746		Wi/IA4 .3 - MAF
Total Repatriated to Belgium to May 1945		215,000***	Billiard, *La Collaboration Industrielle*, p. 14, also cited in Haupt, p.84.

* See Selected Abbreviations and Notes below for explanation of abbreviations of source material citations.
** Citing Der Beauftragte für den Vierjahresplan/Der Generalbevollmächtigte für den Arbeitseinsatz NR. 1/1944.
*** According to Billiard, 275,000 Belgians were repatriated including 60,000 prisoners of war. Therefore the figure of 215,000 includes not just labor draftees but also an unknown number of political prisoners.

The number of Belgian workers in Germany probably attained its peak in the summer of 1943 at a level somewhere between 250,000 and 300,000. By the autumn of 1943, it was down to 220,000 - 230,000 workers. This was somewhat larger than the number of civilians repatriated after the end of the war (215,000), which leads to the conclusion that the additional 86,500 workers recruited for work in Germany between May 1943 and the end of the occupation did not even replace the number of Belgian workers who returned to their country during that period.

Probably the main reason for the decline in labor recruitment was the growing resistance to deportation and the exhaustion of the basic labor pool, but German policies also contributed to the decrease. In the first place, the Military Administration was less than enthusiastic about rigid enforcement of the draft that was likely to drive additional workers into the Resistance. In the second place, by 1943 Speer had gained increasing acceptance for his policy of placing more orders in the occupied territories. This policy in turn provided more Belgian workers with jobs in "blocked" plants which gained them exemption from deportation. In the end, the Germans granted exemptions even to young people born in 1920-1924. In this manner the conflict between two contradictory German policies, added to the growing resistance of Belgian workers to the labor draft, produced the decline in 1943 and 1944 reflected in the statistics.

There remains the question as to whether the imposition of the compulsory labor draft for work in Germany turned out to be a mistake from the German point of view, as the Military Administration had predicted. The political price certainly was heavy. It poisoned the climate of cooperation with Belgian authorities,[202] undermined the position of Belgian collaborationists, and led to a substantial growth of the Resistance movement. (Wags in the Military Administration claimed that Sauckel had been promoted to the position of "Honorary Chief of the Partisans.")[203] Moreover the draft had tied down a considerable number of German and Belgian personnel. Certainly by 1944 the system had lost its justification, as ever fewer draftees responded to call-ups. Thus it would seem that the compulsory draft was successful for the first few months, but that after the middle of 1943 it hardly justified the effort the Germans put into it.

The Management of Finances, Wages and Prices

In the weeks immediately following the capitulation of May 28, 1940, the country faced pressing financial problems. The National Bank (*Banque Nationale*) had not only sent its gold and foreign currency reserves abroad prior to the invasion, but it also had carried with it to France its supplies of bank notes and even the dies from which bank notes were printed.[204] Therefore, authorities left in Belgium had to find a way to pay salaries to government workers and to meet other government obligations such as welfare payments. In addition, a way had to be found to print and issue bank notes in order to sustain economic life in the occupied territory.

As a first step, Belgian authorities, with the approval of the Military Administration, established on June 28, 1940, a lending institution (the *Caisse d'Avances et de Prêts*) with working capital borrowed from large banks and industrial concerns. The declared main purpose of this institution was to make advances to governmental and semigovernmental entities (such as the railroads) so that these could make salary payments and meet their own obligations.[205] In line with instructions given to business leaders by the departing Pierlot government, the *Caisse d'Avances et de Prêts* later also assumed responsibility for supporting individuals who had been dismissed at the behest of German authorities,[206] and it even gave support to emerging Resistance organizations.[207] Its total expenditures were reported to have amounted to BFrs 280 million.[208]

In order to have at their disposal a mechanism for issuing bank notes and for carrying out other financial transactions previously managed by the National Bank, the Germans authorized in a decree of June 27, 1940 the establishment of a "Bank of Issue" (*Banque d'Emission*).[209] This bank was incorporated under Belgian law on July 13 with a Board of Directors which included not only many of the luminaries of Belgian business and banking, but also the two Secretaries-General Leemans and Plisnier.[210]

The initial statutes envisioned the appointment of a president subject to approval and dismissal by the Military Administration. The scope of competence of the *Banque d'Emission* was comprehensively defined. It included from the beginning the authority to buy and sell treasury bonds, to issue short-term loans, and, most importantly in the light of subsequent trends, to conduct exchange operations with other countries. The original charter also stated explicitly that the bank was required to "carry out all banking and cash operations for the administration of the occupied territories and to serve...as the intermediary for financial transactions between public institutions in the...occupied territories."[211]

When the National Bank returned from France in August 1940 with its stock of bank notes and dies, the Bank of Issue continued to operate, even though the National Bank resumed its task as the primary note and credit-issuing institution of the country. Subsequently a differentiation of functions was developed. The National Bank was to continue to carry the normal peacetime functions of a central bank, whereas the *Banque d'Emission* was to become the vehicle through which business transactions in connection with the occupation of the country were to be conducted.[212] It lent itself well to this task in the opinion of the Military Administration because of its more "flexible" statutes.[213] Since traditional banking leaders dominated its governing board, the Germans did not fully trust the leadership of the Bank, out of fear that it would attempt to maintain a degree of control over transactions with Germany. Indeed the administration of the Clearing account between Belgium and Germany and between European countries in the German orbit became the most important task of the bank during the occupation. In essence it used its funds (which were borrowed from the National Bank) to pay Belgian creditors for goods delivered or services rendered to German agencies and enterprises or to enterprises located within the German economic orbit. In this manner, the *Banque d'Emission* became the principal financial instrument of the German economic exploitation of Belgium.[214]

One key decision was made early in the occupation. In order to make it less expensive for Germany to pay for purchases, the Belgian currency was devalued against the German Mark by twenty percent, from a ratio of ten German Marks for one hundred Belgian Francs to a ratio of eight Marks for one hundred Francs.[215] This devaluation also helped to mask the magnitude of the German exploitation of the country by keeping the Clearing deficit smaller than it would have been under the old ratio.[216] The inflation that occurred, including black market prices, may be viewed in part as a reflection of this devaluation of the Belgian Franc.

The overriding objective of German fiscal management was to secure funds for the purchase of goods and services to be extracted from the occupied territory without significantly burdening the German treasury and without destroying the basic financial structure and economic life of occupied Belgium. Its two main fiscal instruments to achieve this goal were (1) payments for (alleged) occupation costs (*Besatzungskosten*) and (2) the German-Belgian Clearing.

The concept of payments for the support of the occupying army and its administrative apparatus had been legitimized by The Hague Convention of 1907.[217] The Germans, however, perverted the use of this mechanism by using funds collected from the Belgian state not only for a variety of "legitimate" military purchases but also for purchases made in the black market, and for other transactions intended to escape the scrutiny of Belgian authorities. Occupation cost payments were set at one billion Francs per month for the period from January 1941 to August 1941, and at 1.5 billion Francs from September 1941 to the end of the occupation. Including two lump payments demanded in 1940, the total amount collected for occupation costs until August 1944 was presented at Nuremberg as coming to approximately sixty-seven billion Francs.[218] These amounts vastly exceeded the cost of maintaining German personnel and troops in Belgium and therefore constituted a war tribute.

Whereas occupation costs were set at fixed amounts after December 1940, the Clearing constituted an open-ended account which allowed the Germans to make unrestrained purchases limited only by the availability of goods and services. German firms and agencies deposited the purchase price of goods acquired in Belgium in German Marks in the Clearing account of the *Reichsbank* in Germany. The Belgian seller in turn received his payment in Belgian Francs from the Clearing account of the Belgian Bank of Issue. Belgian purchases in Germany were governed by the same principle but amounted only to a little more than one third of the amounts spent for German purchases in Belgium. By August 1944, the total payments for goods and services rendered to Belgium by Germany and other countries in the Clearing added up to thirty-six billion Belgian Francs as compared to payments owed to Belgium to the amount of one hundred billion Belgian Francs.[219] Throughout the occupation, the Clearing balance was always in favor of Belgium, particularly so after 1941, when Germany had fewer goods to sell, and when an increasing number of orders was placed with Belgian firms. By the end of the occupation this balance amounted to some sixty-two billion Francs.[220]

The table below shows the state of the Clearing balance at the end of each calendar year.

Table 11[221]

Cumulative Clearing balance

Years	Billion Francs
1940	.881
1941	7.852
1942	24.706
1943	48.775
1944 (August)	62.413

This vast payments imbalance inevitably led to a steady and increasing expansion of the Belgian currency since additional banknotes or bank papers had to be issued to make payments for goods furnished to German agencies and private firms.

According to Belgian government figures submitted at Nuremberg the amount of currency in circulation increased by 236 percent during the occupation.[222] German sources suggest that this increase was more than threefold as shown in the following table.

Table 12[223]

Currency expansion 1940-1944
(in billion Francs)

Dates	Banknotes	Total currency
Oct. 1, 1940		30.000
Jan. 30, 1941	35.626	39.938
Feb.1, 1942	48.834	52.565
Jan. 1, 1943	67.429	71.678
Jan. 1, 1944		87.664
June 22, 1944	95.087	

This expansion of currency presented a serious inflationary threat since the growing scarcity of goods in the occupied territory made it impossible to spend the amounts received as a result of these transactions. Part of this surplus purchasing power was siphoned off by increased taxation and by a growing number of internal loans. By 1944, the tax yield had almost doubled over 1939, and internal loans reached seventy-two billion Francs by the end of June 1944, an amount exceeding the total of charges for occupation costs by eight billion.[224] Price and wage levels were partially controlled through appropriate legislation as will be shown below, but the remaining inflationary pressures made their impact in the rising prices in the black market and of prices for objects that lent themselves to investment purposes. Yet it must be admitted that the increase in currency circulation was not large enough to "destroy" the currency in a runaway inflation.[225] One reason for this accomplishment was the successful refusal of Belgian officials in 1941 to acquiesce in the incorporation of Belgium into the German currency system. The continued separate management of the Belgian Franc allowed the minimum necessary control to avoid the extremes of inflation.[226]

Brief mention needs to be made of two other financial instruments for the exploitation of Belgium, even though the total amounts involved were small as compared to the size of the transactions carried out through the occupation cost and Clearing accounts. In the first place, the Belgian state was required to redeem the German military currency (*Reichskreditkassenscheine*) used until June 1941. According to figures supplied at Nuremberg, the total so redeemed amounted to 3.567 billion Francs.[227] In the second place, the Belgian state was also required to reimburse Belgian local government agencies and individuals and groups for the actual expenses incurred in quartering German troops (*Quartiermachungskosten*), in addition to the fixed sums paid as occupation costs. According to German figures the total of such payments amounted to 5.6 billion Francs by the end of July 1944.[228] These payments did not affect the German-Belgian payments balance but they further increased the national debt.

The following table will summarize the total charges incurred through the payment mechanisms that have been discussed so far. The bottom line sum of 139.488 billion Francs may be viewed as an approximation of the total fiscal impact of the demands for goods and services imposed by the occupying power. If anything it is too low, since numerous transactions never came to the attention of the central record-keeping institutions.

The total fiscal burden imposed on Belgium was obviously staggering, particularly in view of the fact that the total prewar national wealth has been estimated at 450 billion BFrcs.[230] Thus the fiscal cost of the occupation as outlined above can be viewed as having consumed almost one-third of the total national wealth if differences in the value of the Franc between the outbreak of the war and 1944 are disregarded.

Table 13[229]

Fiscal cost of occupation

	Billion Francs
Occupation Costs	67
Clearing Balance	62.665*
Reichskreditkassenscheine	3.567
Miscellaneous Notes	.656
	133.888
Quartiermachungskosten	5.6
Total	139.488

Due to the nature of the two main mechanisms of financing the occupation, the occupation costs extracted from the state *au fond perdu* (without expectation of future reimbursement), and the Clearing which was wiped out with the total bankruptcy of a defeated Germany, the Belgian people in the long run had to pay the entire cost of the occupation from past savings or future earnings, quite apart from other losses suffered by the occupied country. One of the reasons they were able to do so in the immediate postwar years without the catastrophic fiscal dislocations that had occurred in Germany after the First World War was the fact that the basic financial structure of the country was preserved despite the stresses and strains to which it was subjected during the occupation.

Brief mention must be made of the fate of the gold reserves of the National Bank which had been deposited with the *Banque de France*. This gold, which had been sent to Dakar by the French bank was surrendered to Germany by the French in accordance with the provisions of the Franco-German Armistice. Belgian banking authorities in Brussels and the

---

* The small discrepancy between this clearing balance and that furnished in table 11 may be attributed to differences in sources.

Belgian government in London refused to recognize this transfer,[231] and in 1944 the French government assumed responsibility for restoring these gold reserves to Belgium. Thus Belgium weathered the war with a large part of its gold reserves intact and the international position of the Belgian Franc well protected.[232]

The financial stringencies of the occupation and the material shortages of a war economy had a profound impact on wages and prices under the occupation. Before the war, the level of wages and prices in prewar Belgium was one of the lowest among the industrialized countries of Western Europe, as the result of a deliberate policy of keeping prices of manufactured goods competitive in the world market by allowing food and raw material imports to enter without protective duties. Food prices were about thirty to fifty percent lower than in Germany, whereas prices of finished products were only slightly below the level prevailing in the Reich.[233] However, by May 10, 1940 prices had already increased over the 1936-1938 average by an amount variously estimated as being fourteen to nineteen percent.[234]

The key German policy was to maintain existing wage and price levels as far as possible, with only those minimal modifications that would be required to carry out the economic exploitation of Belgium. Since inexpensive food for humans and livestock was no longer available, agricultural prices had to be adjusted upward in order to encourage the amount of agricultural production needed to feed the population. Industrial prices, however, which were much closer to the German level anyway, were to be raised only when production costs increased.[235] Prices for other basic items such as coal and steel, and utility and transportation costs, were to be held to the May 1940 level.[236] Wage increases were to be held to a minimum, well below the inflation that was taking place.

In order to implement these policies, the Germans initially froze all wages and prices at the May 10, 1940 level.[237] During the summer of 1940 they moved to create the machinery for the orderly adjustment of wages and prices in tune with wartime necessities.

When it became necessary to relieve some of the pressure created by the rising cost of living, particularly food prices, the Germans in June 1941 authorized a one-time general wage increase of eight percent for industrial workers.[238] Government officials at the lower echelons whose salaries had been especially depressed in prewar times were given a ten percent increase. In addition, exceptional wage and salary increases were granted to special groups such as mine workers construction workers, and to policemen and officials of various control services.

After this 1941 adjustment no general wage increases were granted during the occupation. However, Belgian employers were most inventive about finding ways of helping their workers to deal with inflation by furnishing free meals in canteens, subsidizing purchases of work clothes, granting pay advances or loans that did not have to be repaid, and increasing on paper the number of hours worked. The Germans occasionally took steps to punish the most flagrant transgressions on the part of the employers, but more generally closed their eyes to all but the most blatant infractions.[239] Baudhuin estimated after the war that the total increase in real wages during the occupation amounted to sixteen percent[240] which must be considered a moderate adjustment given the existing pressures.

The story of price increases poses even more complex problems than that of wages because of the role of the black market. Despite the difficulty of assessing the impact of black market prices on the overall price structure, some generalizations are possible. Price controls were most successful in holding down the cost of certain basic necessities of life such as rents, utilities, fuel (at least in part) and transportation, and least effective with regard to such "discretionary" food items as vegetables, fruit and eggs. Given the fact that black market prices for basic food such as bread, potatoes, butter and meat increased to four to five times above prewar level by the summer of 1942[241] and seven to eight times by 1943[242] it may be estimated that price levels for an "ordinary family" buying a mix of officially-priced and black market food increased between two and four times between May 1940 and August

1944, depending on the proportion of food purchased on the black market. Clearly this burden fell more heavily on the poor than on the well-to-do which meant that the former had to spend most of their income on food in order to survive. This situation also meant that the poorest segments of the population, through the effective reduction of disposable income in the face of black market prices, paid disproportionally for the cost of the German occupation.

External Trade

In the prewar period the Belgian economy had been heavily dependent on foreign trade. More than half of Belgian imports had consisted of industrial raw materials, one quarter of food, and one quarter of finished products. More than one half of all imports came from overseas.[243]

With the German conquest, these overseas imports were cut off completely. Therefore, the Belgian economy had to be reoriented toward the European continent. Germany was to become the principal trading partner, but other European countries, particularly those in the German orbit, also played a part.

In order to retain the cooperation of Belgian authorities, the Germans made a number of concessions designed to allow Belgian administrators to keep track of the size of Belgian exports. In contrast to arrangements in the Netherlands, the Belgian Franc remained a separate currency from the Mark, and a large part of general economic transactions were carried out through the Clearing where a modicum of accounting remained possible. Furthermore, the customs boundary between Belgium and Germany was not abolished, and Belgian administrators initially retained some of control over exports through the requirement of export licenses to be issued by the *Office Central des Licences et Contingents*.[244] Even when the Germans abolished all restrictions on exports to Germany, Belgian customs services continued to record exports except for requisitions and purchases conducted by the military.[245]

The original understanding that Belgium would receive adequate food and other needed supplies in return for surrendering her industrial production to Germany, however sincerely it may have been intended by the Military Administration in 1940, was never fully honored. This original understanding suffered a major setback when Göring ordered a general embargo of exports to occupied territories in August 1941. Central German authorities stubbornly maintained throughout the war that the Belgian people could feed themselves with food raised in their own country and that they could draw on hidden supplies for their other needs.

While most of Belgium's wartime external trade was with Germany, trade with other European countries, including territories under German occupation, was far from insignificant. This "third-country" trade tended to benefit the Belgian consumer more than trade with Germany. According to the Final Report of the Military Administration, exports to third countries amounted to 1.1 billion RM or a little more than one fourth of goods delivered to Germany (4.115 billion RM). However, third countries furnished almost forty-two percent of all imported goods.[246] Trade agreements with these countries usually were made as supplemental protocols to German trade agreements, and payments were made through the central German Clearing in most instances. Food imports from Balkan countries contracted under the auspices of the Winter Help agency were paid for by using blocked Belgian accounts in the countries concerned or in other European countries.[247] Since such a high proportion of imports from third countries consisted of food, third country imports played a vital role in sustaining the Belgian population during the occupation.

Chapter Six

Summary and Conclusion: The German Occupation Regime in Belgium 1940-1944

In this chapter I intend to evaluate the structure, policies and actions of the German administration in Belgium during the second occupation, and to address the broader questions raised in the introduction. In conclusion, I will apply to the German occupation of Belgium my basic assessment of German occupation policies in the Netherlands expressed in my book *The Dutch under German Occupation.*

In this evaluation the distinction between the Military Command and its most important "hybrid" organization, the German Security Police and SD must be discussed once more. The ambiguities of that relationship have been presented in sufficient detail to make it clear that the German police was, and at the same time was not, an integral part of the Military Command, and that discussions of the character, intentions and methods of the Military Command in large measure do not apply fully to the police. While we need to make that differentiation in order to be able to define what was somewhat special about the von Falkenhausen-Reeder administration, the distinction is also subject to criticism because from the point of view of the people in the occupied territory, particularly the Jews, the Military Command and the police were both components of the same German apparatus of oppression, terror and annihilation. There is no way of escaping this ambiguity because any simplified view would do an injustice to the complexity of the situation as it evolved from 1940 to 1944.

Fundamental to an understanding of German policies (and of the Belgian response) was the fact that this was the second occupation for Germans and the people of Belgium alike. The memory of the first occupation, with all of the brutality, suffering and public defiance it had engendered, and the legacy of hatred it had left behind, inclined German military planners and the Belgian elites in 1940 toward caution and compromise. Above all, the view that the mass labor deportations constituted an error of Imperial policy induced von Falkenhausen and Reeder to oppose with all means at their disposal the introduction of the compulsory labor draft. On the part of the Belgian business and government elites the memory of the trauma of forced labor and of the impact on the economic life of the country was a powerful reason in 1940 to accept the proposition that Belgian industry should work for the Germans in return for the understanding that Belgian labor would not be deported to Germany.

The history of the cessation of public services during the First World War continued to haunt German authorities in Belgium during the second occupation and inclined them to make concessions to the legal and constitutional scruples of the Belgian administration, mostly in matters of form, but also sometimes in matters of substance. For instance, in order to prevent a breakdown of the Belgian judiciary system, the Germans in 1942 were willing to accept some restrictions on the ability of the two collaborationist Secretaries-General to take independent action in the future, in return for having past decrees left standing by the judiciary.

The historical context also influenced the course of events in a broader and more diffuse sense. In Belgium alone, of all of the occupied territories in the West, rulers and ruled in 1940 had a historical framework, a set of recent events still very much alive in the memories of mature adults, which could serve as reference point for their actions and reactions. In the other occupied territories in the West, everything was happening in 1940 for the first time, almost entirely "out of the blue", and often the actors were "lost" on the stage. In Belgium, by contrast, there existed a known repertoire, the play had been played out once before, and to a significant degree there was a sense of *déjà vu*. This gave authorities and ordinary people certain points of reference to guide their actions and reactions which the parties concerned in the other occupied territories were lacking.

In the early years of the occupation the historical context clearly benefitted the Germans. It made them more tactful and respectful of legal and moral scruples of the Belgian elites, and in that way increased the willingness of Belgian leaders to work with the Germans. The favorable comparison with the behavior of German soldiers during the first occupation, and, among ordinary people, a surprise that the Germans were "not so bad" helped to create a climate of cooperation in 1940. After the first winter of the war with its deprivations, with the increase of German demands on the economy, and the activities of the German police and SS, this initial sentiment began to dissipate, but it was a significant factor in 1940 when enduring patterns of cooperation were put in place.

The German Administration: Personalities, Policies and Political Effectiveness

There is little doubt that the personality of the two dominant figures in the German administration, von Falkenhausen and Reeder, gave shape to the actions of the occupation authorities and determined, within the rather narrow parameters of differentiation permitted in the Third Reich, the character and nuances of the second occupation of Belgium. Von Falkenhausen and Reeder had a rational and unusually clear perception of the policies they wished to follow, and they managed to communicate that conception to most of their subordinates. They possessed a gift of leadership that engendered a deep loyalty among many of their associates and that had not dissipated after twenty-five years among those of their staff interviewed for this study. The clarity of the basic policy, the compelling quality of their leadership and the hierarchical structure of the Military Command made possible the relatively smooth and effective functioning of the German administration. Most of the conflicts that occurred involved hybrid services within the Command structure which received their orders from, or owed some degree of allegiance to other (state or party) authorities.

In the opinion of this writer, von Falkenhausen's very early insight, probably by September 1940, that Germany might or would lose the war, profoundly influenced his attitude toward his assignment and toward the Belgian people. He stressed quite frequently in his memoirs, admittedly written after the war, the awareness that he had a responsibility for the postwar climate between the two countries. I believe that these sentiments were sincerely held during the war and that they do not merely represent a postwar apologia.

At the same time it must be recognized that von Falkenhausen and Reeder, in the first instance, were officials of Hitler's Third Reich. They were nationalists, authoritarians, and militarists for whom duty perceived in traditional patriotic and military terms came first. But while this was so, their realism and their basic motivation allowed them to put a distinctive mark on the occupation. The clearly perceived priority of the Military Command to maintain security and exploit the country economically induced them to avoid measures that might stir up unnecessary trouble or decrease voluntary cooperation. In particular, it meant avoidance of ideologically motivated political changes which might arouse political passions.

Unfortunately for the military authorities, party and SS aims and policies made it impossible to stick to this policy consistently. Yet the Military Command managed to set definite limits to the ideological transformations that were actually attempted. By and large, most government institutions apart from elective bodies and trade unions were allowed to function, no prominent figure such as Degrelle or Van de Wiele was given an important official position, and advocacy of incorporation into the Greater German Reich was muted at least until 1942.

Through this cautious policy the military authorities succeeded in their key objective to govern the country through the Belgian administration and through cooperation with the elites that were in place in 1940. Though the Germans would accept from time to time refusals by Belgian administrators to issue orders for specific actions the latter considered inadmissible under Belgian law, such as the deportation of the Jews or the forced labor draft for Germany, the Military Administration saw to it that these actions were carried out in the end.

In this manner, government officials and business leaders were kept in the patterns of cooperation established in 1940. Such protests as were made by Belgian authorities against German demands, as a rule were couched in non-inflammatory and conciliatory language designed to avoid arousing political passions. Usually, they were not intended as published statements although many found their way into the underground press. Above all, unlike the situation that prevailed in the First World War, no established authority ever publicly called for resistance to German measures.

Through its "moderation" the German administration also secured the silent consent of the heads of state and church to its rule. Relations with the king were cordial and those with the cardinal respectful. Close liaison with the latter restrained the Primate, if he needed any restraints, from putting any serious obstacles in the way of the occupation authorities, even though on a few occasions (generally involving measures forced upon the Military Command by Reich authorities) the cardinal protested publicly against German actions. At bottom, there existed between the German military administration, the monarchy and the church an effective sense of mutual understanding based on a shared conservative outlook on government and society. Opposed as they might be to each other on specific issues and in their hopes for the outcome of the war, the Military Command and king and Primate shared a common desire for law and order and for the retention of established authority and structures. They also shared a fear of communism and other kinds of left-wing radicalism which might benefit from any kind of disorder. Moreover, none of the three "partners" wanted to precipitate a conflict which in the end would leave the field to Himmler and the SS.

This attitude of King and Primate proved invaluable to the German military administration because signals from court and curia encouraged or confirmed the basic propensity of the administrative and business leadership of the country to enter and remain in a basically cooperative relationship with the German occupation authorities.

A balanced judgment suggests that the policy of the Military Command to coordinate German programs in the occupied territory and to minimize the advocacy or implementation of ideologically motivated political changes was neither fully successful nor a total failure. For instance, Reeder did not manage to prevent the establishment of the Flemish SS in 1940 or of Jungclaus' office in 1942, but he managed, more or less, to mute annexationist propaganda and to support the VNV as the most useful source of Flemish manpower. He did not succeed in keeping effective control over Himmler's police as the years went by, but he did prevent until July 1944 the appointment of an independent police commander (Higher SS and Police Leader) which would have given Himmler and the RSHA a free hand. The Military Command also failed in its original plea to leave the Jews alone because on this issue its preference conflicted with the key concepts that animated national socialism. In the economic field too, success and failure were mixed, with a tendency toward increasing coordination on the German side during the last two years of the war.

In summary: The conflict of competing ambitions and policies typical of the Third Reich was played out in full in Belgium, but the clear goals and strong personalities of the leaders in the Command Area and particularly Reeder's tactical sense tended to offset to some extent the influence of Hitler's competing satraps. For that reason, it probably remains true that the German military regime in Brussels managed to administer its territory with a higher degree of effective coordination than that achieved by the other German proconsuls in the West.

The most unquestionable "political" success of the von Falkenhausen-Reeder regime was the sheer fact of the survival of the Military Command structure until the final weeks of the occupation, despite Hitler's growing dislike of the regime and of the general personally. Apart from accident and sheer luck, some concrete reasons for the survival of the Command structure can be identified. Chief among these was Reeder's success in portraying the economic exploitation of the occupied territory as an impressive, perhaps even unique, success story, and his tactical skill in lining up the old state bureaucracy from Lammers on down behind the retention of the Military Command. Until 1943 all the "old ministries" supported its retention, primarily out of the conviction, carefully engineered by Reeder in his reports and his negotiations in Berlin, that the war effort was best served by leaving things as they were. That conviction held Hitler back and prevailed until July 1944 despite his and Himmler's longstanding preference for a civilian German administration directed by a party figure.

How much did these "practical accomplishments" vaunted by Reeder owe to the so-called "policy of the velvet glove" as von Falkenhausen characterized the initially restrained and nonconfrontational tenor of his administration? While based primarily on pragmatic rather than humanitarian considerations, this policy entailed a degree of sensitivity to the sentiments of the population, and in particular of the administrative and business leaders whose cooperation was vital for the success of the task of running the country with a minimum of German personnel. It meant a recognition particularly in matters of form of the limits to which collaboration could be pushed and an acceptance of such limits. It also meant a degree of restraint in imposing excessively harsh punishments for infractions of German law in order to avoid the creation of a political atmosphere which might imperil the collaboration of Belgian officials and businessmen.

The "policy of the velvet glove" began to break down after the invasion of the Soviet Union in 1941, in part because of the general radicalization of the policies of the Third Reich, and in part because of the changes in the military situation. Resistance activities set off the whole train of mass arrests and of executions and counter-assassinations which went far toward destroying the cooperative climate of the early months. Whatever the personal preferences of the Military Commander, after 1941 German countermeasures against the Resistance, often taken under pressure from Berlin and within the context of the growing independence of police and SS in the

Command area, could hardly be viewed as a part of the policy of the velvet glove.

It may be useful to look at the question whether the Military Command succeeded in the achievement of its paramount objective, the preservation of internal security. In that respect, the Germans could claim almost complete success until the winter of 1941-42. Significant acts of sabotage and political assassinations remained isolated incidents which in no way imperiled public order. On the other hand, the Germans failed to prevent the emergence of an underground press addressing an admittedly still limited audience. They also failed to prevent the formation of scattered underground groups, particularly among patriotic individuals from the military milieu. These groups did not form any immediate threat since they focussed on actions to be taken in connection with a German withdrawal. Despite their mass arrests of known Communists in June 1941, the Germans were unable to prevent the rise of new Communist action groups in the fall of 1941.

The security situation began to deteriorate with the turn of the war and the imposition of the compulsory labor draft, and, as has been described above, effective control over some sectors of the eastern part of the country was lost in 1943-1944. But for the rest of the country, the situation remained pretty well in hand, even though incidents tended to increase significantly during the last year of the occupation. Yet despite the emergence of such Resistance organizations as the Front of the Interior which practiced industrial sabotage and engaged in political assassination, most acts of resistance remained irritants rather than becoming serious threats to law and order for most of the country, with the exception of the Ardennes region in eastern Belgium. Apart from that region the German hold on Belgium was never threatened seriously from within.

While essential German security was maintained, German military authorities were unable to restrain the growing wave of political assassinations and counter-assassinations that occurred in 1943 and particularly in 1944. These indeed constituted a veritable breakdown of civil life, even if German personnel usually were not directly affected.

German intelligence and police were only moderately effective in dealing with escape lines and military espionage. Escape lines for Allied aviators, Belgian patriots and other refugees continued to be operational through France and Spain throughout the occupation, although in that area too the German police caught many clandestine operatives and at least temporarily destroyed functioning networks. Allied intelligence networks operated in Belgium after 1942 with increasing effectiveness, but, as has been said before, none of this posed a serious threat to the security and control of the occupied territory. And above all, the local strikes that occurred in the industrial regions of the country remained of limited duration and scope, and none of the great uprisings that made the Germans lose face and consolidated the hatred of the population in the neighboring Netherlands took place in Belgium.

Our description of German policies towards the Flemish and Walloon language groups ("nationality" or "language" policy) has indicated that ultimately it was a failure. This failure may be attributed to two fundamental reasons. Not only did German intentions and policies conflict but there was simply next-to-no support in Wallonia and in Flanders for annexation to Hitler's Reich, dissatisfied as some of the Flemish people may have been with their place in the prewar Belgian state and society. Therefore Berger and Van de Wiele had to work from a very narrow base in Flanders. In the French-speaking part of the country distrust and hatred of Degrelle and Rex only increased as Degrelle moved closer toward Himmler and the SS. Even if the Germans had been able to agree on a singleminded consistent policy, theirs would have been an impossible job as long as there remained any hope that Germany would not prevail in the war.

Reeder's one distinct success, his ability to recruit a substantial number of Flemish nationalists for German and Belgian administrative and auxiliary police positions, was due to the fact that these assignments provided an income and gave a large number of Flemish men and women an opportunity to work, often in positions of some authority and respect which protected the men from the labor draft. In this respect, German needs and the needs of certain Flemish people coincided.

German military recruitment for the Flemish and Walloon legions which used anti-Bolshevik more than national themes, was only moderately successful. The Germans managed to recruit only half the number of the volunteers secured from the Netherlands, a country of roughly the same size. It must be assumed that skepticism about ultimate German intentions and a basic anti-German stance going back to the First World War put restraints on German recruitment that did not exist in the Netherlands.

It is particularly difficult to resolve the question how effective the Germans were in another area of ethnic or racial policy, the segregation and deportation of the Jews. In this area, the objectives of the Reich to deport all Jews to the East, clearly conflicted with the original desire of the Military Command to leave the Jews alone. Yet the Military Command was bound to implement the measures which laid the groundwork for deportation and extermination. In the end, the deportations were carried out under orders from Eichmann's office in Berlin by the police which was *and* was not under the control of the Military Command.

In view of these complexities, the main conclusion provided by the evidence is that the military regime succeeded in its main goal to avoid a significant disruption of its basic arrangements with the Belgian elites over the "Jewish Question." The evidence also suggests that the Military Command exacted a number of delays and granted or secured for a small number of primarily Belgian Jews exemptions from deportation. The delays secured by Reeder and the reluctance of the Military Command to have the military police or troops freely used for the physical roundup of Jews in the end saved a significant number of lives which provides one part of the explanation why half of the Jews in the 1940 census survived. The evidence also suggests that at least von Falkenhausen and probably Reeder, long before the defeat of Germany, would have found it a moral burden to face the fact that he had played a part in sending more than twenty-five thousand men, women and children to their death. The broader question of moral responsibility, of allowing themselves knowingly or unknowingly to become participants in an operation of mass murder will be discussed below in the section "The Moral Issue."

Most of the other ideologically motivated German enterprises designed to produce political change or new political structures failed or were subverted by the people in the occupied territory. The unified trade union, the UTMI, lost most of its members and remained an empty shell; the Winter Help was captured by the old elites and used for genuinely humanitarian and patriotic purposes; the French-speaking Labor Service kept its nationalist identity and had to be abandoned; only the Flemish Labor Service was captured successfully by Devlag, but its numbers were negligible. Apart from that particular instance, however, the German attempt to subvert existing institutions or create new ones in the image of the Reich met with failure. That failure did not greatly trouble the Military Command since it did not detract from the economic exploitation of the country and since it had been its original preference to defer all such changes until after the war.

Economic Exploitation

The evaluation of the effectiveness of the German economic exploitation of Belgium is faced with another paradox: On the one hand, the Germans succeeded in extracting from Belgium a very substantial contribution to the German war effort but on the other hand, Belgian industry under the occupation operated only at little more than half of its peacetime level of performance. Therefore, German economic management may be viewed as a great success, (as it was presented by Reeder and his associates), or as a failure (as portrayed by Belgian authors after the war in an attempt to minimize the extent of economic collaboration). In the view of the present writer, German economic management should be viewed as a qualified success, limited by the factors described in the preceding chapter and summarized below.

The main physical bases for the degree of success were (1) the ready availability of coal, the main source of industrial energy, (2) the existence of a highly developed industrial plant, (3) the sufficient supply of labor, at least until 1942, (4) the initially substantial supply of raw materials and (5) the operation of a highly developed rail system. To these physical resources must be added the willingness of Belgian management and labor to produce goods for Germany, and the ability of the military regime to coordinate the economic exploitation of the country to some extent. These physical resources and human factors taken together explain the degree of success of the German industrial management of the wartime economy.

The key factors that reduced production to a level well below that of peacetime performance, have also been described in the preceding chapter: (1) the increasing shortage of raw materials for an industry that had been heavily dependent on imports, (2) the progressive wartime deterioration of plant and equipment, and of labor efficiency, (3) the reluctance of German industry to place orders in Belgium, (4) the decreasing willingness of Belgian managers and workers after the turn of the war to work for Germany, and above all (5) the inability of the military authorities to coordinate and rationalize more satisfactorily the economic activities of German business, and of a wide array of military and civilian services and agencies. This latter failure must be considered the single most important obstacle to the successful exploitation of Belgium under wartime conditions. This lack of coordination has been presented as a deliberate design of Hitler's, but on the operating level in Belgium, it appears as a failure of will at the highest level of the German government, a failure of rational management in which the Germans, government, party, the armed forces, industry and business were their own and each others' worst enemies. The military authorities in Brussels saw this problem clearly enough, but they were unable to fully overcome the corrosive impact of this chaotic competition because administrative chaos was built so firmly into the German war economy.

It may be useful to review briefly at this point the effectiveness of German policies and explanations of successes and failures in the specific areas covered in the preceding chapter. The revival of public life and of the economy in 1940 and 1941 was quick and effective because this was a job within the means and competence of the Military Command in which it enjoyed substantial support from Belgian authorities and private persons. The attempt to take over Belgian business enterprises (over the objections of the military regime) in the end came to very little because of the lack of interest by German and Belgian firms. Finances were fairly well managed because German and Belgium authorities had a common interest in avoiding a disastrous runaway inflation. They partially succeeded in this endeavor through wage and price control and through an increase in taxes and a system of internal loans. The inflation that occurred was roughly the size of the payments balance and therefore represented the basic Belgian contribution to the German war effort. This placed a heavy but not unbearable burden on Belgian society and on the economy during the occupation and the immediate postwar period.

The German exploitation of Belgian industry may be summarized in the statement that the Germans managed to exact major and significant contributions from Belgian industry, but that they failed to use fully its productive potential. Their success was limited not only by their failure to establish effective centralized management, but also by inevitable wartime conditions such as the scarcity of customary sources of energy and raw materials from overseas, and the deterioration of plant and equipment.

In the field of agriculture and food, German policies were only indirectly exploitative since the Germans did not try to export food from Belgian production to a significant extent, although the occupation army made purchases in the Belgian market. Instead, the basic 1940 understanding implied that the German administration would see to it that the population would be fed at a minimally acceptable level. The military authorities initially failed to live up to this understanding because they proved unable to persuade authorities in the Reich to import sufficient cereal grains and potatoes to feed the population at an acceptable level of nutrition. The near-famine situation of the first winter of the occupation extended into a second year because the German administration was slow in seeing to it that enough land was put under cultivation to produce the increased amount of basic carbohydrates needed. By the summer of 1942, the reforms in agricultural production and food distribution set in motion had born fruit, and the nutritional situation remained under control until the end of the occupation, admittedly at a marginal level. In summary, the Germans at first failed and subsequently succeeded in feeding the Belgian population at levels that were not substantially detrimental to health except for some marginal groups such as the aged and the very poor.

German successes and failures in the utilization of Belgian labor were also mixed, but the time sequence was the opposite of that observed in the field of nutrition. Here success came first and failure later. In the first year of the occupation recruitment for work in Germany and Belgium went well because of the vast number of unemployed in 1940 and because of the then existing positive attitudes towards working for the victorious Germans. Difficulties came when the labor pool approached exhaustion and when attitudes changed as workers became less and less willing to accept voluntarily assignments in Germany. The final failure in the last eighteen months of the occupation occurred when large numbers of Belgian workers preferred to go underground rather than to submit to deportation to Germany.

At bottom, this failure too was the result of a political decision made by Hitler, and of a basic political flaw in German labor policy. What made the Sauckel slave labor draft necessary was Hitler's deliberate decision not to draft married German women with children for factory work and the failure, at least until 1943, to force German procurement agencies and German industry to place orders in the occupied territories when possible, so that foreign workers could produce goods for Germany in their own country instead of being forced to labor in wartime Germany.

Against these basic failures of policy at the highest level, the reservations and objections of the Military Command in Brussels counted for little. Therefore in the field of labor, as in so many other areas, the causes of policy failure in Belgium must be located in the key political dynamics and structures of the Third Reich.

The Moral Issue

At this point it may not be inappropriate to discuss the issue of the moral responsibility of the two key figures in the German administration. Alexander von Falkenhausen and Eggert Reeder had made their basic decisions and moral choices long before they ever arrived in Brussels in the spring of 1940. Both of them as young men had chosen public service in the army and the Prussian civil service respectively and had risen to positions of authority. Both of them had joined the German Nationalist party before 1933 which sought to destroy the Weimar Republic, the state they were serving and the only democratic government Germany had ever enjoyed. Both of them chose to continue their careers in the Third Reich although von Falkenhausen opted out in 1934 when he went to China. But then again in 1938, admittedly under pressure, he decided to return to a Germany gearing up for war and conquest. In 1939 he accepted an Area Command in Germany because as he put it, "every German has to do his duty", especially in wartime, and in 1940 he took the Command in the Netherlands and Belgium. Thus, by choice and not by necessity, he had put himself in a position where after May 1940 he would become responsible for the actions of the German officials in his Command area and for the repressive measures such as executions he himself ordered in his capacity as Military Commander.

Reeder too continued his career in government service after 1933, even after his conflicts with Himmler, rising to the position of *Regierungspräsident* well before the age of forty. And in 1939 he accepted his position in the army apparently without hesitation to draw up instructions for occupation governments in the West. Finally in 1940 he eagerly accepted the assignment as Chief of the Military Administration in Belgium.

It can be argued that from their point of view von Falkenhausen and Reeder were just following orders in 1939 and 1940 as patriotic Germans subject to military service. But this point of view, even in the contemporary perspective of 1939 and 1940 is an oversimplification. Both of them had more opportunities than most to observe the workings of the Nazi state, and both of them could have found a way out if they had wanted to. The fact is that they did not, and that their willingness to serve the Nazi state (possibly with the hope of improving things "from within") was the decisive act of their lives for which they bear responsibility before history.

It is possible to claim that these arguments are basically unhistorical because the two men did not see their choices in these terms and because mass murder and Auschwitz still lay in the future. There is some truth in this objection but not much. There had been a few Germans, a very few indeed, even from their own German Nationalist party such as Hermann Rauschning who broke with the regime early. Von Falkenhausen had read the message of the Night of the Long Knives correctly and had turned his back on the Third Reich by going to China. Reeder had had a prime opportunity to analyze the character of a system in which the police was trained to disregard law. Concentration camps had existed in Germany since 1933, and the two men were aware of their existence. In 1938, the synagogues had burned and Jews were herded into concentration camps by the thousands without any semblance of legal process. These two men were not innocents in the woods. They knew and understood more accurately than most the character of the state they served.

The fact is that once they accepted their wartime executive positions they became inescapably enmeshed in the evil and crime that constituted the Third Reich even though they tried to limit its worst abuses. Their misfortune was that they did not see, as given the limitations of their own political culture, they indeed hardly could, that cooperation with the absolute evil represented by Nazi Germany was bound to corrupt and contaminate the best intentions of those trying to "work from within" and that such cooperation was bound to turn all persons in positions of authority into accomplices in crime.

Moreover it should be noted that both of them wanted Germany to win the war. But the Germany they served was Hitler's Germany, and German victory would have meant Nazi rule, and terror and mass extermination all over Europe. In the Command area, they labored to the best of their ability to make their contribution toward the achievement of victory. They supported the recruitment of Belgian volunteers for service in the German armed forces, they fought and punished sabotage, espionage and pilot rescue as vigorously as any officer in Hitler's army. And it must also be noted that unlike in Denmark no German official in Belgium warned Jews about impending raids. Their narrow military conception of duty and their oath of loyalty to Hitler made it impossible for them to consider "administrative sabotage" even though they had opposed the deportations in the first place.

The only way in which von Falkenhausen and Reeder could have avoided becoming accomplices in the crimes of the occupation regime which occurred after June 1942, would have been to resign their positions. But here we encounter another level of complexity. When they considered their resignation in 1943, they were aware of the paradox that their resignation would deprive the people living in Belgium of the limited protection against the full force of police terror that the military regime had indeed managed to provide, and that it would turn over the country to Himmler and Sauckel and their minions. In other words, the paradox of the situation was such that they could "keep a clean vest" (in the future) only at the price of "abandoning" the Belgian people. And whatever weight these considerations or rationalizations may have played, we know that both men stayed on until the end. In short, once von Falkenhausen and Reeder had accepted their positions, and once Nazi policy took the turn it took, they were caught in their responsibility for all the actions committed by German services in the Command area, even by such hybrid organizations as the German police. They were caught because their sense of honor and duty to their country as they saw it was stronger than their personal conscience. Through their willingness to serve Hitler's Germany as high executives, Alexander von Falkenhausen and Eggert Reeder became morally responsible for the reprehensible and criminal actions performed by themselves and by German agencies and services in the Command area, even though these services were not fully under their control and even though their actions were contrary to the policies they advocated. Such was the complexity of their position that either unqualified condemnation or simple exoneration would be misplaced.

Final Conclusion

The following summary of the reasons for the successes and failures of the German administration in Belgium will be based on the final comment on the German regime in the Netherlands made in the conclusion of my earlier book:

> The cardinal mistake of the German regime [in the Netherlands] in the opinion of this writer, lay in its insistence on introducing National Socialist principles and institutions into the occupied territory before the war had been concluded.... Through the persecution of the Jews and the insistence on Nazification, German authorities forced a conflict with the most deepseated patriotic, religious, moral and ideological sentiments of the Dutch people without ever fully understanding the strength of these sentiments. The Germans could have continued economic exploitation of the Dutch people and recruitment of men for the war effort, and they could have dealt firmly with sabotage and espionage, without arousing the religious and moral conscience of the nation to the extent they did. Once victory was won, they could have imposed their ideology and institutions without encountering effective opposition, because no resistance of significant proportion is feasible without hope of success.* Thus it must be concluded that the ideological dynamics of the German regime actually interfered with the immediate military and economic considerations of the war effort.**

When I reviewed this passage in the preparation of the present study it occurred to me that the German administration in Belgium, with which I had not been familiar during the period of my work on the occupation of the Netherlands, had followed, to the extent it was allowed to do so by Reich authorities, the policy I advocated some thirty years ago as a more functional alternative to Seyss-Inquart's and Rauter's

---

* I am not sure whether I would make that assertion now (1990) without qualification after the recent events in Central and Eastern Europe.
** *The Dutch under German Occupation* (Stanford, 1963), p. 277.

policy of terror and Nazification, and that the German regime in Belgium had indeed reaped to a significant extent the fruits of its restraint and self-limitation. It did not provoke a city-wide strike through the crude mass arrest of hundreds of young Jewish men in the streets. In fact, by insisting on discretion, it avoided reactions of any political significance to the persecution and deportation of the Jews. It did not provoke a countrywide strike through an unexpected threat of mass deportation of hundreds of thousands of veterans. With one notable exception in Antwerp in 1941 it did not allow Fascist and pro-German organizations a free hand in the streets and it did not give them an official role in the Belgian administration. Hence it had avoided, to a considerable extent, at least in the early years of the war, arousing deeply felt anti-German patriotic passions among large numbers of people in the occupied territory.

Above all, beyond suspending elective bodies, the German regime in Belgium refrained from tampering with the fundamental institutions of the country and minimized to the best of its ability all talk about major structural changes, such as a division of the country or annexation to Germany. It honored the monarchy and avoided major confrontations with the Catholic church. By thus respecting and working through the established institutions of the country it avoided arousing violent anti-German sentiments of that large section of the population which felt a deepseated loyalty to these institutions.

In addition, by doing its best to observe the basic agreement of 1940 to work within the established structures, to feed the Belgian people and to refrain from deporting Belgian labor, the German military regime retained the cooperation of the Belgian elites to the end. Even when it was unable to live up to the commitments made implicitly in 1940, by failing to deliver enough food in 1940-1942, and by failing to prevent the labor deportations of 1942-1944, it managed to let it be known to the governing elites that it had tried to live up to its side of the bargain. It managed to communicate to the Belgian leadership a sense that open resistance which would bring down the military regime would lead to worse suffering and terror than that which prevailed already.

The material in this study shows conclusively that the Military Command could have experienced smoother sailing if outside party and government agencies had not interfered in pursuit of ideological goals. Devlag propaganda for a Greater Germanic Reich and Degrelle's talk about a Burgundian state provoked deep apprehensions that often led to non-cooperation and resistance. The Sauckel compulsory labor draft produced a countrywide underground and an active Resistance. Thus it proved impossible to isolate the occupied territory from Nazi politics. In this manner ideology contributed to the gradual decline of the effectiveness of the military regime.

As has been intimated before, ideology was not the only obstacle to the success of "pragmatic" policy. The turn of military events and the increasingly ruthless exactions of an occupying power on the edge of defeat in time did much to diminish their effectiveness. But in the early years in particular, its relative abstention from ideology allowed the German administration to carry through its primary tasks effectively.

Given this assessment, how to answer the question whether the military regime was a success or a failure in terms of the goals it had set for itself in 1940? The evidence in this study has suggested that it was both, and that the answer depends in essence on the point of view whether the glass was half full or half empty. The greatest success of the military authorities in Belgium in our view was its ability to secure for the duration of the occupation the cooperation of the administrative and business elites and to avoid the major political confrontations with the population at large that characterized the occupation of the Netherlands and of Norway. Through this arrangement the military regime managed to exploit the industrial and economic potential of the country to an impressive extent, given the limitations of wartime conditions and the administrative chaos of Hitler's Reich. Its major failures were those caused by the interference of competing German authorities, by its inability to impose on these agencies a satisfactory degree of coordination, and, above all, toward the end of the occupation, by the approach of German defeat.

Glossary

This glossary contains identifications and brief descriptions of selected Dutch, French and German terms employed in the text.

AWG   ALLGEMEINE WARENVERKEHRSGESELL-SCHAFT. German Trade Assocation. Created in 1940 to regulate trade between Belgium and Germany and German-controlled countries.

AJB   ASSOCIATION DES JUIFS EN BELGIQUE. The Association of Jews in Belgium. An organization created by the Germans as a means of implementing their policies toward the Jews.

CNAA   CORPORATION NATIONALE DE L'AGRICULTURE ET DE L' ALIMENTATION. National Corporation for Agriculture and Food Supply. Organization created to organize the wartime production and distribution of food.

DNB   DEUTSCHES NACHRICHTENBÜRO. German News Agency. The official German government news agency.

DNVP   DEUTSCHNATIONALE VOLKSPARTEI. German Nationalist People's Party. Nationalist party in the Weimar Republic consisting mostly of monarchists. Formed electoral alliance with NSDAP in 1933 and furnished most members of Hitler's original government.

EINSATZGRUPPEN. Special Task Forces of the police and SS formed in 1941 to perform special "political" tasks such as the control and extermination of political opponents and of Jews in conquered territories in the East.

GFP   GEHEIME FELDPOLIZEI. Secret Field Police. The police force of the Germany army concerned with internal and external security.

NSDAP   NATIONALSOZIALISTISCHE DEUTSCHE ARBEITERPARTEI. National Socialist German Workers Party. The German Nazi Party.

OKW   OBERKOMMANDO DER WEHRMACHT. Supreme Command of the German Armed Forces. Created by Hitler to implement his direct command over the German armed forces.

OKH   OBERKOMMANDO DES HEERES. High Command of the Army. The Command of the German Army, taken over by Hitler in December 1941.

ONT   OFFICE NATIONAL DE TRAVAIL. National Labor Office. Belgian government employment office used by Germans to organize deportation to Germany.

REGIERUNGSPRÄSIDENT. Provincial governor in Germany. High civil servant official, appointed by central Reich government.

REICHSKOMMISSARIAT FÜR DIE BESETZTEN GEBIETE BELGIENS UND NORDFRANKREICHS. Office of the High Commisioner for the occupied territories of Belgium and Northern France established in July 1944.

Glossary

The "civilian" German governance structure for the last few weeks of the occupation.

RSHA REICHSSICHERHEITSHAUPTAMT. Reich Main Security Office. The central police office created in Berlin in 1939 to embody the amalgamation of the German police with the S.S.

REX Primarily francophone protofascist movement headed by Léon Degrelle which collaborated with the Germans.

SD SICHERHEITSDIENST. Security Service. The intelligence service of the S.S. and German police.

SIPO SICHERHEITSPOLIZEI. German police concerned with the control of political opponents. An amalgamation of the S.S. and the Prussian political police. Responsible for the deportation of the Jews.

SYBELAC SYNDICAT BELGE DE L'ACIER. Industry Association designed to control production and distribution of iron and steel.

UTMI UNION DES TRAVAILLEURS MANUELS ET INTELLECTUELS. Labor organization established in 1940 to "coordinate" existing unions. Used by Germans in their attempt to create a unitary Labor Front on the German model.

VNV VLAAMSCH NATIONAAL VERBOND. Flemish National League. The Flemish nationalist party which collaborated with the Germans.

ZAST ZENTRALE AUFTRAGSSTELLE. Central Order Office. Designed to control German commercial and industrial orders placed in Belgium.

Selected Abbreviations Employed in Notes and Bibliography

AAPAB	Politisches Archiv, Auswärtiges Amt, Bonn.
BAK	Bundesarchiv, Koblenz.
CGS	Comité des Secrétaires-Généraux. Committee of the Belgian Secretaries General.
CREHSGMB	Centre de recherches et d'études historiques de la seconde guerre mondiale, Brussels.
DGFP	Documents on German Foreign Policy.
HIAS	Hoover Institution Archives, Stanford.
IfZM	Institut für Zeitgeschichte, Munich.
IMT	International Military Tribunal, Nuremburg.
MAF	Militärarchiv/Bundesarchiv, Freiburg.
MBBNF	Militärbefehlshaber für Belgien und Nordfrankreich.
MVCh	Chef der Militärverwaltung (in Belgien und Nordfrankreich).
P.v.F.	Record of the trial of General von Falkenhausen and of Eggert Reeder in Brussels 1950-1951.
RvOA	Rijksinstituut voor Oorlogsdocumentatie, Amsterdam.
SD	Sicherheitsdienst. Intelligence Service of the S.S.

Notes

Chapter One

1 Walter Ford, *Belgian Handbook* (London, 1944), p. 7.

2 Bibliographisches Institut Leipzig, *Schlag nach über Niederlande, Belgien und Luxemburg* (Leipzig, n.d.), p. 19.

3 Ford, *Belgian Handbook*, p. 17.

4 G. N. Clark, *Belgium and the War* (London, 1942), p. 3.

5 John Eppstein, ed., *Belgium*. British Survey Handbooks. (Cambridge [England], 1944), p. 82.

6 Ludwig Pesch, *Volk und Nation in der Geistesgeschichte Belgiens (Berlin, 1944), p. 15;* François Périn, *La Belgique au défi: Flamands et Wallons à la recherche d'un état* (Huy, n.d.), p. 18.

7 Camille Huysmans, *Belgie in den storm* (Antwerp [1944]), p. 13.

8 Robert Senelle, *Constitutional Monarchy in Belgium* (Brussels, 1963), pp. 10-12.

9 Val Lorwin, "Conflict and Compromise in Belgian Politics," Paper presented at the annual meeting of the American Political Science Association, Washington, D.C., September 1965, p. 3. In possession of author. (Hereafter cited as Lorwin, "Conflict and Compromise.")

10 Val Lorwin, "Belgium," in Robert A. Dahl, ed., *Political Oppositions in Western Democracies* (New Haven, 1966), p. 156. (Hereafter cited as Lorwin, "Belgium.")

11 Henri Bernard, *Terre Commune: Histoire des pays de Benelux microcosme de l'Europe* (Brussels, 1961), p. 580.

12 Lorwin, "Belgium," p. 185.

13 Lorwin, "Conflict and Compromise," p. 13.

14 Jules Destrée, quoted in Périn, *La Belgique au défi*, p. 32.

15 Jean Vanwelkenhuyzen, interview with author, Brussels, July 26, 1981.

16 Office of Strategic Services, Research and Analysis Branch, "Survey of Belgium," 1 August 1942, R & A No. 773 j. 2nd ed., (Washington, D.C. 1944), p. 31. (Hereafter cited as O.S.S., "Survey of Belgium.")

17 Eppstein, *Belgium*, pp. 55-56.

18 Ibid., pp. 48-49.

19 Belgium, Ministry of Foreign Affairs and External Trade, *Memo from Belgium: Some Facts about Belgium*, No. 45, February 15, 1964, p. 15; Paul Dresse, *Le complexe belge* (Brussels, 1945), p. 61.

20 Pierre Lafagne, *Sous le signe de la Cross Gammée*, (Spa, 1945), p. [48].

21 Dresse, *Le complexe belge*, p. 64.

22 Senelle, *Constitutional Monarchy*, p. 3.

23 Ibid., pp. 10-12.

24 Ibid., pp. 13-16.

25 Ibid., pp. 16-17; Carl Henrik Höjer, *Le régime parlementaire belge de 1918 à 1940* (Uppsala, 1946), p. 361.

26 Jean Vanwelkenhuyzen, Brussels, June 24, 1975.

27 Höjer, *Le régime parlementaire*, pp. 353-54.

28 Ibid., p. 356; Clark, *Belgium and the War*, p. 5.

29 Höjer, *Le régime parlementaire*, p. 349.

30 Senelle, *Constitutional Monarchy*, p. 11.

31 Raoul van Overstraeten, *Albert I: Leopold III: Vingt ans de politique militaire belge 1920-1940* (Brussels, 1945), p. 674; Paul-Henri Spaak, *Combats inachevés* (Paris, 1969), vol. 1, 64-67.

32 Charles d'Ydewalle, *Le cour et la ville 1934-1940. Les hommes, les faits, les problèmes de ce temps* (Brussels, 1945), p. 18.

33 Ibid., p. 145.

34 Spaak, *Combats Inachevés*, vol. 1, 61.

35 Rudolph Binion, "Repeat Performance: A Psychohistorical Study of Leopold III and Belgian Neutrality," *History and Theory* 8 (1969): 211-59.

36 Charles d'Ydewalle, *La reine et ses soldats* (n.p., n.d.), pp. 153-54.

37 Bernard, *Terre commune*, p. 580.

38 Clark, *Belgium and the War*, pp. 362-63.

39 Pierre Joye and Rosine Lewin, *L'église et le mouvement ouvrier en Belgique* (Brussels, 1967), p. 266.

40 Ibid., p. 251.

41 Höjer, *Le régime parlementaire*, pp. 34-35.

42 Ibid., pp. 39-40.

43 Manu Ruys, *De vlamingen* (Tielt, 1972), p. 115.

44 Eppstein, *Belgium*, p. 52.

45 Ruys, *De vlamingen*, p. 97.

46 Joye and Lewin, *L'église et le mouvement ouvrier*, pp. 269-70.

47 Höjer, *Le régime parlementaire*, p. 51.

48 Ibid., p. 59; Camille Huysmans, *Camille Huysmans: een levensbeeld gevestigd op persoonlijke getuigenissen en eigen werk* (Hasselt, 1961), p. 6, and passim.

49 J. Gérard-Libois and José Gotovitch, *L'an 40: La Belgique occupée* (Brussels, [1971]), p. 17. (Hereafter cited as *L'an 40*.)

50 Peter Dodge, *Beyond Marxism: The Faith and Works of Henri De Man* (The Hague, 1966), pp. 232-36, and passim.

51 Léon Degrelle, *Le cohue de 1940* (Lausanne, [1949]), p. 43.

52 Jakob Herman Huizinga, *Mr. Europe: A Political Biography of Paul-Henri Spaak* (New York, 1961), p. 68.

53 *L'an 40*, p. 16.

54 Eppstein, *Belgium*, p. 51; Höjer, *Le régime parlementaire*, pp. 51, 56-59.

55 Ibid., p. 47.

56 Ruys, *De vlamingen*, pp. 114-15.

57 Joye and Lewin, *L'église et le mouvement ouvrier*, p. 236.

58 Table 5.5, Dahl, *Political Oppositions*, p. 412.

59 Table 5.6, ibid., p. 413.

60 [Raymond de Becker], "La Collaboration en Belgique 1940-1944 ou une révolution avortée," (Inédit attribué à Raymond de Becker [extraits]), Centre de recherche et d'information socio-politique

(CRISP), Courrier hebdomaire No. 497-498: October 30, 1970 (mimeographed), p. 6.

61 Jan de Schuyter, *Geheime bladzijden uit het heldenboek van den weerstand* (Antwerp, 1946), p. 23.

62 Jean-Michel Etienne, *Le mouvement rexiste jusqu'en 1940* (Paris, 1968), p. 47.

63 Jacques Willequet, "Les fascismes belges et la seconde guerre mondiale, *Revue d'histoire de la deuxième guerre mondiale* 66 (April 1967): 96 - 97. (Hereafter cited as Willequet, "Les fascismes belges.")

64 *L'an 40*, pp. 68-69.

65 Ibid., p. 70.

66 Franz Petri, *Die Niederlande (Holland und Belgien) und das Reich* (Bonn, 1940), p. 14.

67 Clark, *Belgium and the War*, pp. 6-7.

68 O.S.S., "Survey of Belgium," pp. 17-18.

69 Paul Lévy, *La querelle du récensement* (Brussels, 1960), p. 131.

70 Lorwin, "Belgium," p. 158.

71 Höjer, *Le régime parlementaire*, pp. 7-8.

72 Eppstein, *Belgium*, p. 47.

73 Willequet, "Les fascismes belges," p. 87.

74 Ibid.

75 Cited in Höjer, *Le régime parlementaire*, p. 7; Lorwin, "Belgium," p. 159.

76 Lévy, *La querelle*, p. 127; Lorwin, "Conflict and Compromise," p. 8.

77 Höjer, *Le régime parlementaire*, pp. 9-10.

78 Périn, *La Belgique au défi*, pp. 89-90.

79 Ibid., pp. 85, 89.

80 Lévy, *La querelle*, pp. 84-85.

81 [Xavier de Grunne], *La Belgique loyale*, No. 1 (n.p. [1941]), p. 68.

82 Périn, *La Belgique au défi*, p. 83.

83   Lévy, *La querelle*, p. 134; A. De Jonghe, interview with author, Brussels, July 15, 1974.

84   Lévy, *La querelle*, p. 21.

85   Höjer, *Le régime parlementaire*, p. 9.

86   Ruys, *De vlamingen*, pp. 84-85.

87   Höjer, *Le régime parlementaire*, p. 14.

88   Emile Cammaerts, *The Keystone of Europe: A History of the Belgian Dynasty, 1830-1939* (London, 1939), p. 301.

89   Ruys, *De vlamingen*, pp. 78-79.

90   I. Schöffer, *Het nationaal-socialistische beeld van de geschiedenis der Nederlanden: een historiografische en bibliografische studie* (Arnhem/Amsterdam, [1957]), p. 53.

91   Höjer, *Le régime parlementaire*, p. 15.

92   Schöffer, *Het nationaal-socialistische beeld*, pp. 53-54.

93   Petri, *Die Niederlande und das Reich*, pp. 33-34; Ruys, *De vlamingen*, p. 89; Jean Gallant, interview with author, Brussels, August 13, 1974.

94   Willequet, "Les fascismes belges," pp. 91-92; *Het process Borginon* (Antwerp, 1948), pp. 148-49.

95   Höjer, *Le régime parlementaire*, p. 16.

96   Ruys, *De vlamingen*, p. 115.

97   Ibid., pp. 95-98.

98   Höjer, *Le régime parlementaire*, pp. 23-24.

99   Franz Petri, interview with author, June 28, 1971.

100 Maurice-Pierre Herremans, *La question flamande* (Brussels, 1948), pp. 105-06.

101 Luçien Marchal, *Histoire de Wallonie* (Brussels, [1952]), p. 296; A Cordewiener, "Les mouvements wallons clandestins et la préparation de la libération," (unpublished m.s., 1974), pp. 1-2, CREHSGMB.

102 Périn, *La Belgique au défi*, p. 33.

103 Huysmans, *Belgie in den storm*, p. 29.

104 Fritz Fischer, *Germany's Aims in the First World War* (New York, 1967), pp. 37-38.

105 Huysmans, *Belgie in den storm*, p. 31.

106 Fischer, *Germany's Aims*, pp. 99-113.

107 Wilfried Wagner, *Belgien in der deutschen Politik des Zweiten Weltkrieges* (Boppard, 1974), p. 68.

108 David Owen Kieft, *Belgium's Return to Neutrality: An Essay in the Frustrations of Small Power Diplomacy* (Oxford, 1972), pp. 1-2.

109 Ibid., pp. 49-51; Jacques Willequet, "Regards sur la politique belge d'indépendance," *Revue d'histoire de la deuxième guerre mondiale* 31 (1958): 4. (Hereafter cited as Willequet, "Regards.")

110 Kieft, *Belgium's Return to Neutrality*, p. 55.

111 R. Devleeshouwer, "Les belges et la drôle de guerre," *Revue générale belge*, May 1960, p. 102; Joye and Lewin, *L'église et le mouvement ouvrier*, p. 269.

112 Spaak, *Combats inachevés*, vol. 1, 49; Kieft, *Belgium's Return to Neutrality*, p. 138; Jane K. Miller, *Belgian Foreign Policy Between the Two Wars* (New York, 1951), p. 226.

113 Emile Wanty, "Les rélations militaires franco-belges de 1936 à Octobre 1939," *Revue d'histoire de la deuxième guerre mondiale*, 31 (1958): 12-18. (Hereafter cited as Wanty, "Les rélations militaires.")

114 Spaak, *Combats inachevés*, vol. 1, 80-81.

115 Wanty, *Les rélations militaires*, pp. 19-21.

116 International Military Tribunal, *Trial of Major War Criminals* (Nuremberg, 1947-49), vol. 39, 33-39. (Hereafter cited as IMT); Willequet, "Regards", p. 7.

117 Ibid.; Spaak, *Combats inachevés*, vol. 1, 54-55; Kieft, *Belgium's Return to Neutrality*, p. 169.

118 *L'an 40*, p. 24; Belgian Information Office, *Thirty Questions about Belgium* (London, 1942), p. 7.

119 Ibid.; Clark, *Belgium and the War*, p. 20.

120 Wanty, "Les rélations militaires," pp. 21-22.

121 Devleeshouwer, "Les belges et la drôle de guerre," pp. 102-03; *L'an 40*, pp. 72-74.

122 Document 375-PS, IMT, vol. 25, 381.

123 Document 58(a)-TC, ibid., vol. 39, 63.

124 Fernand de Langenhove, *La Belgique en quête de sécurité* (Brussels, 1969), p. 44; Spaak, *Combats inachévés*, vol. 1, 70-71; Centre National de la Recherche Scientifique (Paris), *Les rélations militaires franco-belges de mars 1936 au 10 mai 1940* (Paris, 1968), p. 104.

125 "Copie intégrale des documents saisis à Mechelen-sur-Meuse sur un aviateur allemand," (photocopy) Belgium G373, HIAS; P. van Zuylen, *Les mains libres: Politique extérieure de la Belgique 1914-1940* (Paris, 1950), pp. 523-25.

126 H. Pierlot, "Pages d'histoire," twelve articles published in *Le Soir*, reproduced in Commission d'Information instituée par S. M. le Roi Leopold III le 14 juillet 1946, *Note complémentaire, publiée 8 octobre 1947* (Luxembourg, 1948), p. 58. (Hereafter cited as Pierlot, "Pages d'histoire"); Spaak, *Combats inachévés*, vol 1, 77-79.

127 Ibid., pp. 72-76; Pierlot, "Pages d'histoire." pp. 57-58; Willequet, "Regards", p. 10; Centre National, *Les rélations militaires*, p. 107.

128 Van Zuylen, *Les mains libres*, p. 555; Willequet, "Regards", p. 11.

129 *L'an 40*, pp. 36-42; Devleeshouwer, "Les belges et la drôle de guerre," p. 101.

130 Mil Zankin, "Çe qu'on sache: un témoignage," *Le Nouveau Journal*, July 9, 1941.

131 *L'an 40*, pp. 41-43.

132 Ibid., p. 43.

133 Ibid., pp. 43-47.

134 Edmond F.S.A.M.J. Leclef, *Le Cardinal van Roey et l'occupation allemande en Belgique* (Brussels, 1945), p. 14.

135 De Langenhove, *La Belgique en quête de securité*, p. 151.

136 Van Zuylen, *Les mains libres*, p. 553.

137 Spaak, Session of May 10 1940, *Annales parlementaires de Belgique, Chambre des représentants*, p. 1430; Jacques Willequet, *Paul-Henri Spaak: un homme des combats* (Brussels, 1975), p. 102.

138 Spaak, ibid.; Spaak, *Combats inachevés*, vol. 1, 86-87.

139 Spaak, Session of May 10, 1940, *Annales parlementaires*, p. 1431; IMT, vol. 39, 59-61; Belgium, Ministry of Foreign Affairs, *The Official Account of What Happened 1939-1940* (London, n.d.), pp. 28, 100-101; (Germany, Auswärtiges Amt,) *Documents on German Foreign Policy*, Series D, (Washington, D.C. and London, 1947-1964), vol. 9, 301-306. (Hereafter cited as DGFP.)

140 Pierlot, "Pages d'histoire", pp. 59-60; Spaak, *Combats inachévés*, vol. 1, 85.

141 Jacques Pirenne, *Le dossier du Roi Léopold: Livre blanc* (Brussels, 1970), pp. 71-74; Jean Vanwelkenhuyzen, July 26, 1981.

142 Pierlot, Session of May 10, 1940, *Annales parlementaires*, p. 1429.

143 Frans van Cauwelaert, ibid., p. 1428.

144 Fernand Cornil, *Détresse et espérance: les responsabilités du commandement de l'armée et du gouvernement dans la tragédie de mai 1940* (Brussels, 1944), p. 147.

145 R. Capelle, *Au service du Roi* (Brussels, 1949), vol. 2, 23.

146 Pierlot, "Pages d'histoire," p. 72.

147 Armeehauptquartier, "Übergabeverhandlung," May 28, 1940, RW 36/v.49, Militärarchiv-Bundesarchiv, Freiburg, or Microcopy T 501, roll 97, frame 67, Records of German Field Commands: Rear Areas, Occupied Territories and Others, Captured German Records Microfilmed at Alexandria, U.S. National Archives, Washington, D.C. (Subsequent citations from Militärarchiv: location indicated by letters MAF; location citation omitted from RW 36 record group. Subsequent citations from Captured German Records Microfilmed at Alexandria indicated by letters CGRMA; location citation omitted from T 501 record group; hereafter cited as (example) T 501/97/67).

148 Militärbefehlshaber in Belgien und Nordfrankreich, (hereafter cited as MBBNF), Militärverwaltungschef, (hereafter cited as MVCh), Tätigkeitsbericht Nr. 7, August 4, 1940, RW 36/v.165, pp. 49-52, or T 501/102/823-26. (Hereafter cited as T 7 (etc.), with date and documentation data;) *L'an 40*, pp. 110-12, 118.

149 Ibid., p. 112.

150 Ibid., p. 114; Militärverwaltung, Abtlg. Gent, Oberfeldkommandantur 570, Tätigkeitsbericht, October 15, 1940, Rep. 320; Nr. 2920, Reichsministerium des Inneren, BAK; Serge Doring, *L'école de la douleur: souvenirs d'un déporté politique* (Brussels, n.d.), passim.

151 Wim Meyers, interview with author, Brussels, June 25, 1975.

152 Jean Vanwelkenhuyzen and Jacques Dumont, *1940: Le grand exode* (Brussels, 1983), p. 182.

153 Alexander von Falkenhausen, *Memoirs d'outre-guerre* (Brussels, 1974), p. 120; also "Memoiren," Alte Fassung der Memoiren mit handschriftlichen Korrekturen, chap. 12, p. 38, Nachlass Alexander von Falkenhausen, N 246/43, p. 143 (archival pagination), MAF. (Hereafter cited as von Falkenhausen, "Memoiren," N 246, MAF.)

Notes

154 Jean-Léon Charles, *Les forces armées belges au cours de la deuxième guerre mondiale 1940-1945* (Brussels, 1970), p. 53.

155 See *Note complémentaire*, p. 20 for postwar adherence to this line of comment.

156 Basil Bartlett, *My First War: An Army Officer's Journal for May 1940: Through Belgium to Dunkirk* (London, 1940), pp. 59, 65, 80, and 109.

157 Spaak, *Combats inachévés*, vol. 1, 91.

158 G. H. Dumont, *Léopold III, Roi des belges* (Brussels, 1945), p. 294; *Note complémentaire*, p. 20.

159 Pierlot, "Pages d'histoire," pp. 30, 60-61; Paul-Henri Spaak, *The Continuing Battle* (Boston, 1972), p. 38.

160 Spaak, Session of July 25, 1945, *Annales parlementaires*, p. 572; Pierlot, "Pages d'histoire," pp. 63-64, quoting *Rapport de la Commission d'Information institué par S. M. le Roi Léopold III le 14 juillet 1946* (Luxembourg, 1947), p. 51; Spaak, *The Continuing Battle*, p. 43.

161 Ibid., p. 39; Pierlot, "Pages d'histoire," pp. 61, 71.

162 Ibid., pp. 65, 71-72; Pirenne, *Le dossier du Roi*, p. 107.

163 Pierlot, "Pages d'histoire," pp. 60-68; Spaak, *Combats inachévés*, vol. 1, 89-94.

164 Pierlot, "Pages d'histoire," p. 72; Pirenne, *Le dossier du Roi*, p. 104.

165 Capelle, *Au service du Roi*, p. 23; Spaak, *The Continuing Battle*, p. 46; Pierlot, "Pages d'histoire," pp. 71-75.

166 E. R. Arango, *Leopold III and the Belgian Royal Question* (Baltimore, 1963), p. 69.

167 Pierlot, "Pages d'histoire," p. 76.

168 Cornil, *Détresse et espérance*, p. 149; Jean Piron, *Souvenirs* (Brussels, 1969), pp. 40-41; René Didisheim, *L'histoire de la Brigade Piron: au délai de la légende* (Brussels, 1946), pp. 13-14.

169 Secrétariat du Roi, *Recueil de documents établi par le Secrétariat du Roi concernant la période 1936-1949* (n.p., n.d.), Annexe 76, p. 177.

170 "Zusatzprotokoll Nr. 1 zur Übergabeverhandlung mit der belgischen Wehrmacht vom 28. Mai 1940," RW 36/v.49, or T 501/97/69.

171 Pierlot, "Pages d'histoire," pp. 77-79; Arango, pp. 56-57; Albert Kammerer, *La vérite sur l'armistice: Ephéméride de ce qui s'est réellement passé*

(Paris, 1944), pp. 49-53; J. A. Wullus-Rudiger, *La Belgique et la crise européenne 1914-1945* (Paris, 1945), vol. 1, 457.

172 George K. Tanham, "British Press Reaction to the Belgian Surrender, *The Historian*, Autumn 1947, p. 4; Capelle, *Au service du Roi*, vol. 2, 23; Wullus-Rudiger, *La Belgique et la crise européenne*, vol. 1, 460-64.

173 Ibid., pp. 464-67.

174 Pierlot, "Pages d'histoire," pp. 80-81.

Chapter Three

1 Fritz Fischer's *Germany's Aims in the First World War* has been the pioneer effort in this area.

2 Edward N. Peterson, *The Limits of Hitler's Power* (Princeton, N.J., 1969) is a good example of a regional study emphasizing the scope and limits of central authority in the Third Reich.

3 Schöffer, *Het nationaal-socialistische beeld*, pp. 100-101.

4 Ibid., pp. 117-18.

5 Fischer, *Germany's Aims*, pp. 98-100.

6 Ibid., p. 104.

7 Ibid., pp. 109-11.

8 Ibid.

9 Ibid., pp. 112.

10 Gordon Craig, *The Politics of the Prussian Army* (New York, 1970), pp. 340-41.

11 Fischer, *Germany's Aims*, p. 113.

12 Armand J. Wullus-Rudiger, *En marge de la politique belge 1914-1956* (Paris, 1957), pp. 26-27.

13 Wagner, *Belgien in der deutschen Politik*, pp. 66-68.

14 Ibid., pp. 62-63.

15 "Geheimgehaltene Rede Hitlers vor dem politischen Führernachwuchs auf der Ordensburg Sonthofen (Allgäu) am 23.XI.1937 über die deutsche Geschichte und das deutsche Schicksal," Anhang, *Hitlers Tischgespräche im Führerhauptquartier 1941 - 1942*, ed. Gerhard Ritter (Bonn, 1951), pp. 444-47.

16 "Grenzfragen im Westen," [June] 1940, Memorandum submitted to the Military Commander on June 16, 1940, RW 36, v.48, or T501/96/828; Informationsbericht Nr. 42, September 6, 1940, Generalkommissar zur besonderen Verwendung, GkzbV st 73 d., RvOA.

17 Vortragsnotiz betr. Verwaltung der besetzten Gebiete Luxemburgs, Belgiens und Hollands, October 31, 1939, OKW Documents L IV, RvOA.

18 Notiz über eine Besprechung mit Obrstlt. Böhmer vom OKW, June 4, 1940, MBBNF, Der Chef des Kommandostabes, RW 36/v.48, or T 501/96/845.

19 Wagner, *Belgien in der deutschen Politik*, pp. 172-73; Eberhard Jäckel, *Frankreich in Hitlers Europa* (Stuttgart, 1966), 45-47.

20 Keitel to Oberbefehlshaber des Heeres, July 14, 1940, RW 36/v.36.

21 Lammers to Ficker, October 21, 1941, R 43^{II}/678, BAK.

22 Fragments of Goebbels' Diary, May 30, 1942, Nr. III 21g, 16/5c, RvOA.

23 *Reichsgesetzblatt* I, 777, May 20, 1940 (Berlin, 1940); Wagner, *Belgien in der deutschen Politik*, pp. 127-33.

24 Eggert Reeder and Walter Hailer, "Die Militärverwaltung in Belgien und Nordfrankreich," September 1943, reprint from vol. 6 of *Reich, Volksordnung, Lebensraum. Zeitschrift für völkische Verfassung und Verwaltung* (Darmstadt, [1943]), pp. 25-26, RW 36/v.373, or T 501/102/28-29.

25 Wagner, *Belgien in der deutschen Politik*, pp. 169, 254.

26 Interview Dr. Globke, September 23 and October 15, 1945, Document 513-F, IMT, vol. 26, 218-23.

27 Von Falkenhausen to Generalquartiermeister, OKH, April 26, 1941, Volk I/11, MA-167, IfZM; see also memorandum "Unterschiede zwischen Belgien und Nordfrankreich einerseits und dem übrigen Frankreich andererseits," September 30, 1940, RW 36/v.48, or T 501/96/796.

28 Dr. Kahlenberg, "Quellen zur Geschichte Belgiens während der beiden Weltkriege" 1, 1-13, BAK.

29 Eggert Reeder, Proces Verbal (hereafter cited as P.V.), September 29, 1950, Ständiges Kriegsgericht Brüssel/2. Frz. Kammer, Verfahren gegen den ehem. Gen. u. MilBfh. Belgien und Nordfrankreich, Alexander von Falkenhausen, den ehem. MilVerwCh. Belgien und Nordfrankreich Eggert Reeder, den ehem. Gen. u. OFK von Lüttich, Georg Bertram und den ehem. Gen. u. OFK von Lüttich, Bernhard von Claer, v. 25.9.1950 - 27.1.1951 (zit Brüssel, Falkenhausen Prozess), Brüssel, 1950-1951, vol. 1, 23, IfZM. (Hereafter cited as P.v.F. Here-

after location of trial record omitted from citations from the trial of General von Falkenhausen and associates;) Harry von Craushaar, P.V. October 11, 1950, ibid., vol. 2, 121.

30 Vortragsnotiz, October 31, 1939, OKW Documents, L IV, 25009-13 (CDI 113), RvOA; also C.D.I. Kriegstagebuch Nr. 1, December 1939, VI, NG 5347, RvOA.

31 Franz Thedieck, interview with author, Bonn, July 20, 1971.

32 Ibid.

33 "Erlass über die Verwaltung der besetzten Gebiete Frankreichs, Luxemburgs und Belgiens", #213, DGFP, Series D, vol. 9, 301-02. Also OKW Records, T 77/545/720424-25, CGRMA.

34 Von Falkenhausen, "Memoiren," chap. 12, p. 17 a, N 246/43, MAF.

35 MBBNF, MVCh, "Jahresbericht der Militärverwaltung für das erste Einsatzjahr," July 15, 1941, pp. B-1 - B-6, RW 36/v.201, or T 501/104/762-767 (hereafter cited as Jahresbericht 1940-1941); Office of Strategic Services, "German Military Government over Europe" Vol. 2 "Belgium," R&A No. 2500.2 (Washington, D.C., 1945), passim.

36 Werner Best, "Die deutschen Aufsichtsverwaltungen in Frankreich, Belgien, den Niederlanden und im Protektorat Böhmen und Mähren," (mimeographed, [1941]), pp. 76-77, and passim, HIAS.

37 Abschlussbericht, "Die landeseigene Verwaltung," p. 8, RW 36/v.330, or T 501/107/224.

38 Eggert Reeder, "L'organisation de l'Administration Militaire. Ma position dans cette administration et ma position vis-à-vis du Commandant militaire," Rapport remis par le Président Reeder à Monsieur le Substitut de L'Auditeur General Wilmart au date de 19. 7. 1949, P.v.F., vol. 10, 1083 - 84. (Hereafter cited as Reeder, "Grand Report.")

39 Jahresbericht 1940-41, p. B-10, RW 36/v.201, or T 501/104/771.

40 T 12, January 3, 1941, pp. 24-25, RW 36/v.171, or T 501/103/674-675.

41 Ibid., p. 26, or frame 676.

42 Philipp Freiherr von Brand, P.V. October 31, 1950, P.v.F., vol. 4, 358; Karl Graf du Moulin, P.V. October 30, 1950, p. 22, ibid., vol. 3, 342-44.

43 Du Moulin, ibid.

44 Reeder, "Grand Report", P.v.F., vol. 10, 1079-80.

45 Von Falkenhausen, "Memoiren," chap. 12, p. 23 (insert), N 246/43, MAF.; Reeder, "Grand Report", P.v.F., vol. 10, 1077-78; Jahresbericht 1940-41, p. A-5, RW 36/v.201, or T 501/104/695; Petri, June 18, 1971.

46 Reeder, "Grand Report," P.v.F., vol. 10, 1082-83.

47 Interrogation von Falkenhausen, November 27, 1945, Document 015-RF, IMT, vol. 38, 507; Reeder, "Grand Report", P.v.F., vol. 10, 1104.

48 Ibid., pp. 1105-1108.

49 Von Falkenhausen, "Memoiren," chap. 12, p. 2, N 246/43, MAF.; P.V. September 27, 1950, P.v.F., vol. 1, 10-11; "Alexander von Falkenhausen", *Internationales Biographisches Archiv* (Münzinger Archiv), Lieferung 32/66; "Materalien der deutschen Verteidigung zum alliierten Falkenhausen Prozess", Sig. 126, MAF.

50 Alexander von Falkenhausen, "Exposé fait en cause Reeder," MSg 126/2, MAF; Wagner, *Belgien in der deutschen Politik*, pp. 17, 96.

51 Von Falkenhausen, "Memoiren," chap. 1, p. 22, N 246/40, MAF; Friedrich von Baumann, P.V. May 28, 1946, P.v.F., vol. 7, 696; Reeder, "Grand Report", ibid., vol. 10, 1120; Ulrich von Hassel, *Vom anderen Deutschland: Aus den nachgelassenen Tagebüchern 1938-1944* (Frankfurt, 1964), pp. 192-93; Petri, June 18, 1971.

52 Von Baumann, P.v.F., vol. 7, 702; Cecilie von Falkenhausen, interview with author, Nassau, July 9, 1971.

53 Petri, June 28, 1971.

54 Reeder, "Grand Report," P.v.F., vol. 10, 1120; von Falkenhausen, "Memoiren", chap. 12, pp. 68-69, N 246/43, MAF.

55 Ibid., p. 166.

56 Ibid.

57 Ibid., chap. 1, p. 20.

58 Degrelle, *La cohue de 1940* , p. 507.

59 Von Falkenhausen, "Memoiren," chap. 2, pp. 37-38, N 246/40, MAF.; see also Alexander von Falkenhausen, "Memoires," pp. 9-10, JP 1242, CREHSGMB.

60 Von Falkenhausen, "Memoiren," chap. 2, p. 38, N 246/40, MAF; Werner August Graf von der Schulenburg, P.V. October 31, 1950, P.v.F., vol. 4, 354-55.

61 Von Falkenhausen, P.V. September 27, 1950, P.v.F., vol. 1, 12.

62 Interrogation of Constantin Canaris, June 22, 1948, P.v.F, vol. 7, 760.

63 Von Falkenhausen, P.V. September 27, 1950, P.v.F., vol. 1, 12; Hans Speidel, P.V. November 8, 1950, ibid., vol. 4, 447-50.

64 Von Falkenhausen, P.V. September 27, 1950, P.v.F., vol. 1, 12.

65 Von Hassel, *Vom anderen Deutschland*, p. 195; Reeder, "Grand Report", P.v.F., vol. 10, 1129.

66 "Alexander von Falkenhausen", *Internationales Biographisches Archiv*.

67 Von Falkenhausen, P.V. September 27, 1950, P.v.F., vol 1, 12.

68 Von Falkenhausen, "Memoiren," chap. 12, p. 28, N 246/43, MAF; Petri, June 28, 1971: (Petri claimed that von Falkenhausen understood the significance of the cancellation of Operation Sea Lion in September 1940 when he told his officers: "You are wrong to be so happy..."); von Brand, P.V. October 31, 1950, P.v.F., vol. 4, 359-60; Georges Goethals, P.V. November 13, 1950, ibid., vol. 5, 487.

69 Von Falkenhausen, "Memoiren," chap. 12, p. 28, N 246/43, MAF; Hans Speidel, November 8, 1950, P.v.F., vol. 4, 449-50.

70 Von Baumann, P.V. May 28, 1946, P.v.F., vol. 7, 697; von Falkenhausen, September 29, 1950, ibid., vol. 1, 20.

71 Von Falkenhausen, "Memoiren," chap. 12, p. 25, N 246/43, MAF; Harry von Craushaar, P.V. October 13, 1950, P.v.F., vol. 2, 147.

72 Von Falkenhausen, "Memoiren," chap. 12, p. 75, N 246/43, MAF.; Interrogation of Constantin Canaris, June 22, 1948, P.v.F., vol. 7, 762-63.

73 Von Falkenhausen, P.V. October 3, 1950, P.v.F., vol 1, 46-47.

74 A. de Jonghe, June 15, 1975.

75 Elisabeth d'Ursel, P.V. November 17, 1950, P.v.F., vol. 5, 561-62; Albert de Ligne, P.V. November 13, 1950, ibid., 481-82; Jean de Lantsheere, P.V. November 13, 1950, ibid., 492-94.

76 P.v.F., vol. 5, 496.

77 Roger Van Praag, P.V. November 15, 1950, P.v.F., vol. 5, 531-32.

78 Georges Goethals, P.V. November 13, 1950, P.v.F., vol. 5, 489-90.

79 Von Falkenhausen, "Memoiren", chap. 12, p.30, N 246/43, MAF.; von Craushaar, P.V. October 13, 1950, P.v.F., vol. 2, 147.

80 Von Brand, P.V. October 31, 1950, P.v.F., vol. 4, 359-60.

81 Von Falkenhausen, "Memoiren", chap. 12, p. 16, N 246/43, MAF.

82 Affidavit furnished by Eric Warburg, September 13, 1950, Fa Doc 91, Msg 126/4, "Alexander von Falkenhausen", MAF.

83 Gerhard M. Engel, P.V. November 10, 1950, P.v.F., vol. 4, 459.

84 P.v.F., vol. 4, p. 461.

85 Von Falkenhausen, "Memoiren", chap. 12, pp. 30, 115-16, 121, N 246/43, MAF.; von Falkenhausen and von Craushaar, P.V. October 13, 1950, P.v.F., vol. 2, 147.

86 Reeder, "Grand Report", P.v.F., vol. 10, 1128-29; Paul Beyer, P.V. October 17, 1950, ibid., vol. 2, 200; Gregor Geller, P.V. November 7, 1950, ibid., vol. 4, 407.

87 Ständiges Kriegsgericht Brüssel/Kriegsauditorium, Ermittlungsverfahren gegen ehem. Angehörige der Dienststelle C d S Brüssel: KrimDir SS Stubaf Franz Straub, Ltr der Abtlg IV; Krim Sekr SS Ustuf Walter Altenhof, Sachbearbeiter im Ref A der Abtlg IV; Krim Ass. SS OSchaf Heinrich Cuypers, Sachbearbeiter im Ref A der Abtlg IV; Krim Angest. SS Rottenf Helmut Vits, Ref A der Abtlg IV, ([Brüssel], n.d.), vol. 10, 38, IfZM. (Hereafter cited as Process Straub.)

88 Cecilie von Falkenhausen, August 17, 1971.

89 Thedieck, July 20, 1971.

90 Von Baumann, P.V. May 28, 1946, P.v.F., vol. 7, 698; von Brand, P.V. October 31, 1950, ibid., vol. 4, 358.

91 Rapport redigé par Theodore Büchner, October 7-8, 1948, P.v.F., vol. 12, 1387-88.

92 Von Baumann, May 28, 1946, P.v.F., vol. 7, 698.

93 Von Falkenhausen, "Memoiren," chap. 12, p. 31, N 246/43, MAF.

94 Von Baumann, May 28, 1946, P.v.F., vol. 7, 699.

95 Berger to Himmler, October 18, 1940, Records Reichsführer SS und Chief of German Police, T 175/127/2652287-89, CGRMA; Berger to Himmler, September 17, 1941, NS 19/ neu 2140, BAK.

96 Von Baumann, May 28, 1946, P.v.F., vol. 7, 702.

97 Von Falkenhausen, "Memoiren," chap. 12, pp. 117-18 (text and marginalia), N 246/43, MAF.

98 Ibid., pp. 115-16, 121, N 246/43, MAF.

99 Von Brand, P.V. October 31, 1950, P.v.F., vol. 4, 355-58.

100 Von Baumann, May 28, 1946, P.v.F., vol. 7, 703.

101 Reinhold von Thadden - Trieglaff, P.V. October 25, 1950, P.v.F., vol. 3, 307.

102 Günther Plum, "Staatspolizei und innere Verwaltung 1934-36," *Vierteljahrshefte zur Zeitgeschichte* 2/65: 206-07.

103 P.V. September 29, 1950, P.v.F., vol. 1, 21.

104 Reeder, "Grand Report," P.v.F., vol. 10, 1124-25.

105 Biographical information on Reeder drawn from: P.V. September 29, 1950, P.v.F., vol. 1, 21-27; entry "Reeder," contribution by Franz Petri to *Encyclopaedie van de Vlaamse Beweging*, (Tielt, 1973-1975), vol. 2, 1305.

106 Alexander von Falkenhausen, "Exposé fait en cause Reeder," MSg 126/2, MAF.

107 Petri, June 28, 1971; Franz Thedieck, "Ansprache anlässlich der Gedenkstunde für Eggert Reeder am 22. November 1960 in Bonn," TS, p. 11. (In possession of author.)

108 T 26, October-December 1943, p. A-20, RW 36/v.187, or T 501/106/711.

109 Thedieck, "Ansprache," p. 12.

110 Von Baumann, May 28, 1946, P.v.F., vol. 4, 699-700.

111 De Jonghe, June 15, 1975. Franz Petri disagreed with this point of view in 1971 (in interview with author, June 18, 1971).

112 Thedieck, July 20, 1971.

113 Franz Thedieck, P.V. October 18, 1950, P.v.F., vol. 2, 214.

114 Petri, June 18, 1971, and Thedieck, July 20, 1971; F. Wimmers, P.V. January 17, 1950, P.v.F., vol. 12, 1410-11.

115 Schöffer, *Het nationaal-socialistische beeld*, p. 103.

116 Ibid., pp. 155-57.

117 Ibid., pp. 104, 244-45.

118 Franz Petri, *Brüsseler Zeitung*, July 1, 1941, NSDAP, Ordner Belgien, NS 22/vorl., p. 496, BAK.

119 Schoeffer, *Het nationaal-socialistische beeld*, p. 107.

120 Petri, June 18, 1971.

121 Schöffer, *Het nationaal-socialistische beeld*, pp. 103-04, 158, 244.

122 Herbert von Bismarck, P.V. October 31, 1950, P.v.F., vol. 4, 363.

123 Reeder, "Grand Report," P.v.F., vol. 10, 1132-33.

124 Ibid., pp. 1115-16.

125 Von Falkenhausen, P.V. September 29, 1950, P.v.F., vol. 1, 25.

126 Reeder, "Grand Report," P.v.F., vol. 10, 1107-08, 1117, 1132-33.

127 Ibid., p. 1119.

128 Otto Schikarski, P.V. October 30, 1950, P.v.F., vol 3, 337-38.

129 Von Falkenhausen, "Exposé fait en cause Reeder," MSg 126/2, MAF.

130 Reeder, "Grand Report," P.v.F., vol. 10, 1122.

131 Von Falkenhausen, P.V. September 29, 1950, P.v.F., vol. 1, 26.

132 Reeder, "Grand Report," P.v.F., vol. 10, 1128-31 and passim; Von Hassel, *Vom anderen Deutschland*, p. 301.

133 Von Kameke, P.V. October 25, 1950, P.v.F., vol. 3, 253.

134 Reeder, "Grand Report," P.v.F., vol. 10, 1126-27.

135 Reeder, P.V. October 20, 1950, P.v.F., vol. 3, 245; Wagner, *Belgien in der deutschen Politik*, p. 298.

136 Ibid.

137 Vermerk (Report on meeting with Hitler), July 13, 1944, R 43^{II}/678, BAK.

138 Von Falkenhausen, "Exposé fait en cause Reeder,", MSg 126/2, MAF.

139 Reeder, P.V. October 20, 1950, P.v.F., vol. 3, 245.

140 Wagner comes to similar but somewhat more cautious conclusions (Wagner, *Belgien in der deutschen Politik*, pp. 299-300).

141 Arenberg, pers 100/1, November 18, 1944, Abwicklungsstab, RW 25/.173, MAF.

142 The Belgian scholar Albert De Jonghe has devoted detailed attention to the struggle over the introduction of a political "civilian" administration and particularly to the issue of the establishment of the office of Higher SS and Police Leader in Belgium. The results of these studies may be

located in a succession of articles published in the *Cahiers d'histoire de la seconde guerre mondiale*. (Hereafter cited as *Cahiers*.) The first of these was "L'établissement d'une administration civile en Belgique et dans le Nord de la France (document)," *Cahiers* 1 (August 1970): 27-127; a subsequent study "La lutte Himmler-Reeder pour la nomination d'un HSSPF à Bruxelles", which appeared in five installments focusses on the issue of the Higher SS and Police Leader, but also furnishes a great deal of information on the question of the replacement of the Military Administration, (cf. note 26 of bibliographical essay below); see also chap. 4 "Der Streit um die Einführung der Zivilverwaltung", in Wilfried Wagner's *Belgien in der deutschen Politik*.

143 T 175/94/2 615 218, CGRMA, cited in Wagner, p. 132.

144 MBBNF, Der Chef des Kommandostabes, "Notiz einer Besprechung mit Oberstlt. Böhmer vom OKW," June 4, 1940, RW 36/v.48, or T 501/96/845.

145 Stuckart to Lammers, June 4, 1940, R 43^{II}/675, pp. 65-68, BAK; von Falkenhausen, "Von Falkenhausen 1922-45," p. 40, MS # B-289, U.S. National Archives, Washington, D.C.

146 Von Falkenhausen to OKH, June 25, 1940, T 501/94/401-402.

147 OKH to MBBNF, MVCh, July 20, 1940, RW 36/v.39, or T 501/94/479.

148 Stuckart, November 4, 1941, I, Ra10249/41, R 43^{II}/678a, BAK.

149 Wagner, *Belgien in der deutschen Politik*, p. 158.

150 Lammers, October 21, 1941, R 43^{II}/678, BAK.

151 Oberbefehlshaber West to Oberbefehlshaber des Heeres, November 24, 1941, RW 36/v.48, or T 501/96/665-660; Wagner, *Belgien in der deutschen Politik*, pp. 243-46.

152 Lammers, May 14, 1942, R 43^{II}/678, BAK.

153 Stuckart to Lammers, October 9, 1942, ibid.; Wagner, *Belgien in der deutschen Politik*, pp. 250-54.

154 "Betrifft: Umwandlung der Militärverwaltung in Belgien in eine Zivilverwaltung," Rk 775A, October [n.d], 1942, [E245040-48], R 43^{II}/678, BAK.

155 Notation, [E245048], ibid.

156 Wagner, *Belgien in der deutschen Politik*, pp. 265, 270.

157 Von Ribbentrop to Lammers, March 27, 1944, [E43216-19] R 43^{II}/678, BAK.

158 "Erlass des Führers über die Errichtung einer Zivilverwaltung in den besetzten Gebieten von Belgien und Nordfrankreich," July 13, 1944, Rk 852, R 43^{II}/678, pp. 190-94, BAK.

159 Vermerk, (Report on meeting with Hitler), July 13, 1944, R43^{II}/678, pp. 167-71, BAK.

160 Ibid., p. 168.

161 Ibid., p. 169.

162 Ibid., pp. 169-71.

163 A. De Jonghe, "La lutte Himmler-Reeder," 5, *Cahiers* 8 (1984): 200.

164 Keitel to Lammers, October 13, 1941, R 43^{II}/678a, BAK; "Vernehmung des Hans Heinrich Lammers," March 10, 1948, Doc I-1007, RvOA.

165 Von Falkenhausen, "Von Falkenhausen 1922-45," pp. 59-61, MS# B-289, U.S. National Archives.

166 "Betrifft: Umwandlung der Militärverwaltung..," Rk775a, October [n.d.], 1942, [55/E245044], R 43^{II}/678, BAK.

167 Berger to Himmler, July 31, 1944, Tagebuch Nr. 694, NS 19/neu 1541, BAK; De Jonghe, "La lutte Himmler-Reeder" 5, *Cahiers* 8 (1984): 168.

168 Grohé to Himmler, July 29, 1944, NS 19/neu 1541, BAK.

169 Ibid.; Personnel Record Richard Jungclaus, Berlin Document Center, March 17, 1965, RvOA.

170 "Vermerk", Lammers, August 4, 1944, Rk 664 0D, R 43^{II}/678b, pp. 33-34, BAK.

171 Chef des OKW, August 12, 1944, ibid., p. 10.

172 Berger to Himmler, July 31, 1944, Tagebuch Nr. 694, NS 19/neu 1541, BAK.

173 Lammers, Vermerk, August 4, 1944, Rk 664 0D, R 43^{II}/678b., pp. 32-33, BAK.

174 De Jonghe, "La lutte Himmler-Reeder" 5, *Cahiers* 8 (1984): 176-177; George Tanham, *Contribution à l'histoire de la résistance belge 1940-1944* (Brussels, 1971), pp. 179-80.

175 T 14, February 1941, pp. 64-65, RW 36/v.173, or T 501/104/87-88.

176 T 15, March 1941, RW 36/v.174, pp. A-4 - A-5, or T 501/104/158-59.

177 T 13, January 1941, RW 36/v.172, p. A-12, or T 501/103/953.

178 Militärverwaltung, Abschlussbericht "Die landeseigene Verwaltung," p. 77, RW 36/v.339, or T 501/107/226.

179 T 16, April 1941, p. A-15, RW 36/v.175, or T 501/104/344.

180 Jahresbericht 1940-1941, p. 38, RW 36/v.201, or T 501/104/728.

181 T 15, March 1941, p. A-6, RW 36/v.174, or T 501/104/160; Abschlussbericht "Die landeseigene Verwaltung," pp. 51-52, RW 36/v.339, or T 501/107/266-267.

182 Ibid., p. 53, or frame 268.

183 Ibid., p. 34, or frame 249.

184 MBBNF, MVCh, "Verordnung über die Anwendung von Verordnungen der Generalsekretäre." *Verordnungsblatt des Militärbefehlshabers in Belgien und Nordfrankreich für die besetzten Gebiete Belgiens und Nordfrankreichs herausgegeben vom Militärbefehlshaber (Militärverwaltungschef)* 76/3, May 14, 1942. (Hereafter cited as *Verordnungsblatt*.)

185 Abschlussbericht "Die landeseigene Verwaltung," p. 8, RW 36/v.339, or T 501/107/224.

186 Ibid., pp. 7-8, or T 501/107/223-224.

187 Jahresbericht 1940-1941, p. A-18, RW 36/v.201, or T 501/104/708.

188 Ibid., p. B-8, or T 501/104/772.

189 Abschlussbericht "Die landeseigene Verwaltung," pp. 54-56, RW 36/v.339, or T 501/107/269-271.

190 Entry May 8, 1943, Paul de Landsheere and Alphonse Ooms, *La Belgique sous les Nazis*, (Brussels, n.d.), vol. 3, 155-58; May 7, 1943, Séances des Secrétaires - Généraux, 1940-1944, pp. 2 - 4 (photocopy), CREHSGMB. (Hereafter cited as Séances CSG. Reference to location omitted hereafter.)

191 May 21, 1943, Séances CSG, pp. 1-5, and Annexe II, May 20, 1943, ibid., pp. 1-5.

192 Abschlussbericht "Die landeseigene Verwaltung," p. 9, RW 36/v.339, or T 501/107/225.

193 Willequet, "Les fascismes belges," pp. 100.

194 T 7, August 4, 1940, p. 26, RW 36/v.165, or T 501/102/800.

195 T 6, July 18, 1940, p. 26, RW 36/v.165, or T 501/102/549.

Notes

196 Jahresbericht 1940-1941, p. B-12 - B-13, RW 36/v.201, or T 501/104/776-77.

197 T 18, September 1, 1941-December 1, 1941, pp. A-3 - A-4, RW 36/v.177, or T 501/105/242-43.

198 MBBNF, MVCh, "Verordnung gegen die Überalterung der öffentlichen Verwaltung," *Verordnungsblatt* 34/3, March 8, 1941.

199 T 15, March 1941, p. B-4, RW 36/v.174, or T 501/104/194.

200 T 18, September 1, 1941-December 1, 1941, pp. A-3 - A-4, RW 36/v.177, or T 501/105/242-43.

201 Reeder and Hailer, "Die Militärverwaltung in Belgien und Nordfrankreich," p. 33, RW 36/v.373, or T 501/102/36.

202 Abschlussbericht "Die landeseigene Verwaltung," p. 37, RW 36/v.339, or T 501/107/252.

203 Ibid., p. 40, or frame 255.

204 Ibid., p. 28, or frame 243.

205 T 18, September 1, 1941-December 1, 1941, p. A-3, RW 36/v.177, or T 501/105/242.

206 Jahresbericht 1940-1941, p. B-22, RW 36/v.201, or T 501/104/786.

207 T 25, July-September 1943, p. A-36, RW 36/v.186, or T 501/106/515.

208 Jahresbericht 1940-1941, p. 44, RW 36/v.201, or T 501/104/734.

209 Abschlussbericht "Die landeseigene Verwaltung," pp. 20-23, RW 36/v.339, or T 501/107/236-239.

210 T 13, January 1941, p. 46, RW 36/v.172, or T 501/103/989.

211 T 22, September 1 - December 1, 1942, p. B-22, RW 36/v.182, or T 501/105/1261.

212 Jahresbericht 1940-1941, p. B-47, RW 36/v.201, or T 501/104/812.

213 Ibid., p. B-49, or frame 814.

214 Ibid., p. B-52, or frame 817.

215 T 11, December 1, 1940, p. 47, RW 36/v.170, or T 501/103/418.

216 T 27, March 1944, p. B-19, RW 36/v.106, or T 501/106/928.

217 Abschlussbericht der Militärverwaltung in Belgien und Nordfrankreich, "Einführung in das Gebiet der Wirtschaft," pp. 40-41, RW 36/v.249, or T 501/107/158-159.

218 Ibid.; "Verordnung über die Einführung des Ordnungsstrafverfahrens," December 18, 1940, *Verordnungsblatt* 27/2, and "2.Verordnung über das Ordnungsstrafrecht," August 2, 1941, ibid. 51/1.

219 Abschlussbericht "Wirtschaftslenkung und Wirtschaftskontrolle," pp. 93-94, RW 36/v.328, or T 501/107/1051-1052.

220 Séances CSG, February 17, 1941 and February 19, 1941.

221 Abschlussbericht "Wirtschaftslenkung und Wirtschaftskontrolle," p. 95, or T 501/107/1053.

222 T 28, April 1944, p. B-13, RW 36/v.189, or T 501/106/987.

223 Jahresbericht 1940-1941, p. B-57, RW 36/v.43, or T 501/96/525.

224 September 29, 1950, P.v.F., vol. 1, 19.

225 C. Lohest and G. Kreit, *La défense des belges devant le conseil de guerre allemand* (Liège, 1945), pp. 10, 14.

226 Ibid., p. xiv, and p. 3.

227 Ibid., p. 17.

228 Jahresbericht 1940-1941, p. B-56, RW 36/v.43, or T 501/96/524; September 29, 1950, P.v.F., vol. 1, 20.

229 November 27, 1950, P.v.F., vol. 6, 631.

230 T 11, December 1, 1940, p. 47, RW 36/v.170, or T 501/103/418.

231 T 27, March 1944, p. B-21, RW 36/v.188, or T 501/106/930.

232 P.V. November 7, 1950, P.v.F., vol. 4, 404.

233 W. van Randenborgh, P.V. October 18, 1950, P.v.F., vol. 2, 224-25.

234 Jahresbericht 1940-1941, p. B-115, RW 36/v.201, or T 501/104/880.

235 Generalquartiermeister, Oberkommando des Heeres Nr. 800/40, "Merkblatt ueber die Aufgaben und Befugnisse der G.F.P. beim Oberquartiermeister der Heeresgruppe," pp. 1-2, Wi VIII, 331, MAF.

236 P.V. November 10, 1950, P.v.F., vol. 6, 468-73; P.V. November 21, 1950, ibid., pp. 489-90.

237 Cf. Lohest and Kreit, *La défense des belges*, p. 20; Edmond Hoton, *Leurs gueules: essai de zoologie germanique* (Brussels, 1944), p. [14].

238 De Jonghe, "La lutte Himmler-Reeder," 1, *Cahiers* 3 (October 1974): 117-23.

239 Ibid., pp. 148-49.

240 Der Beauftragte der Sicherheitspolizei und des SD für den Bereich des Militärbefehlshabers in Belgien und Nordfrankreich, Brüssel, February 25, 1943, Nr. 698/43g, R 70/1, BAK.

241 De Jonghe, "La lutte Himmler-Reeder," 1, *Cahiers* 3 (October 1974): 132-33.

242 Jahresbericht 1940-1941, p. B-118, RW 36/v.201, or T 501/104/853.

243 Ibid., pp. B-118 - B-119, or frames 883-884.

244 Reeder, P.V. October 20, 1950, P.v.F., vol. 3, 230-234.

245 De Jonghe, "La lutte Himmler-Reeder," 1, *Cahiers* 3, (October 1974): 130.

246 Reeder, P.V. October 20, 1950, P.v.F., vol. 3, 232-33; Interrogation of Constantin Canaris, June 22, 1948, ibid. vol. 7, 763.

247 "Die nachrichtendienstliche Arbeit der Dienststelle Brüssel und die wesentlichsten Probleme auf dem Arbeitsgebiet der Wirtschaft," Reichssicherheitshauptamt, October 28, 1942, R 58/977, BAK.

248 J.F. Duntze, P.V. October 23, 1950, P.v.F., vol 3, 260; Interrogation of Constantin Canaris, P.V. July 7, 1949, ibid., vol. 10, 1063.

249 Miscellaneous testimony of Belgian witnesses, P.v.F., vol. 3, 260-63.

250 De Jonghe, "La lutte Himmler-Reeder," 5, *Cahiers* 8 (October 1984): 133-34

251 Jahresbericht 1940-1941, pp. B-116 - B-117, RW 36/v.201, or T 501/104/881-82.

252 "Die belgische Polizei," Polizeidenkschrift, March 1943, pp. 9, 19-20, RW 25 .171, MAF; T 18, September 1-December 1, 1941, p. B-48, RW 36/v.203, or T 501/105/644.

253 "Die belgische Polizei," p. 27, RW 25 .171, MAF.

254 Ibid., p. 32.

255 O.S.S., "Survey of Belgium," pp. 33-34; "Die belgische Polizei," p. 1, RW 25 .171, MAF.

256 Ibid., pp. 20-26; T 17, June 1-September 1, 1941, p. B-51, RW 36/v.176, or T 501/105/83.

298 Notes

257 Ibid., pp. B-35 - B-36, or frames 113-14.

258 T 25, July-September 1943, pp. B-13 - B-14, RW 36/v.186, or T 501/106/542-543; T 26, October-December 1943, pp. 38-39, RW 36/v.187, or T 501/106/769-770; T 27, March 1944, p. B-20, RW 36/v.187, or T 501/106/929.

259 T 29, May 1944, p. C-21, RW 36/v.190, or T 501/106/1078.

260 T 30, June 1944, RW 36/v.191, p. C-4, RW 36/v.191, or T 501/106/1175.

261 Séances CSG, June 16, 1944, p. 13.

262 Ibid., September 2, 1944, p. 5.

263 T 20, March 15-June 1, 1942, p. B-26, RW 36/v.178, or T 501/105/868.

264 T 21, June 1-September 1, 142, p. B-24, RW 36/v.180, or T 501/105/1069.

265 "Die belgische Polizei," p. 38, RW 25 .177, MAF.

266 MBBNF, MVCh, Gruppe Politik, "Einsatz von Landeseinwohner (*sic!*) in unmittelbaren Wehrmachtsdiensten," June 24, 1943, p. 8, NS 19/neu 1541, BAK.

267 Ibid., p. 12.

268 Ibid., p. 3.

Chapter Four

1 Jahresbericht 1940-1941, pp. A-7, A-15, RW 36/v.201, or T 501/104/697, 705; see also Reeder to von Bargen, April 29, 1942, pp. 1-2, NS 19/neu 1541, BAK.

2 T 13, January 1941, p. 14, RW 36/v.172, or T 501/103/955.

3 T 20, March 15 - June 1, 1942, p. A-38, RW 36/v.178, or T 501/105/826; F. Duntze, P.V. October 23, 1950, P.v.F., vol. 3, 259; F. Thedieck, P.V. October 18, 1950, ibid., vol. 2, 214; Dienststelle des Auswärtiges Amtes in Brüssel, December 10, 1943, Nr. 2846/43, Abtlg. Inland I-D, Belgien Kirche, 3, Auswärtiges Amt, Politisches Archiv, Bonn, AAPAB.

4 MBBNF, Kommandostab Ia, November 30, 1941, Nr. 4500/41, T 501/95/002; see also MBBNF, Kommandostab Ia, August 22, 1940, T 501/94/515; MBBNF, Kommandostab Ia, May 14, 1941, T 501/93/413; MBBNF, MVCh, Gruppe Politik to OKH, June 22, 1942, RW 25 .1, MAF.

5 T 8, September 15, 1940, pp. 12-13, RW 36/v.166, or T 501/102/905-06; Reeder and Hailer, "Die Militärverwaltung in Belgien und Nordfrankreich," pp. 14-15, RW 36/v.373, or T 501/102/16-17.

6 T 14, February 1941, p. 3, RW 36/v.173, or T 501/104/12; MBBNF, Der Chef des Kommandostabes an den Chef des Generalstabes A.O.K. 16, August 31, 1940, T 501/94/532.

7 T 8, September 15, 1940, p. 12, RW 36/v.166, or T 501/102/905.

8 T 16, April 1941, p. A-13, RW 36/v.175, or T 501/104/342.

9 Reeder, "Grand Report," P.v.F., vol. 10, 1119.

10 Petri, June 28, 1971; Reeder to von Bargen, April 29, 1942, p. 7, NS 19/neu 1541, BAK.

11 Ibid., pp. 4-5; Sammelmappe Gelb NG 53470, RvOA.

12 Reeder to von Bargen, April 29, 1942, pp. 6-7.

13 Reeder in *Brüsseler Zeitung* Nr. 149, May 31, 1942.

14 OKH to Militärverwaltungschef, Brüssel, July 20, 1940, RW 36/v.39, or T 501/94/479.

15 Chef OKW to Oberbefehlshaber des Heeres, July 14, 1940, RW 36/v.36.

16 *Brüsseler Zeitung*, quoted in *Journal de Charleroi*, May 29, 1941, Folder 1M, N 277, HIAS.

17 Pirenne, *Le dossier du Roi*, p. 259.

18 A. de Jonghe, *Hitler en het politieke lot van Belgie* (Antwerp, 1972), vol. 1, 109-113.

19 "Compte rendu établi par le Dr. Schmidt," Pirenne, *Le dossier du Roi*, pp. 270-77; "Compte rendu établi par le Roi," Annexe 163, Secretariat du Roi, *Recueuil de documents*, pp. 406-07.

20 Pirenne, *Le dossier du Roi*, p. 282.

21 Entry of June 27, 1942, *Hitler's Secret Conversations* (New York, 1961), p. 503.

22 Kiewitz to von Falkenhausen, December 17, 1941 and July 24, 1942, RW 36/v.49, or T 501/97/18 and frame 4.

23 Rapport Büchner, P.v.F., vol. 12, 1392.

24 "Massnahmen gegen Unruhen in Laeken," October 6, 1941, RW 36/v.49, or T 501/97/37.

25 Himmler to Jungclaus, July 30, 1943, NS 19/neu 75, BAK, or T 175/19/2522991.

26 Himmler to Berger, January 20, 1943, NS 19/neu 1541, BAK.

27 Vortragsnotiz: Betr. Besetzte Gebiete West, Sammelmappe Gelb 25038-39, RvOA; "Arbeitsrichtlinien für die Militärverwaltung," Wi, VIII, 331, MAF.

28 Jahresbericht 1940-1941, pp. 35-36, RW 36/v.201, or T 501/104/725-26.

29 *Volk en Staat*, August 4, 1940.

30 Séances CSG, September 10, 1940, pp. 1-2.

31 Zweiter Bericht Abtlg. Kultur, November 15, 1940, pp. 4-5, VJ Staat, 2170/42, RvOA.

32 Séances CSG, July 25, 1940, August 27, 1940, January 31, 1941, and March 21, 1941.

33 Reeder to Himmler, October 18, 1943, p. 8, NS 19/neu 1530, BAK.

34 T 16, April 1941, p. A-14, RW 36/v.175, or T 501/104/343; T 17, June 1-September 1, 1941, p. A-33, RW 36/v.176, or T 501/105/64.

35 Reeder to Himmler, October 18, 1943, p. 2, NS 19/neu 1530, BAK.

36 Ibid., p. 12.

37 T 18, September 1-December 1941, pp. A-53 - A-54, RW 36/v.177, or T 501/105/303-304.

38 T 20, March 15-June 1, 1942, p. A-30, RW 36/v.178, or T 501/105/818; T 22, September 1-December 1942, pp. B-18 - B-19, RW 36/v.182, or T 501/105/1254-55.

39 Schöffer, *Het national-socialistische beeld*, p. 93.

40 Jahresbericht 1940-1941, p. 35, RW 36/v.201, or T 501/104/725.

41 *Schlag nach*, p. 22.

42 T 6, July 18, 1940, RW 36/v. 164, p. 20, or T 501/102/536.

43 Jahresbericht 1940-1941, p. B-89, RW 36/v.201, or T 501/104/854.

44 Von Bargen to Auswärtiges Amt, January 18, 1943, RW 25 .1, MAF.

45 Sicherheitsdienst (SD), "Meldungen aus Belgien", 12/44, June 15, 1944, R 70/Belgien 5, BAK. (Hereafter cited as SD, Meldungen.)

46 T 11, December 1, 1940, p. 35, RW 36/v.170, or T 501/103/406.

47 T 13, January 1941, p. 28, RW 36/v.172, or T 501/103/970.

48 Petri, June 28, 1971.

49 Von Bargen to Auswärtiges Amt, April 9, 1941, NG 2769, IfZM.

50 T 9, October 1, 1940, pp. 4-5, RW 36/v.167, or T 501/102/1285-86.

51 Séances CSG, August 29, 1941, p. 3; Louis de Lentdecker, *Het proces Romsée* (Antwerp, 1950), p. 89.

52 Ibid.; William Ugeux, "The Press under the Occupation," Jan-Albert Goris, ed., *Belgium under Occupation* (New York, 1947), p. 126.

53 T 11, December 1, 1940, pp. 34-35, RW 36/v.170, or T 501/103/405-406.

54 T 8, September 5, 1940, p. 35, RW 36/v.166, or T 501/102/928; Hoton, *Leurs gueules*, p. 85; Jahresbericht 1940-1941, p. B-90, RW 36/v.201, or T 501/104/855.

55 Ibid., p. B-89, or frame 854.

56 T 26, October-December 1943, Anlage A-3, p. 1, RW 36/v.87, or T 501/106/721.

57 Jahresbericht 1940-1941, p. B-91, RW 36/v.201, or T 501/104/856.

58 Ibid., p. B-92, or frame 857.

59 T 10, October 16, 1940, p. 6, RW 36/v.169, or T 501/103/146.

60 *Verordnungsblatt* 65/1, December 23, 1941; Joseph Bronckart, *Cinq ans d'occupation: Verviers pendant la guerre 1940-1945* (Verviers, 1946), vol. 2, 3.

61 MBBNF, Abtlg Ia, Nr. 89/41, Anlage 2, January 7, 1941, RW 36/v.336, or T 501/98/821.

62 H. Singer, *La vérité sur les juifs* (Brussels, n.d.), p. 4.

63 Propagandaabteilung Belgien, Abtlg. Presse, Box 7, Folder 1 I, N 277, HIAS; Bronckart, *Cinq ans d'occupation*, vol. 3, 94.

64 Propagandaabteilung Belgien Abtlg. Presse, Box 4, Folder III A, N 277, HIAS.

65 Fernand Demany, *Mourir debout: Souvenirs du maquis* (Brussels, [1945]), pp. 185-86; Pierre Bodart, *Avec l'armée belge des partisans* (Brussels, 1948), p. 223.

66 Oberkommando des Heeres, *Heeresgruppen-Verordnungsblatt für die besetzten Gebiete*. Herausgegeben von der Heeresgruppe. Nr. 1, May 10, 1940, Verordnung Nr. 2; *Verordnungsblatt* 65/2, December 27, 1941.

67 Ibid. 14/4, September 2, 1940.

68 Ibid. 17/4, October 19, 1940.

69 Ibid. 2/18, June 17, 1940.

70 Ibid. 53/2, August 25, 1941.

71 Ibid. 70/4, March 18, 1942.

72 Ibid. 56/1, September 24, 1941.

73 Ibid. 101/1, May 10, 1943.

74 MBBNF, Abtlg. Ia, Kriegstagebuch, July 22, 1941, T 501/93/484. (Hereafter cited as KTB.)

75 T 18, September 1-December 1, 1941, p. A-42, RW 36/v.177, or T 501/105/292.

76 MBBNF, (Kdo. St/Verw. St), Ia to Gen. Qu, OKH, August 22, 1940, Nr. 3394/40, T 501/94/520; February 27, 1941, Nr. 857/41, T 501/94/948.

77 T 18, September 1-December 1, 1941, p. A-37, RW 36/v.177, or T 501/105/282.

78 KTB, June 22, 1941, T 501/93/452; Jahresbericht 1940-1941, p. B-120, RW 36/v. 201, or T 501/104/885.

79 KTB 733, SSD July 9, 1943; T 501/95/1312; KTB 741, SSD July 15, 1943, ibid., frame 1325; KTB 750, July 22, 1943, ibid., frame 1335; [Parti Communiste de Belgique] "Guide du militant," October 1943, R 70/Belgien 4, pp. 350-51, BAK.

80 *Brüsseler Zeitung*, April 8, 1944, Anlage 1, T 28, April 1944, RW 36/v.189, or T 501/106/985.

81 Leitender Feldpolizeidirektor beim MBBNF, Tätigkeitsbericht für den Monat April 1944, p. 13, RW 36/v.155, or T 501/108/783; SD, Meldungen 12/44, June 15, 1944, R 70/Belgien 5, BAK; 14/44, July 15, 1944, ibid.; 15/44, August 1, 1944, R 70/Belgien 6, BAK; 16/44, August 15, 1944, ibid.

82 José Gotovitch, interview with author, Brussels, August 10, 1981.

83 T 25, July-September 1943, p. B-11, RW 36/v.186, or T 501/106/540.

84 OKW, February 15, 1940, Documents 9, P.v.F., vol. 16, 1758-59; Von Falkenhausen, ibid., vol. 1, 32.

85 Constantin Canaris, June 22, 1948, P.v.F., vol. 7, 766-67; Von Craushaar, P.V. October 11, 1950, ibid., vol. 2, 131; Von Falkenhausen, "Memoiren," chap. 12, p.75, N 246/43, MAF.

86 Reeder, September 5, 1949, P.v.F., vol. 12, 1355-56.

87 Judgment, P.v.F., vol. 19, 2036-37.

88 Belgium, Commission d'enquête sur les violations des règles du droit des gens, des lois et des coutumes de guerre, 1944; *Les crimes de guerre commis sous l'occupation de la Belgique, 1940-1945: L'arrestation, la déportation et l'exécution des ôtages* (Liège, 1948), pp. 29-30.

89 Ibid.

90 Der Stuf. Killing, Vermerk, June 4, 1944, Betr. politische Aktionen in Belgien (Vortrag beim RFSS am 2.6.44), T 175/131/2657509, CGRMA.

91 Marcel Houtman, *Après quatre ans d'occupation* (Brussels, 1945), p. 270.

92 Killing, Vermerk, June 4, 1944, T 175/131/2657510, CGRMA.

93 T 30, June 1944, p. A-13, RW 36/v.191, or T 501/106/1149.

94 Aktenmaterial über Massnahmen zur Aufrechterhaltung der öffentlichen Ordnung einschl. Sühnemassnahmen, April 15, 1943, p. 2, RW 36/v.53, or T 501/97/475.

95 T 26, October-December 1943, p. A-35, RW 36/v.187, or T 501/106/742.

96 Killing, Vermerk, June 4, 1944, T 175/131/2657510 - CGRMA.

97 SS Hauptsturmführer Killing, Betr. Politische Aktionen in Belgien, June 20, 1944, T 175/131/2657514, CGRMA.

98 MVCh-pol, Nr. 1126/43, September 22, 1943, R 70/Belgien 6, pp. 52-54, BAK.

99 Von Falkenhausen, P.V. October 6, 1950, P.v.F., vol. 1, 82.

100 General z.b.V. beim OKH, Nr. III/99/42, July 5, 1942, RW 36/v.48, or T 501/96/591-92.

101 SD Brussels to MVCh, April 26, 1944, R 70/Belgien 6, pp. 65-66, BAK.

102 Belgium, Commissie voor Oorlogsmisdaden, *De oorlogsmisdaden bedreven onder de bezetting van Belgie 1940-1945: Het folteringscamp Breendonck* (Luik, 1949), p. 15, and passim.

103 Ibid., p. 20.

104 Ibid., pp. 56-57.

105 P.v.F., vol. 9, 1025.

106 OKH, Generalstab des Heeres, Generalquartiermeister, "Arbeitsrichtlinien für die Militärverwaltung," p. 2, RW 19, MAF.

107 Alexander von Falkenhausen, "Exposé fait en cause Reeder," p. 97, MSg 126/2, MAF.

108 Henri De Man, *Gegen den Strom: Memoiren eines europäischen Sozialisten* (Stuttgart, 1953), p. 245.

109 T 5, July 7, 1940, p. 32, RW 36/v.163, or T 5/102/494; Jahresbericht 1940-1941, p. A-62, RW 36/v.201, or T 501/104/752.

110 F. W. Wimmers, February 23, 1948, P.v.F., vol. 12, 1421 - 22.

111 Ibid., p. 1420.

112 Maxime Steinberg, *1942: Les cent jours de la déportation des juifs de Belgique* (Brussels, 1984), p. 92. (Hereafter cited as Steinberg, *Les cent jours*.)

113 Von Hahn, P.V. October 24, 1950, P.v.F., vol. 3, 280.

114 Steinberg, *Les cent jours*, pp. 13 - 15.

115 Maxime Steinberg, *La traque des juifs 1942 - 1944* (Brussels, 1986), vol. 2, 218. (Hereafter cited as Steinberg, *La traque*.)

116 Ibid., p. 206.

117 SIPO/SD Brüssel IV B-3 Erd(mann)/Plum, Einsatzplan September 1, 1943, Beweisdokument 1446, Eichmann Prozess, IfZM.

118 Steinberg, *La traque*, vol. 2, 207 - 208; Steinberg, *Les cent jours*, pp. 197 - 98, 203 - 204.

119 Steinberg, *La traque*, vol. 2, 203 - 204.

120 Maxime Steinberg, *La question juive 1940 - 1942* (Brussels, 1983), p. 126. (Hereafter cited as Steinberg, *La question juive*.)

121 Ibid., p. 177.

122 *Verordnungsblatt* 18/1, October 25, 1940.

123 Ibid. 20/1, October 28, 1940.

124 Ibid. 20/2, October 28, 1940.

125 Ibid. 44/1 and 44/2, May 31, 1941.

126 "Abschlussbericht Treuhandvermögen," RW 36/v.337, p. 141, or T 501/107/1277; RW 36/v.185, pp. D-31 - D-32, or T 501/106/426-427.

127 "Abschlussbericht Treuhandvermögen," pp. 153 - 54, or T 501/107/1289-1290.

128 RW 36/v.182, p. D-21, or T 501/105/1321.

129 "Abschlussbericht Treuhandvermögen," p. 218, or T 501/107/1354.

130 Ibid., p. 167.

131 Belgium, Commission des Crimes de Guerre, *Les crimes de guerre commis sous l'occupation de la Belgique 1940-1945: Le persécution anti-sémitique en Belgique* (Liège, 1947), pp. 19 - 21.

132 *Verordnungsblatt* 63/4, December 1, 1941.

133 Ibid. 63/3, November 25, 1941.

134 *La question juive*, p. 127.

135 *La traque*, vol. 1, 257.

136 *Verordnungsblatt* 73/3, April 22, 1942.

137 "Abschlussbericht Gruppe VII," p. 79, RW 36/v.317, Wi/IA4 .24, MAF.

138 *Verordnungsblatt* 79/1, May 27, 1942; P.v.F., vol. 3, 272.

139 *Verordnungsblatt* 79/4, June 1, 1942.

140 RW 36/v.178, p. A-50, or T 501/105/838.

141 Steinberg, *Les cent jours*, pp. 15 - 16.

142 Ibid., p. 156; Von Hahn, P.V. April 21, 1948, Process Straub, vol. 4, 10; Von Falkenhausen, "Exposé fait en cause Reeder," p. 90, MSg 126/2, MAF.

143 Steinberg, *Les cent jours*, p. 139.

144 Ibid., p. 178.

145 RW 36/v.180, p. 38, or T 501/105/1042.

146 Steinberg, *Les cent jours*, photographic reproduction, opp. p. 185.

147 Ibid., pp. 207 - 208.

148 Ibid., p. 228.

149 Ibid., pp. 216 - 17.

150 Steinberg, *La traque*, vol. 2, 73 - 74.

151 Commission d'enquête, *Les crimes de guerre: La persécution anti-sémitique*, pp. 30 - 34.

152 Steinberg, *Les cent jours*, p. 229.

153 Ibid., p. 144.

154 Ibid., p. 148 - 49.

155 Steinberg, *La traque*, vol. 1, 9.

156 Ibid., p. 213, 219.

158 Ibid., vol. 2, 191 - 94.

159 Ibid., vol. 1, 219.

160 Ibid., vol. 2, 218 - 20, 223.

161 Ibid., p. 222.

162 Ibid., p. 227.

163 Ibid., p. 229.

164 Ibid., p. 223.

165 Ibid., p. 225.

166 Singer, *La verité sur les juifs*, pp. 12 - 14; Steinberg, *La traque*, vol. 2, 224-27.

167 Ibid., p. 230.

168 Ibid., pp. 231 - 34.

169 Ibid., pp. 234 - 36.

170 T 16, April 1941, RW 36/v.178, p. A-21, or T 501/104/352.

171 Luther to Dienststelle Auswärtiges Amt Brüssel, October 29, 1942, Inland IIg "Judenfrage in Belgien 1939 - 1944", AAPAB.

172 Luther telegram, January 22, 1943, Beweisdokumente 969, Eichmann Prozess, IfZM.

173 Richtlinien 25, Akten betr. Belgien 1942/43, Handbuch III, Innenpolitik Habu 307, AAPAB.

174 Luther to von Bargen, October 24, 1942, Inland II g, AAPAB.

175 Luther to von Bargen, September 22, 1942, ibid.

176 Lucien Steinberg, *Les autorités allemandes en France occupée: Inventaire commenté de la collection des documents conservés au C.D.J.C.* (Paris, 1966), p. 148.

177 Office of Strategic Services, R & A No. 2500.2 "German Military Government over Europe: Belgium," p. 109; Lucien Steinberg, *La révolte des justes* (Paris, 1970), p. 238; Steinberg, *La question juive*, p. 83 and n. 55, p. 101.

178 Steinberg, *La traque*, vol. 2, 259.

179 Steinberg, *La question juive*, p. 84.

180 Jahresbericht 1940 - 1941, RW 36/v.201, p. A-63, or T 501/104/753; Steinberg, *La question juive*, p. 83.

181 Ibid., p. 84.

182 See Table 3.

183 Steinberg, *La traque*, vol. 2, 259.

184 Ibid., pp. 247, 256.

185 Ibid., n. 13, p. 261.

186 Table provided October 1967 by Mlle. Yvonne Braem, Chef de Service, Administration des Victimes de la Guerre, Ministère de la Santé Publique, Brussels. In possession of author.

187 Source: Steinberg, *La traque*, vol. 2, 259.

188 Eppstein, ed. *Belgium*, p. 65.

189 *L'an 40*, p. 275.

190 T 11, November, 1940, RW 36/v.170, pp. 9 - 10, or T 501/103/380 - 381.

191 See Victor Matthys in *Le Pays Réel*, December 4, 1940.

192 T 17, June 1 - September 1, 1941, pp. A-41 - A-42, RW 36/v.176, or T 501/105/74 - 75.

193 T 19, December 1, 1941 - March 15, 1942, pp. A-9 - A-10 RW 36/v.203, or T 501/105/611 - 612.

194 T 22, September 1 - December [31], 1942, p. A-38, RW 36/v.182, or T 501/105/1234.

195 *L'an 40*, p. 279.

196 T 20, March 15 - June 1, 1942, p. A-44, RW 36/v.178, or T 501/105/832.

197 *L'an 40*, pp. 468 - 69.

198 T 20, March 15 - June 1, 1942, pp. A-48 - A-49, RW 36/v.178, or T 501/105/836 - 837.

199 *L'an 40*, p. 471.

200 Hierl to von Falkenhausen, November 18, 1942, NS 19/neu 2078, BAK.

201 RFSS Pers. Stab to Berger, June 14, 1943, NO 5784, IfZM.

202 *La Belgique loyale*, p. 53; RW 36/v.178, p. A-49, or T 501/106/298.

203 T 20, March 15 - June 1, 1942, pp. A-46 - A-48, RW 36/v.178, or T 501/105/834 - 836.

204 T 25, July - September 1943, pp. A-45 - A-46, RW 36/v.178, or T 501/106/524-525.

205 Hierl to von Falkenhausen, NO 5780, IfZM.

206 Himmler to Reeder, February 16, 1943, NS 19/neu 1866, BAK.

207 Hierl to Himmler, June 9, 1943, NO 5786, IfZM.

208 Séances CSG, July 3, 1942, pp. 4 - 5; July 9, 1942, pp. 11-12; June 25, 1943, p. 6; T 25, July - September 1943, p. A-46, RW 36/v.186, or T 501/106/525.

209 T 26, October - December, 1943, p. A-41, RW 36/v.187, or T 501/106/748.

210 Der Reichsarbeitsführer, January 13, 1944, NS 19/neu 1568, BAK.

211 T 11, November 1940, RW 36/v.170, p. 24, or T 501/103/395.

212 Abschlussbericht "Fürsorgewesen," pp. 37 - 40, RW 36/v.338, or T 501/107/321-324.

213 Ibid., p. 46, or frame 331.

214 Reichskommissar für die besetzten Gebiete von Belgien und Nordfrankreich, (sic!) Gruppe Fürsorge III, 615 (Sept. 20, 1943), RW 25 .175, RW 36/v.340.

215 E.g. *Volk en Staat*, December 22 and 25, 1940.

216 Von Falkenhausen, "Memoiren," chap. 12, pp. 53-54, N 246/43, MAF.

217 T 18, September 1 - December 1, 1941, pp. 63 - 65, RW 36/v.177, or T 501/105/313 - 315.

218 Abschlussbericht "Fürsorgewesen," p. 45, RW 36/v.338, or T 501/107/329.

219 T 14, February 1941, p. 29, RW 36/v.173, or T 501/104/50.

220 Jahresbericht 1940 - 1941, pp. B-54 - B-55 and p. B-67, RW 36/v.201, or T 501/104/819 - 20, and 832.

221 "Zweiter Bericht, Abtlg. Kultur," November 25, 1940, VJ Staat 2170/42, RvOA.

222 Jahresbericht 1940 - 1941, p. B-57, RW 36/v.201, or T 501/104/822.

223 T 22, September 1 - December [31], 1942, p. B-15, RW 36/v.182, or T 501/105/1251.

224 Lammers to Büchner, July 23, 1942, (Folder Kulturschutz), RW 36/v.206, or T 501/98/204-205.

225 Abschlussbericht "Kulturschutz," pp. 43 - 44, RW 36/v.333, or T 501/98/383-384.

226 Ibid., p. 58 or frame 398.

227 T 1, June 4, 1940, pp. 16 - 21, RW 36/v.204, or T 501/102/132 - 37; Franz Petri, June 28, 1971; testimony van der Essen, IMT, vol. 5, 534.

228 Belgium, Commission des Crimes de Guerre, *Les crimes de guerre commis lors de l'invasion du territoire national May 1940: La déstruction de la bibliothèque de l'Université de Louvain* (Liège, 1946).

229 "Zweiter Bericht, Abtlg. Kultur," VJ Staat 2170/42, RvOA.

230 Jahresbericht 1940 - 1941, p. B-79, RW 36/v.201, or T 501/104/844.

231 T 17, June 1 - September 1, 1941, p. B-29, RW 36/v. 176, or T 501/105/107.

232 T 24, April - June 1943, p. B-38, RW 36/v.185, or T 501/106/338; T 26, October - December 1943, pp. B-20 - B-21, RW 36/v.187, or T 501/106/781-782; Leclef, *Le Cardinal van Roey*, p. 189.

233 *Le Soir*, September 6/7, 1941.

234 Jahresbericht 1940 - 1941, pp. B-74 - B-75, RW 36/v.201, or T 501/104/839 - 840.

236 T 12, December 1940, p. 37, RW 36/v.171, or T 501/103/687.

237 Jahresbericht 1940 - 1941, p. B-63, RW 36/v.201, or T 501/104/828.

238 *Volk en Staat*, September 18, 1941, p. 1.

239 T 15, March 1941, pp. B-15 - B-16, RW 36/v.174, or T 501/104/205 - 206; see also Jean Willems, "The Universities under the Occupation," Goris, *Belgium under Occupation*, pp. 135 - 37.

240 "Zweiter Bericht, Abtlg. Kultur," pp. 33 - 34, VJ Staat 2170/42, RvOA.

241 Ibid., pp. 72 - 73.

242 Willems, "The Universities under the Occupation," Goris, *Belgium under Occupation*, p. 137; Franz Petri, June 28, 1971.

243 T 18, September 1 - December 1, 1941, pp. B-28 - B-29, RW 36/v.177, or T 501/105/363 - 364.

244 T 21, June 1 - September 1, 1942, p. B-9, RW 36/v.180, or T 501/105/1056.

245 T 23, January - March 1943, pp. B-12 - B-13, RW 36/v.183, or T 501/106/90-91.

246 Letter Draft, May 22, 1944, RW 36/v.208, or T 501/98/515-516.

247 "Vermerk," Gruppe Kultur, Az Wiss 2070, February 9, 1944, RW 36/v.208, or T 501/98/549.

248 Franz Petri, June 28, 1971.

249 T 501/95/672.

250 OKW, WFA L (IV a), Nr. 22015/40, January 11, 1940, Sammelmappe OKW, RvOA.

251 Order MBBNF, June 6, 1940, RW 36/v.108, or T 501/97/232.

252 Kiewitz to von Weizsäcker, September 21, 1940, p. 2, RW 36/v.49.

253 T 501/94/468, 683.

254 T 501/94/786.

255 Degrelle, *La cohue de 1940*, pp. 134 - 35.

256 Jahresbericht 1940 - 1941, p. B-47, RW 36/v.201, or T 501/104/812.

257 Ivan Gérard, *Armée Sécrète: Souvenirs du Commandant* (Brussels, 1962), p. 56; Guy Bastien, *L'Armée Sécrète* (Brussels, 1965), p. 9.

258 T 26, October - December 1943, p. B-2, RW 36/v.187, or T 501/106/757.

259 Charles, *Les Forces Armées*, p. 56.

260 Belgium, *Memorandum du gouvernement belge relatif aux pertes et dommages subis par la Belgique par suite de l'aggression allemande*, October 1, 1945 (Brussels, 1945).

261 United States, Chief of Counsel for Prosecution of Axis Criminality, *Nazi Conspiracy and Aggression, Supplement A*, (Washington, D.C., 1947),

p. 874; also cited in Edward L. Homze, *Foreign Labor in Nazi Germany* (Princeton, N.J, 1967), p. 195.

262 Charles, *Les forces armées*, p. 56.

Chapter Five

1 Jahresbericht 1940 - 1941, pp. C-11 - C-12, RW 36/v.201, or T 501/104/918 - 920.

2 Reeder and Hailer, "Die Militärverwaltung in Belgien und Nordfrankreich," p. 28, RW 36/v.373, or T 501/102/31.

3 MBBNF, MVCh, Wirtschaftsabteilung, "Gesamtbericht über die Tätigkeit auf den wichtigsten Industriegebieten in der Zeit vom Einsatz bis zum 31.8.40," p. 3, RW 36/v.242, or T 501/102/1078. (Hereafter cited as Wirtschaftsabteilung, "Gesamtbericht... bis zum 31.8.40.")

4 T 9, September 1940, pp. 2 - 3, RW 36/v. 167, or T 501/102/1283-1284; Jahresbericht 1940 - 1941, p. 27, RW 36/v.201, or T 501/104/717.

5 Early MS (in possession of author) of John R. Gillingham, "The Economic New Order in Belgium" (Ph.D. diss., University of California, Berkeley, 1973), p. 289.

6 John Gillingham, *Belgian Business in the Nazi New Order* (Ghent, 1977), p. 107.

7 Jahresbericht 1940 - 1941, pp. A-3 - A-4, RW 36/v.201, or T 501/693-694; T 21, June 1 - September 1, 1942, p. A-13, RW 36/v.180, or T 501/105/992; Abschlussbericht "Gewerbliche Wirtschaft," pp. 84-90, RW 36/v.321, or T 501/107/611-617.

8 Jahresbericht 1940 - 1941, p. B - 126, RW 36/v.201, or T 501/104/891.

9 Ibid., p. B-32 and pp. C-73 - C-74, RW 36/v.201, or T 501/104/796 and 996 - 997; Bronckart, *Cinq ans d'occupation*, vol. 1, 36.

10 Abschlussbericht "Energiewirtschaft," p. 8, RW 36/v.275.

11 T 10, October 1940, p. 1, RW 36/v.169, or T 501/103/151.

12 *Jahresbericht 1940-1941*, p. B-108, RW 36/v.201, or T 501/104/873; Abschlussbericht "Das Fürsorgewesen," p. 2, RW 36/v.338, or T 501/107/286.

13 Séances CSG, July 29, 1940, p. 1; Jahresbericht 1940 - 1941, p. B-108, RW 36/v.201, or T 501/104/873.

14 Abschlussbericht "Fürsorgewesen," p. 6, RW 36/v.338, or T 501/107/290.

15 T 10, October 1940, p. 1, RW 36/v.169, or T 501/103/151.

16 Jahresbericht 1940 - 1941, p. B-109, RW 36/v.201, or T 501/104/874.

17 T 18, September 1 - December 1, 1941, p. B - 65, RW 36/v.177, or T 501/105/404.

18 T 10, October 1940, p. 64, RW 36/v.169, or T 501/103/69; T 11, November 1940, p. 47, RW 36/v.170, or T 501/103/420.

19 Allgemeine Übersicht, December 1, 1941 - March 15, 1942, pp. 77 - 78, RW 36/v.203, or T 501/105/721-722.

20 T 28, April 1944, p. 46, RW 36/v.18, or T 501/106/1020.

21 T 29, May 1944, p. A-8, RW 36/v.190, or T 501/106/1042.

22 T 30, June 1944, p. A-9, RW 36/v.191, or T 501/106/1145.

23 Ibid., pp. E-20 - E-22, or frames 1215-1216.

24 Jahresbericht 1940 - 1941, Anlage, p. B-5, RW 36/v.201, or T 501/104/896.

25 T 4, June 29, 1940, Anlage 3, RW 36/v.162, or T 501/102/441.

26 T 26, October - December 1943, p. B - 31, RW 36/v.187, or T 501/106/793.

27 NID 8083 and NID 10698, Nuremberg Documents, IfZM; Reichswirtschaftsministerium, Abteilung Bergbau, R 7, VIII, 207, BAK.

28 Von Falkenhausen, "Memoiren," chap. 12, p.58, N 246/43, MAF.

29 NG - 3693, p. 5, Nuremberg Documents, IfZM; Document Dr. Rasche, Nr. 144, pp. 1-2, Nuremberg Documents Case XI, N 128/2, RvOA.

30 Reichswirtschaftministerium, Abteilung Bergbau, R 7, VIII, 207, BAK.

31 Rademacher to Luther, November 22, 1941, NG 3693, Nuremberg Documents, IfZM; NID 10698, p. 11, Nuremberg Documents, IfZM.

32 Jahresbericht 1940 - 1941, p. C-59, RW 36/v.201, or T 501/104/979.

33 Document Dr. Rasche, Nr. 144, p. 4, Nuremberg Documents Case XI, N 128/2, RvOA.

34 Abschlussbericht "Auswärtiger Warenverkehr," RW 36/v.251, pp. 25 - 26, or T 501/107/434-435.

35 Fernand Dellicour, *La politique du travail pendant la guerre: un problème angoissant* (Brussels, 1946), p. 60.

36 Geschichte der Rüstungs-Inspektion in Belgien vom 1.X. 1940 bis zum 31.XII.1941, pp. 41 - 43 and p. 109, RW 25 .33, MAF.

37 Abschlussbericht "Gewerbliche Wirtschaft," pp. 18 - 19, RW 36/v.321, or T 501/107/545-546; Edmond Henusse and Jean van den Bossche, *La repression du travail sous l'occupation allemande de 1940 à 1944* (Brussels, 1946), p. 76.

38 Lageberichte der Rüstungs-Inspektion in Belgien vom 15.VII.1940 - 2.XII.1940, pp. 15-16, RW 25 .34, MAF.

39 Der Reichswirtschaftminister, II L 2592/40, June 15, 1940, NG 056, Nuremberg Documents, IfZM.

40 Wirtschaftsabteilng, "Gesamtbericht... bis zum 31.8.40," pp.9, 14, RW 36/v.242, or T 501/101/1074 and 1079.

41 Abschlussbericht "Gewerbliche Wirtschaft," p. 9, RW 36/v.321, or T 501/107/536.

42 T 12, January 3, 1941, p. 63, RW 36/v.171, or T 501/102/714.

43 Gillingham, "The Economic New Order," p. 290.

44 Hoton, *Leurs gueules*, p. 19.

45 T 23, January 1 - March 31, 1943, p. D-17, RW 36/v.183, or T 501/106/159.

46 Wirtschaftsabteilung, "Gesamtbericht...bis zum 31.8.40," pp. 14 - 15, RW 36/v.242, or T 501/101/1079 - 1080.

47 OKW, Gen. Q., Rechenschaftsbericht der AWG, p. 3, MA 190/2, IfZM, or T 77/571/749461, CGRMA.

48 Jahresbericht 1940 - 1941, p. B - 45, RW 36/v.201, or T 501/104/810.

49 Abschlussbericht "Textilwirtschaft," pp. 5 - 9, RW 36/v.326, or T 501/107/900-904.

50 Jahresbericht 1940-1941, p. C-9, RW 36/v.201, or T 501/104/916.

51 Ibid., p. C-4, or frame 911.

52 Abschlussbericht "Gewerbliche Wirtschaft," pp. 8 - 9, RW 36/v.321, or T 501/107/535-536.

53 Der Reichswirtschaftminister, S 1a/23125/40, August 26, 1940, R 7, VIII/207, BAK.

54 Der Reichswirtschaftminister, S 1/1125/41, OKW WiRüAmt/Rü II d, Reichskanzlei, R 43 II/675a, BAK.

55 Gillingham, "The Economic New Order," p. 304; Abschlussbericht "Leder - und Rauchwarenwirtschaft," p. 46, RW 36/v. 278.

56 NI - 10164, August 23, 1940, Nuremberg Documents, IfZM.

57 Geschichte der Rüstungs-Inspektion in Belgien von 1.X.1940 bis zum 31.XII.1941, pp. 14-15, RW 25 .33, MAF.

58 T 15, March 1941, pp. A-8 - A-9, RW 36/v.174, or T 501/104/164-165.

59 Abschlussbericht "Wirtschaftsleitung und Wirtschaftskontrolle," pp. 118 - 19, RW 36/v.328, or T 501/107/1076-1077.

60 T 24, April - June 1943, pp. A-16 - A-17, RW 36/v.185, or T 501/106/244-245; MVCh, Abt. Wirtschaft, "Die von der Militärverwaltung gesteuerten, im deutschen Interesse 1943 aufgebrachten Leistungen Belgiens und Nordfrankreichs," p. 6, RW 36/v.250, or T 501/107/16. (Hereafter cited as Leistungen 1943.)

61 Zentralauftragsstelle in Belgien und Nordfrankreich, "Die Ergebnisse der Auftragsverlagerungen von Mai 1940 bis Ende Juli 1943," RW 36/v.186.

62 Wirtschaftsabteilung "Gesamtbericht...bis zum 31.8.40," pp. 20-21, RW 36/v.242, or T 501/102/1093-1094.

63 Abschlussbericht "Bergbau/Kohlenwirtschaft," pp. 77-79, RW 36/v.329, or T 501/107/755-757.

64 Ibid., p. 56, or frame 734.

65 Wirtschaftsabteilung, "Gesamtbericht...bis zum 31.8.40," p. 36, RW 36/v.242, or T 501/102/1109-1101.

66 Dellicour, La politique du travail, p. 70.

67 T 23, January - March, 1943, pp. D-33 - D-37, RW 36/v.183, or T 501/106/117-184; Abschlussbericht Gruppe VII, pp. 115-19, RW 36/v.317, Wi/IA4 .24, MAF.

68 "Kohlewirtschaft, Förderung von Steinkohle, Koksgewinnung und Herstellung von Briketts," RW 36/v.329, p. [119], or T 501/107/797.

69 Abschlussbericht "Eisenschaffende Industrie," p. 3, RW 36/v.330, or T 501/107/805.

70 Fernand Baudhuin, "Economy under the Occupation," Goris, Belgium under Occupation, p. 30; Wirtschaftsabteilung: "Gesamtbericht...bis zum 31.8.40, Referat 4: Eisen," p. 1, RW 36/v.242, or T 501/102/1175.

71 Jahresbericht 1940 - 1941, p. C-92, RW 36/v.201, or T 501/104/1020.

Notes

72 Eidesstattliche Erklärung Otto Steinbrinck, January 30, 1947, p. 1, NI 3551, Nuremberg Documents, IfZM; Henusse and van den Bossche, *La repression du travail*, p. 64.

73 Abschlussbericht "Eisenschaffende Industrie," p. 30, RW 36/v.330, or T 501/107/831.

74 Ibid., pp. 13 - 14, or frames 814 -15.

75 Wirtschaftsabteilung: "Gesamtbericht...bis zum 31.8.40, Referat 4: Eisen," pp. 1 - 2, 6, RW 36/v.242, or T 501/102/1175-1176, 1180.

76 Fernand Baudhuin, *Belgique 1900 - 1960* (Louvain, 1961), p. 198.

77 "Zeittafel über wichtige Begebenheiten auf dem Gebiete der Wirtschaft," Anlage II, Abschlussbericht der Militärverwaltung in Belgien und Nordfrankreich, p. 6, RW 36/v.249, or T 501/107/198. (Hereafter cited as Zeittafel.)

78 Baudhuin, *Belgique 1900 - 1960*, p. 198.

79 Ibid.

80 T 27, March 1944, p. B-40, RW 36/v.188, or T 501/106/950.

81 Zeittafel, p. 20, RW 36/v.249, or T 501/107/212.

82 Gillingham "The Economic New Order," p. 239.

83 Baudhuin, "Economy under the Occupation," Goris, *Belgium under Occupation*, p. 36.

84 T 20, March 15 - June 1, 1942, p. 15, RW 36/v.178, or T 501/105/781.

85 Abschlussbericht "Eisenschaffende Industrie: Gesamtlieferungen der eisen - und metallverarbeitenden Industrie," Anlage 3, RW 36/v.330, follows p. 50, or T 501/107/857.

86 Abschlussbericht "Nichteisenmetalle," pp. 4-7, RW 36/v.327, or T 501/107/866-869.

87 Jahresbericht 1940 - 1041, pp. C-96 - C-98, RW 36/v.201, T 501/104/1027-1029.

88 Abschlussbericht "Nichteisenmetalle," p. 28, RW 36/v.327, T 501/107/890.

89 Abschlussbericht "Die Edelmetallbewirtschaftung," pp. 8 - 9, 13 - 14, [66 - c - 12 - 12 - 69b], RW 36/v.276.

90 T 26, October - December 1943, p. D-24, RW 36/v.187, or T 501/106/840.

91 Gillingham, ""The Economic New Order," p. 239.

92 Wirtschaftsabteilung, "Gesamtbericht...bis zum 31.8.1940," Referat 6: Chemie, p. 1, RW 36/v.242, or T 501/102/1191.

93 Abschlussbericht "Chemische Industrie," pp. 2 - 3, [66 - c - 12 - 12/69c], RW 36/v.277.

94 Wirtschaftsabteilung, "Gesamtbericht...bis zum 31.8.1940," Referat 6: Chemie, pp. 3 - 4, RW 36/v.242, or T 501/102/1193-1194.

95 Abschlussbericht "Chemische Industrie," p. 25, [66 - c - 12 - 12 - 69c], RW 36/v.277.

96 Jahresbericht 1940 - 1941, pp. C-115 - C-116, RW 36/v.201, or T 501/104/1046-1047.

97 *Ibid.*, pp. C-105 - C-106, RW 36/v. 201, or T 501/104/1036-37; Abschlussbericht "Textilwirtschaft," pp. 16 - 17, RW 36/v.326, or T 501/107/911-912.

98 T 26, October - December 1943, p. D-25, RW 36/v.187, or T 501/106/841.

99 Abschlussbericht "Energiewirtschaft," pp. 23-24, [66 - c - 12 - 12 - 69a], RW 36/v.275.

100 Wirtschaftsabteilung, "Gesamtbericht...bis zum 31.8.40," Referat 3: Energie, p. 1, RW 36/v.242, or T 501/102/1147.

101 Abschlussbericht "Energiewirtschaft," p. 21, [66 - c - 12 - 12 - 69a], RW 36/v.275.

102 T 26, October - December 1943, p. D-40, RW 36/v.187, or T 501/106/856.

103 Abschlussbericht "Energiewirtschaft," pp. 32-34, [66 - c - 12 - 12 - 69a], RW 36/v.275.

104 *Ibid.*, pp. 13-14; T 23, January 1 - March 31, 1943, p. D-43, RW 36/v.183, or T 501/106/190.

105 U. S. Army Services Forces, *Civil Affairs Handbook*, Vol. 3, *Belgium*, (Washington, D.C., 1943), p. 76.

106 Eppstein, *Belgium* , p. 82.

107 Fernand Baudhuin, *L'économie belge sous l'occupation 1940 - 1945*, (Brussels, 1945), pp. 232 - 38.

Notes

108 Baudhuin, *Belgique 1900 - 1960*, pp. 190 - 91; T 7, August 4, 1940, p.37, RW 36/v.165, or T 501/102/811; Jean Colard, *L'alimentation de la Belgique pendant l'occupation allemande 1940 - 1944* (Louvain, 1945), p. 37.

109 T 7, August 4, 1940, pp. 18 - 19, RW 36/v.165, or T 501/102/792 - 793.

110 Jahresbericht 1940 - 1041, pp. C-19 - C-20, RW 36/v.201, or T 501/104/926 - 927.

111 T 8, September 4, 1940, pp. 67 - 68, RW 36/v.166, or T 501/102/960-961.

112 Baudhuin, "Economy under the Occupation," Goris, *Belgium under Occupation*, pp. 40 - 41.

113 Colard, *L'alimentation*, pp. 39 - 41.

114 "Entwicklung der Anbauflächen, Belgien," R 14/231, BAK.

115 MVCh, Abt. Wirtschaft, "Die von der Militärverwaltung gesteuerten, im deutschen Interesse 1942 aufgebrachten Leistungen Belgiens und Nordfrankreichs," p. 7, RW 36/v.246, or T 501/106/1293. (Hereafter cited as Leistungen 1942.)

116 Leistungen 1943, p. 11, RW 36/v.250, or T 501/107/21.

117 Leistungen 1942, p. 7, RW 36/v.246, or T 501/106/1270.

118 Leistungen 1943, pp. 11 - 12, RW 36/v.250, or T 501/107/21-22.

119 "Entwicklung der Viehbestände, Belgien," R 14/231, BAK.

120 Leistungen 1942, p. 8, RW 36/v.246, or T 501/106/1271.

121 Leistungen 1943, p. 12, RW 36/v.250, or T 501/107/22.

122 "Entwicklung der Viehbestände, Belgien," R 14/231, BAK.

123 Ibid.

124 T 26, October - December 1943, p. D-1, RW 36/v.187, or T 501/106/825.

125 Anlage, p. 2, KTB 632/41, T 501/94/865.

126 Baudhuin "Economy under the Occupation," Goris, *Belgium under Occupation*, pp. 33-34.

127 Jahresbericht 1940-1941, pp. C-23 - C-24, RW 36/v.201, or T 501/104/931-932.

128 T 17, December 1940, p. 1, RW 36/v.170 or T 501/103/650.

129 Colard, *L'alimentation*, pp. 74 - 75; Bronckart, *Cinq ans d'occupation*, vol. 1, 93.

130 Jahresbericht 1940-1941, pp. C-26 - C-27, RW 36/v.201, or T 501/104/934-935.

131 T 17, June 1, 1941 - September 1, 1941, pp. C-3 - C-5, RW 36/v.176, or T 501/105/133, 135.

132 G. Jacquemyns, *Privations et espoirs: La société belge sous l'occupation allemande 1940 - 1944* (Brussels, 1945), p. 210.

133 Zeittafel, pp. 16 - 19, RW 36/v.249, or T 501/107/208-211.

134 SD, "Meldungen aus Belgien" Nr. 13, June 1, 1944, R 70/Belgien 5, BAK.

135 Bronckart, *Cinq ans d'occupation*, vol. 3, 102.

136 Abschlussbericht Abt. Wirtschaft, "Einführung," p. 12, RW 36/v.249, or T 501/107/130.

137 Abschlussbericht "Tabakbewirtschaftung," p. 26, [66 - c - 12 - 12 - 69f], RW 36/v.280.

138 T 13, January 1941, p. 9, RW 36/v.172, or T 501/103/948.

139 T 16, April 1941, p. C-12, RW 36/v.175, or T 501/104/415.

140 Abschlussbericht "Tabakbewirtschaftung," pp.34 - 35, [66 - c - 12 - 12 - 69f], RW 36/v.280.

141 Abschlussbericht "Wirtschaftslenkung und Wirtschaftsführung," pp. 145 - 46, RW 36/v.328, or T 501/107/1103-1104.

142 Guillaume Jacquemyns, *Mode de la vie: Comportement moral et social*, p. 212, vol. 2 of *La société belge sous l'occupation allemande 1940-1944*, (Brussels, 1950).

143 Abschlussbericht "Tabakbewirtschaftung," p. 26, [66 - c - 12 - 12 - 69f], RW 36/v.280.

144 Abschlussbericht "Wirtschaftslenkung und Wirtschaftsführung," RW 36/v.328, pp. 113-14, or T 501/107/1071-1072.

145 Colard, *L'Alimentation*, p. 98; Eric Pertz, "Oorlog en ekonomie: Belgie 1940 - 1944" (Thesis, Katholieke Universiteit Leuven, 1976), pp. 81 - 82.

146 Abschlussbericht, "Währung und Finanzen," pp. 20 - 21, RW 36/v.325, or T 501/107/392-393; Comité d'enquête chargé d'informer le Gouvernement sur la situation et les opérations de la Banque d'Emission pendant l'occupation allemande, *Rapport* (Brussels, 1946), vol. 2, 215. (Hereafter cited as Comité d'enquête, *Rapport.*)

147 Abschlussbericht "Wirtschaftslenkung und Wirtschaftskontrolle," pp. 120 - 26, RW 36/v.328, or 501/107/1078-1084.

148 Extract from Circular of the MBBNF, 19 Je 1943, Document ECH 9, Nuremberg Documents, IfZM.

149 Jahresbericht 1940 - 1941, p. C-20, RW 36/v.201, or T 501/104/938.

150 "Die belgische Polizei," p. 34, RW 25 .171, MAF; Abschlussbericht "Wirtschaftslenkung und Wirtschaftskontrolle," pp. 90 - 92, RW 36/v.328, or T 501/107/1048-1050.

151 Ibid., pp. 108 - 110, or frames 1066-1068.

152 Ibid., p. 158, frame 1116.

153 [Piet L.] Potargent, *La mise au travail de la main-d'oeuvre belge dans le pays et à l'étranger durant l'occupation*, (Brussels, n.d.), p. 10.

154 Ibid.

155 Bart Brinckman, "De schakel tussen arbeid en leiding: Het Rijksarbeidsambt (1940 - 1944)," *Cahiers*, vol. 12 (May 1989), 139 - 40.

156 Ibid., pp. 121 - 22, and pp. 126-130; Mathias G. Haupt, *Der "Arbeitseinsatz" der belgischen Bevölkerung während des Zweiten Weltkrieges*, (Bonn 1970), pp. 66 - 67.

157 Potargent, *La mise au travail*, p. 10.

158 T 9, October 1, 1940, p. 84, RW 36/v.167, or T 501/102/1365.

159 Potargent, *La mise au travail*, p. 11.

160 Ibid., pp. 16 - 17.

161 Ibid., p. 11.

162 Ibid., pp. 14 - 15.

163 Jahresbericht 1940-1941, pp. C-32 - C-35, RW 36/v.201, or T 501/104/943-46.

164 T 17, June 1 - September 1, 1941, p. C-12, RW 36/v.175, or T 501/105/142; Haupt, *Der "Arbeitseinsatz,"* p. 83.

165 Potargent, *La mise au travail*, pp. 25 - 27.

166 Ibid., p. 12.

167 Abschlussbericht Gruppe VII, p. 178, Wi/IA.24, RW 36/v.317, MAF; Potargent, *La mise au travail*, p. 29.

168 *Verordnungsblatt* 68/2, March 6, 1942.

169 "Travail obligatoire en Belgique," Séances CSG, March 12, 1943.

170 *Verordnungsblatt* 75/2, April 30, 1942; Potargent, *La mise au travail*, p. 34.

171 Ibid., p. 36.

172 Ibid., p. 45; *Verordnungsblatt* 75/9, May 7, 1942.

173 Haupt, *Der "Arbeitseinsatz,"* p.206.

174 Potargent, *La mise au travail*, pp. 42 - 44.

175 *Verordnungsblatt* 87/7, October 6, 1942.

176 Ibid. 87/6, October 6, 1942.

177 Haupt, *Der "Arbeitseinsatz,"* p. 116.

178 Brinckman, "Het Rijksarbeidsambt," *Cahiers*, vol. 12, 120.

179 Potargent, *La mise au travail*, pp. 58 - 60.

180 Ibid., p. 73; Brinckman, "Het Rijksarbeidsambt," *Cahiers*, vol. 12, 126.

181 Abschlussbericht Gruppe VII, pp. 202-204, Wi/IA .24, RW 36/v.317.

182 *Verordnungsblatt* 87/4, October 6, 1942.

183 Ibid., 87/5, October 6, 1942.

184 Potargent, *La mise au travail*, p. 65.

185 *Verordnungsblatt* 96/2, March 5, 1943.

186 Potargent, *La mise au travail*, pp. 66 - 67.

187 *Verordnungsblatt* 14/2, June 28, 1943.

188 Potargent, *La mise au travail*, pp. 67 - 68.

189 Abschlussbericht Gruppe VII, p. 253, Wi/IA .24, RW 36/v.317, MAF; Bronckart, *Cinq ans d'occupation*, vol. 2, 241.

190 Potargent, *La mise au travail*, p. 77.

191 T 30, June 1944, p. C-17, RW 36/v.191, or T 501/106/1188.

192 Haupt, *Der "Arbeitseinsatz,"* pp. 143 - 46.

193 T 23, January 1, 1943 - March 31, 1943, pp. B-12 - B-13, RW 36/v.183, or T 501/106/90-91.

194 T 24, April - June 1943, p. B-30, RW 36/v.185, or T 501/106/330; Haupt, *Der "Arbeitseinsatz,"* p. 142.

195 Potargent, *La mise au travail*, p. 70.

196 Bronckart, *Cinq ans d'occupation*, vol. 2, 218; vol. 3, 106 - 107.

197 E. Lousse, *The University of Louvain during the Second World War* (Bruges, 1946), pp. 19 - 24; Haupt, *Der "Arbeitseinsatz,"* p. 153.

198 T 26, October - December 1943, pp. B-14 - B-15, RW 36/v.187, or T 501/106/775-776; Lousse, *The University of Louvain*, p. 28.

199 T 24, April - June, 1943, pp. B-31 - B-32, RW 36/v.185, or T 501/106/331-332.

200 Haupt, *Der "Arbeitseinsatz,"* pp. 82 - 84.

201 Homze, *Foreign Labor in Nazi Germany*, p. 195.

202 Abschlussbericht "Die landeseigene Verwaltung," p. 46, RW 36/v.339, or T 501/107/261.

203 Friedrich Baumann, P.V. May 28, 1946, P.v.F, vol. 7, 701.

204 Maurice Masoin, "Public Finances and Currency," Goris, *Belgium under Occupation*, p. 49.

205 R. Billiard, *La contrainte économique sous l'occupation 1940 - 1944* (Brussels, 1946), pp. 9 - 16; Dellicour, *La politique du travail*, p. 43.

206 *Ibid.*, pp. 54 - 55.

207 Masoin, "Public Finances and Currency," Goris, *Belgium under Occupation*, p. 49.

208 Dellicour, *La politique du travail*, p. 44.

209 T 5, July 7, 1940, p. 18, RW 36/v.163, or T 501/102/480; Comité d'Enquête, *Rapport*, vol. 4, 1 - 6.

210 Billiard, *La contrainte économique*, pp. 13 - 16; Comité d'Enquête, *Rapport*, vol. 1, 1 - 2, and Annexe, pp. 16 - 17.

211 *Ibid.*, vol. 4, 3 - 4.

212 Dellicour, *La politique du travail*, p. 52.

213 Jahresbericht 1940 - 1941, p. C-56, RW 36/v.201, or T 501/104/976.

214 Masoin: "Public Finances and Currency," Goris, *Belgium under Occupation*, p. 50.

215 T 7, August 4, 1940, pp. 45 - 47, RW 36/v.165, or T 501/102/819-820; Baudhuin, *Belgique 1900 - 1960*, p. 193.

216 T 5, July 7, 1940, p. 27, RW 36/v.163, or T 501/102/489.

217 Abschlussbericht "Währung und Finanzen," pp. 10 - 13, RW 36/v.325, or T 501/107/382-385.

218 Prosecution statement, January 31, 1946, IMT, vol. 5, 637.

219 Comité d'Enquête, *Rapport*, vol. 1, 13.

220 Prosecution statement, January 31, 1946, IMT, vol. 5, 642.

221 Comité d'Enquête, *Rapport*, vol. 1, 173.

222 Prosecution statement, January 21, 1946, IMT, vol. 5, 566.

223 Zeittafel, passim, RW 36/v.249, T 501/107/193-212.

224 Billiard, *La contrainte économique*, p. 17; Abschlussbericht "Währung und Finanzen," p. 20, RW 36/v.325, or T 501/107/392.

225 Ibid., pp. 30 - 31, or frames 402-403.

226 *Ibid.*, p. 18, or frame 390.

227 Prosecution statement, January 31, 1946, IMT, vol. 5, 642.

228 Abschlussbericht "Währung und Finanzen," p. 13, RW 36/v.325, or T 501/107/385.

229 Prosecution statement, Janaury 31, 1946, IMT, vol. 5, 642.

230 Baudhuin, "Economy under Occupation," Goris, *Belgium under Occupation*, p. 29.

231 Übersicht December 1, 1941 - March 15, 1942, p. 69, RW 36/v.103, or T 501/105/712.

232 Masoin "Public Finances and Currency," Goris: *Belgium under Occupation*, p. 60.

233 Abschlussbericht "Wirtschaftslenkung und Wirtschaftskontrolle," pp. 1 - 2, RW 36/v.328, or T 501/107/959-960.

234 Abschlussbericht Gruppe VII, p. 5, RW 25 .24, RW 36/v.317, MAF; Baudhuin, *La Belgique 1900 - 1960*, p. 188.

235 Abschlussbericht "Wirtschaftslenkung und Wirtschaftskontrolle," p. 17, RW 36/v.328, or T 501/107/975.

236 Jahresbericht 1940 - 1941, p. C-65, RW 36/v.201, or T 501/104/986.

237 *Ibid.*, pp. C-38 - C-39, or frames 954-955.

238 *Ibid.*, pp. C-39 - C-40, or frames 956-957.

239 Abschlussbericht "Wirtschaftslenkung und Wirtschaftskontrolle," p. 21, RW 36/v.328, or T 501/107/979; Bronckart, *Cinq ans d'occupation*, vol. 2, 84.

240 Baudhuin, *Belgique 1900 - 1960*, p. 189.

241 T 21, June 1 - September 1, 1942, pp. D-22 - D-23, RW 36/v.180, or T 501/105/1129-1130; Jacquemyns, *Privations et Espoirs*, p. 104.

242 T 24, April - June 1943, p. D-28, RW 36/v.185, or T 501/106/423.

243 Abschlussbericht "Auswärtiger Warenverkehr," pp. 1 - 3, RW 36/v.251, or T 501/107/410-412.

244 Ibid., pp. 8 - 9, or frames 417-418.

245 Übersicht December 1, 1941 - March 15, 1942, p. 62, RW 36/v.203, or T 501/105/702.

246 Abschlussbericht "Auswärtiger Warenverkehr," p. 23, RW 36/v.251, or T 501/107/432.

247 Abschlussbericht "Fürsorgewesen," pp. 63 - 64, RW 36/v.338, or T 501/107/348-349.

Bibliography

Bibliographies and Reference Works

Agence Dechenne. *Bibliographie*. Brussels. August 1941 - July 1944.

Belgium. Archives generales du royaume. "Liste de noms et d'addresses de personalités et d'instituts susceptibles de détenir de la documentation au sujet de la Belgique pendant la deuxiéme guerre mondiale." Brussels, 1967.

Bibliographisches Institut Leipzig. *Schlag nach über Niederlande, Belgien und Luxemburg*. Leipzig, n.d.

Centre de recherches et d'études historiques de la seconde guerre mondiale. *Inventaires*. 1) José Gotovitch, ed. *Fond Leo Lejeune*. Brussels, 1971. 3) J. Gallant, ed. *Archief J. Grauls*. Brussels, 1973.

Dujardin, Jean, José Gotovitch, and Lucia Rymenans. *Inventaire de la presse clandestine (1940 - 1944) conservée en Belgique*. Brussels, 1966.

Encyclopaedie van de Vlaamse Beweging. 2 vols. Tielt, 1973 - 1975.

Heyse, Theodore. *Une documentation belge de l'époque 1939 - 1950: classements et tables*. Brussels, 1954.

Hove, Julien van. *Répertoire des organismes de documentation en Belgique*. Brussels, 1947.

International Biographisches Archiv. (Münzinger Archiv). Lieferung 32/66.

Kahlenberg, Friedrich. "Quellen zur Geschichte Belgiens während der beiden Weltkriege." BAK.

Meyers, W.C.M. *Belgie in de Tweede Wereldoorlog: Bibliografie (1970 - 1975)*. Brussels, 1977.

Published Government Documents

Belgium. *Annales parlementaires de Belgique. Chambre des représentants*. Session ordinaire. 1939-1940, 1944-1945.

Belgium, Commission des Crimes de Guerre, *Les crimes de guerre commis lors de l'invasion du territoire national mai 1940: La déstruction de la bibliothèque de l'Université de Louvain*. Liege, 1946.

Belgium. Commissie voor Oorlogsmisdaden. *De oorlogsmisdaden bedreven onder de bezetting van Belgie 1940 - 1945: Het folteringscamp Breendonck*. Luik, 1949.

Belgium. Commission d'Enquête sur les violation de règles du droit des gens, des lois et des coutumes de guerre. *Les crimes de guerre: La persécution anti-sémitique en Belgique*. Liège, 1947.

___. ___. *Les crimes de guerre commis sous l'occupation de la Belgique, 1940 - 1945: L'arrestation, la déportation et l'exécution des ôtages*. Liège, 1948.

___. *Memorandum du gouvernement belge relatif aux pertes et dommages par suite de l'aggression allemande*. October 1, 1945. Brussels, 1945.

___. Ministry of Foreign Affairs and External Trade. *Memo from Belgium: Some Facts about Belgium*. No. 45. February 15, 1964.

___. Ministry of Foreign Affairs. *The Official Account of What Happened 1939 - 1940*. London, n.d.

___. *Übersetzung der im "Moniteur belge - Belgisch Staatsblad" erscheinenden Verordnungen.* Brussels, June 1940 - June 1944.

Germany. Auswärtiges Amt. *Documents on German Foreign Policy.* Series D. 19 vols. Washington, D.C. and London, 1947-1964.

___. *Reichsgesetzblatt.* Berlin, 1940.

International Military Tribunal. *Trial of Major War Criminals.* 42 vols. Nuremberg, 1947-1949.

Militärbefehlshaber (Militärverwaltungschef). *Verordnungsblatt des Militärbefehlshabers in Belgien und Nordfrankreich für die besetzten Gebiete Belgiens und Nordfrankreichs.* Brussels, 1940-1944.

Oberkommando des Heeres. *Heeresgruppen-Verordnungsblatt für die besetzten Gebiete.* Herausgegeben von der Heeresgruppe. May 10, 1940.

United States. Chief Counsel for Prosecution of Axis Criminality. *Nazi Conspiracy and Aggression.* 8 vols. Washington, D.C., 1946; Supplements A, B. 1947-1948.

United States. Army Services Forces, *Civil Affairs Handbook.* Vol. 3, *Belgium.* Washington, D.C., 1945.

Unpublished Materials

Abtlg. Inland I-D, Belgien Kirche 3, AAPAB.

Akten betr. Belgien 1942/43, Richtlinien 25, Handbuch III, Innenpolitik Habu 307. AAPAB.

[Becker, Raymond de.] "La Collaboration en Belgique 1940 - 1944 ou une révolution avortée." (Inédit attribué a Raymond de Becker [extraits]). Centre de recherche et d'information socio-politique. CRISP. Courrier hebdomaire No. 497-498. October 30, 1970. Mimeographed.

Belgium. Comité des Secrétaires-Genéraux. Séances 1940 - 1944. Photocopy. CREHSGMB.

Best, Werner. "Die deutschen Aufsichtsverwaltungen in Frankreich, Belgien, den Niederlanden und im Protektorat Böhmen und Mähren." [1941]. Mimeographed. HIAS.

Braem, Yvonne. Chef de Service, Administration des Victimes de la Guerre, Ministère de la Santé Publique, Brussels. "Numbers of deportees on each convoy departing from Malines 1942 - 1944." (In possession of author.)

"Copie intégrale des documents saisis à Mechelen-sur-Meuse sur un aviateur allemand." Photocopy. Belgium G373. HIAS.

Cordewiener, A. "Les mouvements wallons clandestins et la préparation de la libération." Mimeographed. 1974. CREHSGMB.

Falkenhausen, Alexander von. "Memoiren." Alte Fassung der Memoiren mit handschriftlichen Korrekturen, Nachlass Alexander von Falkenhausen. MS. N 246/40-44. MAF.

___. "Memoires." JP 1242. CREHSGMB.

___. "Exposé fait en cause Reeder." MSg 126/2. MAF.

___. "Von Falkenhausen 1922-1945." MS #B289. United States National Archives, Washington, D.C.

File, Abtlg. Inland I-D, Belgien Kirche, 3. PAAAB.

Fouck, Charles. "Rapport sur la mission d'évacuation de la population civile belge." May 28, 1940. Ts Belgium. F 673 (Vault). HIAS.

Gillingham, John. "The New Economic Order in Belgium." Ph.D diss., University of California, Berkeley, 1973. (MS-photocopy in possession of author.)

Goebbels, Paul Joseph. Fragments of Goebbel's Diary. May 30, 1942. Nr. 3 21g, 16/5c. RvOA.

Halstead, Charles R. "The Rexist Movement: A Study of One Aspect of Belgian Fascism." Ph.D. diss., University of Virginia, 1959.

Hierl to von Falkenhausen. November 18, 1942. NS 19/neu 2078. BAK.

Informationsbericht Nr. 42. September 6, 1940. Generalkommissar zur besonderen Verwendung. GkzbV st 73 d. RvOA.

Klemm, Peter Fritz. "German Economic Policies in Belgium from 1940 to 1944." 2 vols. Ph.D. diss., University of Michigan, 1973.

Knoebel, Edgar Erwin. "Racial Illusion and Military Necessity: A Study of SS Political and Manpower Objectives in Occupied Belgium." Ph.D. diss., University of Colorado, 1965.

Kriegstagebuch Nr. 1, December 1939, p. 4. NG 5347. RvOA.

Lorwin, Val R. "Conflict and Compromise in Belgian Politics." Paper presented at the annual meeting of the American Political Science Association, Washington, D.C., September, 1965. In possession of author.

Luther to Dienststelle Auswärtiges Amt Brüssel. October 29, 1942. Inland 2g "Judenfrage in Belgien 1939 - 1944." AAPAB.

"Materialien der deutschen Verteidigung zum alliierten Falkenhausen Prozess." Sig. 126. MAF.

Microfilms. MA 3(8), MA 60, MA 123, MA 144/4, MA 167, MA 190/2, MA 285, MA 295, MA 332, MA 333. IfZM.

Militärverwaltung, Abtlg. Gent, Oberfeldkommandantur 570, Tätigkeitsbericht. October 15, 1940. Rep. 320. Nr. 2920. Reichsministerium des Inneren. BAK.

Nuremberg Documents. Series NG, NI, NID, NO. IfZM.

Nuremberg Documents. N 128/2. RvOA.

Oberkommando des Heeres. Sammelmappe Gelb. NG 53470. RvOA.

OKW Documents L IV. RvOA.

Personnel Record Richard Jungclaus. March 17, 1965. Berlin Document Center. RvOA.

Pertz, Eric. "Oorlog en ekonomie: Belgie 1940 - 1944." Ph.D. diss., Katholieke Universiteit Leuven, 1976.

Petri, Franz. MS entry "Reeder," contribution to *Encyclopaedie van de vlaamse beweging*.

Propagandaabteilung Belgien, Abtlg. Presse, N 277. HIAS.

Record Group NS 19. Persönlicher Stab Reichsführer SS. BAK.

Record Group NS 22. Reichsorganisationsleiter der NSDAP. BAK.

Record Group R 58. Reichssicherheitshauptamt. BAK.

Record Group R 70. Polizeidienststellen in eingegliederten und besetzten Gebieten. BAK.

Record Group RW 19 (previously Wi VIII). Oberkommando der Wehrmacht/Wehrwirtschafts- und Rüstungsamt. MAF.

Record Group 25 (previously Wi/1A4). Rüstungsdienststellen in Belgien - Nordfrankreich. MAF.

Record Group RW 36. Militärbefehlshaber in Belgien und Nordfrankreich. MAF.

Record Group R 7. Reichswirtschaftsministerium. BAK.

Record Group R 14. Reichsministerium für Ernährung und Landwirtschaft. BAK.

Record Group. R 43 II/675, 678. Reichskanzlei. BAK.

SIPO/SD Brüssel IV B-3 Erd (mann)/Plum, Einsatzplan September 1, 1943. Beweisdokument 1446. Eichmann Prozess. IfZM.

Ständiges Kriegsgericht Brüssel/2. Frz. Kammer, Verfahren gegen den ehem. Gen. u. MilBfh. Belgien und Nordfrankreich, Alexander von Falkenhausen, den ehem. MilVerwCh. Belgien und Nordfrankreich Eggert Reeder, den ehem. Gen. u. OFK von Lüttich, Georg Bertram und den ehem. Gen. u. OFK von Lüttich, Bernhard von Claer, v. 25.9.1950 - 27.1.1951 (zit Brüssel,) 1950-1951. 29 vols. IfZM.

Ständiges Kriegsgericht Brüssel/Kriegsauditorium, Ermittlungsverfahren gegen ehem. Angehörige der Dienststelle C d S Brüssel: KrimDir SS Stubak Franz Straub, Ltr der Abtlg IV; Krim Sekr SS Ustuf Walter Altenhof, Sachbearbeiter im Ref A der Abtlg IV; Krim Ass. SS OSchaf Heinrich Cuypers, Sachbearbeiter im Ref A der Abtlg IV; Krim Angest. SS Rottenf Helmut Vits, Ref A der Abtlg IV, [Brüssel], n.d.), 52 vols. IfZM.

Thediek, Franz. "Ansprache anlässlich der Gedenkstunde für Eggert Reeder am 22. November 1960 in Bonn." Photocopy in possession of author.

United States of America. Office of Strategic Services. Research and Analysis Branch. "German Military Government over Europe." Vol. 2 "Belgium." R & A No. 2500.2. Mimeographed. Washington, D.C., 1945.

___. "Survey of Belgium." 1 August 1942. R & A No. 773 j. Mimeographed. Washington, D.C., 1944.

United States. National Archives. Captured German Records Microfilmed at Alexandria. Record Group T 71. Records of the Reich Ministry of Economics.

___. Record Group T 77. Records of German Armed Forces High Command.

___. Record Group T 84. Miscellaneous German Records Collection.

___. Record Group T 175. Records of the Reich Leader of the SS and Chief of the German Police.

___. Record Group T 501. Records of German Field Commands, Rear Areas, Occupied Territories and Others.

"Vernehmung des Hans Heinrich Lammers." March 10, 1948. Doc I-1007. RvOA.

Warburg, Eric. Affidavit furnished on September 13, 1950. Fa Doc 91. Msg 126/4. MAF.

"Zweiter Bericht, Abtlg. Kultur." November 25, 1940. VJ Staat 2170/42. RvOA.

Newspapers and Periodicals

Archives et Bibliothèques de Belgique. 1969.

Belgian Information Service, New York. *Belgium.* 1940 - 1945.

___. *News from Belgium.* New York, 1941 - 1945.

Brüsseler Zeitung. 1940 - 1944.

Centre de recherches et d'études historiques de la seconde guerre mondiale. *Bulletin* Nos. 2 -   . Also published as *Mededelingen.* Brussels. 1970 -   .

___. *Cahiers d'histoire de la seconde guerre mondiale.*   Nos. 1 -   . Brussels, 1970 -   . Also published as *Bijdragen tot de geschiedenis van de Tweede Wereldoorlog.*

Centre national d'histoire des deux guerres mondiales. *Cahiers d'histoire de la deuxième guerre mondiale.* No. 1. Brussels. 1967.

The Historian. 1947.

History and Theory. 1969.

Journal de Charleroi. 1941.

The Journal of Modern History. 1945 -   .

Nationalsozialistische Monatshefte. 1941.

Le Nouveau Journal. 1940 - 1944.

Le Pays Réel. 1940 - 1944.

Reich. Volksordnung. Lebensraum. Zeitschrift für völkische Verfassung und Verwaltung. 1943.

Res Publica. 1978.

Revue générale belge. 1960.

Revue d'histoire de la deuxième guerre mondiale. Paris. 1950 -

Vierteljahrshefte für Zeitgeschichte. 1953 -   .

Volk en Staat. 1940-1944.

Monographs and Special Studies

Arango, E. R. *Leopold III and the Belgian Royal Question.* Baltimore, 1963.

Ardenne, R. (pseud.). *The German Exploitation of Belgium.* Washington, D.C., 1942.

Bährens, Kurt. *Die flämische Bewegung: Europäisches Problem oder innerbelgische Frage?* Berlin, 1935.

Bartlett, Basil. *My First War: An Army Officer's Journal for May 1940: Through Belgium to Dunkirk.* London, 1940.

Bastien, Guy. *L'Armée Sécrète.* Brussels, 1965.

Baudhuin, Fernand. *Belgique 1900 - 1960.* Louvain, 1961.

___. *L'économie belge sous l'occupation 1940 - 1945.* Brussels, 1945.

___. *Les finances de 1939 à 1949: La Belgique et la Hollande.* Paris, 1950.

Belgian American Foundation. *The Belgian Campaign and the Surrender of the Belgian Army, May 10 - 28, 1940.* New York, 1940.

Belgian Government Information Center, New York. *A New Code for Mayors.* New York, 1942.

Belgian Information Office. *Thirty Question about Belgium.* London, 1942.

Bernard, Henri. *Terre Commune: Histoire des pays de Benelux microcosme de l'Europe.* Brussels, 1961.

Billiard, R. *La contrainte économique sous l'occupation 1940 - 1944.* Brussels, 1946.

Binion, Rudolph. "Repeat Performance: A Psychohistorical Study of Leopold III and Belgian Neutrality." *History and Theory* 8 (1969): 213-259.

Bodart, Pierre. *Avec l'armée belge des partisans.* Brussels, 1948.

Boels, Jean Frédéric Amédée. *Deux guerres, une vie.* Brussels, 1954.

Bronckart, Joseph. *Cing ans d'occupation: Verviers pendant la guerre 1940 - 1945.* 4 vols. Verviers, 1946.

Cambrelin, Georges. *Le drame belge 1940 - 1950.* Paris, 1951.

Cammaerts, Emile. *A History of Belgium from the Roman Invasion to the Present Day.* New York, 1921.

___. *The Keystone of Europe: A History of the Belgian Dynasty, 1830 - 1939.* London, 1939.

Capelle, Robert. *Au service du Roi.* 2 vols. Brussels, 1949.

___. *Dix - huit ans auprès de roi Léopold.* Paris, 1970.

Centre National de la Recherche Scientifique. *Les rélations militaires franco-belges de mars 1936 au 10 mai 1940.* Paris, 1968.

Chambard, Marcel. *Ombres et clartés de la campagne belge de 1940.* Brussels, 1946.

Charles, Jean - Léon. *Les forces armées belges au cours de la deuxième guerre mondiale 1940-1945*. Brussels, 1970.

Chlepner, Ben Serge. *Cent ans d'histoire sociale en Belgique*. Brussels, 1956.

Clark, G. N. *Belgium and the War*. London, 1942.

Clough, Shepard B. *A History of the Flemish Movement in Belgium*. New York, 1930.

Colard, Jean. *L'alimentation de la Belgique pendant l'occupation allemande 1940 - 1944*. Louvain, 1945.

Comité d'enquête chargé d'informer le Gouvernement sur la situation et les opérations de la Banque d'Emission pendant l'occupation allemande. *Rapport*. 3 vols and Annexe. Brussels, 1946.

Commission d'Information institué par S.M. le Roi Léopold III le 14 juillet 1946. *Rapport*. Luxembourg, 1947.

____. *Note complémentaire, publiée 8 le octobre 1947*. Luxembourg, 1948.

Commission of Information constituted by H.M. King Leopold III on the 14th of July, 1946. *The Royal Question: Rapport*. London, 1949.

Cornil, Fernand. *Detrésse et espérance: Les responsabilités du commandement de l'armée et du gouvernement dans la tragédie de mai 1940*. Brussels, 1944.

Craig, Gordon. *The Politics of the Prussian Army*. New York, 1970.

Dahl, Robert A., ed. *Political Oppositions in Western Democracies*. New Haven, 1966.

Degrelle, Léon. *Le cohue de 1940*. Lausanne, [1949].

[De Grunne, Xavier.] *La Belgique loyale*. No. 1. N.p., [1941].

De Jong, L. *The German Fifth Column in the Second World War*. Chicago, 1956.

———. *Het Koninkrijk der Nederlanden in de Tweede Wereldoorloog*. 14 vols. The Hague, 1969-1991.

De Jonghe, A. *Hitler en het politieke lot van Belgie*. Vol. 1. Antwerp, 1972.

———. "Berchtesgaden (19 November 1940): voorgeschiedenis, inhoud en resultaat." *Res Publica* 20, no. 1 (1978): 41-54.

———. "De strijd Himmler-Reeder om de benoeming van een HSSPF te Brussel (1942 - 1944)," Parts 1, 2. *Bijdragen tot de geschiedenis van de Tweede Wereldoorlog* 3 (October 1974), 4 (December 1976): 9-81, 5-160.

———. "De vestiging van een burgerlijk bestuur in Belgie en Noord-Frankrijk." *Bijdragen tot de Geschiedenis van de Tweede Wereldoorlog* 1 (August 1970): 69-132.

De Landsheere, Paul and Alphonse Ooms. *La Belgique sous les Nazis*. 4 vols. Brussels, n.d.

De Langenhove, Fernand. *La Belgique en quête de sécurité*. Brussels, 1969.

De Launay, Jacques and Jacques Offergeld. *Belgen en bezetters: Het dagelijkse leven tijdens de bezetting 1940 - 1945*. Antwerp, 1983.

De Lentdecker, Louis. *Het proces Romsée*. Antwerp, 1950.

Dellicour, Fernand. *La politique du travail pendant la querre: un problème angoissant*. Brussels, 1946.

De Man, Henri. *Après coup*. Brussels, 1941.

___. *Cavalier seul*. Geneva, 1948.

___. *Gegen den Strom: Memoiren eines europäischen Sozialisten*. Stuttgart, 1953.

Demany, Fernand. *Mourir debout: Souvenirs du maquis*. Brussels, [1945].

De Putter, Jos. *La constitution de la libre Belgique*. N.p., [1945].

De Schuyter, Jan. *Geheime bladzijden uit het heldenboek van den weerstand*. Antwerp, 1946.

D' Ydewalle, Charles. *Le cour et la ville, 1939 - 1940: Les hommes, les faits, les problèmes de ce temps*. Brussels, 1945.

___. *La reine et ses soldats*. N.p., n.d.

Didisheim, René. *L'histoire de la Brigade Piron: Au délai de la légende*. Brussels, 1946.

Dodge, Peter. *Beyond Marxism: The Faith and Works of Henri de Man*. The Hague, 1966.

Doring, Serge. *L' école de la douleur: Souvenirs d' un déporté politique*. Brussels, n.d.

Dresse, Paul. *Le complexe belge*. Brussels, 1945.

Duchesne, Jean. *1934 - 1940 un tournant dans l'histoire belge: Vingt-deux crises gouvernementales*. Brussel, 1967.

Dumont, G. H. *Léopold III, roi des belges*. Brussels, 1945.

Eichholtz, Dietrich. *Geschichte der deutschen Kriegswirtschaft 1939 - 1945*. Berlin, 1969.

Eppstein, John, ed. *Belgium*. British Survey Handbooks. Cambridge [England], 1944.

Etienne, Jean-Michel. *Le mouvement rexiste jusqu'en 1940.* Paris, 1968.

Falkenhausen, Alexander von. *Memoires d'outre-guerre.* Brussels, 1974.

Fischer, Fritz. *Germany's Aims in the First World War.* New York, 1967.

Ford, Walter. *Belgian Handbook.* London, 1944.

Garfinkels, Betty. *Les belges face à la persécution raciale 1940 - 1944.* Brussels, 1965.

Gérard, Ivan. *Armée sécrète: Souvenirs du Commandant.* Brussels, 1962.

Gérard-Libois, J., and José Gotovitch. *L'an 40: La Belgique ocupée.* Brussels, 1971.

___. *Leopold III: De l'an 40 a l'effacement.* Brussels, 1991.

Gillingham, John. *Belgian Business in the Nazi New Order.* Ghent, 1977.

Goffin, J. *De overgave van het Belgisch leger.* Ghent, [1940].

___. *La reddition de l'armée belge: La verité.* Ghent, [1940].

Goffin, Robert. *Le roi des belges: A-t-il trahi?* New York, 1940.

Goris, Jan-Albert. *Belgium in Bondage.* Antwerp, 1946.

___. ed. *Belgium under Occupation.* New York, 1947.

Gotovitch, J. "Histoire de la déportation: Le convoi du 22 septembre 1941." *Cahiers d'histoire de la deuxième guerre mondiale* 1 (1967): 95-126.

___. "L'opinion et le roi." *Res Publica* 20, no. 1 (1978): 55-98.

___. "Die Rüstungs-Inspektion Belgien." *Archives et Bibliothèques de Belgique* 40, no. 3-4 (1969): 436-48.

Hassel, Ulrich von. *Vom anderen Deutschland: Aus den nachgelassenen Tagebüchern 1938 - 1944*. Frankfurt, 1964.

Haupt, Mathias G. *Der "Arbeitseinsatz" der belgischen Bevölkerung während des Zweiten Weltkrieges*. Bonn, 1970.

Henusse, Edmond, and Jean van den Bossche. *La repression du travail sous l'occupation allemande de 1940 à 1944*. Brussels, 1946.

Herremans, Maurice-Pierre. *La question flamande*. Brussels, 1948.

Het proces Borginon. Antwerp, 1948.

Hitler's Secret Conversations. New York, 1961.

Höjer, Carl Henrik. *Le régime parlementaire belge de 1918 à 1940*. Uppsala, 1946.

Homze, Edward. *Foreign Labor in Nazi Germany*. Princeton, N.J., 1967.

Hoton, Edmond. *Leurs gueules: Essai de zoologie germanique*. Brussels, 1944.

Houtman, Marcel. *Après quatre ans d'occupation*. Brussels, 1945.

Huizinga, Jakob Herman. *Mr. Europe: A Political Biography of Paul Henri Spaak*. New York, 1961.

Huysmans, Camille. *Belgie in den storm*. Antwerp, [1944].

___. *Camille Huysmans: een levensbeeld gevestigd op persoonlijke getuigenissen en eigen werk*. Hasselt, 1961.

Jäckel, Eberhard. *Frankreich in Hitlers Europa*. Stuttgart, 1966.

___. *Hitlers Weltanschauung: Entwurf einer Herrschaft.* Tübingen, 1969.

Jacquemyns, Guillaume. *La société belge sous l'occupation allemande 1940 - 1944.* 3 vols. Vol 1 *Alimentation et état de santé.* Vol 2 *Mode de vie. Comportement moral et social.* Vol 3 *Les travailleurs déportés et ses familles.* Brussels, 1950.

___. *Privations et espoirs: La société belge sous l'occupation allemande 1940-1944.* Brussels, 1945.

Jacquemyns, Herwig. *Een bezet land.* Part 2 of *Belgie in de Tweede Wereldoorlog.* Antwerp, 1982.

Joye, Pierre, and Rosine Lewin. *L'église et le mouvement ouvrier en Belgique.* Brussels, 1967.

Kammerer, Albert. *La vérité sur l' armistice: Ephéméride de ce qui s'est réellement passé.* Paris, 1944.

Kieft, David Owen. *Belgium's Return to Neutrality.* Oxford, 1972.

Knight, Thomas J. "Belgium Leaves the War." *The Journal of Modern History.* vol. 41, no. 1 (March 1969): 46-67.

Lafagne, Pierre. *Sous le signe de la Cross Gammée.* Spa, 1945.

Lamberty, Max. *Filosofie der vlaamsche beweging en der overige stromingen in Belgie.* 3d ed. Brugge, 1944.

Leclerc, Antoine. *Traité des dommages de guerre 1940: Commentaire théoretique et practique des arrêtes du Commissariat général à la restauration du pays en matière de dommages aux biens.* Brussels, 1941.

Leclef, Edmond F.S.A.M.J. *Le Cardinal van Roey et l'occupation allemande en Belgique.* Brussels, 1945.

Legros, Elisée. *A la recherche de nos origines wallones.* Liège, 1945.

Lévy, Paul. *La querelle du récensement.* Brussels, 1960.

Lijphart, A. *The Politics of Accomodation: Pluralism and Democracy in the Netherlands*. Berkeley, 1968.

Lohest, C., and G. Kreit. *La défense des belges devant le conseil de guerre allemand*. Liège, 1945.

Lousse, E. *The University of Louvain during the Second World War*. Bruges, 1946.

Lufft, Hermann August Leonhard. *Die Wirtschaft Hollands und Belgiens sowie Luxemburgs*. Berlin, 1941.

Marchal, Luçien. *Historie de Wallonie*. Brussels, 1952.

Miller, Jane K. *Belgian Foreign Policy Between the Two Wars*. New York, 1951.

Mortier, Firmijn. *Politieke moorden ongestraft tijdens de duitse bezetting bedreven door Rexisten en andere handlangers van de Nazis*. Antwerp, 1945.

Oberkommando der Wehrmacht. *Kriegstagebuch des Oberkommandos der Wehrmacht 1940 - 1945*. 4 vols. Frankfurt, 1961-67.

Ockrent, Roger. *Les crises constitutionelles du pouvoir législatif en Belgique: Les pouvoirs des Secrétaires-Généraux sous l'occupation ennemie*. Brussels, 1944.

Overstraeten, Raoul van. *Albert I: Leopold III: Vingt ans de politique militaire belge 1920 - 1940*. Brussels, 1945.

Périn, Francois. *La Belgique au défi: Flamands et Wallons à la recherche d'un état*. Huy, n.d.

Pesch, Ludwig. *Volk und Nation in der Geistesgeschichte Belgiens*. Berlin, 1944.

Peterson, Edward N. *The Limits of Hitler's Power*. Princeton, N.J., 1969.

Petri, Franz. *Die Niederlande (Holland und Belgien) und das Reich.* Bonn, 1940.

Peuckert, Fritz. "Flanderns Volkstum in Vergangenheit und Gegenwart." *Nationalsozialistische Monatshefte* 12 No. 131 (February 1941): 99-111.

[Pirenne, Jacques]. *L'attitude de Léopold III de 1936 à la libération.* Paris, 1949.

___. *Le dossier du Roi Léopold: Livre blanc.* Brussels, 1970.

Piron, Jean. *Souvenirs.* Brussels, 1969.

Plum, Günther. "Staatspolizei und innere Verwaltung 1934 - 1936." *Vierteljahrshefte für Zeitgeschichte* 2 (1965): 193-224.

Potargent, [Piet L.]. *La mise au travail de la main-d'oeuvre belge dans le pays et à l'étranger durant l'occupation.* Brussels, n.d.

Reeder, Eggert, and Walter Hailer. "Die Militärverwaltung in Belgien und Nordfrankfreich." *Reich. Volksordnung. Lebensraum. Zeitschrift für völkische Verfassung und Verwaltung* 6 (1943): 1-46.

Reusch, Walter. *Die Sprachgesetzgebung auf dem Gebiete der Verwaltung in Belgien.* Giessen, 1935.

Ritter, Gerhard, ed. *Hitlers Tischgespräche im Führerhauptquartier, 1941-1942.* Bonn, 1951.

Ruys, Manu. *De vlamingen.* Tielt, 1972.

Schöffer, I. *Het nationaal-socialistische beeld van de geschiedenis der Nederlanden: Een historiografische en bibliografische studie.* Arnhem/Amsterdam, [1957].

Secrétariat du roi. *Recueil de documents établi par le Secrétariat du Roi concernant la période 1936 - 1949.* N.p., n.d.

___. *Recueil de documents concernant la période 1936 - 1949. Supplement.* Ixelles, 1950.

Selleslagh, F. *L'emploi de la main d'oeuvre belge sous l'occupation.* Brussels, 1970.

Senelle, Robert. *A Survey of Political and Administrative Development in Belgium.* Memo from Belgium No. 48. [Brussels], 1964.

___. *Constitutional Monarchy in Belgium.* Brussels, 1963.

Servais, Jean, and F. Mechelynck. *Les codes et les lois spéciales les plus usuelles en vigueur en Belgique.* 4 vols. Brussels, 1958.

Singer, H. *La vérité sur les juifs.* Brussels, n.d.

Smolders, Th., ed. *La législation belge depuis le 10 mai 1940: Textes, commentaires et jurisprudence.* 2 vols. Brussels, 1941.

Spaak, Paul-Henri. *Combats inachevés.* 2 vols. Paris, 1969.

___. *The Continuing Battle.* Boston, 1972.

Steinberg, Luçien. *La révolte des justes.* Paris, 1970.

___. *Les autorités allemandes en France occupée: Inventaire commenté de la collection des documents conservés au C.D.J.C..* Paris, 1966.

Steinberg, Maxime. *Dossier Bruxelles Auschwitz: La police SS et l'extermination des juifs de Belgique.* Brussels, 1980.

___. *L'étoile et le fusil.* 3 vols. Brussels, 1983 - 1986. Vol 1 *La question juive 1940 - 1942,* 1983. Vol 2 *1942: Les cent jours de la déportation,* 1984. Vol 3 (parts 1 and 2) *La traque des juifs 1942 - 1944,* 1986.

Struye, Paul. *L'évolution du sentiment public en Belgique sous l'occupation allemande.* Brussels, 1945.

Tanham, George. *Contribution à l'histoire de la résistance belge 1940 - 1944*. Brussels, 1971.

Van Den Wijngaert, M. *Een koning geloofd, gelaakt, verloochend*. 2 vols. Leuven, Amersfoort, 1984.

Van Kalken, F. *Entre deux guerres: Equisse de la vie politique en Belgique de 1918 a 1940*. Brussels, 1944.

Van Langenhove, Fernand. *Le Belgique en quête de securité 1920 - 1940*. Brussels, 1969.

Vanwelkenhuyzen, Jean. *Les universités belges sous l'occupation allemande (1940 - 1944)*. Brussels, n.d.

Vanwelkenhuyzen, Jean, and Jacques Dumont. *1940: Le grand exode*. Brussels, 1983.

Von Hassel, Ulrich. *Vom anderen Deutschland*. Frankfurt, 1964.

Vidalenc, Jean. *L'exode de mai - juin 1940*. Paris, 1957.

Wagner, Wilfried. *Belgien in der deutschen Politik des Zweiten Weltkrieges*. Boppard, 1974.

Warmbrunn, Werner. *The Dutch Under German Occupation 1940 - 1945*. Stanford, 1963.

Weber, Wolfram. *Die innere Sicherheit im besetzten Belgien und Nordfrankreich 1940 - 1944*. Düsseldorf, 1979.

Willemsen, A. W. *Het vlaams- nationalisme 1914 - 1940*. Groningen, 1958.

Willequet, Jacques. *La Belgique sous la botte: Résistances et collaborations 1940 - 1945*. Paris, 1986.

___. "Les fascismes belges et la seconde guerre mondiale, *Revue d'histoire de la deuxième guerre mondiale*, 66. 1967.

___. *Paul-Henri Spaak: Un homme des combats.* Brussels, 1975.

Wullus-Rudiger, Armand J. *En marge de la politique belge 1914 - 1956.* Paris, 1957.

___. *La Belgique et la crise européenne 1914 - 1945.* 2 vols. Paris, 1945.

___. *Les origines internationales du drame belge de 1940.* Brussels, 1950.

___. *Les memoires de P. Reynaud et la Belgique: Un appel à Winston Churchill et Général de Gaulle.* Brussels, 1946.

Zuylen, Pierre van. *Les main libres: Politique extérieure de la Belgique 1914 - 1940.* Paris, 1950.

Appendix

Willem C. M. Meyers*

**The German Occupation of Belgium:
A Bibliographical Essay**

Since Belgian historical publications reflect the cultural diversity of the country, most studies are published in French or Dutch. Obviously within the scope of this essay, only a limited selection could be made.

The annual bibliography published by the Centre de recherches et d'études historiques de la seconde guerre mondiale in Brussels so far comprises some five thousand titles[1]**. For even more detailed information a number of bibliographies are available.[2]

A late start
By way of introduction, it seems useful to take a closer look at the history of the historiography of the Second World War in Belgium. Belgium, contrary to its neighbors Holland, France, and the Federal Republic of Germany, took a late start where the history of the Second World War is concerned. What would be the reason for this? In 1971, Herman Balthazar, Professor of History at the University of Ghent wrote:

---

* Librarian, Centre de recherches et d'études historiques de la seconde guerre mondiale/Navorsings - en Studiecentrum voor de Geschiedenis van de Tweede Wereldoorlog, Brussels.

** The notes for this bibliographical essay may be located below, following the text of the essay.

> Three preliminary conditions are necessary to study the history of the Second World War - and this goes for any historical subject: a climate, options and documents. "Climate" is the ability to synthesize scientific analyses without being under emotional stress or pressure; 'options': one knows what one is studying and why; a perspective and finality are essential for research; 'documents' have to be available, which assumes the accessibility and public nature of the source material, and the readiness of the actors and the victims to testify.[3]

In 1976, José Gotovitch was able to write that there had been an acceleration in the historiography of the Second World War since 1970. He also analyzed the question which political, sociological, and scholarly historical phenomena slowed down research before 1970.[4]

What were these factors which delayed historical research? The immediate postwar period did not bring pacification in Belgium. The Royal Question, the issue of the punishment of collaborators and traitors, the Cold War, and the revival of the Flemish movement all provided obstacles to attempts at objective historiography.

Apart from these considerations, there was what we could call a technical reason: the diffidence of the historians themselves. The Belgian historical school traditionally has based its reputation primarily on the critical investigation of sources, with a preference for medieval history. Therefore historians at first hesitated to do research for which few documentary sources were available.

At that time, archives were not open to the public. During this early postwar period, archives remained closed to the public for fifty years (and judicial documents even up to one hundred years.) When "Oral History" became more widely practiced, and when private archives had become more accessible in the wake of the publication of memoirs, a more liberal policy was adopted for official archives as well.

The increase of studies on the war period was also due to the foundation in 1968 of the Center[5] and to the media. Radio and television in particular took a renewed interest, in response to various anniversaries of wartime events. Radio and television producers discovered in the years 1965-1968 that there existed no general synthesis of the history of the Second World War in Belgium which they could use as a basis for their programs. Such a study does not yet exist as of this writing. The interested reader still has to be satisfied with general surveys of Belgian history[6].

He also has the option to consult for the first year of the occupation the pioneering work *L'An 40*, published in 1971.[7] This social and political history turned out to be a great success which appealed to the layman and at the same time opened the door for the media.

After 1970, Belgian radio and television (the Dutch-speaking broadcasting company) started ambitious programs dealing with the history of the occupation. These series met with favorable response among the general public. Some programs, especially those on the "New Order" and the "Collaboration" provoked many reactions and controversies. Each series was accompanied by a text which provided a useful study guide.[8] These programs were rebroadcast in translation on the francophone Radio-Télevision Belge. In 1990 RTBf also started an ambitious five-year series on both radio and television, likewise accompanied by texts, under the general title "Jours de guerre" (days of war).[9]

A pattern for further research and an unexpected research result

To provide a survey of the most important studies of the beginning of the seventies: the already mentioned *L'An 40* and A. De Jonghe's *Hitler en het politieke lot van Belgie*.[10] *L'An 40*, although no longer completely up-to-date is an example of the search for an overall picture of Belgian society during the first year of the war. Main topics of this work were (1) the widening gap between King Leopold III and the government (which was to become one of the issues of the "Royal Question"), (2) the organization and the aims of the German authorities, (3) the attempts of the political and economic establishment to adapt to the New Order in occupied Europe, and (4) the initial willingess of the population to collaborate with the Germans. It also described the hesitating beginnings of resistance, the growing popular anger at the problems of everyday life caused by the occupation, and the actions of the government-in-exile in London. By doing so, this book created a new pattern for further research.

De Jonghe's study of Hitler and the political future of Belgium is the other milestone in the historiography of the Second World War. The author's aim was to define Hitler's vision of the position of Belgium in the new Europe. The results of De Jonghe's research, an eminent example of historical source critique, were the following: in a Europe dominated by Germany there was no room for a Belgian state. Flanders was, in one way or another, to become a part of the Greater Germanic Empire. The fate of Wallonia remained an open question. To prepare the *Anschluss* of Flanders, a civilian administration headed by a German Nazi party official was to be installed.[11] However, the installation of this civilian administration was delayed until July 1944, six weeks before the liberation. De Jonghe shows that the presence of the king in Belgium was an important factor delaying Hitler's decision to establish such a civilian administration.[12]

The "Royal Question"

In the nineteen seventies, De Jonghe's study and less explicitly, *L'An 40*, again brought the Royal Question to the attention of the public. Which were the main issues of this "Royal Question"? Did the Belgian policy of neutrality, as it was attributed to the king, distance the country from Belgium's "natural" allies? Was the capitulation of the army on May 28, 1940 inevitable or was it treason to the allied cause? Was the king prepared, despite the objections of the government, to install an authoritarian regime in occupied Belgium? Did the king embrace the Resistance or did he, on the contrary, advocate some form of collaboration with the Germans?

After many years of studies these questions can be answered in a more differentiated way. It is a fact that Leopold III fully supported the policy of independent neutrality prior to May 1940. The developments that led to this policy, which originated from domestic as well as external considerations were examined by Guido Provoost.[13] Through official and nonofficial contact with other neutral European nations the king tried to prevent the outbreak of the war.[14] This "double" diplomacy caused intense stress within the cabinet led by Prime Minister Hubert Pierlot. Jean Vanwelkenhuyzen treats at great length the goodwill of both parties which he claims reacted differently for psychological and potential reasons to the events occurring during and after the campaign of May 1940.[15]

Lord Roger Keyes, then admiral and British liaison-officer to Leopold III during the eighteen-day campaign, immediately took up the defense of the king against the allegations made by Churchill and especially by the French Prime Minister Paul Reynaud, to the effect that Leopold III, on May 28, 1940 capitulated in an unlawful and - towards the Allies - traitorous way. His son, Sir Roger Keyes, also a friend of the king, published a biased, but well-documented defense of Leopold's attitude before and during the war.[16]

Jean Stengers analyzes the different approaches of king and cabinet from the May days of 1940 until the drafting of the "political testament" of Leopold III in 1944 which revealed that he did not understand the political evolution in the allied world.[17] The recent study by Michel Brelaz provides additional information on Leopold's entourage, and especially on his relations with Henri De Man, a friend of the monarch and the leader of the Socialist party in 1940.[18] Also to be mentioned are the account of the king's secretary Count Robert Capelle[19] and the bitter diary of General Raoul Van Overstraeten, Leopold's aide de camp.[20]

The reactions of the church to the capitulation of May 1940 and the subsequent denunciation of the king by the government have been studied by Etienne Verhoeyen.[21] The role of the church during the first year of the occupation, and especially of Cardinal Van Roey, hesitating between acceptance of, and resistance to, the Germans, has been studied by Alain Dantoing.[22] Finally, Mark Van Den Wijngaert has analyzed Leopold's declining popularity in the occupied country.[23]

The German administration
Without any doubt the penetrating and well documented studies of A. De Jonghe are of the greatest importance to a

scholar wanting to understand German occupation policies. Starting with the study of the structure of the military administration[24] explaining the background of the objectives of the change from a military into a civilian administration[25] the author examines meticulously the interaction between the occupying authorities and the collaboration in his study on the controversy between the SS leader Himmler and the head of the Military Administration Reeder.[26] An attentive and patient reader becomes acquainted with the problems of public security and the hostage policy, the keen rivalry within the Flemish Collaboration, the relations between the German occupation forces and the different structures of the Belgian establishment such as the church, the judiciary and the higher administrative officials, especially the Secretaries-General.[27]

Wilfried Wagner attempts to gain a clear understanding of the German occupation policy,[28] whereas Wolfgang Weber studies the policies and actions of the German security police.[29] The reactions of the Belgian gendarmerie are examined by Willy Van Geet.[30] A special aspect of the maintenance of public order are the contacts since 1936 of some Belgian police officials with the German police in an attempt to control communism in Belgium.[31]

Racial persecution

In Belgium, as in other occupied territories, the German authorities implemented the Nazi racial program. Jews and Gypsies were the primary victims.[32] Lucien Steinberg treats the attempts of the Belgium Jewish community to adjust to occupation and persecution and he describes the rise of Jewish resistance.[33/34] Maxime Steinberg has written a comprehensive work on the persecution of the Jews and of the Jewish response to the German attempt to deport all Jews living in Belgium. He has examined in great detail the submission and even collaboration of the Jewish "establishment" and the emerging Jewish resistance to the German directives, and to the deportation which began in 1942.[35] Israel Shirman has studied the inevitable accompanying phenomenon of economic profiteering.[36]

Despite the increasing number of scholarly studies of the history of Belgium during the Second World War executed by a younger generation of historians born after the war, a continuing need exists for additional objective work, especially for a comprehensive history of the occupation. The time may have come when an objective scholarly examination of this period will be less difficult than it has been in the past.

Notes

1 The following bibliographies by the author, Willem C. M. Meyers: *Belgie in de tweede wereldoorlog: Bibliographie 1970-1980* (Brussels, 1983); "Bibliografie van de in 1981 verschenen publikaties betreffende Belgie tijdens de tweede wereldoorlog," CREHSGM, *Bulletin* 12 (1982); "Bibliografie van de in 1982, 1983 en 1984 verschenen publikaties betreffende Belgie tijdens de tweede wereldoorlog," CREHSGM, *Cahiers d'histoire de la seconde guerre mondiale* 9 (1985): 375-466; subsequent bibliographies in *Cahiers*: for 1985, *Cahiers* 10 (1986): 223-63; for 1986, ibid. 11 (1988): 215-31; for 1987, ibid. 12 (1989): 253-85; for 1988 and 1989, ibid. 13 (1990): 235-76.

2 By the same author: "New Research on the History of Second World War in Belgium," in Jürgen Rohwer and Hildegard Müller, *Neue Forschungen zum Zweiten Weltkrieg: Literaturberichte und Bibliografien* (Koblenz, 1990), pp. 22-44; "Belgie in de tweede wereldoorlog: Een poging tot kritische selectie van de voornaamste werken gepubliceerd sinds 1970," in *Bijdragen en mededelingen betreffende de geschiedenis der Nederlanden* 105 (1990), afl. 2: 280-94.

3 "De stand van het geschiedenisonderzoek betreffende de tweede wereldoorlog in Belgie," in *Ons Erfdeel*, 14, 3, (1971): 55-59.

4 "Problèmes de l'historiographie de la Belgique pendant la seconde guerre mondiale," in *Septentrion: Revue de culture néerlandaise* 3, (1976): 5-15.

5 Since 1970 the Centre de recherches et d'études historiques de la seconde guerre mondiale has produced twenty issues of its *Bulletin*, thirteen issues of its *Cahiers*, twenty-six inventories of archival record groups, as well as a variety of other reference works.

6 Herman Balthazar, "België onder Duitse bezetting 10 mei 1940 - 8 september 1944," in *Algemene geschiedenis der Nederlanden*, vol. 15 (Haarlem, 1982); E.H. Kossmann, *De Lage Landen 1780-1980: Twee eeuwen Nederland en België*, vol. 2 (Amsterdam/Brussels, 1986), pp. 141-205; Willem C. M. Meyers, "De tweede wereldoorlog," in *Twintig eeuwen Vlaanderen*, vol. 6, *De vlaamse beweging*, 3 (Hasselt, 1979), pp. 13-75; Jacques Willequet, "La IIe guerre mondiale," in *Histoire de la Belgique contemporaine 1914-1970* (Brussels, 1974), pp. 131-51.

7 Jules Gérard-Libois and José Gotovitch, *L'An 40: La Belgique occupée* (Brussels, 1971).

8 General title of the series: *Belgie in de tweede wereldoorlog*. Published so far by DNB-Pelckmans in Kapellen: Paul Louyet, *De verloren vrede 1918-1939* (1973); Herwig Jacqemyns, *Een bezet land* (1980); Maurice De Wilde, *De Nieuwe Orde* (1982); Paul Louyet, *Het verzet*, [vol. 1] (1984); Maurice De Wilde, *De kollaboratie*, vol. 1 (1985); Herman Van De Vijver, Rudi Van Doorslaer, Etienne Verhoeyen, *Het verzet*, vol. 2, (1988); *Het cultureel leven tijdens de bezetting* (1990); Etienne Verhoeyen et al., *Het minste kwaad* (1990); Luc De Vos and Frank Decat, *Mei 1940, van Albertkanaal tot Leie* (1990). The series was accompanied by two encyclopedias: Philippe Van Meerbeeck, Etienne Verhoeyen, Herman Van De Vijver, Rudi Van Doorslaer, *Lexicon. De tijd der vergelding en het verzet* (Brussels, 1988); Frank Van Laeken and Etienne Verhoeyen *Politieke en jeugdcollaboratie* (Brussels, 1985).

9 Under the direction of Francis Balace. Published so far by Crédit Commercial, Brussels: *Jours de sursis* (1990); *Les dix-huit jours* (1990); *Jours de défaite*, [vol. 1] (1991); *Jours de défaite*, vol. 2 (1991); *Jours de chagrin*, vol. 1 (1991).

10 Albert De Jonghe, *Hitler en het politieke lot van België (1940-1944): De vestiging van een Zivilverwaltung in België en Noord-Frankrijk*, vol 1, *Koningskwestie en bezettingsregime van de kapitulatie tot Berchtesgaden (28 mei - 19 november 1940)* (Antwerp/Utrecht, 1972).

11 ___, "De vestiging van een burgerlijk bestuur in België en Noord-Frankrijk: De slotbespreking in het Führerhauptquartier 12 Juli 1944," *Cahiers* 1 (1970): 69-128.

12 A skillful summary of the entire problem in the interview "De weg naar Berchtesgaden: De verhouding Koning Leopold III - Rijkskanselier Hitler van 31 mei tot 19 november 1940: Dr. Albert De Jonghe in gesprek met Gaston Durnez, *De Standaard* (1991).

13 *Vlaanderen en het militair politiek beleid in België tussen de twee wereldoorlogen*, 2 vols. (Leuven 1976-1977).

14 Christian Koninckx, *Koning Leopold II: Diplomaat voor de vrede* (St. Niklaas, 1987).

15 *Quand les chemins se séparent: Mai-juin-juillet 1940: Aux sources de la question royale* (Paris-Gembloux, 1988).

16 *Outrageous Fortune: The Tragedy of Leopold III of the Belgians 1901-1941* (London, 1984). This publication was translated in Belgium in French and Dutch.

17 *Aux origines de la question royale: Léopold III et le gouvernement: Les deux politiques belges de 1940* (Paris-Gembloux, 1980).

18 *Leopold III et Henri de Man* (Geneva, 1988.)

19 *Dix-huit ans auprès du Roi Leopold* (Paris, 1970).

20 *Léopold III prisonnier* (Brussels, 1986).

21 "La lettre pastorale du Cardinal Van Roey sur la capitulation du 28 mai 1940: Le role du barreau et de la magistrature," *Cahiers* 5 (1978): 221-42.

22 *La "collaboration" du Cardinal: L'Eglise de Belgique dans la guerre 40* (Brussels, 1991).

23 *Een Koning geloofd, gelaakt, verloochend: De evolutie van de stemming onder de katholieke bevolking ten aanzien van Leopold III tijdens de bezetting (1940-1944)*, 2 vols. (Leuven, 1984).

24 See note 10.

25 See note 11.

26 "De strijd Himmler-Reeder om de benoeming van een HSSPF te Brussel (1942-1944)," *Cahiers* 3 (1974): 9-91; 4 (1976): 5-152; 5 (1978): 5-178; 7 (1982): 97-187; 8 (1984): 5-234.

27 See also A. De Jonghe, "De personeelspolitiek van de Militärverwaltung te Brussel gedurende het eerste halfjaar der bezetting (juni-december 1940): Bijdrage tot de studie van de Duitse *Flamenpolitik* in Wereldoorlog II," *Belgisch tijdschrift voor nieuwste geschiedenis* 1/2 (1972): 1-49.

28 *Belgien in der deutschen Politik während des Zweiten Weltkrieges* (Boppard, 1974).

29 *Die innere Sicherheit im besetzten Belgien und Nordfrankreich 1940-1944* (Düsseldorf, 1978).

30 *De Rijkswacht tijdens de bezetting 1940-1944* (Antwerp, 1985).

31 Rudi Van Doorslaer and Etienne Verhoeyen, "L'Allemagne nazie, la police belge et l'anti-communisme en Belgique (1936-1944): Un aspect des relations Belgo-Allemandes," *Belgisch tijdschrift voor nieuwste geschiedenis* (1986): 61-125.

32 For the persecution of the Gypsies see José Gotovitch, "Quelques données relatives à l'extermintion des Tziganes de Belgique," *Cahiers* 4 (1976): 161-80.

33 *Le Comité de défense des Juifs en Belgique 1942-1944* (Brussels, 1973).

34 See Claire Prowizur-Szyper, *Conte à rebours: une résistance juive sous l'occupation* (Brussels, 1979).

35 *L'Etoile et le fusil*, 3 vols. (Brussels, 1983-1986).

36 "Un aspect de la 'Solution finale'. La spoliation économique des Juifs de Belgique," *Cahiers* 3 (1974): 65-83.

Index

Abbeville, 45
Abschlussbericht, 96
Activity Reports (*Tätigkeitsberichte*), 93-96; effectiveness of, 95; intentionality of, 95; organization and design of, 94
Activists, 30
Administration Division of Military Administration (*Verwaltungsabteilung*), 74
Agence Dechenne, 137
Agricultural production, 216-19
Aktion Iltis, 161
Aktion Sonnenwende, 143
AJB. *See* Association of Jews in Belgium
Albert I, King, 13, 16, 29-30
Allgemeine Warenverkehrsgesellschaft (AWG), 203
Antwerp, 5-6, 20, 27, 60, 61, 112-13
Antwerp Easter pogrom 1941, 165
Antwerp diamond workers, 163
Arbeidsorde, 172, 173
Archbishop of Malines, 22, 43, 141, 158, 253
Ardennes, 45, 256
Army (Belgian), 33, 38-39, 47-48
Asche, Kurt, 151
Assemblé Wallonne, 34
Association of Jews in Belgium (*L'Association des Juifs en Belgigue* or AJB), 155, 157-58, 162, 163, 164
Astrid, Princess, 16, 57
Auftragsverlagerung, 204, 211
Auskämmungsaktion, 231
Avenarius, Colonel, 175

Baels, Lilian, 57
Banque d'Emission (Bank of Issue), 203, 238-39
Banque Nationale, 238, 239
Battle of the Bulge, 61
Bauchau, Henri, 174, 175, 177
Baudhuin, Fernand, 216
Beer rationing, 221
Belgian Congo, 13
"Belgicist", 135
Belgium, 5, 8-9, 34; constitution of, 9, 17-18; constitutional problems of, 13-15, 37-38; fundamental institutions of, 6; gold reserves, 244; government in the thirties, 22; interwar government, 21-24; national characteristics, 10-12
Bergen-Belsen concentration camp, 164
Berger, SS General Gottlob, 84, 104, 257; and nationality policies, 131
Bernhardi, Friedrich, 35
Besatzungskosten, 240
Bethmann Hollweg, Theobald von, 65
Binion, Rudolph, 16
Black market, 222-25
Borchardt, Werner, 152
Bormann, Martin, 64, 99, 100, 101
Borms, Auguste, 30, 32, 131
Brauchitsch, General Walther von, 64, 76
Breendonck concentration camp, 116, 120, 147, 148-49
Bruges, 112
Brüsseler Zeitung, 138, 139
Brussels, 27-28, 45, 60, 68, 112; and language frontier, 24; characterization of inhabitants, 27; population of, 5
Bülow-Schwante, V.K. Alexander von, 43
Burger, Anton, 164

Caisse d'Avances et de Prêts, 238
Canaris, Konstantin, 151
Capitulation of May 28, 1940, 51
Caserne Dossin, Malines, 157, 158
Cassandre, 138
Catholic church, 8, 22, 125, 175, 178; influence over schools, 182
Catholic party, 17, 18, 22, 23
Catholic trade union (*Confédération des Syndicats Chrétiens*), 19, 172
Catholic University of Louvain, 183, 234
Chancellery of the Military Administration (*Präsidialbüro*), 74
Central Production Placement Agency (*Zentralauftragsstelle* or ZAST), 204, 206, 207, 210
Charleroi, 146
Charles, Jean Léon, 188, 189
Charles, Prince, 17
Chemical industry production 1940-1944, 212, 213
Churchill, 52
Ciano, Galeazzo, 40
Civilian Administration (*Reichskommissariat*), 60, 96-104
Claeys, Gaston, 108
Clearing, German-Belgian, 203, 239-41, 247
CNAA. See National Corporation for Agriculture and Food Supply
Coal production 1940-1944, 207-208
Colonial University of Antwerp, 184
Comité de Défense des Juifs, 160
Commission for Repatriation, 194
Committee of Secretaries-General, 105-106; German view of, 106
Communauté Culturelle Wallonne, 135
Communist party, 143
Compromise of the Belgians (*Compromis des Belges*), 32

Compulsory labor draft for Germany October 1942, 231-34, 268
Confédération des Syndicats Chrétiens, 19, 172
Confédération Générale des Syndicats Liberaux, 172
Confédération Générale des Travailleurs de Belgigue, 172
Construction industry 1940-44, 212
Coordinating Purchasing Agency (*Zentralmeldestelle*), 223
Corporation Nationale de l' Agriculture et de l'Alimentation. See National Corporation for Agriculture and Food Supply
Council of Flanders (*Raad van Vlaanderen*), 30
Counter-terror (*Gegenterror*), 146-47
Cour de Cassation, 7, 58, 106, 113
Courtrai, 147
Court, royal, 24, 178
Craushaar, Harry von, 70, 74, 89
Cultural Councils (*Kulturräte*), 180
Currency expansion 1940-1944, 242
Currency Police (*Devisenschutzkommando*), 152

Decree against the Superannuation of the Public Administration (*Verordnung gegen die Überalterung der öffentlichen Verwaltung*), 110
Decree concerning the Exercise of Public Functions (*Verordnung über die Ausübung öffentlicher Tätigkeit*), 109
de Becker, Raymond, 23
Degrelle, Léon, 22, 46, 70, 187; *Gauleiter* Grohé's attitude toward, 104; Reeder's attitude toward, 135; service on the Eastern front, 57; Walloon attitudes toward, 257

Index

Delhaye, Raymond, 194
de Ligne, Albert, Prince, 148
Delvo, Edgar, 173, 174
De Man, Henri, 20, 150, 173, 174
Denis, General Henri, 37, 43, 50
Département de l'Agriculture et du Ravitaillement, 215
Département du Nord, 65, 69
Département du Pas-de-Calais, 65, 69
Département du Travail et de la Prévoyance Sociale, 226
Department of Agriculture and Food Control (*Département de l'Agriculture et du Ravitaillement*), 215
Department of Labor and Social Welfare (*Département du Travail et de la Prévoyance Sociale*), 226
Destrée, Jules, 33-34
Deutsches Nachrichtenbüro, 137
Deutsch-vlämische Arbeitsgemeinschaft. See Devlag
Devaluation of the Belgian Franc, 240
Devèze, Albert, 19
Devlag (*Deutsch-vlämische Arbeitsgemeinschaft*), 100, 111, 134, 146, 175; and German SS, 134-35
De Vlag, 133
De Winter, Emile, 108, 216
Dienststelle Jungclaus. See Service Jungclaus
Dietsland, 31
Dixmuide, 30
DNB (*Deutsches Nachrichtenbüro*), 137
Dunkirk, 24, 25

Eben-Emael, Fort, 45
Economics Division of Military Administration (*Wirtschaftsabteilung*), 72, 191
Economic policies of Military Administration, basic understanding with Belgian business, 191-93; economic regulations: enforcement of, 224-25; operating mode of Belgian industry, 201; labor recruitment: 1940 agreement with Belgian authorities, 227-29
Ehlers, Ernst, 151, 162
Eichmann, Adolf, 156, 157
Elisabeth, Queen Mother, 16, 81, 161
Energy production 1940-1944, 213-14
Erdmann, Fritz, 152
Eupen-Malmédy, 67, 68
Exodus of refugees May 1940, 46-47
Exports to Germany, 204-207

Falkenhausen, General Alexander von, 53, 71, 75, 103, 116; and Belgian judicial system, 116-17; and execution of hostages, 145; and King Leopold, 81, 129; and persecution of Jews, 150, 156, 162; and problem of moral responsibility, 82, 252, 263-66; as future President of Germany, 80; attitude towards Belgian population, 126; career, 77; cooperation with Reeder, 90-93; personal characteristics of, 77-79, 83-84; political views of, 79-81; quality of leadership of, 251
Falkenhausen, Ludwig von, 77
Feldgendarmerie, 117
Feldkommandantur, 74
Festung Europa, 141
Fiduciary Company, (*Treuhandgesellschaft*), 154
Field Gendarmerie (*Feldgendarmerie*), 117
Final Report of the Military Administration (*Abschlussbericht*), 96
Fischer, Fritz, 35, 63, 65
First World War, 14, 29, 55, 133, 183; influence on German policies in Belgium 1940-1944, 63-65

360 Index

First World War Memorials, 181
Fiscal cost of occupation, 243-45
Flamenpolitik, 65, 66
Flanders, 32, 50, 68, 110, 180; and the language question, 25-28; support for annexation to Germany, 257
Flemish language, 26
Flemish Legion, 133
Flemish nationalism, 26, 28-30
Flemish National League (*Vlaams Nationaal Verbond* or VNV), 33, 111, 134, 172; and the German occupation regime, 57, 59; as manpower source for Germans, 254; *Gauleiter* Grohé's view of, 104; Himmler's views of, 100, support of Winter Help, 178
Flemish SS, 59, 111, 134, 254; and counter-terror, 146; and deportation of Jews, 152
Food supply 1940-1944, 219-21
Foreign trade 1940-1944, 247
Fortress Europe (*Festung Europa*), 141
France, 24, 38, 69; and invasion of Belgium May 1940, 49-54; interwar relations with Belgium, 34, 35-36, 38
Franco-Belgian Military Agreement, 36
Free University of Brussels, 183, 184-85
"Frontier University," 183
Front movement (*Frontbeweging*), 29
Front party (*Frontpartij*), 30

Galopin, Alexandre, 54, 146
Gebhardt, Karl, 128
Geheime Feldpolizei, 117, 118, 119
Gendarmerie Nationale, 121-22
Gérard-Libois, Jules, 23-24, 46
German foreign policy aims, continuity of, 63
German Labor Front, 172, 173
German propaganda, 140-41

German Labor offices (*Werbestellen*), 225-26, 230; and labor draft for Germany, 231; and labor draft for Belgium, 229-30
German Labor Service, 174
Germanic SS in Flanders, 132
Germanisches Volkserbe in Wallonien und Nordfrankreich, 89
German policies, summary of: cooperation with Belgian elites, 252-53, 267; economic policies, 259-63; internal security, 256-57; memory of first occupation, 250; nationality policies, 257-58; persecution of Jews, 258-59
GFP. See Secret Field Police
Ghent, 5, 6, 20, 112
Ghent altar tryptich, 181
Gillingham, John, 55, 192
Goebbels, Joseph, 64, 74, 137
Göring, Hermann, 64, 203, 204, 225; as "high apostle of German consumerism," 202; prohibition of black market purchases, 223
Grammens, Florimond, 131
Grase, General Martin, 99, 103
Gotovitch, José, 23-24, 46
Grenzlandsuniversität, 183
Grohé, *Gauleiter* Josef, 99, 103, 104, 164
Groot-Dietsland, 31
Gruppe Kultur, 180

Hahn, Baron Wilhelm von, 151
Hainault, province of, 6
Harbou, Theodor von, 84-85
Hasselt-Merxplas, 147
Hendriks, Fr. J., 226
Het Laatste Nieuws, 138
Heym, Günther, 88, 151
Heymans, Paul, 178, 179, 194
Hierl, Konstantin, 174, 176, 177
High Command of the Army (*Oberkommando des Heeres* or OKH), 70, 97, 145

Index

Higher SS and Police Leader (*Höherer SS und Polizeiführer*), 99, 103, 118, 254
Himmler, Heinrich, 187, 254; and counter-terror, 120, 146, 147; and establishment of *Reichskommissariat*, 60, 97, 99, 100-103; and nationality policies, 131, 257; and Reeder, 85-86, 176; and voluntary labor services, 177
Hindenburg, Paul von, 66
Hitler, Adolf, and Belgian prisoners of war, 186-87; and King Leopold, 127-30; and *Reichskommissariat*, 97-104; attitude toward military regime, 82-83, 254; method of governance, 63-64; policy toward Belgium, 66-68, 99
Höherer SS and Polizeiführer. See Higher SS and Police Leader
Holland. See Netherlands
Holm, Erich, 152, 162
Hoover, Herbert, 52, 181
Hotel Plaza, 75, 76, 78
Huy, Fortress of, 116, 147

Idée belge, 15
Ipsen, Hans Peter, 184, 186
Ijzerbedevaarten, 30

"January crisis" 1940, 40
Jeunesse Romane, 135
Jungclaus, Richard, 103, 118, 180; and counter-terror, 146-47

Kapitalverflechtung, 198-99
Kaufmann, *Gauleiter* Karl, 97
Keitel, Field Marshal Wilhelm, 64, 76, 98-99, 102, 105
Keyaerts, Maurice, 188
Keyes, Roger, 52
Kiewitz, Werner, 129
Kommandostab, 71, 91, 94, 118

"Labor Book" (*Arbeitsbuch*), 232
Labor draft, compulsory placement for students, 233-34; compulsory placement in Belgium, 229-30; compulsory placement in Belgium and Germany, 231-34; "voluntary" phase, 226-29
Labor recruitment, results of, 235-38
Labor Order (*Arbeidsorde*), 172
Laeken, 51
Lammers, H.H., 64, 98-99, 100
Language distribution, 25
Language laws, 32-33
Language Question, 12, 21, 24-34; and Brussels, 27; economic and social dimensions of, 28; historical evolution of, 25-29
Leemans, Victor, 105
Le Nouveau Journal, 138
Leopold I, King, 9, 13
Leopold II, King, 9, 13
Leopold III, King, 14-16, 21, 48, 57; and capitulation, 45; and January 1940 crisis, 40-41; and Parliament May 10, 1940, 44: and Pierlot government May 1940, 48-51; and policy of independent neutrality, 37; attitude toward Germany May 1940, 49-50; attitude toward German military regime, 253; Berchtesgaden interview with Hitler November 1940, 128; deportation to Germany June 1944, 129; May 1940 decision to remain in Belgium, 50-51; May 28, 1940 proclamation, 51
La Nation Belge, 138
Le Pays Réel, 136, 138
Le Soir, 138
Liberal Party, 17, 19, 21
Liebe, Max, 42
Liège, 5, 65
Liège (province), 6, 20
Linguistic Commission, 131
Louvain, 147
Ludendorff, Erich, 66
Luxembourg, 69

Malines, 147, 157, 161, 163, 169
Marie-José, Princess, 16, 40
Mechelen-sur-Meuse, 40
Meridian Circle, 186
"Manifesto of the Thirteen", 41
Mayors, replacement of, 110
Max, Adolphe, 42
Meissner, Otto, 128
Metallurgical production 1940-1944, 208-12
Militärverwaltung. See Military Administration
Militärbefehlshaber. See Military Commander
Military Administration (*Militärverwaltung*), 71-72; and Belgian government agencies: judiciary, 114-15; police, 121-23; Secretaries-General, 108-109; and educational institutions, 182-86; and language question, 127; and the media, 136-40; attitude towards VNV, 131; Divisions of: Control Corps, 224; Cultural Division (*Gruppe Kultur*), 180; *Dienststelle Hellwig*, 172; Economics Division (*Wirtschaftsabteilung*), 159, 191, 203; Economic Investigative Service (*Wirtschaftlicher Fahndungsdienst*), 224; *Gruppe Arbeit*, 225; Purchasing Offices (*Warenstellen*), 200; political complexion of, 75; priorities of, 125
Military Command, and anti-German incidents, 125-26, 142; and Belgian hostages, 145-46; and German police, 119-20, 249; and internal security, 141-44; and prisoners of war, 186-88; internal cooperation and morale, 75; military courts, 115-16; relationship with Belgian Establishment, 253; replacement of, 102; structure of, 71-75; view of Winter Help, 179
Military Commander (*Militärbefehlshaber*), 71

Military events May 1940, 45; human losses as a result of, 47
Military Police (*Feldgendarmerie*), 152
Moresnet, 68

Nagel, Colonel, 70
Namur, 5, 6
Namur, province of, 6
National Bank (*Banque Nationale*), 238, 239
National Corporation for Agriculture and Food Supply (*Corporation Nationale de l'Agriculture et de l'Alimentation* or CNAA), 58, 112, 215-16
National Gendarmerie (*Gendarmerie Nationale*), 121-22
National Labor Office (*Office National du Travail* or ONT), 226; and "voluntary" labor recruitment, 228; and labor draft for compulsory placement in Belgium, 229-30
Nazi-Soviet Non-Aggression Pact, 143
Netherlands (The), comparisons with: confiscation of radios, 139; designation of chief authority, 67; institutional changes, 113; police rule, 120, 149; political activities, 125; operation of universities, 185, 234; overall evaluation, 266-67; shock of invasion and defeat, 54
Normandy invasion, 60
Norway, 149, 234
Nyns, Marcel, 182

Oberfeldkommandantur, 74
Oberkommando der Wehrmacht. See Supreme Command of the Armed Forces
Oberkommando des Heeres. See High Command of the Army
Occupation costs (*Besatzungskosten*), 240

Index

Office Central des Licences et Contingents, 247
Office National de Placement et de Contrôle, 226
Office National du Travail. See National Labor Office.
OKH. See High Command of the Army
ONT. See National Labor Office
OKW. See Supreme Command of the Armed Forces
Operation Sea Lion, 80
Operation Solstice (Aktion Sonnenwende), 143
Ordnungsstrafverfahren, 115
Organization Todt, 123
Ortskommandantur, 74
Oster, Hans, 40

Parti Ouvrier Belge, 17, 19
"Peace through Neutrality," 42
Persecution of Jews, administrative arrangements, 151-52; Antwerp region, 164-65; economic despoliation, 154-55; exemptions from deportation, 157, 163-64; imposition of Yellow Star, 156; mass deportations August-October 1942, 157; policy conflicts, 150; round-up of Belgian nationals September 1943, 161-63; treatment of persons of foreign nationality, 165-66; summary of outcome, 166-69.
Petri, Franz, 89-90, 180, 186
Phoney War period 1939-1940, 33, 38, 42
Pierlot, Hubert, 19, 40, 41, 48, 51; and the invasion May 10, 1940, 43-44; becomes Prime Minister 1939, 22; radio address May 28, 1940, 52
Pierlot government, attitude toward Allies, 50; support of Winter Help activities, 178
Pirenne, Henri, 15, 42
Pirenne, Jacques, 42
Plan de Travail, 20

Plisnier, Oscar, 108
Police forces (Belgian), 121-24
Policy of independent neutrality (politique d'independance), 37
Policy of the lesser evil (politique du moindre mal), 102
Policy of the velvet glove (Politik der weichen Hand), 126, 255
Politique d'indépendance, 37
Politique du moindre mal, 102
Prisoners of war in Germany, 91, 188-89
Propagandaabteilung, 74, 137, 138, 140, 141

Quartiermachungskosten, 243

Rauschning, Hermann, 264
Reconstruction, 193-94
Red Cross (Belgian), 148, 178
"Red Donkey", 70
Reeder, Eggert, 70, 75, 103; administrative philosophy of, 76, 86, 87; and counter-terror, 147; and German policy, 118-19; and Himmler, 85-86; and persecution of Jews, 156, 157, 161; and voluntary labor services, 177; career of, 85-86; cooperation with von Falkenhausen, 90-93; opinion of Degrelle, 135; personal characteristics of, and political views of, 85-87; problem of moral responsibility, 252, 263-66; quality of leadership of, 251
Reeder-von Falkenhausen team, effectiveness of, 92
Reich Main Security Office (Reichssicherheitshauptamt or RSHA), 118, 161, 254
Reichskommissariat, 60, 96-104
Reichskreditkassenscheine, 243
Reichssicherheitshauptamt. See Reich Main Security Office
Repatriation of Refugees 1940, 194-95

364 Index

Restitution Commission (*Wiedergutmachungskommission*), 131
Reynaud, Paul, 47, 51
Rex, 22, 46, 57, 111, 135, 138; and counter-terror, 146; and Walloon population, 257; support of Winter Help, 178
Rex Security Forces, 152
Romsée, Gérard, 112, 122, 195; and Association of Journalists, 137; and schools, 183; and voluntary labor services, 175, 177; appointment of, 105; as the Germans' most reliabale collaborator, 106, 111
Royal Observatory Uccles, 186
RSHA. *See* Reich Main Security Office
Ruspoli, Princess Elisabeth, 83
Rüstungsinspektion Belgien (Army Procurement Agency), 205, 235

Salon Didier, 42
Sauckel, *Gauleiter* Fritz, 99; and compulsory labor draft for Germany, 231; appointment as Plenipotentiary for Labor, 229; as "honorary chief of the partisans", 237
Sauckel organization, and labor draft of university students, 185, 186
Schmitt, Philipp, 148
Schultze, Dr., 225
Schutzverordnung von 1943, 142
SD (*Sicherheitsdienst*), 118, 146, 147
Secours d'Hiver, 178-80, 259
Secret Field Police (*Geheime Feldpolizei* or GFP), 117, 118, 119
Secretaries-General, 71, 72, 105-109, 125, 176; protest against labor deportation of women, 232
Security Deeree of 1943 (*Schutzverordnung von 1943*), 142
Security Police (Sicherheitspolizei or SIPO), 118-19, 148, 157-58,

164; and Communist party, 143; effectiveness of battle against Resistance, 143-44; methods, 144-45
Sedan, 45, 48
Seneffe, castle of, 78
"September Manifesto", 41
Service Jungclaus (*Dienststelle Jungclaus*), 133
Service Volontaire du Travail pour la Wallonie, 175-76, 259
Seyss-Inquart, Dr. Arthur, 70, 71, 76, 149
Sicherheitspolizei. *See* Security Police.
SIPO. *See* Security Police.
Socialist party (*Parti Ouvrier Belge*), 17, 19
Societé Générale de Belgique, 7, 54, 146
Somme, 67
Spaak, Paul-Henri, 20-21, 41-43, 48, 51; and *"Moi d'abord!"*, 43
Speer, Albert, 64, 199, 237
Sperrbetriebe (blocked factories), 199
SS, 57, 85, 180, 187
Stages of economic exploitation, 198-99
Stahlwerksverband, 209
Steel production 1940-1944, 209-10
Steinberg, Maxime, 149, 166, 167
Steinbrinck, Otto, 209
St. Gilles prison, 116, 147
Straub, Franz, 118, 151
Stuckart, Wilhelm, 67, 69, 98
Studienkommission 1939, 70
Supreme Command of the Armed Forces (*Oberkommando der Wehrmacht* or OKW), 67, 76, 98, 116, 145, 204
Syndicat Belge de l'Acier or SYBELAC, 209

Tätigkeitsberichte. *See* Activity Reports
Terboven, *Gauleiter* Josef, 149
Textile industry 1940-1944, 213

The Dutch under German Occupation, 249, 266
Thedieck, Franz, 70, 88
Thyssen, August, 65
Tirpitz, Alfred von, 66
Tobacco rationing, 221-22
Transportation 1940-1944, 195-97
Treaty of London 1839, 34-35
Treuhandgesellschaft, 154

Überwachungsstelle, 223
Ullmann, Grand Rabbi Salomon, 158
Union of Manual and Intellectual Workers (*Union des Travailleurs Manuels et Intellectuels* or UTMI), 173, 174, 259
University of Ghent, 30, 32, 183, 184, 234
University of Liège, 183, 234
University of Louvain, library of, 181

Verzuiling, 10
Visé, 24
VNV. See Flemish National League
Volk en Staat, 136, 138
"Voluntary" labor recruitment 1940-1942, 228-29
Voluntary Labor Service for Flanders (*Vrijwillige Arbeidsdienst voor Vlaanderen*), 175-76, 259
Voluntary Labor Service for Wallonia (*Service Volontaire du Travail pour la Wallonie*), 175-76, 259
Van Cauwelaert, Frans, 19, 44
van Coppenolle, Adriaan, 122
Van de Wiele, Jef, 100
Vandervelde, Emile, 20
Van den Berghe, Edouard, 40
Van Overstraeten, Raoul, 38, 40, 43

Van Severen, Joris, 31, 46
van Zeeland, Paul, 22, 36
Verbrekingshof. See Cour de Cassation
Verdinaso, 31
Verordnung gegen die Überalterung der öffentlichen Verwaltung, 110
Verordnung über die Ausübung öffentlicher Tätigkeit, 109
Verviers, 65
Verwaltungsabteilung, 74
Verwilghen, Charles, 194

Waffen-SS, 133, 176
Wage and price policies, 245-47
Wagner, General Eduard, 76, 93
Wallonia, 20, 28, 67-68, 110, 180, 257
Walloon nationalism, 33-34
Wannsee Conference, 149
Warenstellen, 200
Waterloo, 24
Weidmann, Felix, 152
Werbestellen. See German labor offices
Wehrmachtsbefehlshaber, 103
Weygand, General Maxime, 50
Wiedergutmachungskommission, 131
Willems, Jan Frans, 26
Willequet, Jacques, 23, 109
Winter Help (*Secours d'Hiver* or *Winterhulp*), 178-80, 259
Wirtschaftlicher Fahndungsdienst, 224
Wirtschaftsabteilung, 159, 191, 203
Woestijn, Etienne, 224
Wynendaele, 50

Yellow star, 153
Ypres, 50

ZAST or *Zentralauftragsstelle*, 204, 206, 207, 210
Zentralmedestelle, 223